NIETZSCHE'S CASE

Philosophy as/and Literature
NIETZSCHE'S
CASE
Bernd Magnus,
Stanley Stewart, &
Jean-Pierre Mileur

ROUTLEDGE
NEW YORK LONDON

Published in 1993 by

Routledge
An imprint of Routledge, Chapman and Hall, Inc.
29 West 35 Street
New York, NY 10001

Published in Great Britain by

Routledge
11 New Fetter Lane
London EC4P 4EE

Library of Congress Cataloging in Publication Data
Magnus, Bernd.
    Nietzsche's case : philosopy as/and literature / Bernd Magnus,
Jean-Pierre Mileur, Stanley Stewart.
      p. cm.
    Includes bibliographical references.
    ISBN 0-415-90094-8   ISBN 0-415-90095-6
    1. Nietzsche, Friedrich Wilhelm, 1844–1900. 2. Literature-
Philosophy. I. Mileur, Jean-Pierre. II. Stewart, Stanley, 1931-
B3317.M254 1992   92-6454
193--dc20   CIP

British Library cataloging in publication data is available

FOR

Lore

Kelly

Barbara

Contents

Bibliographic Note

References to Nietzsche's writings will be documented parenthetically in the text, with abbreviated titles followed by the number of the part of the work, then the title (if any) of the section, followed, finally, by the number of the partition within that section. Unless otherwise indicated, we quote from the English translations of Walter Kaufmann and R. J. Hollingdale as indicated in abbreviated form below. In a few instances, we substitute our own translation. We have regularized i/j and u/v, eliminated meaningless italics and small capitals, and silently corrected obvious printer's errors. Beneath titles of Nietzsche's works we have, for the convenience of readers, arranged abbreviations of sections alphabetically rather than in the order in which they occur in Nietzsche's works.

Abbreviations

A   *The Antichrist* (*PN*)

BWN   *Basic Writings of Nietzsche*. Translated and edited by Walter Kaufmann. New York: Random House, 1968.

BGE   *Beyond Good and Evil* (*BWN*)
        "RN"   "The Religious Nature"
        "WS"   "We Scholars"

BT   *The Birth of Tragedy From the Spirit of Music* (*BWN*)
        "Attempt"   "Attempt at Self-Criticism"

EH   *Ecce Homo* (*BWN*)
        "WIAD"   "Why I am a Destiny"
        "WIASC"   "Why I am So Clever"

	"WIASW"	"Why I am So Wise"
	"WIWSGB"	"Why I Write Such Good Books"
GM	*Toward the Genealogy of Morals (BWN)*	
	"GBC"	"'Guilt,' 'Bad Conscience,' and the Like"
	"GEGB"	"'Good and Evil,' 'Good and Bad'"
	"NP"	"Nietzsche's Preface"
	"WMAI"	"What is the Meaning of Aescetic Ideals?"

GS   *The Gay Science: with a prelude in rhymes and an appendix of songs.* Translated by Walter Kaufmann. New York: Random House, 1974.

HATH   *Human All Too Human.* Translated by R. J. Hollingdale. Cambridge: Cambridge University Press, 1986.

PN   *The Portable Nietzsche.* Selected, translated, and edited by Walter Kaufmann. New York: Viking Press, 1983.

PTAG   *Philosophy in the Tragic Age of the Greeks.* Translated by Marianne Cowan. New York: Regnery/Gateway, 1987.

TI   *Twilight of the Idols (PN)*

	"EP"	"Editor's Preface"
	"FGE"	"The Four Great Errors"
	"HTWBF"	"How the 'True World' Finally Became a Fable"
	"MA"	"Maxims and Arrows"
	"MAN"	"Morality as Anti-Nature"
	"PS"	"The Problem of Socrates"
	"RP"	"'Reason' in Philosophy"
	"SUM"	"Skirmishes of an Untimely Man"
	"WGL"	"What the Germans Lack"
	"WIOA"	"What I Owe to the Ancients"

UDHL   *On the Uses and Disadvantages of History for Life (UT)*

UT   *Untimely Meditations.* Translated by R. J. Hollingdale. London: Penguin Books, 1968.

WP   *The Will to Power.* Translated by Walter Kaufmann and R. J. Hollingdale. New York: Random House, 1967.

Z   *Thus Spoke Zarathustra (PN)*

	"AF"	"The Ass Festival"

"Awakening"   "The Awakening"
"CWK"   "Conversations With the Kings"
"Cry"   "The Cry of Distress"
"DB"   "On the Despisers of the Body"
"DS"   "The Drunken Song"
"IP"   "On Immaculate Perception"
"Leech"   "The Leech"
"Magician"   "The Magician"
"OA"   "On the Afterworldly"
"OFD"   "On Free Death"
"OHM"   "On the Higher Man"
"ONT"   "On Old and New Tablets"
"OR"   "On the Rabble"
"PB"   "On Passing By"
"RW"   "On Reading and Writing"
"Sign"   "The Sign"
"SS"   "The Seven Seals"
"TM"   "On the Three Metamorphoses"
"UM"   "The Ugliest Man"
"VB"   "The Voluntary Beggar"
"VR"   "On the Vision and the Riddle"
"Welcome"   "The Welcome"

Acknowledgments

Any conscientious attempt on our part to acknowledge all who have influenced the content of this monograph would result in a list as long as this book itself. In consequence, while we silently acknowledge our indebtedness to all unnamed individuals, we have nevertheless elected to mention and thank a less expansive list of institutional support structures. We acknowledge with gratitude the generous assistance of David P. Gardner's University of California Humanities Research Initiative, without which our collaboration could never have begun; the UC Riverside Humanities Initiative Committee; UCR's Center for Ideas and Society; UCR's Senate Committee on Research; The National Endowment for the Humanities; the British Academy; the University of California Humanities Research Institute; Robert Schlosser and the Huntington Library.

Bits and pieces of Chapter I have appeared in predecessor versions in: *Reading Nietzsche*, Robert C. Solomon and Kathleen Higgins eds. (Oxford University Press, 1988); *Philosophical Topics*, Vol. 19 No. 2, Fall 1991; and of Chapter 2 in *New Aspects of Lexicography: Literary Criticism, Intellectual History, and Social Change*, ed. by Howard D. Weinbrot (Carbondale and Edwardsville: Southern Illinois University Press, 1972).

Finally, having declined to list individuals to whom we are indebted, we nevertheless cannot permit this occasion to pass without acknowledging the important, facilitating role played by our research assistant during the first two years of our collaboration. Without Dr. Shari Starrett's unstinting devotion to the success of our project, it might never have come to fruition.

Pre(post)face: Confessing/Professing Collaboration

For humankind is more sick, uncertain, changeable, indeterminate than any other animal, there is no doubt of that—it is *the* sick animal: how has that come about?[1] GM (III, 13).

That there is once again a crisis in the humanities has become a cliché. The alleged crisis is a result of a changed and changing cultural environment, an environment characterized by radically conflicting general features. On the one hand, humanists have recently experienced a sense of increasing influence, responsibility, accountability, technological innovation, and "relevance" to other segments of our intellectual culture and society at large. The recent explosion in applied philosophy, in critical legal studies, in gender studies, in cultural studies, and in public humanities programs such as those funded by the NEH and other agencies—state councils for the humanities, library, film, and museum development programs and funding—all testify to this renewed sense of urgency. On the other hand, many humanists have at the same time experienced a loss of disciplinary authority; disaffection from disciplinization and departmentalization; the marginality of the humanities as cultural powers, when measured in terms of status (power, prestige, profit, perks); the simultaneous public and often highly visible criticisms of humanities faculty for the alleged abdication of their responsibility to the citizenry; the challenges of feminism and multicultural studies (including issues of race, gender, sexual orientation, and ethnicity), especially as these bear on questions of methodology and canon formation.

It is the best of times; it is the worst of times.

Two themes, among others, have emerged with regularity in this crisis atmosphere: (1) the inadequacy of current forms of humanistic knowledge acquisition, production, transmission, and dissemination; and (2) the name of Friedrich Nietzsche. Indeed, one highly visible critic, Allan Bloom, joined both themes by connecting "the closing of the American mind"—the misedu-

1

cation and misconstruction of America's public philosophy—directly to the hegemony of Nietzsche's philosophy.

Without endorsing Bloom's specific view either of the failure of the humanities or the connection of that alleged failure to Nietzsche, opinions with which we would in any case disagree, we have felt for some time that the prevailing paradigm of humanistic knowledge production privileges the solitary, individual, isolated researcher, and that this has become somewhat anachronistic, given the accelerated fragmentation of knowledge since the Renaissance and the emergence of sub-disciplinary "experts" in every field of human inquiry. In contrast, collaborative research has become a commonplace in the modern university in the natural and social sciences; but it has never become an accepted research genre in the humanities, except in narrowly defined domains such as editing texts. Multidisciplinary, theoretical research which deals with root questions of central importance to the humanities has seldom been undertaken collaboratively.[2]

This jointly-authored study of Nietzsche and his literary interlocutors—*Nietzsche's Case: Philosophy as/and Literature*—combines the perspectives of a philosopher and Nietzsche scholar, a critical theorist/Romanticist, and a Renaissance literary scholar. Conceptually, our book occupies the interface of philosophy and literature, bringing conventionally marked "philosophical" and "literary" texts into conversation with one another in a way never done before. Nietzsche's texts are brought into productive conversation with the New Testament, with the texts of Sidney, Bacon, Shakespeare, George Herbert, Milton, Spenser, Browning, Wordsworth, Blake, Shelley, Coleridge, Carlyle, Whitman, and Lawrence—to mention only a few previously unmentioned or seldom discussed texts/names with which Nietzsche's texts share an elective affinity—not only with the standard texts of the philosophical tradition and the tradition of criticism from Plato to Derrida. Because we hope we have established in the pages that follow a more robust and nuanced treatment of Nietzsche's texts than has been done by individual authors and commentators in the recent past, we expect our collaboration to illustrate and to help justify the need for collaboration in humanistic research and study, especially collaboration on theoretical topics in criticism. The deep, substantive diversity of our academic areas of specialization, which are nevertheless complementary for purposes of this project, became an instrument for multiplying perspectives in a way perhaps uniquely appropriate to a thinker like Nietzsche, a thinker steeped in the classical, Renaissance, and modern traditions in philosophy and literature, in religion and in science.

Despite the differences in our fields of specialization, our shared interests in Nietzsche and in theoretical issues of criticism constantly transgress (or transcend) disciplinary divisions of intellectual labor. These shared interests, plus a healthy respect for the importance of substantive differences in specialization and perspective, drew us to one another. Nevertheless, if there exist obstacles to meaningful collaboration in general and to joint authorship in particular, these pale when contrasted with deeply held and internalized disciplinary assumptions and constraints which tend to promote isolation and cross-disciplinary incomprehension. Finding a way of making the voice of the other one's *own* can be as difficult as it can be rewarding. This is especially true in a case such as ours, one in which our theoretical views and metaphilosophical convictions are already matters of published record. The voice which emerges in the pages that follow, therefore, is genuinely the voice of a four-year collaboration, a voice which is no one's in particular and yet is each of ours.

This difficulty of blending the voices of philosophy and literature mirrors the felt difficulty of fruitful collaborative inquiry into root questions within one's own discipline. In philosophy, for example, the mutual incomprehension between "analytic" and "continental" approaches has gained hegemony, with results that have been bemoaned by the Council for Philosophical Studies, on behalf of the American Philosophical Association, as follows:

> For several generations the American philosophical community has been split in an artificial and counterproductive way between traditions loosely termed "analytic" and "continental." This is costly not only to philosophers and their students, but also to the many students in other disciplines who can or could profit from the study of philosophy. But the schism itself is so integrated into the institutional structure of philosophical education that it is self-perpetuating.
>
> Whatever the cause, the analytic/continental antagonism has now become institutionalized. Representatives of the two persuasions usually do not communicate. Each side has its own departments, its own journals, its own annual conventions, and, most important, its own students. Mutual ignorance and mistrust are thus preserved and handed down. In one university existentialists and phenomenologists are caricatured as fuzzy-headed pompous obscurantists, who might better write novels or sermons than their so-called "philosophy." Down the street, however, Anglo-American "scholasticism" is denounced as a vast desert of necessary and sufficient conditions for knowing that p, saying that p, or dancing on the head of a p. Departmental curricula perpetuate this artificial, suspicion-blinded, and philosophically shallow categorization. The resulting narrowness has a stultifying effect on both teachers and students. (1982)

If the mutual shunning which has come to characterize philosophy in America has had undesirable consequences, the conflict in literary studies between those committed to traditional historico-critical methods and those pursuing recent developments in "theory" has been no less unfortunate. Indeed, the educational and political consequences of mutual shunning may have been and may continue to be as baleful in literary criticism as the analytic/continental split has been to philosophy.

To repeat (while stating for the first time) the two paragraphs which will bring this study to (self-circling) closure, current critical discussion of

Nietzsche in the English-speaking world has suffered—and our shared culture's imagination has, in consequence, been impoverished—not only as a result of the mutual shunning of "analytic" and "continental" approaches to philosophy in general and to Nietzsche's texts in particular, to the body of his thought. There is another, deeper, older, even more pervasively institutionalized mutual shunning so ubiquitous that it hides in plain view: the separation of "literary" from "philosophical" discourse. That mutual shunning is as old, as unquestioned (and hence as "venerable") as Plato's decision to banish "poets" from the polis the "philosopher" is destined to rule. And it is only a slight exaggeration to say that this very shunning is the founding gesture of philosophy as it has been delivered over to us: "I, Plato, *am* the truth," Nietzsche reminds us helpfully in *Twilight of the Idols*. The impact on Nietzsche has been lamentable, however, for each—"poet" and "philosopher" (or writer and thinker, critic and philosopher)—continues to regard the other with suspicion. As a result of this hermeneutics of suspicion philosophers—especially those inclined to what we will call "the Official View" in chapter 1—typically regard "literary critical" appropriations of Nietzsche as, at best, simpleminded misappropriations, or, at worst, practicing without a license. And for most "literary critics" the philosopher's carefully domesticated "Nietzsche" either looks hopelessly naive, uninteresting, or both; he looks hopelessly "thin"; he looks like someone to place in the wax museum of great dead (white male) "philosophers." The philosopher typically looks for coherent meaning in Nietzsche's texts, and, above all, for evidence of rigor; the critic looks for novel new ideas, new insights, for fractures, fissures, and ambiguities in Nietzsche's texts, for opportunities or connections missed. Thus, mutual shunning of our literary and philosophical cultures continues.

This book marks our first attempt to contest this baleful shunning, or, to vary the figure, to suture the body of Nietzsche's institutionally dismembered literary/philosophical thought. To extend this figure, we have treated the body of Nietzsche's thought as thoroughly permeable and suturable, available to thoughtful intervention whether the means be marked "literary" or "philosophical." Only in this way, in our view, can there be a genuine recuperation, a convalescence, a restoration of the body of Nietzsche's (institutionally dismembered) literary/philosophical thought that is both robust and nuanced. We have, to put it simply, attempted in the pages that follow a kind of suturing, even a kind of healing, but above all a kind of thinking that has a rigor of its own—a rigor which, one hopes, will have left mortis behind.

In *Beyond Good and Evil*, Nietzsche tells his reader that every great philosophy is really only "the personal confession of its author and a kind of involuntary and unconscious memoir" (*BGE* 6). This leads his reader, naturally enough, to two questions expressible as one: What does the greatness of Nietzsche's philosophy consist in and what is it confessing? Further, of what—

or in what sense—is it an involuntary and unconscious memoir? And doesn't the admission that a philosophy is a personal confession undermine its aspiration to voice impersonal truth arrived at through lucid, disinterested reflection? Isn't an involuntary and unconscious memoir the very opposite of the God's-eye-view to which philosophy aspires?

Our book inhabits these questions yoked as one. Even the title of our book is itself intended to capture, underscore, and reinscribe these essential tensions, the essential ambiguity inscribed in the expression "Nietzsche's case." For "Nietzsche's case" means both the case Nietzsche prosecutes, his critiques of our shared tradition, as well as the case Nietzsche himself *is*. In the first sense, "Nietzsche's case" points beyond the philosopher's brief, even points beyond its author, to the objects the brief interrogates—traditional religion, philosophy, and morality. In the second sense, "Nietzsche's case" is token-reflexive; it interrogates its subject, the proper name "Nietzsche." To put this same point differently: if Nietzsche has given us a new sense of the genealogy of our shared tradition, then he has also insinuated a genealogy of that genealogy, one which points us back to its authorship. So, while unravelling the greatness of Nietzsche's philosophical achievement we aspire at the same time to unravel the unconscious and involuntary memoir it constitutes, by interrogating its voice, its authority, its authorship.

Such a reading does not replace more conventionally philosophical readings. Rather, it supplements them at precisely those points where philosophical discourse fails to connect satisfactorily with what and how Nietzsche actually wrote. Our goal is not to prosecute a project of literary *ressentiment* against philosophy but to establish a mode of intimacy that does not ultimately require us to make a choice between satisfying the disciplinary requirements of one or the other, that allows us to say something of value to both without trivializing either. Whether our project succeeds or not will depend, in part, upon our success in rendering no longer interesting or appropriate the question, Is it philosophy or is it literature?

1

The "Problem of Style" in Nietzsche's Philosophy The "Problem of Philosophy" in Nietzsche's Style

My propositions serve as elucidations in the following way: anyone who understands me eventually recognizes them as nonsensical, when he has used them—as steps—to climb up beyond them. (He must, so to speak, throw away the ladder after he has climbed up it).

He must transcend these propositions, and then he will see the world aright. —Wittgenstein, *Tractatus Logico-Philosophicus*

The Body of Thought

In recent years "the problem of style" has moved from the margins to something more nearly like the center of concerns among Nietzsche critics. In instance, philosophers as varied in approach, tradition, and temperament as Arthur Danto, Jacques Derrida, and Alexander Nehamas have made the problem of style central to their discussions of Nietzsche.[1]

It has not always been so.

To appreciate how much the philosophic climate has changed in the past two and a half decades, we need only recall that in his influential 1965 study, *Nietzsche as Philosopher,* Arthur Danto was able to write:

In the course of his piecemeal elaborations he [i.e., Nietzsche] touched on most of the problems that have concerned philosophers, and he discussed them interestingly, and even profoundly. If one takes the trouble to eke his philosophy out, to chart the changes in signification that his words sustain in their shifting from context to context and back, then Nietzsche emerges *almost* [our italics] as a systematic as well as an original analytical thinker. This task is not a simple one. His thoughts are diffused through many loosely structured volumes, and his individual statements seem too clever and topical to sustain serious philosophical scrutiny. Nietzsche seems distrustful and almost officially defiant of philosophic rigor, and he has, in fact, often been the thinker *de choix* of men who find academic and professional philosophy too circumspect or meticulous for their bold and bohemian tastes. Moreover, Nietzsche's not altogether undeserved reputation as an intellectual hooligan, as the spiritual mentor of the arty and the rebellious, and, more darkly, as the semicanonized proto-ideologist of Nazism, has made it difficult *even* [our italics] for philosophers to read him as one of their own.[2]

This attitude, this philosophic pose or stance—which, incidentally, does not even capture Danto's current view twenty-six years later—this blend of philosophical chauvinism, of condescension coupled with political and moral disapproval, reinforced the view current at the time that Nietzsche is basically unsound—interesting though he may be to those unused to or incapable of the rigors of analytical philosophy. And it was *not* only self-congratulatory—"meticulous," "circumspect," "rigorous," "serious," that is to say English-speaking—philosophers who thought that there is something peculiar about Nietzsche's way of doing philosophy. The French philosopher, Eric Blondel, was puzzled by a similar attitude he found prevalent in Europe, in France in particular, and remarked on this in 1971: "Until now, most critics have insisted on considering Nietzsche's 'poetic' and metaphorical style of writing as either the simple and often tasteless ornamentation of philosophical prose produced by good-natured poets, or as the kind of decoration that is favored by 'men of letters,' but that philosophers try desperately to forget. . . ."[3] To be fair, Blondel adds almost immediately the following important point: "Because of his deliberate use of polysemantic metaphors rather than neutral concepts it would seem more judicious, or perhaps even more philosophic, to ask if Nietzsche's 'style' does not necessarily embody a philosophic choice. . . ."

As the locution, "tasteless ornamentation," suggests, Blondel initially shares with Danto the perception that Nietzsche's way of writing tends to get in the way of the philosophic point he is trying to make, that if Nietzsche had only been a different sort of writer—a serious, systematic, rigorous one—we would all have been better off, that *even Nietzsche himself would have been better off*. The difference between Danto's 1965 view and Blondel's in 1971 is that Danto endorses this opinion while Blondel finds it puzzling. This divergence in attitude is one central difference between much English-speaking and non-English-speaking philosophy over the past two decades. The attitude implied in Danto's remark won out in America towards those whose style of writing, those whose way of doing philosophy, does not conform to our own professional conventions, while, during the same period, serious reflection on the connection between style and content, expression and meaning, became a central topic of discussion in much European philosophy.

The picture of the relationship of philosophy to its expression, the prevailing picture in analytic philosophy, is a familiar one. It is that of sober, deep thought on a recognizable topic of concern to us entombed within unfortunate and distracting rhetorical devices and facades. One is reminded of Gottlob Frege's dismissive habit of calling style "mere coloration" (*Farbung*). On this model of philosophic anti-style, the distinction between a philosopher's thought and the text which expresses it is to be treated on the analogy of the relation of wheat to chaff, kernel to husk, or diamond to coal.

It is this picture of philosophic thought—a model in deep bondage to a "scientific" picture of textual motivation and production—which led Danto to his extravagant surmise that Nietzsche's texts, published as well as *Nachlass*, are pretty much of a piece, that any tableau could pretty much substitute for any other:

> Any given aphorism or essay might as easily have been placed in one volume as in another without much affecting the unity or structure of either. And the books themselves, except for their chronological ordering, do not exhibit any special structure as a corpus. No one of them presupposes an acquaintance with any other. Although there undoubtedly was development in Nietzsche's thought and in his style, his writing may be read in pretty much any order, without this greatly impeding the comprehension of his ideas.[4]

These extraordinary assertions are inattentive not only to the structure(s) and genres[5] of Nietzsche's published texts but to the distinction between published and unpublished writings.[6] Just as importantly, these remarks derive their energy—their presumed obviousness and their self-confident force—from Whiggish philosophical condescension:

> In recent years, philosophers have been preoccupied with logical and linguistic researches, pure and applied, and I have not hesitated to reconstruct Nietzsche's arguments in these terms. . . . Because we know a good deal more philosophy today, I believe it is exceedingly useful to see his analyses in terms of logical features which he was unable to make explicit, but toward which he was unmistakably groping. His language would have been less colorful had he known what he was trying to say, but then he would not have been the original thinker he was, working through a set of problems which had hardly ever been charted before. Small wonder his maps are illustrated, so to speak, with all sorts of monsters and fearful indications and boastful cartographic embellishments![7]

The conception of the relationship of philosophic thought to its expression which informed and motivated Danto's remarks in 1965 is of a piece with Russell's much earlier article which wore its thesis on its sleeve, its ideology on its title: "Logic As the Essence of Philosophy." Ideally, philosophical propositions ought to be grouped like set-theoretic constants, in this scenario, like axiomatic deductive systems, or perhaps like arithmetic expressions, such as $5+7=12$, $8+4=12$, $-7+19=12$ and perhaps expressions such as $5+7=8+4=-7+19$. The thought of the number 12 can be regarded as captured equally well by any of these expressions. On the other end of the linguistic continuum, in sharp contrast perhaps, one finds certain sentences whose "thought" just is their expression, just *is* the style itself. Think of Browning's "Childe Roland to the Dark Tower Came," for instance. Can we with critical impunity disentangle its form from its content, its thought from its style? Or could it be that such terms as "form," "content," "thought," "style" and "expression," are in some contexts awkward and unhelpful—by which we mean only that they might be ineffective in elucidating the particulars of the text in question?

For present purposes, let us call this "the Official View." On this Official View, historians of philosophy are conceptual archaeologists, digging and sifting through remnants of the past for treasures which may help to illuminate our times. Or, to vary the metaphor, we are all digging for conceptual gold hoping to find a vein in otherwise filthy philosophical mines.

To get a sense of how much this philosophic scene has changed in the past two decades, to get a sense of the extent to which the Official View is now contested, one need only consider the transformations in Danto's own opinions on the topic under consideration, namely, that of the relationship between a philosopher's thought, on the one hand, and its mode of expression, on the other.

While delivering his presidential address to the American Philosophical Association's Eastern Division in 1985, Arthur Danto bemoaned the Official View, as the following quotation indicates, thereby distancing himself from a perspective he himself had once endorsed:

> A lot of what I have read on Plato reads much as though he to whom the whole of subsequent philosophy since is said to be so many footnotes, were in effect a footnote to himself, and being coached to get a paper accepted by *The Philosophical Review*. And a good bit of the writing on Descartes is by way of chivying his argumentation into notations we are certain he would have adopted had he lived to appreciate their advantages, since it is now so clear where he went wrong. But in both cases it might at least have been asked whether what either writer is up to can that easily be separated from forms it may have seemed inevitable to be presented in, so that the dialogue or meditation flattened into conventional periodical prose might not in the process have lost something central to those ways of writing. *The form in which the truth as they understood it must be grasped just might require a form of reading, hence a kind of relationship to those texts, altogether different from that appropriate to a paper, or to what we sometimes refer to as a "contribution."* [our italics]

This observation of Danto's represents a virtual about-face in the course of twenty years. Danto's 1965 treatment of Nietzsche still expressed the Official View, still expressed the Whiggish one about which he later came to have doubts, the view that there is a single, paradigmatic form of philosophical discourse (namely "conceptual analysis") which we are fortunate enough to have discovered, one which would have been used by our predecessors in place of their crude dialectical instruments if only they had been smart enough or lucky enough to have been born in our English-speaking century. On the contrary, Danto now suggests, "it might at least have been asked whether what either [any] writer is up to can that easily be separated from forms it may have seemed inevitable to be presented in, so that the dialogue or meditation flattened into conventional periodical prose might not in the process have lost something central to those ways of writing."

In what follows, a reflection is begun on what Blondel's remark and Danto's recent suggestions have in common—that to understand the truth as Nietzsche saw it requires a certain relation to the text, one in which Nietzsche's polysemantic metaphors are not perceived as distractions but are instead thought to be required by his very thought itself, indeed may perhaps be said to *be* the thought itself. In short, we want to convert Blondel's and Danto's assertions into a question by asking: What does it mean to say that Nietzsche's style necessarily embodies a philosophic choice? And how is this question to be understood? And what does it mean to say that to understand a past philosopher's text is to be related to it in a certain way, a way which gets flattened out in treating it as a precursor of the current Official View?

To gesture in the direction of a preliminary response to the questions just asked, in the pages that follow we shall be turning time-honored philosophical analyses inside out by refusing to read Nietzsche's written sentences as "the expression" of "his ideas," vehicles for the transcription of thought, embodiments of prior philosophical convictions. We shall refuse to read the written grapheme as the body of thought. This reversal may instead be read with greater profit therefore as an attempt to pose and answer a different question: How else would one expect someone who writes like this to think?[8]

Baiting the Hook: Digressing to Derrida

The writings of many philosophers and critics have contributed to the gradual transformation in recent approaches to philosophical writing itself, a transformation which is reflected in the changed tone and problematic of the two Danto quotes cited above which frame the argument of this chapter. Philosophical writing, qua writing, has recently become problematized in important and interesting ways, ways which will have to influence one's understanding of a writer and thinker as complex as Nietzsche. And no one has had a greater influence on the reconceptualization of the relationship of philosophy to its writing than has Jacques Derrida. So we digress to Derrida at the outset, since his writings play a role in the argument which constitutes the body of this text.[9]

There are more than ordinary obstacles to locating Derrida in interpretive space. That is because it is a part of Derrida's substantive strategy to call into question the notion that thinkers can either be neatly located or paired-off in conceptual space, to challenge the view that they represent "philosophical positions" (what Nietzsche called "a dance of bloodless categories"), to call into question the unstated but powerful assumption that there exists over and above one's interpretive practices a neutral ideal space which one's categories of reflection merely exemplify: a kingdom of Platonic natural kinds never tiring of yet another instantiation. Further, Derrida's writings often suggest—as do those of Richard Rorty, who follows him in this—that the seemingly innocuous task of paraphrasing a thinker, or of attempting to characterize his work, is itself part and parcel of "the metaphysics of presence," that one's critical procedures which may seem natural—even necessary and inevitable—are instead optional products of a specific institutionalized vocabulary, of, as Wittgenstein put it, "a form of life."[10] Derrida's writings suggest that the tasks of paraphrase and characterization of philosophical views are themselves the optional products of vocabulary choice.[11] Once chosen (either consciously by us or tacitly through our cultural traditions and acculturation) one's critical practices may come to feel natural, even inevitable; they carry in their wake the unspoken conviction that one's most fundamental interpretive strategies and categories are inevitable for any rational inquirer, that they derive this power from their essential correctness, from their correspondence to the way things (or texts) are in themselves. One begins to feel as if there were a fact of the matter about which vocabulary, taken as a whole, is the right one. In this way, Derrida's writings seem to insist that an optional vocabulary hides its origins from itself.

If Nietzsche's work resists paraphrase, and Heidegger's work suggests that paraphrase must purchase its success by obscuring the matter of thought—descending to chatter, to idle talk (*Gerede*)—Derrida's writings may be read as extended reflections on the impossibility of paraphrase and characterization. They may alternatively be read as an extended performance in which the received categories of literary and philosophical reflection are successively called into question. And yet—or perhaps "therefore"—the most neutral and apparently uncontroversial characterization of the conceptual space Derrida occupies can be made problematic, as is illustrated by his own remarks on the term "deconstruction":

> the word "deconstruction" has always bothered me. . . . When I made use of this word . . . I had the impression that it was a word among others, a secondary word in the text which would fade or which in any case would assume a non-dominant place in a system. For me, it was a word in a chain with many words . . . as well as with a whole elaboration which is not limited only to a lexicon, if you will. It so happens that this word which I had only written once or twice . . . all of a sudden jumped out of the text and was seized by others who have since determined its fate in the manner you well know. . . . For me "deconstruction" was not at all the first or the last word, and certainly not a password or slogan for anything that was to follow.[12]

Derrida's reluctance notwithstanding, one may usefully begin by relating his texts not only to those he explicitly discusses but to those he assumes have shaped his interlocutors' vocabulary as well. Saussure is one such absent pres-

ence, consideration of which is not without significance, since the movement
from rigorous phenomenology in the Husserlian manner—with its stress on a
perceptual vocabulary—to structuralism and semiology is mediated through
Saussure. In contrast, Anglophone philosophy of language and German hermeneutics remained, at least initially, relatively untouched by acquaintance
with Saussure. In marked contrast, Derrida's vocabulary shifted after 1967
from terms such as consciousness, intentional object, intentional act, and in-
tuition of essences to the language of sign, signifier, and signified.

Saussure's *Course of General Linguistics* had claimed that "in language there
are only differences without positive terms,"[13] an insight which strikes at the
heart of the representational picture of language apparently acquired with
mothers' milk. Indeed, as Saussure observed, "there are only differences. Even
more important, a difference generally implies positive terms between which
the difference is set up."[14] Yet just that is what is being set aside, displaced.
How to think of language non-representationally—how to think of difference
without presupposing identity—mirrors Nietzsche's difficulty of thinking
"world" as will to power, thinking of "things" as families of events, as consisting
of and constituted *by* no-thing in particular, thinking "things" as relations without relata.

Saussure's implicit challenge to referential semantics accords well with J. L.
Austin's generative thought—to which Derrida frequently attends—that language, which was typically treated as descriptive and hence as the medium for
bringing thoughts into correspondence with facts, might as usefully be regarded as a performative instrument and as the vehicle of a kind of action. So
Austin is lauded (in "Différance") for combating what he called "the descriptive fallacy," for having exploded the concept of communication as a purely
semiotic, linguistic, or symbolic concept. Nevertheless, the concept exploded
is required to detonate the charge. Hence, argues Derrida, performativity is
parasitic on descriptivity after all.

Consider the standard example: When one says "I promise," one is not describing anything: one is *doing* something; promising consists in *saying* "I
promise." However, we have in effect just said "I promise" without making any
promise at all, merely showing instead with which instrument of language it is
done. Thinking primarily of stage-actors, Austin dismisses such citational
cases as themselves parasitic. But Derrida insists that if an action is to consist
in saying something, then there must be a rule which transforms the saying
into doing; and the rule must *cite* the expression: therefore, no citation, no
performance. This elegant example of "deconstruction" can be understood as
a demonstration that a thesis actually requires as one of its conditions the very
thing it means to reject; and focus on this conundrum is a recurrent feature of
Derrida's work.[15]

This self-deconstructing parasitology, this mutual dependence of action upon citation and citation upon action (or speech upon "writing"), is but a single instance of a broader tendency: Derrida's general transformation of our sense of the stability and autonomy of the world itself into a textual exigency, as if self and world were themselves inscriptions.

Within the received view, within what Heidegger had called the ontotheological tradition, Derrida invites us to think of the dream of philosophy as inhabited by three unwobbling pivots, consisting of (1) the world (or becoming, appearance, *hyle, res extensa*, object, phenomena, etc.), (2) the philosopher (or subject, person, observer, theorist), and (3) the in-principle correct account of the world, Reality's Own Vocabulary. Nietzsche had argued that (3) is a function of a self-deceptive will to power. And Heidegger had agreed with Nietzsche that no discourse can be reality's canonical self-description. Philosophers cannot play the role of Charlie McCarthy for reality's Edgar Bergen. However, this now places Derrida in a position to say that "there is nothing outside the text," that notions of truth, meaning and reference only make sense when the dream of philosophy—the ternary "metaphysics of presence"—is assumed, only when there exists something *more* than interpretations, only when the word/world connection can be stitched together again: but we "cannot legitimately transgress the text toward something other than it, toward the referent (a reality that is metaphysical, historical, psychobiographical, etc.) or toward a signifier outside the text whose content could take place, could have taken place outside of language, that is to say, in the sense that we give here to that word, text."[16]

Put differently, Derrida is able to thematize the end of philosophy, conceived as the theory of accuracy of representation, as an event within writing, by recognizing that its dream of three unwobbling pivots applies to reading and writing as well. For think now of a book as a ternary relation between (1) a text (an inscription), (2) a reader, and (3) the meaning of the text (the in-principle correct interpretation, the Text's Own Self-Description). Invoking Saussure's linguistic insight and Nietzsche's perspectivism, Derrida asserts that (3) is undecidable, that there can be no such thing as the univocal, canonical, absolute meaning of a text. Even divine inscriptions require optional encodings. Indeed, under the pressure of Nietzsche's perspectivism, all we are left with is "the text" and texts "about" texts. "The idea of the book," in contrast,

is the idea of a totality, finite or infinite, of the signifier; this totality of the signifier cannot be a totality, unless a totality constituted by the signified preexists it, supervises its inscriptions and its signs, and is independent of it in its ideality. The idea of the book, which always refers to a natural totality, is profoundly alien to the sense of writing. . . . If I distinguish the text from the book, I shall say that the destruction of the book as it is now under way in all domains, denudes the surface of the text.[17]

This somewhat oblique entry into Derrida manages to underscore the claim that we are left with a Nietzschean domain of intertextuality only, a perspectival space, a domain in which no spectator standpoint is available to distinguish the conceptual from the literary, a domain in which literal speech is understood as dead metaphor, metaphors we have forgotten were metaphors, desiccated poetry, a framework in which philosophy is [just] one more literary genre.

Nietzsche here as elsewhere anticipated Derrida when he wrote—in answer to the question, What is truth?

> a mobile army of metaphors, metonymes, and anthropomorphisms—in short a sum of human relations, which have been enhanced, transposed and embellished poetically and rhetorically and which after long use seem final, canonical, and obligatory to a people; truths are illusions about which one has forgotten that this is what they are; metaphors which are worn out and without sensuous power; coins which have lost their pictures and now matter only as metal, no longer as coins.[18]

Derrida shares with Heidegger and Nietzsche the view that the history of philosophy is a narrative of presence, closure, and totality—the dream of a unique, complete, and closed explanatory system—fueled by binary oppositions. Each agrees, in his own way, that the dream at the heart of philosophy begins paradigmatically with Plato. And just as Heidegger absorbs Nietzsche into the history of philosophy as the closure of nihilism rather than its confrontational overcoming (as Nietzsche would have it), Derrida's strong misreading (his misprision) absorbs Heidegger within the metaphysics of presence too. Heidegger's magic inscription—*Sein*—betrays his vestigial yearning for unmediated vision (perhaps better: for unmediated hearing) beyond intertextual discourses: "There will be no unique name, even if it were the name of Being. And we must think this without *nostalgia*, that is, outside of the myth of a purely maternal or paternal language, a lost native country of thought. On the contrary, we must *affirm* this, in the sense in which Nietzsche puts affirmation into play, in a certain laughter and a certain step of the dance."[19]

Derrida's relation to Heidegger can therefore be characterized hyperbolically as castration of the father-figure and a reassertion of the grandfather Nietzsche—reassertion of a perspectivism which is not a concealed yearning to be more than perspectivism itself—or as patricide. And just as Heidegger reverses our ordinary work-a-day conception of the relation between primordial and founded, basic and derived, host and parasite, Derrida also applies this tool, whether it be in suggesting the priority of writing over speech-acts, the metaphorical over the literal, *bricolage* over engineering, or signifier over signified. But unlike Heidegger, and crucially we think, Derrida's reversals are not offered to establish or to argue that the derivative *is* primordial. Derrida's reversals always appear to be strategic, concerned to reverse the dominance relation between opposed concepts, as in the male/female reversal in *Spurs*, to annul the privileging of presence itself. Heidegger's profound linguistic and archaeological suggestions of origins remain, for Derrida, necessarily part and parcel of the metaphysics of presence.[20]

Inscribing the Textual Body

It has been said that to understand the truth as Nietzsche saw it requires a certain relation to his text, one in which Nietzsche's polysemantic metaphors are not perceived as distractions but are instead thought to be required by his very thought itself, that his style is itself the expression or embodiment of a philosophic choice. So we want to begin by asking again: What does it mean to say that Nietzsche's style necessarily embodies or expresses a philosophic choice? And how is this question to be understood? Further, what does it mean to say—as Derrida, Barthes, Nehamas, Danto and Taylor have suggested, each in his own way—that to understand a past philosopher's text is to be related to it in a certain way, a way which gets flattened out in treating it as the expression of philosophic positions which can be captured adequately in paraphrase and recharacterization? What does it mean to set aside the view that Nietzsche's writings are the expressions of prior philosophical convictions, and how is this to be understood?

We can think of least five ways in which Nietzsche's "thought" is *inseparably* tethered to his style. First, there is the characteristic form of Nietzsche's writing, which Alexander Nehamas has recently identified correctly as the trope *hyperbole*.[21] Second, there is the feature of *undecidability* which inhabits almost all of his writings as a sort of spectral presence. Third, Nietzsche's writings resist *paraphrase* and they do so in a special way. Fourth, most of his published writings virtually *embody* the theses for which they argue, they represent, incarnate their thought, they are instances of their own kind, tokens of their own type; they are self-referring simulacra. We shall call this feature of Nietzsche's style "tokening." Fifth, a defining feature of Nietzsche's central philosophical gestures is that they are self-consuming concepts.

Let us say a word or two about each of the first four characteristics of Nietzsche's style we have just mentioned—i.e., hyperbole, undecidability, resistance to paraphrase, and tokening its type—before pausing a bit longer over the fifth one, namely the self-consuming character of Nietzsche's thought.

Concerning the first feature which tethers thought to style, hyperbole, or exaggerated overstatement, the importance of Nietzsche's use of this trope is not its contrast and comparison with literal speech—with what ought to be said instead of its exaggeration; nor is Nietzsche hyperbolic in the methodological sense in which Descartes uses this trope to arrive at the truth. Rather the important contrast in Nietzsche's use of hyperbole is with the trope *litotes*, the contrast with ironic understatement.

To take but a single instance of Nietzsche's hyperbole, when one reads him there is never any question who is speaking. It is almost impossible for Nietzsche's reader *not* to have a reaction. In a reversal characteristic of Nietzsche's use of this trope, his hyperbolic discourse almost always immediately puts his readers defenses up, flags their enthusiasms and aversions, and makes his persona unforgettable. One way of thinking of Nietzsche's hyperbolic style, therefore, is to contrast it with the litotic voice of Socrates which speaks in Plato's dialogues. In Plato's case, a case of litotes which seldom makes itself the object of Socratic irony, the reader is left deliberately with the impression that impersonal, disembodied reason speaks here, that there are no distorting persona at all, or better, that Plato's interlocutors are merely place-holders for the voice of Reason itself, place-holders for Reality's Own Vocabulary. The reader of Plato's dialogues, especially those of his middle period, is supposed to think that disinterested, impersonal Truth, Knowledge and Virtue find a voice, indeed *are* voiced at that dialogue site. The picture is that of philosophers playing the role of Charlie McCarthy to reality's Edgar Bergen. Notice, however, that litotes, the appearance of ironic understatement, does all the work for Plato here. Paradoxically, Plato's arrogant dream of a transparent voice of reason obscures and conceals the dogmatist's dream of universality and neutrality—what Nietzsche called the will to power clothed in the form of the will to truth. Nietzsche's discourse, in contrast, always assails and assaults his readers. There is no pretended neutrality. This is an enormous risk for a writer to take, because without the appearance of neutrality prose threatens very quickly to degenerate into propaganda, which is always a forgettable genre after the circumstances which gave rise to it no longer obtain. And yet Nietzsche always takes this risk; he never tires of asking his readers: This is *my* truth; where is yours? "And above all, do not mistake me for someone else," he berates his reader in *Ecce Homo*.[22]

This way of reading Nietzsche's hyperbolic voice, as a site which contests and reverses received notions of arrogance and modesty, has the effect of transvaluing the reader's preconceptions about Plato's and Nietzsche's rhetoric, their respective discourse. On a surface reading, Nietzsche's writings solicit instant and strong reactions. His prose exaggerates, sometimes merely to solicit a response, sometimes to wound. Everywhere, however, his presence makes itself felt as *his* presence. Who else in the common tradition could have written a mock spiritual "autobiography" whose chapters bear the titles: "Why I Am So Wise"; "Why I Am So Clever"; "Why I Write Such Good Books"; and "Why I Am a Destiny." And who if not Nietzsche could have ended such a book with the sentence: "Have I been understood?—*Dionysus versus the Crucified.*"[23]

This apparent conceit, this megalomania gravis, contrasts vividly with the

litotic voice of Plato's Socrates—as well as with the ministering voices of virtually all others in the philosophic canon. Since Plato parted company from the
wise men of his day (the *sophoi* were, by definition, wise men after all), knowledge and opinion, logic and rhetoric, truth and persuasion are thought to have
gone their separate ways. Indeed, Plato's is perhaps the first transvaluation of
Greek values, a reversal which turns wise men (*sophoi*) into "sophists," turns
the possession of wisdom into the defeated cultural rival of those who love it
but do not possess it, the lovers of wisdom—philosophers. Our language retains an inherited ambivalence which is reflected in the fact that "sophist" and
"sophistication"—nay and yea—derive from the same term.

This Platonic demotion of rhetoric was purchased with a promissory note,
however. That promissory note was this: Among all the competing self and
world descriptions one and only one could be picked out as the vocabulary
reality would itself choose to describe itself, if it could. And yet, although that
promissory note remains uncashed, the binary oppositions of knowledge/
opinion, logic/rhetoric, truth/persuasion derive their force entirely from the
assumed value of that promissory note. It would not be too much to conclude,
therefore, that Nietzsche's hyperbolic discourse strategically reverses the dominance relation of received conceptions of philosophic modesty and conceit.
Litotic philosophic voices seduce and succeed through their pretended neutrality, through the conceit that they are disinterested sites in which reality
itself achieves its true voice. Nietzsche's shrill voice is modest, in contrast, because it speaks for no one save its proper name.

Nietzsche's prophetic voice, especially his gospelizing Zarathustra, should
also be read as an instance of hyperbole in the sense specified, should therefore be read as a gospel to end all gospelizing, a gospel which consumes itself
in its very iteration.

Concerning undecidability, the second feature which tethers thought inseparably to style, Nietzsche's published writings challenge closure at every turn.
Even after one has assigned a sense to any single entry or aphorism of his, the
relation of this entry to the remainder of the work in which it is domiciled can
always be made problematic. This uncertainty of the relationship of part to
whole is a spectral other which haunts every proffered interpretation. For
even after a sense has been assigned to a work as a whole, Nietzsche's subtitles
will give the careful reader pause. For example, even if one figured out what
Thus Spoke Zarathustra means, one might still wonder why it is subtitled "a book
for everyone and no one"; and why *Zur Genealogie der Moral* is subtitled "a
polemic" (*Eine Streitschrift*) when it is the one work of his whose drift and argument are recognizable, even a touch familiar. Even the title itself is often
simply mistranslated *The Genealogy of Morals*. Nietzsche's title does not begin
with the definite article, however. Had he wanted to convey *the* genealogy of
morals, the book's title would instead have been *Die Genealogie der Moral*. Instead, *zur* in the title functions at the same time as a preposition and an article.

The *zu* of *zur* suggests either the English preposition "toward" or the preposition "on" (in some specific contexts even "to" or "for"); and the concluding letter "r" is a contraction of the German definite (dative case) article *"der"* ("the"). It is undecidable in principle, therefore, whether the preposition "toward" or "on" was intended by Nietzsche. At best, therefore, the title of Nietzsche's text might be either *Toward the Genealogy of Morals* or *On the Genealogy of Morals*, but certainly not *The Genealogy of Morals*. Walter Kaufmann, incidentally, seemed to be quite conscious of this difficulty, for he translated the title *On the Genealogy of Morals* in his *Basic Writings* edition of some of Nietzsche's works, having earlier translated the same title as *Toward the Genealogy of Morals* in the selections he included in the *Viking Portable Nietzsche*. This undecidable difference between the prepositions "toward" and "on" in Nietzsche's title is not without significance, because "on the genealogy of morals" suggests a topic upon which one is remarking; whereas "toward the genealogy of moral" does not imply the prior existence of the subject upon which Nietzsche is remarking. The one preposition ("toward") suggests that Nietzsche is working in the direction of the genealogy of morals in a way that the preposition "on" does not suggest. Indeed, the preposition *zu*, which always takes the dative case, implies direction as often as not, as in *zum Bahnhof*, when one is going "to the railroad station." But to repeat and underscore the two points made here: (1) Whatever the prepositional intent of *zu* in *Zur Genealogie der Moral*, the title cannot bear the substitution of the definite article ("the"); and, (2) it is undecidable whether *zur* means to convey "toward" or "on" the genealogy of morals. The provisional, tentative, and future-directed character of some of Nietzsche's other subtitles during this period lead us to prefer "toward" to "on." Nor is it at all obvious to the reflective reader why *Beyond Good and Evil* bears the subtitle "Prelude to a Philosophy of the Future" (*Vorspiel einer Philosophie der Zukunft*), which suggests that Nietzsche's text itself neither constitutes a philosophy of the future—since it is its prelude—nor envisions that future philosophy. Nor does it express its hegemony either, since Nietzsche is careful to write the German indefinite article (*einer*: a) rather than the definite article (*der*: the). *Beyond Good and Evil* is a prelude to *a* philosophy of the future, not to *the* philosophy of the future. It is a prelude to one of many conceivable future philosophies, in short.[24] And, as with *Ecce Homo*, one always wonders whether and when Nietzsche is playing it straight or is being ironic. Consider how much mischief has been done by the remark of the old woman made *to* (not *by*) the character Zarathustra, a remark typically passed off as if it were Nietzsche's official view on this subject: "*Wenn du zum Weib gehst vergess die Peitsche nicht*"—"when going to women do not forget the whip."[25] Moreover, all of his writings evoke the feeling that their author places every reader's interpretation in scare quotes, is always undermining an interpretation in the very act of suggesting it.

Concerning resistance to paraphrase as a feature of Nietzsche's writing, the third characteristic of his style which cannot be divorced from the thought it expresses, there are two senses in which this characterization applies to which we wish to draw your attention. There is, first, the sense in which even when a successful gloss *can* be offered of the item up for discussion, the feeling nevertheless persists that the item, just as it was written, is more important than its paraphrase, in the sense that the specific words cannot be improved upon and that the force of the utterance is lost even in a successful paraphrase of its meaning. This is especially true of some of Nietzsche's memorable one-liners, aphorisms in the true sense of the word, such as: "Was mich nicht umbringt macht mich stärker"—"what does not destroy me makes me stronger."[26] In this respect, Nietzsche's writing is properly characterized as poetic, in just the sense that no sane person would prefer a successful paraphrase of the cognitive content of Browning's poem "Childe Roland to the Dark Tower Came" in place of the poem itself. To prefer a successful paraphrase to the poem would be to prefer one hundred imaginary dollars to one hundred real ones. And it seems to us that this same relation obtains between Nietzsche's text as a whole and its gloss or its paraphrase. As Nietzsche reminds us in another text, great writers want to be learned by heart, to be memorized. Perhaps memorization is more than memorialization, since in memorizing a line we incarnate it; it becomes, in a manner of speaking, a part of us.

The second sense in which Nietzsche's writings resist paraphrase, however, is this. One gets the feeling that, for almost any commentary on any aspect of Nietzsche's work, that commentary fails to represent its subject, that there are equally valid and deeply incompatible alternative reconstructions, that no one of them is the final word. One may be tempted to say that this is true of any commentary on any work of philosophy or literature; and we would be inclined to agree. However, in the Nietzsche case, resistance to paraphrase is different.

This difference can be brought out by saying that in the case of, say, Kant's first *Critique*, one also has the feeling that if one subtracts the commentary from the text something is left over which that commentary fails to capture, fails to represent accurately, and that what is left over is what escapes conceptual reconstruction. But the feeling persists here that a Kant commentary has failed to represent its contents only as an empirical matter, not that one *could not* substitute the commentary for the original, at least in principle.[27] In the Nietzsche case, one feels that no such substitution is possible in principle. In this respect, the relationship which holds between Nietzsche's philosophizing, on the one hand, and an account of that philosophy, on the other hand, is rather like the relationship which holds between a great novel and its plot summary; one learns everything and nothing from it.

This is an important point, because it begins to acknowledge that reading *can* be a matter of being related to a text in a certain way, as the quote from

Arthur Danto (1985 version) suggested above. To appreciate the force of this point one need only recall one's favorite pornographic novel or sex manual, or one need only recall those driven to despair and even suicide upon reading Goethe's *The Sorrows of Young Werther*. Or consider how differently we and the Trappist monk Thomas Merton are related to the Gospel according to John, or how differently our colleagues in religious studies departments read the *Koran* or the *Tao Te Ching* than those for whom these *biblios*, these books, are the saving vessel of truth, are truth's incarnation.

Concerning tokening, the fourth sense in which Nietzsche's texts instantiate—embody—their theses, one can contrast his texts with the more typical traditional discursive philosophical procedures (procedures of the sort in which an author frequently tells his or her reader where s/he is headed and how s/he proposes to get there). In contrast, Nietzsche favors an accumulation of self-sufficient insights, epigrams, maxims, aphorisms, fragments, and notes, which require the reader to provide the missing logical ligatures, the connectives which unify his books. In consequence, the reader's constructed ligature has the force of both establishing and, paradoxically, dissolving authorial identity and intention. "Nietzsche" becomes Nietzsche as-read-by-*x*-on-occasion-*y*. Since the task is to give an account of what Nietzsche is up to in his many notes, genres, and styles, their connection—"his" theses—appear always to be provided by his reader: "Provided" in the strong sense that the difference between making and finding, creating and discovering is out of place here. In answer to the question "Is this what Nietzsche meant?" the answer is always both yes and no. Yes, because we really cannot in practice separate what is said in a text from what is meant by it; no, because what is meant only becomes explicit in the reader's (re)construction of the text's meaning. The fact that Nietzsche only published entries he himself numbered without providing bridge passages between and among them imposes upon his reader the need to provide connections between entries, to provide logical ligatures—safe passage among unsafe passages—that are not provided by grammatical or structural features of the published works. In the Nietzsche case, "reading" *is* interpretation with a vengeance.

Finally, fifth, there is the self-consuming character of Nietzsche's concepts and tropes to consider, to which we now turn.

A Fish Story: Self-Consuming Concepts

Self-Consuming Artifacts[28] draws a suggestive distinction between self-satisfying,[29] dialectical,[30] and self-consuming artifacts[31] which we want to misappropriate, i.e., adopt and transform for our own purposes. Stanley Fish argues that it is characteristic of dialectical works to involve the reader in discursive activities—to involve the reader in attempting to arrive at "the meaning of the text"—and then to declare invalid or premature the conclusions of such discursive undertakings. The result is disquieting because the reader's interpretation is always being challenged at the very same time that it is being enabled, until the very possibility of understanding in the conventional vocabulary is itself contested or opened to serious question. Works of this sort are self-consuming in two senses. First, they undermine their own structure; and, second, in undermining their own structure they also undermine the reader's self-confidence.

Fish then connects this strategy to what he calls the aesthetic of the good physician. He argues that the good physician may be a poet, preacher, philosopher, or pamphleteer, but is identifiable by an intention to minister to his or her patients by inflicting pain, by wounding them. The good physician pains the readership (patient) by forcing it to confront the inadequacy of the views s/he believes it to hold and by forcing a transformation in those views, to the extent of rejecting the system of values they exemplify and express.

There are inconveniences in Fish's story (some of which he has addressed in subsequent works) but they need not concern us here. What we want to suggest is that most of Nietzsche's central philosophic notions—eternal recurrence, the *Übermensch*,[32] perspectivism, will to power—can be understood as self-consuming concepts, notions whose very articulation simultaneously invites and refuses meaning and coherence, with an effect upon his readership apposite to that described by Fish.

By the expression "self-consuming," we shall mean that for any given concept it requires as a condition of its intelligibility (or even its iteration) the very contrast it purports to set aside or would have the reader set aside.[33] A familiar illustration might help.

As we all know, Descartes's hyperbolic doubt tries to argue at a critical point that our waking and dreaming states are logically interchangeable and that, in consequence, all perception and bodily-state reports might be delusory dreams rather than veridical perceptions. This is supposed to show that there may be no bodies at all and no spatiotemporal perceptions either.

Many philosophers, beginning with Descartes's own critics, have pointed out that Descartes's hyperbolic doubt requires the very contrast between waking and dreaming he seeks to set aside in order to undermine the distinction between them. To be able to distinguish waking states from dreaming states *requires* the contrast between actual perceptions as opposed to imagined, dream-state, ones. To have the concept "dream-perception" requires as a condition of its intelligibility the contrast with "waking-state perception." Thus, all that Descartes's argument *could* show is that, for any perception taken in isolation, one cannot be certain whether one is waking or dreaming. However, that uncertainty itself is parasitic upon the prior more general certainty that at some determinate point someone's perceptions must be waking-state perceptions, must be veridical.

The details of this reconstruction of Descartes's argument can, of course, be disputed. In fact, that contestability is an arresting feature of what we are calling self-consuming concepts. Self-consuming concepts remain perennially fresh and plausible in an important sense, even *after* it has been pointed out that their intelligibility and force are purchased at the cost of presupposing the very concepts to be displaced or set aside. In this respect self-consuming concepts differ from paradoxes, self-contradictions, and self-reference fallacies. Their appeal is not diminished by exposure.

When early logical positivists announced the principle of verification, for example—the principle that to be cognitively meaningful a proposition must be capable of verification in principle—it was widely debated whether historical explanations, as a species, would go the way of metaphysics and poetry into the dark night of cognitive meaninglessness. This situation changed abruptly, however, the moment it was pointed out that positivism itself—that is to say its vaunted principle of verifiability—was *itself* unverifiable, a consequence which rendered the principle itself cognitively meaningless.

And no one mistook it for poetry either.

The point of assembling this reminder from the history of recent analytic philosophy is to underscore the difference between self-consuming concepts, as we are using that term, and the self-exempting fallacy, of which the principle of verification is but one instance.

Self-consuming concepts arrest our attention. They seem plausible somehow, they continue to recommend themselves to us—even *after* it has been pointed out that they purchase their sense, their plausibility and their force, at the expense of reinscribing the very contrasts they wish to set aside. Thus we remain fascinated by Descartes's elegantly flawed argument about the logical interchageability of the waking and dreaming states.

And yet even putting the matter this way misleads. In the example of the logical interchageability of the waking and dreaming states in Descartes's argument, two seemingly opposed and independent notions were seen to require one another. Self-consuming concepts, as we are using the term, differ in that the resources for dissolution are resources for *self*-dissolution. The negation of self-consuming concepts is their self-negation, and is inscribed within the body of these concepts themselves.

A better series of examples, therefore, could have derived from Hegel, whose philosophy as such may exhibit this form, as in his classic Being-Nothingness-Becoming triad. To illustrate this point briefly and superficially, Hegel's insight, in the *Science of Logic*, is that the concept "Being"—when properly understood—does not merely exclude the concept "Nothingness" but requires it, projecting it from itself as it were. For the distinction between Being

and particular beings, particular existents, can be drawn by removing determinations successively from particular beings. In this respect, Hegel's discussion of Being retrieves, recapitulates and recuperates the logic of the debate
about "substance" which divided Descartes, Locke, Berkeley, Hume and Kant.
To remove all determinations, all specifying conditions, from beings is to arrive at the notion of Being by stripping determinate beings of their particular-
ity, removing all of their predicates. To strip away all predicates, however,
leaves only a vacant possibility of being, an empty possibility of being, an
empty X awaiting predication, awaiting determination and specification.
These are, then, the "features" of no thing at all. Indeed, they are the features
of Nothingness.

It is not only Hegel's *Science of Logic* that exhibits some of the central features we are here calling self-consuming concepts. For just recall that the unconditional certainty (*Gewissheit*) that attaches to sense-certainty (*Die Sinnliche
Gewissheit*) is successively and successfully undermined from within in *The Phenomenology of Spirit*. Hegel accomplishes this by showing us just how the concept of certainty that attaches to our most directly evident sensations and locution—indexicals such as "here" and "now," "this" and "that"—are really
universals in disguise, applicable to anything in the universe. Each perception
and locution requires as a condition of its iteration and of its intelligibility the
very notion it wishes to contest or set aside. Each one implodes, requiring its
own concrete negation in order to make sense, in order even to be a candidate
for iteration. Indeed, the whole of *The Phenomenology* exhibits this form. Each
of its affirmations is self-negating, it has often been suggested, a self-
diremption which propels the text itself into a pretext for his *Science of Logic*.

As in the Descartes example, the details of these reconstructions can be debated. They are rehearsed here for two reasons: First, to underscore the point
that self-consuming concepts are self-negating, not negated by external comparison, that the resources for their self-negation are always already there,
waiting to surface and to be surfaced; second, as in the Being-Nothingness
diad, the diad is in reality a self-propelling triad. In Hegel's example, the oscil-
lation of Being and Nothingness yields the sublated concept "Becoming."
And, we would argue, self-consuming concepts, concepts which are self-
negating in a special sense, also entail a moment of recuperation in which the
content of the original unmediated concept and its negation are both can-
celled and preserved, annulled while retained (although *not* necessarily ele-
vated).[34]

But, again, even this comparison with Hegel's *Aufhebungen* can be misleading. In the case of the Being-Nothingness-Becoming triad, for example, we
are tempted to think that at each moment of self-negation something different
has been grasped conceptually, that the synthetic concept "Becoming" is a notion different from its progenies, Being and Nothingness. In the case of self-

consuming concepts, however, it is not the case that we see something *different* when we recognize that a given concept requires as a condition of its intelligibility the very contrast it wishes to set aside or would have us set aside. Rather, it would be far less misleading to say that in the case of self-consuming concepts *we see the same thing, only differently.*[35]

The recognition, therefore, that a given self-consuming concept requires as a condition of its intelligibility the very contrast it wishes to set aside or would have us set aside is not the recognition of a flaw, a lack, or an absence. It is, rather, the recognition that the concept entails its own negation, in a special sense, the recognition of which, in turn, is a negation of the negation. It seems to us that Nietzsche's notions of perspectivism, will to power, eternal recurrence, and the ideal life are self-consuming in this sense. The notion of will to power as relation(s) without relata, for example, is self-consuming in the sense specified, as is invoking the analogy between seeing and knowing—which Nietzsche's perspectivism explicitly does—in order to set aside the dominating visual metaphorics of traditional epistemology.

Permit us to turn briefly, therefore, to an examination of eternal recurrence and the ideal life, two of Nietzsche's most significant and dramatic self-consuming notions; both of which may also be usefully viewed—in our preliminary approximation—as self-consuming concepts. Nietzsche's presentation of eternal recurrence is central to his philosophic project. It is the generating thought of his *Zarathustra*, the thought which most divides commentators. It is unarguably the subject of two of Zarathustra's speeches—"On the Vision and the Riddle" and "The Convalescent"—and it is fully rehearsed in *The Gay Science* under the heading "*Das Grösste Schwergewicht.*" That entry (341) concludes by asking its interlocutors two questions framed as one:

> If this thought were to gain possession of you, it would transform you, as you are, or perhaps crush you. The question in each and every thing, "Do you want this once more and innumerable times more?" would weigh upon your actions as the greatest stress. Or how well disposed would you have to become to life and to yourself to *crave nothing more fervently* [*um nach nichts mehr zu verlangen*] than this ultimate eternal confirmation and seal?[36]

Nietzsche refers to this very aphorism in *Ecce Homo* when he writes "my *Gaya Scienza* . . . contains hundreds of signs of something incomparable; in the end it even offers the beginning of *Zarathustra*, and in the penultimate section of the fourth book the basic idea of *Zarathustra*."[37] So the aphorism just cited is "the basic idea of *Zarathustra*," a book Nietzsche characterized with predictable hyperbole in *Twilight of the Idols* as "the most profound book [humankind] possesses."[38]

The doctrine of eternal recurrence seems to be self-consuming in all of its versions,[39] including the cosmological/metaphysical and the many normative versions which try to derive one imperative or another from it. A closer look at the cosmological version which some commentators have asked us to imagine reveals rather quickly that the concept of eternal recurrence requires a notion of linear time to distinguish a specific configuration from its recurrence—the very mundane conception of time the doctrine allegedly contests and displaces. The state-of-the-universe at this instant, for example, will recur, if it is to recur, on some other identical June 30, 1991. But if this state of the universe can occur at some other time, on some other June 30, 1991, then it is not a recurrence of the same but a recurrence of the exactly similar—an argument already anticipated by Isaac Newton, when he remarked that even if all particles in the universe were one day to achieve the identical configuration they exhibit today these would not be identical states, since the time of their occurrence would differ. Therefore, as was argued elsewhere long ago, either occurrence is the case or circular time is the case; but if circular time, then only a single cycle; hence occurrence again rather than recurrence.[40] (We shall return to this question in a different context.) The only thing needed for the cosmological version of recurrence to exhibit that it is self-consuming is that it must purchase its intelligibility by asserting a condition it wishes to set aside. The concept of the recurrence of identical, datable events, indeed the concept of recurring datable identical times, is one such conceptual oxymoron, is one such self-consuming notion.

The favored normative version of eternal recurrence is self-consuming in much the same way. In this interpretation one is admonished to behave as if recurrence were true. Typically, the emphasis is on the putative psychological consequences which the teaching of eternal recurrence is thought to have upon one's actions if one believes it to be true—if one behaves as if recurrence were a cosmic "fact." The motivating point of this strategy is the belief that if one acts as if recurrence were true the psychological effect would be momentous.

It is not at all clear, however, what it is that one is being asked to imagine. If one is asked to behave as if recurrence were true, it is not clear that there can be *any* consequences. For one is then being asked to behave in ways that one has behaved an infinite number of previous recurrences. The point is that behaving as if recurrence were true entails behaving as if this moment not only will recur again but actually has recurred. This seems to follow from believing the truth of recurrence, from behaving as if it were true. So behaving as if recurrence were true entails behaving as if this moment, how one lives, is how one lived in an infinite number of previous recurrences. Moreover: How one now lives, this moment, *must* be how one has lived this moment an infinite number of previous times, if it is to count as a recurrence of "the same." But then what consequences can be said to follow? If believing that recurrence were so entails believing the sort of fatalism which is here proposed, then it is not clear that one can ever decide to believe (or not believe) it, and, accordingly, that any consequences follow from believing it to be true, since a fortiori believing it or not believing it is also fated in advance. One can only act as if recurrence were true if one believes that in a previous recurrence one behaved as if it were true, and so on ad infinitum.[41]

One could say that whatever causes one to behave as one does, it can only be oneself. That is, if this moment repeats a past recurrence, "necessarily," then one's present choices are a repetition of one's past choices. The choices are no less ours for having been past. But if any weight is to attach to such personal pronoun references a different difficulty arises. The self-consuming difficulty is this: The psychological weight, the stress which one is to experience, if recurrence is true, is said to be a consequence of one's believing that what one does now seals the future, imposes the seal of eternal repetition upon this very event. It is as if one were choosing one's eternal future self in the very act of choosing one's present self. But if we change our vantage point, it becomes quickly apparent that one's "present self" has here the same logical relation to one's "future self" as one's "past self" has to one's "present self." Their relationship is precisely symmetrical. So while one is at this very moment to experience the psychological weight, the enormous stress which attaches to choosing one's eternally recurring future self, how is one to avoid the deflating psychological impact which follows from recognizing that one's present self has already been chosen eternally, has already been constructed? It would appear that, on this normative reading, we cannot have it only one way. If we are to behave as if we are sealing future recurrences by writing these words, and if this is to be both a stressful and liberating thought, then why is this same thought not also supremely deflating—as the Stoics seem to have recognized—once it is realized that with whatever words we do write we are merely repeating the very phrases we have written an infinite number of previous times? Why is it not just sound and fury signifying yet another repetition?

The principle difficulty with the normative reading is closely related to that of the cosmological version. Both interpretations are irrevocably attached to the truth function of eternal recurrence. The cosmological version argues that Nietzsche thought recurrence was true. The normative version argues that Nietzsche invites us to behave as if it were true. The two versions—the cosmological and the normative—require as a condition of their intelligibility the very distinctions they wish to avoid or set aside.

If recurrence is a true account of the way things are, it ought to make no difference to our present lives, since these lives then will recur as other lives at other "identical" times and places. It seems clear that these future recurring "lives" quite simply have no conceptual or psychological grip on our present "lives." If, on the other hand, we are to behave as if recurrence were true, the giddying liberation of justifying ourselves to ourselves unto eternity founders on the dismaying flip-side that our present self-justifications are just a repetitious rehearsal of past eternities of self-justification.

In Nietzsche's published writings we are invited to think through the notion of eternal recurrence. We are asked the question "How well disposed would one have to become to oneself and to life to crave nothing more fervently than the infinite repetition, without alteration, of each and every moment?" Nietzsche invites his reader, first, to imagine a finite number of possible states of the universe, each destined to recur eternally, and then react to this imagined state of affairs. Presumably most people would find such a thought shattering because they would always find it possible to prefer the eternal repetition of their lives in an edited version rather than to crave nothing more fervently than the recurrence of their actual lives with each of its horrors. Only a superhuman being (an *Übermensch*), Nietzsche tells us in the Prologue to *Thus Spoke Zarathustra*, could accept recurrence without emendation, evasion, or self-deception, a being whose distance from conventional humanity is greater than the distance between man and beast.

What sort of creature would desire the unaltered repetition of its exact life, would prefer each and every moment of its life just as it is, and would prefer this to any alternative possibility it could imagine? What sort of attitude is suggested by a person, a quester, who could regard his or her life as Leibniz's God regarded the world: the best of all possible worlds?

Perhaps all of us have at one time or another experienced a tremendous moment whose repetition we would will unto eternity were this within our power and for the sake of which we would exchange our lives for no other. Artists at work in every medium have been known at one time or another to experience that enormous satisfaction when their work achieves their standard of perfection, when they would not trade places with the gods. Less esoterically, it is said that the agony of the long distance runner is sometimes replaced—after "the wall" has been hit—by an incredible sense of euphoria, well-being and achievement, which is not easily replaced. Most mundane of all, perhaps, human sexual satisfaction can sometimes be so intensely pleasurable that one would will its eternal repetition, and at that instant exchange lives with no one.

These illustrations are contestable, to be sure. Some may be inclined to argue that peak experiences, whether artistic, athletic, or sexual, are seldom without self-deception or pathology. We need not enter that debate here, however; for the burden of the remark is not that we know what it is like to achieve *Übermenschlichkeit*, only that we may on rare occasions perceive it as through a glass darkly.

But, again, what sort of creature could live its life under this description? For what sort of creature would this be its defining disposition? What sort of creature would desire the unaltered repetition of its exact life, we ask again, would prefer each and every moment of its life just as it is, and would prefer this to any alternative possibility it could imagine? And again, what sort of attitude is suggested by a person, a quester, who could regard his or her life as Leibniz's God regarded the world: the best of all possible worlds?

One way to approach these questions would be to argue that to want each moment unconditionally is to want it for its own sake, not because of something else or as a means to something else. When Aristotle argues, for example, that happiness is the highest good, he argues that it alone is wanted unconditionally, for its own sake. On this view, health and medicine are not wanted for their own sakes but because they promote happiness, they are desired as means to ends, are desired in order to achieve happiness. Even pleasure is not the highest good for Aristotle, just because it is pursued not only for its own sake but as a means of achieving happiness. It is not wanted simply and only for its own sake. On this reading of Nietzsche's eternal recurrence—by no means the only possible reading, to be sure—each moment must be wanted, as Aristotle thought happiness was wanted, for its own sake, neither because of something else nor as a means to something else.

To make the enormity of this task more transparent and more vivid, imagine or recall for one moment the most entirely satisfactory sexual experience of your life, the moment in which you preferred your beloved to any possible alternative beloveds, a moment in which you also urgently preferred to be the lover you were just then. Imagine further that, upon reflection, you would welcome the eternal recurrence of that experience, just as it is, without addition, subtraction, or remainder. Let us say of this unconditionally cherished sexual ecstasy—real or imagined, it does not matter which—that you desired it for its own sake. Now also imagine, in contrast, the moment of your deepest despair, or the searing pain of your most unfulfilled longing, or the shattering blow of your most ruinous humiliation, or the self-deceptive acid of your most secret envy. Finally, if you can, imagine having just the same attitude toward the catalogued moments of your greatest anguish that you were asked to imagine of your most cherished sexual ecstasy or fantasy. Just *that* is what Nietzsche's eternal recurrence requires of each and every moment wanted for its own sake, it seems to us, and just *that* is what turns this requirement itself into a self-consuming human impossibility, a conceptual and existential oxymoron. It ought to give pause to those who think that Nietzsche's thought of eternal recurrence taught us to "celebrate" each moment: *carpe diem.*

In Nietzsche's first published text on the trope of eternal recurrence, "*The Greatest Stress,*" from which we quoted earlier, there are two questions posed by the notion of eternal recurrence. Stated schematically, the questions are: (1) For any x, "do you want this once more and innumerable times more?"; (2) For any x, "do you crave nothing more fervently than this eternal confirmation and seal?" The first question specifies what is to be placed under the yoke of eternal repetition—not a life taken as a whole, but each and everything within that life. The second question asks how well disposed one would have to be to one-self and to life to crave nothing more fervently than the eternal recurrence of each moment of one's life—not even imagined alternative lives, alternative selves, and worlds.

But who could live, as some of us have had to do, in the midst of extermi-nation camps and love *that* unconditionally? And who among us would not will the recurrence of our lives minus the deaths of tens of thousands of innocent children who died and still are dying brutal deaths in Iraq, Kuwait, El Salva-dor, and elsewhere throughout the Third World—and not only there? Who among us, in brief, would not prefer some other possible life and world, no matter how content one may be with one's present lot? How can eternal recur-rence be willed after Dachau, Auschwitz, and Katyn Woods?

The point is that no matter how content we may be with our lives we can always imagine a better one, for example, our lives plus a reduction in the total sum of the world's pain and suffering, or our lives plus an attitude of *Übermen-schlichkeit* for those we love and admire, or for none. But there is still more required by this self-consuming notion. An *Übermensch* must not only affirm unconditionally each and every moment but must, as a sign of his or her re-sponsive self-love, be willing to eternalize each moment. To love each moment unconditionally, for the *Übermensch*, just *is* to will its eternal return. The *Über-mensch* alone, like the God whose death Nietzsche announces, wants nothing more fervently than the eternity of each and every moment of his or her life.

Only God and *Übermenschen* love each moment unconditionally, want noth-ing to be different, not forward, not backward, not in all eternity. Only for God, Leibniz and *Übermenschen* is this the best of all possible worlds. And Nietzsche was right to characterize this as his most abysmal thought; for it is abysmal![42]

On this reading, an *Übermensch* alone loves life unconditionally, without emendation, evasion or self-deception. We mortals should always be able to imagine a better possible life and world, if we allow our imaginations free reign. But that is just to say that Nietzsche's famous injunction, "become who you are," is far more difficult than simply coming to terms with one's own life and destiny. On this reading, only an *Übermensch* sincerely wills his or her own life. The rest of us will our lives and the world's in an edited version, if we are honest with ourselves. We live edited lives. We are virtually always the heroes of our lives.

Maudemarie Clark[43] has recently attempted to rescue Nietzsche from this (as she sees it) unhappy conclusion by applying the analogy of what she calls "the marriage test" to the questions put by Nietzsche's demon in "*Das Grösste Schwergewicht*." She suggests that the demon's question—"would you be willing to live this same life eternally?"[44]—is like the question, "if you had it to do all over, would you marry me again?"[45] Although this is not the place to enter into a protracted discussion of this alleged analogy, the following points need at least to be mentioned: (1) Clark's "test of affirmation"—which, for Clark as for Nehamas, is what Nietzsche's eternal recurrence teaches at bottom—is not a single but a plural test in the Nietzsche text she cites as evidence. We are asked by Nietzsche's demon not only if we would be *willing* to live the same life eternally but whether we *crave nothing more fervently* (in italics in Nietzsche) than this possibility, what he calls "this eternal confirmation and seal." Perhaps a more appropriate marital analogy would therefore have been this: "If you had it to do all over again, and you could marry anyone who ever lived, will ever live, or could ever live possessing whatever traits you wished, would you marry me again?" (2) Clark's analogy rests, as she herself admits, on suspending reflection rather than engaging in it: "Nietzsche's use of the demon to proclaim recurrence suggests that passing his test depends on one's uncritical response to recurrence. . . . To use eternal recurrence as a test of affirmation, one must be willing to 'play the game,' to imagine eternal recurrence in an uncritical and preanalytic manner, suspending all doubts concerning its truth or conceivability."[46] This sounds suspiciously like the proverbial doctor performing surgery upon a patient, then proclaiming the operation's unqualified success, save for the minor point that the patient died beneath the knife. (3) If the upshot of Nietzsche's central teaching makes sense on the condition that thoughtful deliberation and critical reflection are to be suspended in assessing one's life— horrific suggestions for any Nietzschean, it seems to us—then it is hard to see how anyone could fail to pass Clark's proposed "test of affirmation." After all, it is not too hard to guess how most people would respond to the question "would you be willing to live this same life eternally?" What, after all, is the alternative? If the alternative is nothingness, as it will undoubtedly have to be for the majority of Nietzsche's readers, who will say no? The heaviest of burdens (*das Grösste Schwergewicht*) is not, on Clark's view, a question of choosing between this life and thoughtfully imagined alternative versions of it. It is simply an unreflective *überhaupt* assessment of one's life. She might as well have written: "On balance, would you want the recurrence of your life?" As in her version of the "marriage test" she does not allow measuring that life against all possible alternatives. Clark's problem, like that of all philosophers who insist on converting eternal recurrence into a test of affirmation, is that it trivializes Nietzsche's insight. It converts Nietzsche's most horrific and most burdensome measure of a life into a stroll in the park on a sunny afternoon, something to be enjoyed by everyone save those afflicted with pathological self-loathing or self-directed necrophilia. For it seems to us that the force of her "affirmation test" is to convert most of humanity into *Übermenschen*. On the view offered here, in contrast, Nietzsche was not in the affirmation test business at all.

Maudemarie Clark is by no means alone in trying to rescue Nietzsche from our (to their minds unhappy) conclusion that Nietzsche was not in the affirmation test business at all, was not the Ann Landers of philosophers. For example, despite the fact that, in *Nietzsche: Life as Literature*, Alexander Nehamas (unlike Clark) confines himself to a single and singular instance of Nietzsche's "life affirmation test"—reading it as realized only in the authorial construct "Nietzsche"—eternal recurrence is nevertheless a philosophical principle of affirmation and justification for him too. Indeed, the doctrine of eternal recurrence simultaneously marks and is the mark of the ideal life for Nehamas:

> Eternal recurrence is a view of the ideal life. It holds that *a life is justified only if one would want to have again the same life one had already had, since, as the will to power shows, no other life can ever be possible* [our italics]. The eternal recurrence therefore holds that our life is justified only if we fashion it in such a way that we would want it to be exactly as it had already been.[47]

Important notions are on epigrammatic display here. One is that eternal recurrence is a view of the ideal life, that a "life is justified only if one would" wish its unaltered repetition; a second notion is that, as the will to power presumably shows, "*no other life can ever be possible*" (our italics). These two suggestions need to be uncoupled, it seems to us. Nehamas conflates these two notions—the idea that there is a test involved in the thought of eternal recurrence on which *Übermenschen* receive the highest grade in the class "human beings," and the quite different idea that no other life can ever be possible for human beings *simpliciter* than the ones they live. However, these two notions neither entail nor imply one another, from a logical point of view; and the textual evidence to support such an entailment is shaky at best (as we shall show in the next section). And yet Nehamas seems to think that there is an entailment, as when he argues that when we accept eternal recurrence "at that point we accept all we have done, *since* [our italics] every part of the past is by itself necessary and in combination sufficient for us to be what we are."[48] But surely the recognition that "every part of the past is by itself necessary and in combination sufficient for us to be what we are" is not strong enough to move us, by itself, to accept all we have done and all we have become. Indeed, the alleged recognition is either trivially true or contentiously and probably false. For in its benign form, to say that "every part of the past is by itself necessary and in combination sufficient for us to be what we are" is simply to assert that we are products of our past, that to be who we are is, among other things, to have made precisely the choices we made in the circumstances and time-space continuum which are the measure of our lives. And what it means to be "us" just *is* to be the result of these particular choice matrices, not some other ones. To be Caesar is, necessarily, to have crossed the Rubicon. Had "he" not crossed the Rubicon, there would have been a different "Caesar." Different choices, different lives. Different lives, different selves.[49] This benign sense of necessity is very like Sartre's later notion that we *are* our choices, nothing else besides. To have chosen otherwise would be to have been a different person. Notice, however, that this certainly does *not* entail the stronger thesis Nehamas needs—the thesis that we *could* not have had different pasts, *could* not have been different selves, *could* not have made different choices. Moreover, and ironically, Nehamas's conflation consumes itself, for *to want* the life we "necessarily" have already had *requires* a comparison of what has been the case with what *might have been* the case, requires comparing our (at least partly) chosen selves and our lives against rejected or missed alternative possible lives and selves. Surely, even on Nehamas's view, to *want* what must be the case in any case requires an imaginative comparison between the selves we have become and their unrealized alternatives, alternative "selves" we *could not* have become on Nehamas's view. After all, that is the point of his argument that when we accept eternal recurrence "*at that point we accept all we have done* [our italics], since every part of the past is by itself necessary and in combination sufficient for us to be what we are."[50] It is the imaginative comparing of alternative selves (unrealized *or* impossible) that does all the work here, however, not the recognition of an alleged cosmic fatalism. Indeed, the recognition requires the comparison. Another way to put this same point is just to say that when Nehamas has Nietzsche claim that "*no other life can ever be possible*" he trades on two very different senses of "possible." For, to repeat, it is trivially true that for something to count as "your" life it must consist of the events—the past—that constitute it and individuate it as "yours." So, it is true that to count as your life no other life is possible; the life of a "Caesar" who did not cross the Rubicon is not the possible subject of Shakespeare's play. But surely it is as "possible" for you to have lived your life differently, as "possible" to have become a different person than the one you are, as it is for Caesar not to have crossed the Rubicon.

Since Nehamas is no doubt aware of the force of objections such as these, he employs a philosopher's standard artifice, that is to say, he makes the notion of the recurrence test *parasitic* on an independent ontology of will to power, one that he then ascribes to Nietzsche (implausibly, as we shall argue in the next section of this chapter). For if you reconstruct the relevant sentence of the first Nehamas passage quoted above, its logical form is this: *since, as the will to power shows, no other life can ever be possible, a life is justified only if one would want to have again the same life one has already had.* Our disagreement with Nehamas is just that an *Übermensch*'s reason for wishing most fervently the repetition of each unaltered moment is *not* that she recognizes the alleged necessity which alone has made her who she is, but rather that she would prefer to be—wants eternally to be—the very person she already is, and she wants this more fervently than any alternative possibilities she can imagine.[51]

Like the *höhere Menschen* Zarathustra encounters, seduces, misleads, teaches, and—finally—escapes, philosophers typically want Nietzsche to be a sublime

Ann Landers. On the diagnostic reading suggested here, the heaviest burden Nietzsche asks us to recognize and to bear is not that of our fated destiny. Rather, it is the realization that our highest aspirations and yearnings turn against themselves in spite of themselves in the endless carnival of the ascetic ideal.

The suggestion made earlier that we live edited lives was intended to throw into sharper relief the ground-shifting, perspectivizing force of Nietzsche's figure of eternal recurrence. The thought of eternal recurrence, viewed in this way, surfaces in what Harold Bloom has called "the urge to be elsewhere." Eternal recurrence understood in this way chimes well with the Romantic tradition's insistence that the most radical of all desires is to possess the name one has already been given, as in Browning's "Childe Roland to the Dark Tower Came," which was mentioned earlier. Put differently, Nietzsche's thought of eternal recurrence suggests that the most radical of all desires is to want unconditionally to be the very person one already is.

The upshot of these remarks is that if one identifies the ideal life with the *Übermensch*—and identifies an *Übermensch* as the person who could sincerely say yes to eternal recurrence without self-deception or pathology—then this conception of the ideal life, too, may be self-consuming—or self-deconstructing—in the sense that it requires one to regard each and every moment of one's life as Leibniz's God viewed it, namely, as the best of all possible moments. Only self-deception of theological proportions could affirm the unconditional worth of every moment of one's life, it seems to us.

We can sum up what we have been saying as follows: According to the Official View, the distinction between a philosopher's thought and the text which expresses it is to treated on the analogy of the relation of wheat to its chaff, kernel to its husk, or diamond to coal. The case of Nietzsche may be marshalled to complicate this Official View, by pointing out features of his style which are not easily detached from the thought they express—perhaps cannot be detached from it. Indeed, one motivating point of our book is to call into question the traditional philosophical notion that thought and its embodiment mark contrasts that go all the way down. Perhaps it is better to understand "philosophical" writing as subject to and emerging out of the experience and the exigencies of writing itself rather than to understand graphemes as the vehicle for the expression of antecedent philosophical "ideas."[52] And the central stylistic features mentioned to begin to motivate this argument have been hyperbole, undecidability, resistance to paraphrase, tokening, and the self consuming character of Nietzsche's concepts and tropes.

The upshot of this preliminary excursion, in "the Nietzsche case," can be put in the form of an a single sentence with which we should like to conclude this section. If hyperbole is the most useful trope to characterize the literariness of Nietzsche's texts, then self-consuming concepts may be the most useful way of recuperating the philosophical content of Nietzsche's literariness.

The Corpus of Thought:
A Textual/Philological Supplement

The distinction we shall begin to focus on in this section is neither a distinction between analytic and non-analytic nor between "philosophical" and "literary" accounts of Nietzsche's works.[53] It is, in fact, quite indifferent to these distinctions. Nor is the distinction very deep, at least not at first glance. It is, instead, primarily a philological distinction, one not unusual in discussion of canon formation. We can distinguish between those who treat Nietzsche's *Nachlass* as if these materials were philologically unproblematic—that is, those who treat the *Nachlass* as on at least a par with his published writings, for instance—from those who do not. For purposes of this section we will call those commentators who regard the use of Nietzsche's *Nachlass* as unproblematic "lumpers." The fact that Nietzsche elected neither to publish nor to polish most of the *Nachlass* seldom bothers a lumper, so it is not surprising that, with them, the reasons *why* he did so will not appear to be a problem. A lumper is inclined to assume, as does Richard Schacht in his instructive book, for example, that "these un-published writings . . . contain much more of his expressed thinking on certain important matters than do his finished work."[54]

Lumpers are drawn to Nietzsche's *Nachlass*, to his literary estate, and are especially fond of *Der Wille zur Macht*. In Schacht's case, for example, there are 1,718 quotations from Nietzsche in his 546 pages of text. 861 out of 1,718 quotations—more than half—are from the anthology of notes, *Der Wille zur Macht*. Moreover, in his interesting chapter titled "The World and Life" (a chapter which deals with such matters as "Toward a Philosophical Cosmology," "The World and 'Will to Power'," "Life and Will to Power," and "The Eternal Recurrence"), where Schacht quotes Nietzsche 199 times, 152 of these quotations derive from *Der Wille zur Macht*, better than three out of four on the average. *Thus Spoke Zarathustra*, in contrast, frequently poses something of an embarrassment. It is quoted by Schacht, again for example only, a total of thirty-four times throughout his book in part because "it [i.e., *Thus Spoke Zarathustra*] does not readily lend itself to the sort of analysis undertaken here."[55] The aim of most lumpers—from Jaspers and Heidegger to Danto and Schacht—is to place Nietzsche's writings squarely within the commentator's conception of the philosophical tradition. And that is no small accomplishment! Indeed it can be, as it is in Heidegger's case, a major accomplishment. It does not matter especially for our purposes either whether the commentator's tradition is regarded as the metaphysics of presence—in which Nietzsche becomes its closure, as in Heidegger's suggestion—or whether Nietzsche's prose is regarded instead as making disguised yet substantive traditional philosophical recommendations, recommendations which can be recast in argument form defined by an antecedent philosophical agenda, such as truth and knowledge, ontological commitments, the nature of the ideal life, and the nature of morality. It is therefore not at all surprising that for many lumpers Nietzsche's style is regarded as an obstacle to understanding his philosophical intentions. Under this rubric the relatively flat and familiar prose of the *Nachlass*, devoid of literary embellishment, is often thought either to be less ambiguous than work Nietzsche chose to publish or authorized for publication or—in the extreme case—to be his real philosophy. To quote Heidegger:

> But Nietzsche's philosophy proper, the fundamental position on the basis of which he speaks in these and in all the writings he himself published, did not assume a final form and was not itself published in any book. . . . What Nietzsche himself published during his creative life was always foreground. . . . *His philosophy proper was left behind as posthumous, unpublished work.*[56]

Lumpers come in all shapes and traditions. Heidegger, Jaspers, Deleuze, Müller-Lauter, Danto and Schacht are, for our purposes, paradigmatic lumpers. In contrast to lumpers there are what we call "splitters." Hollingdale, Alderman, Montinari, Higgins, Clark, and Strong are splitters. Parenthetically, the late Walter Kaufmann was a special case in this taxonomy. He generally claimed to be a splitter but in practice was typically a lumper; and Alexander Nehamas's excellent book, *Nietzsche: Life as Literature*[57] contains the same ambivalence as Kaufmann's. While it should not affect the thrust or force of Nehamas's overall argument—with which we are in considerable sympathy— he, too, relies heavily on *The Will to Power* on those occasions when it alone will get the argumentative job done. This is especially true, for example, in chapter 3, "A Thing is the Sum of Its Effects," whose title and argument would collapse without *The Will to Power* as the primary source material. Nehamas then relies heavily on this chapter in subsequent ones—for example in his discussion of eternal recurrence in chapter 5—as when he argues, for instance, that for Nietzsche to change anything is, for any X, to change everything. But, to repeat, Nehamas's fine book might have been argued to most of its conclusions with virtually equal force without the *Nachlass*.

Splitters, in contrast to lumpers, tend to distinguish sharply between published and unpublished writings in Nietzsche's case. Moreover, such commentators occasionally read Nietzsche as struggling in his published writings to set aside the felt need to offer canonical ontological descriptions, theories of knowledge, theories of morality, and theories of the ideal life.[58]

As we can see in discussions of eternal recurrence, perspectivism and will to power, this methodological difference between lumpers and splitters—this difference of opinion about the use and value of Nietzsche's literary estate— can become substantive. For instance, lumpers tend to argue that eternal recurrence is a normative and/or empirical concept, even when the term "empirical" is equated with "metaphysical." In its normative version, it is argued that eternal recurrence admonishes us to behave as if recurrence were true, because believing it to be true will be the greatest weight upon our actions. In its empirical version, Nietzsche is sometimes thought to propose a "mistaken be-lief [that] science compels us to accept the [eternal recurrence] hypothesis."[59] Then, too, lumpers tend to construe will to power, in some sense or other, as an ontology or cosmology, and are inclined to treat Nietzsche's perspectivism as a theory of knowledge.[60]

Typically, the views of splitters are more difficult to characterize. Some split-ters are persuaded that Nietzsche neither had nor wished to offer a theory of knowledge, nor an ontology, nor an ethics. However, they have difficulty ex-plaining why he ought to be taken seriously by philosophers if he had none of these things to offer us. Most splitters will also insist, *contra* lumpers, that Nietzsche's philosophy cannot be divorced from his style, that the mode of expression and what is expressed are in some sense inseparable; yet they have difficulty explaining how this claim is to be understood and why this should be so. For while it may be true that authentic poetry dissolves in paraphrase, it is hard to see why philosophy would or could dissolve in recharacterization.[61]

The uncomfortable upshot for much Nietzsche scholarship to date, partic-ularly in the English-speaking world, seems therefore to be this: if splitters are right in their textual claims, and we think that they generally are, the purchase price of their textual probity may be to move Nietzsche out of discursive phi-losophy altogether or perhaps into its margins. Lumpers, on the other hand, move Nietzsche squarely into the wax museum of the great dead philosophers, but at the purchase price of promoting to primacy and priority many of the very texts and theses Nietzsche seems to have abandoned.

What we propose to do in the pages that follow, therefore, is to sketch briefly the present philological situation in Nietzsche studies as we understand it. The result of that sketch will be the by now familiar suggestion that, in his 1888 manuscripts, Nietzsche performed what may be called an epistemectomy rather than offering us an epistemology, that he seems also to have abandoned the will to power and eternal recurrence as ontological principles, and that an *Übermensch* was perhaps not to be construed as yet another version of the hu-man ideal. Of course, that will leave us with the questions: Is our Nietzsche still a philosopher? And if so in what sense? Our preliminary conclusion in this chapter will be disappointingly sketchy and programmatic. We shall suggest that a splitter's Nietzsche—rescued from philological triviality—may usefully situate him as the first full-blooded postmodern, nonrepresentational thinker, the fountainhead of a tradition which flows from him to Heidegger, Derrida, Foucault, Rorty and much recent literary theory. For the moment this must remain a promissory note, which we hope to cash out in subsequent chapters.

The Present Philological Situation

The Colli-Montinari editions[62] supersede, expand and correct all prior Nietzsche editions. The *Nachlass*, for example, is expanded from roughly

3,500 pages in the *Grossoktavausgabe* and *Musarionausgabe* to more than 5,000 pages out of a corpus of about 8,000 pages. Moreover, the materials are presented in a strictly chronological order as a result of which it has become clear that Nietzsche had not only abandoned his intention to write a book called *Der Wille zur Macht*, but that *even while he was entertaining the notion of writing such a book* its content was *not* to be the pseudo-canonical 1,067 sections gathered under that title by Elisabeth Förster-Nietzsche, Heinrich Köselitz, Otto Weiss, et al.[63] The book *Der Wille zur Macht*—even in its projected version before Nietzsche conclusively rejected the idea of writing such a book—is probably *not* the one frequently cited. Rather, by February 1888 Nietzsche had settled on 374 previously written entries as raw material for a future book to be titled *Der Wille zur Macht*.[64] One hundred and four of these entries never found their way into pre-Montinari editions at all; and of the remaining 270 fragments only 133 are included in unaltered form in the collection of 1,067 sections which appear under the Förster-Nietzsche title *Der Wille zur Macht*. In brief, 934 out of 1,067 entries in the lumpers's favorite book appear to have been intended for no book at all; or, on the most generous construal, 270 notes may have been intended initially for further polishing, only to have been abandoned in the end. The implications of this, as we will try to show, may be serious.

It might be useful at this point to recall that Nietzsche's literary estate from roughly 1885 to January 1889 (*The Will to Power* period) was culled by Colli and Montinari from twenty-two handwritten sources which consist of fifteen very large exercise books, three large notebooks, and four substantial loose-leaf portfolios.[65] These add up to thousands of pages and items, including materials taken up in previous critical editions as well as materials not included. Over the years some commentators have taken inventory from accounts of the materials from which different critical editions have been culled, an inventory which consists of more than twenty-five distinguishable categories, including fragments, aphorisms, plans, outlines, titles, prefaces, virtually finished initially unpublished writings such as *Ecce Homo*, *The Antichrist*, and the Basel *Schriften*, memoranda, sketches, drawings, doodles, bills, receipts, fiscal questions, investment information, notices of sales, cost-accounting notes, notices of prices and notices of awards and contests, travel notes and routes, descriptions of walks and paths, snippets of conversations real or imagined, gossip about visits and visitors, weather reports, pages of quoted materials transcribed from other authors and discussions of same; and, of course, there is an endless stream of letters to and from Nietzsche. Sometimes Nietzsche's pages are stained. Some pages are torn. Some are illegible, having been rewritten many times. Some are opaque inscriptions. Sentences set off in quotation marks such as one of Derrida's favorites, "*Ich habe meinen Regenschirm vergessen*," are not unique. That sentence is to be found for the first time in the Colli-Montinari critical edition while Nietzsche's quoted laundry lists typically are not to be found in any critical editions.

From 1886 forward—that is for the last three years of Nietzsche's mental life—the evidence suggests that he began to review systematically all his published writings and unpublished notes for what seems to have been the first time.[66] He appears to be preoccupied with copyright questions, wishing to have them secured in his behalf, in part because he is eager to revise *Menschliches Allzumenschliches* and perhaps all of his other works as well. Chiefly, however, he is preoccupied with future works, particularly with a book project whose title he changes often, sometimes perhaps to be called *Der Wille zur Macht*.

Space does not permit a thorough chronicle of the fascinating rise, decline and fall of *Der Wille zur Macht* as a literary project.[67] What merits reiteration, however, is the fact that in mid-February 1888 Nietzsche gathered together and himself numbered 374 entries under the rubric *Der Wille zur Macht*. The mere fact that Nietzsche numbered unpublished entries was unusual for him. He typically did not do so. His later editors introduced that convention. At any rate, these 374 entries appear in two quarto notebooks—notebooks with four leaves per page—and one folio loose-leaf notebook. The first quarto notebook is 142 pages long and contains—among other things—Nietzsche's numbering of entries 1–136 for the planned book *Der Wille zur Macht*. Nietzsche then numbered serially entries 137–300 in a second 142-page quarto notebook. Sections 301–372 are numbered in a loose-leaf folio page book, constituting the first 40 pages among 200 folio sheets.[68] A third quarto notebook then establishes rubrics for all 374 entries for the planned book *Der Wille zur Macht*.

One very interesting contrast between the earlier March 1887 plan which Elisabeth Förster-Nietzsche employed as the basis for her edition and the superseding February 1888 plan may be found in the 1888 outline for *Der Wille zur Macht*, which consists of twelve rubrics for four books:

[zum ersten Buch]
  1. Der Nihilismus, vollkommen zu Ende gedacht.
  2. Cultur, Civilisation, die Zweideutigkeit des "Modernen."

[zum zweiten Buch]
  3. Die Herkunft des Ideals.
  4. Kritik des christlichen Ideals.
  5. Wie die Tugend zum Siege kommt.
  6. Der Heerden-Instinkt.

[zum dritten Buch]
  7. Der "Wille zur Wahrheit."
  8. Moral als Circe der Philosophen.
  9. Psychologie des "Willens zur Macht" (Lust, Wille, Begriff usw.)

[zum vierten Buch]
10. Die "ewige Wiederkunft".
11. Die grosse Politik.
12. Lebens-Recepte für uns.[69]

Among the most interesting contrasts, it seems to us, is the one between the published 1887 version of Book Three—from the plan Elisabeth followed—and the supervenient 1888 version. The 1887 version, the one which was published and has become an important text for lumpers, remember, has four parts for Book Three of *Der Wille zur Macht*:

1. The Will to Power as Knowledge
2. The Will to Power in Nature
3. The Will to Power in Society
4. The Will to Power as Art

Contrast that with the later 1888 plan for Book Three once again:

1. The "Will to Truth."
2. Morality as Circe of Philosophers.
3. Psychology of the "Will to Power" (Pleasure, Will, Concept, etc.).

This 1888 latter plan self-consciously supersedes Nietzsche's March 1887 plan, the one on which the pseudo-canonical *Der Wille zur Macht* is based, since Nietzsche had the 1887 outline before him while writing the supervening 1888 plan. Moreover, 104 entries designated by Nietzsche for inclusion in *Der Wille zur Macht* in 1888 never found their way into that 1,067-entry non-book, and 137 others are incomplete or are incorrectly cited or incorrectly edited.

More significantly for our purposes, the rubric of the will to power in *nature* silently slips from view in *all* eight or so post–1887 plans. Equally important perhaps, the 1888 materials we have just described are those Nietzsche took with him to Sils Maria four months later, in June 1888, and some of even these materials he seems to have instructed his landlord, Durisch, to dispose of in September 1888 when he left Sils, having abandoned *Der Wille zur Macht* as a literary project.[70]

Quite apart from the stunning disparity between what Nietzsche had planned to retain and polish in February 1888 but ultimately discarded anyway and what Förster-Nietzsche retrieved and published using earlier, rejected rubrics, there are the equally stunning entries Nietzsche really did not plan to publish. These include, for example, the famous last entry, 1,067, of the Förster-Nietzsche edition, an entry Nietzsche jotted down in July *1885* but had set aside by February 1888 as material for which he had no further use.

And do you know what "the world" is to me? Shall I show it to you in my mirror? This world: a monster of energy, without beginning, without end; a firm, iron magnitude of force that does not grow bigger or smaller, that does not expend itself but only transforms itself as a whole, of unalterable size, a household without expenses or losses, but likewise without increase or income; enclosed by "nothingness" as by a boundary; not something blurry or wasted, not something endlessly extended, but set in a definite space as a definite force, and not a space that might be "empty" here or there, but rather as force throughout, as a play of forces and waves of forces, at the same time one and many, increasing here and at the same time decreasing there; a sea of forces flowing and rushing together, eternally changing, eternally flooding back, with tremendous years of recurrence, with an ebb and a flood of its forms; out of the simplest forms striving toward the most complex, out of the stillest, most rigid, coldest forms toward the hottest, most turbulent, most self-contradictory, and then again returning home to the simple out of this abundance, out of the play of contradictions back to the joy of concord, still affirming itself in this uniformity of its courses and its years, blessing itself as that which must return eternally, as a becoming that knows no satiety, no disgust, no weariness: this, my *Dionysian* world of the eternally self-creating, the eternally self-destroying, this mystery world of the twofold voluptuous delight, my "beyond good and evil," without goal, unless the joy of the circle is itself a goal; without will, unless a ring feels good will toward itself—do you want a name for this world? A *solution* for all its riddles? A *light* for you, too, you best-concealed, strongest, most intrepid, most midnightly men?—*This world is the will to power—and nothing besides!* And you yourselves are also this will to power—and nothing besides![71]

   The reasons for going on at such length are a bit complex. They include the conviction that many lumpers have perhaps been elevating the wrong texts, that when it comes to will to power as a first-order conception—a cosmology, ontology, or what-have-you—they can find very little support in Nietzsche's published writings. Discussion of will to power in larger ontological contexts, in contexts other than the psychological or organic, occur primarily in only *two* entries Nietzsche chose to publish, *Zur Genealogie der Moral* II, 12 and *Jenseits von Gut und Böse* 36. The pertinent snippet from a rather lengthy aphorism is typically excised as follows from *GM* II 12:

I have emphasized this point of historical method all the more strongly because it runs counter to our current instincts and fashions, which would rather come to terms with the absolute haphazardness or the mechanistic meaninglessness of events than with the theory of a will to power mirrored in all process. The democratic bias against anything that dominates or wishes to dominate our modern misarchism (to coin an ugly word for an ugly thing) has gradually so sublimated and disguised itself that nowadays it can invade the strictest, most objective sciences without anyone's raising a word of protest.

The other aphorism in question, *BGE* 36, reads, in part:

Suppose nothing else were "given" as real except our world of desires and passions, and we could not get down, or up, to any other "reality" besides the reality of our drives . . . Suppose, finally, we succeeded in explaining our entire instinctive life as the development and ramification of *one* basic form of the will—namely, of the will to power, as *my* proposition has it; suppose all organic functions could be traced back to this will to power and one could also find in it the solution of the problem of procreation and nourishment—it is *one* problem—then one would have gained the right to determine *all* efficient force univocally as—*will to power*. The world viewed from inside, the world defined and determined according to its "intelligible character"—it would be "will to power" and nothing else.

The meaning and intention of these two entries is scarcely clear. Even if they were clear they would only constitute two slender reeds out of more than 8,000 pages of text on which to hang an ontology or cosmology of will to power. Similarly, little or no support can be found for eternal recurrence as a cosmology or ontology in works authorized or intended by Nietzsche for publication, as far as we can tell.

But even if one were to take the sensible-sounding route of treating the *Nachlass* as a thought-laboratory—as Walter Kaufmann originally suggested when publishing the English translation of *The Will to Power*—the issue is scarcely settled. For which notes are to count as experiments for which published notions? Can such notes not be read with equal justice as *failed* experiments, ideas Nietzsche elected not to follow up, such as *Der Wille zur Macht* 1,067? That is, should the literary estate not be read as one reads rough drafts of papers, plays, novels or dialogues, as *predecessor* versions in which the published word just is the last word? And even if one could read the *Nachlass* as Nietzsche's thought-laboratory, it is far from clear what that would tell us about any single thought-experiment—other than that it was unacceptable in its *Nachlass* form.

An illustration may help here.

1. In the late summer of 1882 Nietzsche wrote a note which reads: "'But how could you behave that way! a friend said to a very clever person—it was stupidity.' It has become difficult enough for me too, he replied."[72] (*Es ist mir auch schwer genug geworden.*)

2. A year later a note strikingly similar to this one appears in the summer 1883 *Nachlass*: "'But how could you behave that way? It was stupidity'—'It has become difficult enough for me too.'"[73] (*Es ist mir auch schwer genug geworden.*)

3. Less than 18 months later, in the winter 1884–85 *Nachlass* to *Z* we read: "—but Zarathustra, said the serpent, you clever one, how could you behave that way! That was stupidity!—It has become difficult enough for me too."[74] (*Es ist mir auch schwer genug geworden.*)

4. And less than thirty pages later, in the same winter 1884–85 *Nachlass* one reads: "'But you clever one, how could you behave that way! It was stupidity'—'It has become difficult enough for me too.'"[75] (*Es ist mir auch schwer genug geworden.*)

5. Finally, in the published 1885 Part IV of *Thus Spoke Zarathustra* one reads

the following, in the section called "The Ass Festival": "And you, said Zarathustra, you wicked old magician, what have you done! Who should hereafter believe in you in this free age, when you believe in such gods-asininities?

"It was stupidity what you did; how could you, you clever one, commit such a stupidity!

"O Zarathustra, the clever magician replied, you are right, it was stupidity—it has become difficult enough for me too."[76] (*Es ist mir auch schwer genug geworden.*)

That this chain of five quoted passages which recur in modified form over a three-year period is connected is clear. Notice that the events, speakers, circumstances and content change. What is unclear, however, is how or why any of these *Nachlass* fragments may be said to shed *any* light on the published *Zarathustra* remark. And our sense is that the remainder of the *Nachlass* bears much the same relationship to the published works, a thesis we cannot hope to demonstrate here, of course. The methodological point suggested should be clear, however: Substituting *Nachlass* for published materials confuses an explanation with that which requires one.

Nevertheless, lumpers have often suggested in reply that the *Nachlass* is "representative" of Nietzsche's thinking. However, this is either trivially true or misleading. For it is trivially true to say that Nietzsche's rejected draft notes "represent" his thinking, because the term "represent" may merely mean "what he thought." If they are Nietzsche's thoughts, they represent Nietzsche's thinking rather than someone else's. But notice that even this is oversimple and misleading, because some of the *Nachlass* consists of pages of the writings of *others* which Nietzsche dutifully copied, for example the dozens of pages of Baudelaire he copied in 1888. Are Baudelaire's thoughts to be construed as Nietzsche's thoughts then? And if not, how do the former "represent" the latter?

More typically, however, there are three distinguishable senses in which Nietzsche's *Nachlass* may be said to "represent" his thinking:

1. Sometimes the *Nachlass* "represents" his thought in the sense that the published writings and *Nachlass* are virtually identical, e.g., as in the case of the notes surrounding *Die Geburt der Tragödie*, which are almost *verbatim* the published text. There are virtually no editorial revisions in this case.

2. Sometimes Nietzsche's *Nachlass* has been said to "represent" his thinking in an inappropriate sense, in the sense that he produced these plans and/or entries at time T but elected *not* to pursue them further at time Tn, i.e., Nietzsche deliberately abandoned them (e.g., as in the case of the five prefaces for five unwritten books Nietzsche prepared for Lou Salome, or the *Der Wille zur Macht* plan of March 1887 which he abandoned in February 1888, or the bulk of the entries published under the *Der Wille zur Macht* title).

3. Sometimes the *Nachlass* "represents" Nietzsche's published thought in the

sense that the notes are raw materials which are modified, typically substantially, in the published *oeuvre*, as in the *Zarathustra* chain quoted earlier. These are the hardest cases and ones for which no algorithm will serve. Such entries should be treated with great care.

These three distinctions or something like them seem basic. We predict more with hope than with confidence that future Nietzsche studies will take them into account, so that sense (2) of the term "represent" will not be conflated with senses (1) and (3).

Before concluding these philological reflections it might be useful to review the general shape and fate of Nietzsche's projects during the summer and fall of his highest hope and deepest despair, his last summer in Sils Maria, 5 June 1888 to 20 September. Here are its highlights, in outline:

1. Nietzsche had begun to gather some of his notes together in early May, 1888 for a new work to be titled *Der Fall Wagner*. He works on these notes, writes many new ones, and by mid-August has a finished version to show his publisher as well as his admirers, chiefly Heinrich Köselitz (a.k.a. Peter Gast). By mid-September printers copies are ready.

2. At the same time, having reached Sils in June, he now begins to write a somewhat different work whose end result is as yet not clear to Nietzsche himself; for he is at work from June on not only on *Der Fall Wagner* but on a set of notes which he thinks, at first, will be called *Müssiggang eines Psychologen*, but he relents and later decides on the title *Götzendämmerung* instead.

3. At the beginning of September 1888 Nietzsche segregates his entries into those which will appear as *Gotzendämmerung*. He excludes from them what will eventually appear as entries 1–28 of *Der Antichrist*; and at the same time he replaces the conception of a project called *Der Wille zur Macht* with that of a new work in four parts, to be called *Umwerthung aller Werte*.

4. The book *Der Antichrist* is worked on. It contains the 28 mentioned entries which were not included in *Götzendämmerung*; and sections 29–62 are written. Nietzsche leaves Sils on 20 September unclear about the shape of the *Umwerthung*. Sometimes *Der Antichrist* is to be part one, to be followed by a second title, *Der Immoralist*. The suggestion occurs to Nietzsche for the first time at the end of September that perhaps *Götzendämmerung* is the synopsis of his views, his "philosophy" in outline form.

5. *Ecce Homo* is begun on or about October 15, his 44th birthday. He works on it continuously, along with *Der Antichrist*. *Ecce Homo* is revised for the last time and sent to the printer on 2 January 1889.

6. From the end of November on *Der Antichrist* displaces the *Umwerthung* as the title of that "major" planned work. In the end, even the *Umwerthung* subtitle is dropped in favor of "Fluch auf das Christenthum." And, as is well known, *Der Antichrist* does not appear in print until 1895, in the edition Elisabeth Förster-Nietzsche supervised. It appears in volume eight of the Nau-

mann edition of the *Grossoktavausgabe*, mistakenly as Book One of *Der Wille zur Macht*. Finally, the first edition of *Ecce Homo* is not published until 1908, twenty years after its composition.

We take it that the philological evidence shows that by the end of Nietzsche's stay in Sils Maria no *Hauptwerk* called *Der Wille zur Macht* was forthcoming, and that by the year's end no *Hauptwerk* of any sort was forthcoming.

A lumper who views Nietzsche's *The Will to Power* as the distilled essence of his thought, its alembic, may nevertheless wish to avail himself or herself of a distinction to avoid having to set his or her privileged text aside. One might adopt the strategy often urged by poststructuralist thinkers—from Barthes to Foucault, Nehamas, and Derrida—and distinguish the author of Nietzsche's texts from the efficient cause of them, namely, from the historical person Friedrich Nietzsche. The term "author" is in this case a quasi-technical term, the complex product of the interaction of text and audience/critic. An "author" is an abstract object, as it were, only contingently connected to the "writer" who stands as the text's efficient cause. Viewed in this light, the "author" Nietzsche is—among other things—the producer of *The Will to Power*. Eighty years of commentary has produced a state of affairs in which Nietzsche's name is linked to that text. It is a part of his canon after all therefore.

It is unclear what to make of such a gambit. One might reply by saying that mistaken attributions of "authorship" are also a central element in canon-formation, and are, in consequence, subject to revision. Consider, for example, the number of dialogues and letters mistakenly attributed to Plato—the author—in the past two hundred years which have subsequently been read out of the canon. Moreover, if "Nietzsche's" diary—*My Sister and I*—which was demonstrably spurious had instead become the subject of commentary, would Nietzsche have become its "author" too? And, finally, what is one to make of the author Nietzsche who had set aside the notes and outlines of *The Will to Power*? Is this to be a permanent contest of authors, Nietzsche versus "Nietzsche"?[77]

We have gone on at such length about the *Nachlass* because most lumpers shall need to treat those materials as final versions if they are to get an ontology of will to power or eternal recurrence out of Nietzsche and perhaps if they are to collapse *Übermenschen* into higher humanity.[78]

Most commentators who treasure the *Nachlass*, most lumpers, do so because it is there that the representational, foundationalist Nietzsche is to be found, the Nietzsche who does *not* conflate art and philosophy, the Nietzsche who worries about the way the world's intelligible character is itself to be characterized, the Nietzsche who worries about facts and perspectives, truth and reference, the Nietzsche who worries about which virtues we should value and what we ought to strive for. And it is there that Nietzsche writes relatively straightforward declarative sentences, rather than endless hypotheticals and subjunctive conditionals.

Splitters, we are suggesting, need not be seduced by this picture. They may instead honor Nietzsche by placing his published work at the head of that philosophical genealogy which says that there is no ultimate contrast to mark genealogy off from ontology, no point in asking about the way the world is in itself apart from what we make of it. That is the Nietzsche who speaks with many voices in his many published texts, not with a single voice governing every concern. This "postmodern"[79] Nietzsche does not merely reject the view that "philosophy" is a natural kind term; rather, he is the thinker who also gave us a genealogical account of how we came to believe that "philosophy" must name a natural kind, that it must have a transcendental standpoint and a metahistorical agenda. He is, in short, the philosopher who showed in his own published writings what philosophy is, has been and perhaps can only be—its own time written in thought and thought by writing.

2

Prophecy's Voice/Voicing Prophecy: A Genealogy of Literary-Philosophical Prophetics[1]

If at the foundation of all there lay only a wildly seething power which writhing with obscure passions produced everything that is great and everything that is insignificant, if a bottomless void never satiated lay hidden beneath all—what then would life be but despair? If such were the case, if there were no sacred bond which united mankind, if one generation arose after another like the leafage in the forest, if the one generation replaced the other like the song of birds in the forest, if the human race passed through the world as the ship goes through the sea, like the wind through the desert, a thoughtless and fruitless activity, if an eternal oblivion were always lurking hungrily for its prey and there was no power strong enough to wrest it from its maw—how empty then and comfortless life would be! But therefore it is not thus, but as God created man and woman, so too He fashioned the hero and the poet or orator.
—S. Kierkegaard, *Fear and Trembling*

The Rhetoric of Crisis

When G. E. Moore conceded that he knew of no philosophical problem that he did not get from other philosophers,[2] he implied that, as the product of social engagement, philosophical problems are optional activities. The attitude toward philosophy expressed here contrasts sharply with that of rhetoricians who hold that poetry or criticism or learning or philosophy—whatever cultural phenomenon is in question—is in a state of crisis. Although we are thinking primarily of Nietzsche, many authors from many epochs employ a rhetoric of crisis. Moore's self-deprecating remark implies that his chosen subject may be of parochial interest only, while the theme of crisis often encountered in Nietzsche's prose—and in the writings of Bacon, Milton, Shelley, Wagner, Ruskin, Eliot, de Man and others—seems, in contrast, to elevate the subject. The suggestion is that the author understands, can explain, and even resolve the crisis. These rhetorical perspectives imply quite different attitudes toward the texts in which they are imbedded. If philosophical problems are of little consequence, it follows that present discussion of these problems will not exercise much audience appeal. But if a crisis exists, the exhortations of an informed speaker take on a commensurate sense of urgency.

The good news has two parts: (1) the discipline is under siege, and (2) an articulate champion has arrived in time. Historically, defenders of poetry appear in adversarial roles. Contention is a source of interest in a drama engaging critics and their interlocutors. Would Zarathustra be as interesting without his perpetually obtuse disciples and the asinine multitude? To what extent is the rhetoric to Sidney's *Defence of Poesy* (1595) parasitic upon the assault of Gosson's *School of Abuse* (1579)? For that matter, what would we know of Socrates's opinions on poetry without the active engagement of such characters as Ion and Phaedrus? And yet our sense of the contention between mentor and novitiate is only a preparative to the dramatic *peripitea*: the telling historical analysis, rhetorical unmasking, political directive, philosophical turn.

As a trope, the heraldry of crisis may include any of a constellation of messianic figures: the prophet as crier in the wilderness[3]; the prophet as diviner of false gods[4]; the diviner of false gods as redeemer[5]; and the redeemer as a resurrected deity or demi-god.[6] While all of these characters share a special relationship to the Deity, Zarathustra is unusual among them in that, as a gospeller, he bears the good news that "God is dead." But the ethos of all these characters derives from their special access to knowledge of or about God. With respect to the sense of crisis in their utterances, they possess a divining spirit which enables them to perceive the stresses behind their historical situation, and which enables them to perceive relevant aspects of the future, the latter often in the form of a shift in human consciousness. Not only does the diviner perceive that shift, but his own words become an important part of the transformation, which will ease the sense of crisis. These gospellers are, of course, outsiders. But, more than loners, they come forth as shaping figures in the progress of the human race. In this mode, the philosopher of *Beyond Good and Evil* speaks as nothing less than "the conscience for the collective evolution of humankind" (*BGE* 68). Even when alone,[7] they are the alike scourges of the established order. Hence, the recurring figures of transformation in their work: "*The Advancement of Learning*"; "to *save* mankind"; "*Revaluation of all values*" (*A* 62).

The rhetoric of crisis often invokes what Michael Lieb eloquently calls "the poetics of the holy."[8] Even when the seer decries the received sacred text, he does so in the incantatory rhetoric of the Bible: "And I saw a new heaven and a new earth" (Rev. 21:1). Underlying the oracular, prolocutionary cadences of this rhetoric of crisis we recognize the figure of Christ, proclaiming the end of one age, one law, one Word, and the beginning of a new: "I am the way, the truth, and the life; no man cometh unto the Father, but by me" (John 14:6). As

Michael Lieb observes,[9] salvation makes itself known by a new order which must and shall replace the old: "But the hour cometh, and now is, when the true worshippers shall worship the Father in spirit and in truth: for the Father seeketh such to worship him. . . . The woman saith unto him, I know that Messiah cometh, which is called Christ: when he is come, he will tell us all things. Jesus saith unto her, I that speak unto thee am he" (John 4:23–26).

In *Zarathustra*, the proclamation of the Word may appear to be strikingly different in tone and contrary in substance to that in the New Testament. But the family resemblance is the *sine qua non* of its rhetorical power. Nietzsche's nineteenth-century audience would have recognized the narrative analogue to Zarathustra's encounter with a hunchback, who challenges the preacher to convince him and the other cripples that he can do what Jesus had done before him: "You can heal the blind and make the lame to walk" (Z II "On Redemption"). They would have remembered that, after the execution of John the Baptist, Jesus "departed by ship into a desert place apart," where, moved by compassion for the multitude, he walked on the sea, stilled the tempest, and gave other signs in order that the suffering might understand: "Insomuch that the multitude wondered when they saw the dumb to speak, the maimed to be whole, the lame to walk, and the blind to see: and they glorified the God of Israel" (Matt. 15:31). In contrast, Zarathustra responds to the hunchback's temptation (the implied promise that, should Zarathustra remove their suffering, the multitude will convert to his doctrine) by teaching the doctrine on non-healing. The last thing the hunchback needs is a Messiah to remove his hump, and by doing so reduce him to a grateful, anesthetized nullity, with no appreciation for the actual ("real," "apparent") hunchback condition of life. In effect, Zarathustra rejects the conditions prescribed for public acceptance of his ideas by insisting that the worst thing he could do for cripples would be to heal them. Zarathustra's method of proselytizing, which may appear as a refusal to proselytize, is to deny the premise of the Gospel narrative, and with it the "new" law of Christianity, which is now the "old" law. Jesus healed the sick. But suppose that, rather than working restoration, healing were a pernicious assault on the character of the individual. Zarathustra would remove the hump from everyone *except* the hunchback, who needs it for "his spirit."[10]

And yet in another way Zarathustra is quite like the sacrificed Christ, for by recognizing the hunchback within himself he internalizes the suffering of his ersatz disciple. Zarathustra is the bridge as well as the one who crosses the "bridge to the future." In the gospel narrative, they ask Jesus if he is in fact John the Baptist, returned to life. Zarathustra answers a similar question ("What shall we call him?" [Z II "On Redemption"]) by saying that he is an imaginative amalgam of time-segments from the future: "And this is all my creating and striving, that I create and carry together into One what is a fragment and riddle and dreadful accident." Zarathustra's "doctrine" would liberate the hunchback, not from his hump, but from his "*ressentiment*" against life, the experience of which cannot be detached from the world of which his hump is a necessary part. The hump is stubborn evidence of his and only his existence, which explains why he must separate himself forever from the idea that the hump exists because of some order or justice decreed outside of the event—or rather "accident"—itself. The hunchback and all cripples (that is, everyone who has come to Zarathustra to be healed from their personal history) must learn this new gospel of the "will to power," which "must will something higher than any reconciliation" (Z II "On Redemption"), nothing less in fact than to "teach him [humankind] also to will backwards." Zarathustra teaches the new gospel of a will beyond reconciliation and resentment:

> "I led you away from these fables when I taught you, 'The will is a creator.' All 'it was' is a fragment, a riddle, a dreadful accident—until the creative will says to it, 'But thus I willed it.' Until the creative will says to it, 'But thus I will it; thus shall I will it.'" (Z II "On Redemption")

One could with some justice regard Zarathustra's new gospel as a reiteration of themes in the New Testament. What good is it to heal the body if the spirit languishes? Zarathustra recognizes the biblical source of the hunchback's challenge, but he strikes through it to reject its callow, traditional (or Philistine) reading of the text, or, to put the same thought another way, to address the anomaly of acts of healing in Christ's ministry. For the emphasis on compassion and healing of the physical body does not seem to follow from Christ's own declaration, that "the hour cometh, and now is, when the true worshippers shall worship the Father in spirit and in truth . . ."; and, again, "God is a Spirit: and they that worship him must worship him in spirit and in truth" (John 4:23–24). Hence, Zarathustra's reconstruction of the received Word of the New Testament exposes the old gospel's underlying insistence on the importance of the physical body, this despite emphatic protestations to the contrary.

Hence, Zarathustra sees the hunchback and all of the other cripples as expressions of the same fragmented human spirit. His Goyaesque description of the "tremendous ear . . . attached to a small, thin stalk" (Z II "On Redemption") draws attention to the human penchant to be controlled by an impulse to get even, to exact, as Kathleen Higgins convincingly demonstrates, revenge against the past.[11] As Nietzsche suggested in *Untimely Meditations*, part of the problem derives from the intimidating prestige of precedent: "Monumental history is the masquerade costume in which their hatred of the great and powerful of their own age is disguised as satiated admiration for the great and powerful of past ages, and muffled in which they invert the real meaning of that mode of regarding history into its opposite; whether they are aware of it or not, they act as thought their motto were: let the dead bury the living" (*UDHL* 2). But this problem is not a necessary condition of existence. The good news that Zarathustra brings appears to be "the will to power" (Z II "On

Redemption"), not mere acceptance of the past or acquiescence to its cumulative effects, but triumph over a passive acquiescence to the tyranny of the past, this elicited by an assertive willing it—affirming "All" that has ever happened anywhere, hump on the back and every other discrete moment or condition of life, suffering no less than joy.

If Zarathustra were to heal the hunchback—he never does deny the hunchback's assertion, "You can heal" (Z II "On Redemption")—he would not only encourage in others the ancient rage against time, but fall victim to it himself. Hence, by resisting the temptation to "overgo" the predecessor Messiah, he exposes healing of the sick as a pernicious instance of resentment against time: "'Everything passes away; therefore everything deserves to pass away. And this too is justice, this law of time that it must devour its children.' Thus preached madness" (Z II "On Redemption"). Zarathustra teaches the new gospel of a creative alternative to "the spirit of revenge and all gnashing of teeth," namely, "that will which is the will to power," which is not focused on the past, but the future. And here Zarathustra reveals the mark of the diviner of what will be: "The now and the past on earth—alas, my friends, that is what *I* find most unendurable; and I should not know how to live if I were not also a seer of that which must come. A seer, a willer, a creator, a future himself and a bridge to the future—" (Z II "On Redemption").

Clearly, this rhetorical stance presents less of a problem in fiction qua fiction than in generic expressions commonly designated as "philosophy," and this is a fortiori so in the case of Nietzsche's anti-metaphysical project. For, as Gary Shapiro argues,[12] even when Nietzsche is at his most Nietzschean, spewing out venom in *The Antichrist*—we are tempted to say, indeed, especially then—as he calls for the criminalization of Christianity and the razing of it temples, even then his apocalyptic rhetoric evokes the cadences of St. John at Patmos in the critic's description: "The idea of a new time and a new history. . . ."[13] Thus, as Shapiro shrewdly observes, Nietzsche signs himself "*The Antichrist*."[14] Shapiro points out, too, that probably Nietzsche's editors had their reasons for excluding the section with this signature from *The Antichrist*, but in the context of the text's interrelation to other texts, as Shapiro suggests, this signature extends the fictive horizon broadly presented throughout the work. The new gospel is more like a public poster announcing a new regime or an anonymous graffito on a wall than a solemnly inscribed sacred "Word" set out to replace an outworn creed: "This eternal indictment of Christianity I will write on all walls, wherever there are walls—I have letters to make even the blind see" (A 62). The effusion of hyperbole is not meant to cover but to expose this instance of recuperation of the lost (and only) Christian, who taught a forgotten (if modest) truth that this immediate world is the only one we have. And by recuperating this perspective, this fictive "Antichrist" would raze the temples built by the priests, who falsified the predecessor text ("the kingdom of god is at hand") by instituting a horrid assault on the body, and in its place restore the

promised "holy spirit of life"[15] Thus, the old becomes new, death is transfig-
ured to life, the filthy is made clean, and, by the power of "the holy spirit," the
Pharisees are cast out: "the rest follows from the above."

The familiarity with which Nietzsche's audience would have perceived this
cryptic message, as Shapiro rightly points out, derived from a variety of contexts, especially those concerning the felt tension in the late nineteenth century between religion and science: "Like other texts, but in a self-conscious
way, *The Antichrist* makes sense only in relation to other texts. It is a book that
recalls a number of similar genres (lives of Christ, polemical histories of religion) which were an important part of nineteenth-century thought."[16]

Shapiro's trenchant analysis of *The Antichrist* could be extended to other
works which similarly treat a fictive character (sometimes thought to be the
historical Nietzsche) who sees the future, discerns unclean spirits, and in many
ways conducts his life as the saints and martyrs had through the ages con-
ducted theirs. Thus, it might be helpful to think of all of these texts in relation
to similar fictions in which prophets are endowed with power to see the future
and to read minds (the theme of knowing when another lies), and so on. It
may help, that is, to think of certain philosophical perspectives as belonging,
at least in part, to literary genres. One advantage of this might be that, in such
a context, we may question the need for such assertions as Shapiro's: "So, like
all of Nietzsche's books, *The Antichrist* is self-referential."[17] For literary purposes, we wish to know, not that all works are alike, but how they differ as well.
Do the "self-referential" features of *The Antichrist* differ noticeably from those
of *The Birth of Tragedy* and *Ecce Homo*?

But a more important issue is involved in Shapiro's—we think helpful—
reminder that Nietzsche's texts are radically part of their own textual history
with its attendant interrelations to other texts. The prophetic stance has a generic history, just as does the quest for the "historical Jesus," and Nietzsche's
fictions are shaped by and shape the use of Scripture in generating literary
forms. The prophetic mode is employed to impose a sense of urgency on the
reader. It emphasizes, even if only to deprecate the literary source, a temporal
relation of the immediate word to the ultimate historical order, even if that
order is, as Shapiro writes, a "ring of becoming."[18] The prophet-speaker
knows the future, and he knows the present and past as they control that future. Above all, this speech is rendered under the unction of a power accorded
only to authors: the Muses, God, "the holy spirit of life."

Knowledge and the Sacred Text

Early in the thirteenth century a young scribe began copying the Vulgate in
even lines of small, neat characters. We don't know who he was, but he must

have been young, for, according to scholars at the Franciscan Institute at St. Bonaventure, he spent the next forty years—in effect, his entire vocational life—reproducing a single copy of the sacred text.[19] No one has found a single error in the finished product. In retrospect, this apparently pristine text seems to us a sublime feat of patience attesting to a felt sense of the intrinsic value of the Bible as opposed to all other texts. Our wonder at the sacrifice involved is a sign of our modernity: Why would anyone spend or subsidize a life transmitting a single copy of one text? But at the same time medieval scholars valued biblical interpretation no less than textual preservation. St. Bernard's more than eighty homilies on the Canticles make our current application of the spatial figure, "close reading," seem curious if not inappropriate, especially considering the fact that in his exegesis St. Bernard never quite got through the second chapter of the Song of Songs.[20]

As we have suggested, in "On Redemption," Zarathustra's gospel is characterized in large part by its antithetical relation to the narrative the hunchback invokes as he attempts to maneuver the Preacher into a useful competition with his predecessor. Obviously, Zarathustra's gospel repudiates the ethical aims of the predecessor text as well as the associated acts of Christ's healing ministry. Of course, this revision of gospel teaching is evidence of Nietzsche's knowledge of the Bible, which, in turn, is important to our appreciation of *Thus Spoke Zarathustra* as well as to our understanding of his interpretive theory, including his radical historical views and his critique of received morality. Without the gospel narrative of the life of Jesus, we would have no Zarathustra; thus (or so it seems to us) we must not take literally Nietzsche's expression of contempt for anything remotely reminiscent of the asceticism that has developed upon and been otherwise associated with the teachings of Jesus: "*De imitatione Christi* is one of those books which I cannot hold in my hand without a physiological reaction; it exudes a perfume of the Eternal-Feminine which is strictly for Frenchmen—or Wagnerians" (*TI* "SUM" 4). Or, again (and perhaps more tellingly), attentive readings must pause at the suggestion "That one does well to put on gloves when reading the New Testament," which fits Nietzsche's insistence, in one context at least, that in the whole of the volume he can find "only a *single* figure [Pilate] who commands respect" (*A* 46). For elsewhere the same "Nietzsche" speaking with much the same fervor insists that Jesus's symbolist practice seems to have foreshadowed his own emphasis on psychological "reality" and the idea of "becoming" so important in his doctrine of eternal recurrence:

> If I understand anything about this great symbolist, it is that he accepted only *inner* realities as realities, as "truths"—that he understood the rest, everything natural, temporal, spatial, historical, only as signs, as occasions for parables. The concept of "the son of man" is not a concrete person who belongs in history, something individual and unique, but an "eternal" factuality, a psychological symbol redeemed from the concept

of time. The same applies once again, and in the highest sense, to the *God* of this typical symbolist, to the "kingdom of God," to the "kingdom of heaven." . . . I am ashamed to recall what the church has made of this symbolism: Has it not placed an Amphitryon story at the threshold of the Christian "faith"? (*A* 34)

Our point is that, here, Nietzsche accuses his world-historical adversaries, the theologians, of employing a metaphoric strategy—of interpreting "this great symbolist" symbolically, that is, with a figurative method that would not be far out of place, given its Greek origins, in *The Birth of Tragedy*. We know that Nietzsche's speaker moves here toward an admirable representation of the New Testament protagonist, an attitude which can hardly be thought to dominate in *The Antichrist*.

We need not look for univocal sentiments—the literary analogues to "clear and distinct ideas"—in Nietzsche's representation of scriptural tradition. The rhetorical web of figures and feelings may be highly reticulated, and, further, it may not remain constant from one work to another, nor even from one part to another of the "same" work. In *Zarathustra*, Nietzsche depends on audience recognition of its Christian original, and the tone is not vituperative, but even benign: "'To be sure: except ye become as little children, ye shall not enter into *that* kingdom of heaven. (And Zarathustra pointed upward with his hands.) But we have no wish whatever to enter into that kingdom of heaven: we have become men—*so we want the earth*'" (*Z* IV "AF" 2). Similarly, what outrages Nietzsche in *The Dawn* is not the Bible, but its interpreters. He is exasperated by the "impudent arbitrariness" with which "the Bible is picked and pulled and *the art of reading badly* formally inculcated upon the people," the most egregious example being "the attempt to pull away the Old Testament from under the feet of the Jews—with the claim that it contains nothing but Christian doctrine and *belongs* to the Christians as the *true* Israel, while the Jews had merely usurped it." And for the Nietzsche of *The Antichrist* the problem is not the biblical text, but what one makes of it:

> Another sign of the theologian is his *incapacity for philology*. What is meant here by philology is, in a very broad sense, the art of reading well—of reading facts without falsifying them by interpretation, without losing caution, patience, delicacy, in the desire to understand. Philology as *ephexis* in interpretation—whether it is a matter of books, the news in a paper, destinies, or weather conditions, not to speak of the "salvation of the soul." (*A* 52)

This passage may not sort well with Nietzsche's well-known remark on "facts" in *The Will to Power*: "Against positivism, which halts at phenomena—'There are only *facts*'—I would say: No, facts is precisely what there is not, only interpretations" (*WP* III 481). But it should be pointed out that even here Nietzsche explores the complexity of the concept of "factuality" insofar as it assumes that a fact is immediately apprehended (the "thing-in-itself"). "Philology as *ephexis*": what Nietzsche seeks here is a poised state of suspended judgment, a Pyrrhonian ethics of reading. And, for him, an ephectic theologian is a contradiction in terms. Theologians quickly leap from certain text to certain interpretation: the hermeneutic counterparts of "the good and the just." The upshot of the challenge to the idea of The Fact *simpliciter* is another instance of Nietzsche's recurring theme of perspectivism. Even if we suppose for the moment that *The Will to Power* can be relevant to such a discussion (and this supposition is, as we argued in chapter 1, by no means obvious), we might argue that entry number 479 is as relevant—or perhaps more relevant—to the question of Nietzsche's theory of interpretation: "I call that a *lack of philology*; to be able to read off a text as a text without interposing an interpretation is the last-developed form of 'inner experience'—perhaps one that is hardly possible—" (*WP* III 479). As in the passage already cited from *The Antichrist*, here Nietzsche is more concerned with the peremptory function of the interpretive act in creating what passes for fact than with the usefulness or vacuity of the concept itself.

In Nietzsche's time, the interpretation of Scripture had resumed an importance that it had not enjoyed since the Renaissance, partly because of controversy surrounding the work of Schleiermacher and Strauss. Earlier, we remarked on the medieval scribe who surrendered his vocational life to the task of duplicating a single, error-free copy of the sacred text. It is a commonplace of intellectual history that, in the Renaissance—the post-Eleatic period with which Nietzsche most closely identified himself—technology rendered the scribe redundant, as what had once taken forty years could, once the type was locked in the chase, be accomplished hundreds of times over in as many weeks. But the same printing press that made the sacred text available to the many in many languages also provided an audience for legions of interpreters, which provision, depending on one's point of view, could be seen as an open-ended opportunity to enrich or to corrupt the sacred text. In a comment bearing a distinctly "perspectivist" ring, one Renaissance interpreter writes: "*It cannot be denied, but that there are many who, Spider-like, suck the poyson of sin and error out of these sweet and precious flowers* [of Scripture]."[21] The idea here is that, unlike Nietzsche, Wilson thinks of the proliferation of perspectives, not as an enrichment of human possibilities, but as an opening toward corruption and error.

Even thinkers whom Nietzsche admired could share this suspicion of individuality in interpretation. For instance, Bacon and Hobbes had philosophical and political objections to interpretive procedures which provided no check on the imagination. Nietzsche was more flexible. He could, at one time, express skepticism concerning the way in which individual character could vitiate the interpretation of events no less than of the biblical text (A 52), and at another, affirm the most radical latitudinarianism toward the individual, imaginative creation of events.

We could account for this difference by saying that Bacon and Hobbes were of a different time. Renaissance dictionary builders and biblical commentators from Thomas Wilson and John Cowell to George Herbert and John Milton confronted the problems arising from the status of language as a medium of public communication, which may or may not fit the idiosyncrasies of individual perception and usage. The printing press had only extended the possibilities of promulgation of a theoretically unbound range of individual interpretation. Generally, Renaissance theorists held that there were two major modes of biblical interpretation. Lexicographers, Wilson and Cowell, for instance, held that the first ("*ministeriall*")[22] method provided such helps as dictionaries, while the second (private prayer), although the more powerful of the two, by virtue of its being private, remained immune to challenge. Similarly, Milton, who attacked others for their "notorious abuse of Scripture,"[23] nevertheless held Scripture to be the "sole interpreter of itself to the conscience."[24]

The distinction between the two approaches to Scripture bears a family resemblance to the apposition in recent critical theory between "meaning" and "relevance." E. D. Hirsch[25] follows Husserl, Frege, and Quine in discussing the implications of this pair in recent criticism and philosophy. Although the issue is still a lively one, it seems fair to say that, if pressed, historical critics think of their work in much the same way that Cowell and Wilson did theirs—more a set of classifications than a class (to use Nietzsche's figure in *Twilight of the Idols*) of "novels." They are uncomfortable with what Milton describes as the "Spirit within."[26] Today, historicists may seem, with Milton, to deny the final say to any given interpretation; but, at least implicitly, they must concede that rules enable them to discriminate between those critical or interpretive assertions about a text in need and those not in need of correction. For, as Stanley Fish concedes, when they deny this they necessarily affirm the priority of private experience. Hence, they hold that the best interpretation is private and therefore—like Thomas Wilson's mental prayer—silent. We need not think of this remark as polemical, but such an assumption, when imposed on Renaissance texts, leads not as Stanley Fish supposes to solipsism, but, as Bacon and Nietzsche seem to agree, to unhelpful fictions, or, as we might say, to distortions of the historical text. Another Renaissance interpreter, John Hales, observed that epistemological difficulties arise when readers, coming to Scripture "fore-possest with some opinion ... see the image of their owne conceits."[27] For Hales, Cowell, and Wilson, interpretation of the Bible and of all other texts similarly conceived and composed worked in the opposite way: "Other Expositions may give rules and directions for understanding their Authors, but Scripture gives rules to Exposition it self, and interprets the Interpreter."[28] It is this sense of the inevitable intertwining of one's life with the sacred text that informs Herbert's sonnet, "The H. Scriptures. II":

> Such are thy secrets, which my life makes good,
> And comments on thee: for in ev'ry thing

Thy words do finde me out, and parallels bring,
And in another make me understood.[29]

We can infer from the rhetoric of Renaissance biblical exegesis that interpretive theory and practice became the focus of many social, political, and philosophical tensions. They were expressions of the prevailing intellectual situation, which Richard Popkin characterizes as the epistemological crisis of the Renaissance.[30] How interpretations become stabilized is integral to the canonization of knowledge, and therefore of intellectual and scientific projects. Sometimes moderns perceive the issue of knowledge and the curriculum through the prism of the Victorian sense of mutually exclusive institutional claims to the privileged domain of knowledge: the "warfare between religion and science." But in the Renaissance religion was not always antagonistic to scientific research. The stories of Galileo and Giordano Bruno are well-known, but religion's sponsorship of scientific "projectors" is less recognized.[31]

Bacon is, rightly, a key figure in the inevitable split between science and religion, and he figures prominently in Nietzsche's canon of contributors to the advance of philosophy. But in many ways—in his attitude toward the sacred text, for instance—Bacon was a man of his time, and therefore did not think of his work as hostile toward, but rather complementary to the domain of Scripture: the Book of God's Word *and* the Book of God's Works. Thus, critics often cite Bacon's eloquent prayer prefixed to *The Great Instauration*:

Wherefore, seeing that these things do not depend upon myself, at the outset of the work I most humbly and fervently pray to God the Father, God the Son, and God the Holy Ghost, that remembering the sorrows of mankind and the pilgrimage of this our life wherein we wear out days few and evil, they will vouchsafe through my hands to endow the human family with new mercies. This likewise I humbly pray, that things human may not interfere with things divine, and that from the opening of the ways of sense and the increase of natural light there may arise in our minds no incredulity or darkness with regard to the divine mysteries; but rather that the understanding being thereby purified and purged of fancies and vanity, and yet not the less subject and entirely submissive to the divine oracles, may give to faith that which is faith's.[32]

The prayer is so familiar that we tend to forget that Bacon repeats its last phrase in his famous discussion in *Novum Organum* (1620) of the four Idols of the Mind. Moreover, it is not often noted that Bacon, who affords a place for biblical exegesis in his scheme of universal knowledge, was nevertheless uneasy with what he called "the free way of interpreting Scripture."[33] This problematic procedure followed two possible lines of thought, which invariably led to the confounding of both science *and* theology. For Bacon, when applied to history or the cosmos, biblical commentary falsified the aims of secular no less than of divine knowledge: "For to seek the materiate heaven and earth in the word of God, (whereof it is said, 'Heaven and earth shall pass away, but my word shall not pass away'), is rashly to seek for temporary things amongst eternal; and as to seek divinity in philosophy is to seek the living among the dead, so to seek philosophy in divinity is to seek the dead among the living."[34]

Neither do critics often recognize how completely Bacon's works are infused with biblical language and lore. Although he seems to argue strenuously that the worlds of speculation and fiction be held separate from that of "second causes" (which insistence explains his reservations about the fusion of biblical lore with science in the work of such thinkers as Pico della Mirandola and Robert Fludd), Bacon nevertheless *himself* combines the two domains of discourse in his final effort to explain his program for society. *New Atlantis: A Worke unfinished* (1626)[35] is the regnant case in point, but by no means the only one. Elizabeth McCutcheon has shown how deeply this work depends on the literature and iconography of Christian and Hebraic thought.[36] William Rawley, the earliest critic of *New Atlantis*, states that Bacon "designed [the] *Fable*" to be published with the ten centuries of *Sylva Sylvarium, or, Naturall History* (1626), a work which even Rawley admits might seem to be "an Indigested Heap of Particulars."[37] But, as he claims in his Preface "To the Reader," this seeming deluge of details must depend on a generous audience sympathetic to Bacon's inductive claims. The apparent lack of "Method" is, in this rhetorical context, a systematic reaction to the present state of philosophy:

> And hee knew well, that ther was no other way open, to unloose Mens mindes, being bound; and (as it were) Maleficiate, by the Charmes of deceiving Notions, and Theories; and therby made impotent of Generation of Workes.[38]

For this reason Bacon's strategy is of necessity that of the builder: "the Scope which his Lordship intendeth, is to write such a *Naturall History*, as may be Fundamentall to erecting and Building of a true *Philosophy*."[39] The "*Naturall History*," projected as Part III of *The Great Instauration*, was to follow *Novum Organum*, which laid out the general plan of the building which Bacon now proposes to build.

It seems clear that Rawley is trying to answer in advance any criticism directed at the experiments as "Vulgar and Triviall."[40] But this figurative matrix of Rawley's defense looks beyond *Sylva Sylvarum* to *New Atlantis*, with which it was published in 1626. The reiteration of Bacon's appeal to the senses may seem predictable in light of such previous works as *Novum Organum* and *The Advancement of Learning*, but the figure employed in describing Bacon's contribution is something of a non sequitur:

> That his Lordship (who thinketh hee deserveth to be an Architect in this building,) should be forced to be a Work-man and a Labourer; And to digge the Clay, and burne the Brick, and more then that, (according to the hard Condition of the *Israelites* at the latter end) to gather the Strawe and Stubble, over all the Fields, to burn the Bricks withall.[41]

And yet the invocation of Old Testament contrasts is very much a part of Baconian rhetoric. Bacon sought to associate the Fall of Man with the methods of his philosophical predecessors, especially Aristotle. The implication here is that science, developed along Baconian lines, promised to restore man to his proper relation with the Deity, finally, to his original condition: "relief of man's estate" as a literal doctrine of Pelagian restoration to innocence and self-sufficiency. It seems clear that this is how Rawley understood Verulam's project in 1626. The value of scientific knowledge—"the true *Axiomes* must be drawne from plaine Experience"[42]—is "the producing of many Noble *Works* and *Effects*,"[43] which, as seen in *New Atlantis*, is "Knowledge to that perfection, whereof the Nature of Mortall men is capable."[44] Rawley understood this project and this end as a form of worship: "I will conclude with an usuall Speech of his Lordships, That this Worke of his *Naturall History*, is the *World*, as God made it, and not as Men have made it; For that it hath nothing of Imagination."[45]

Not only does William Rawley bring out the first editions of *Sylva Sylvarum* and *New Atlantis* together, but he links the two pieces here and in his Preface to Bacon's utopia, which suggests that he construes the scientific work as a gloss on the "Fable's" subtitle: *A Worke unfinished.* J. Weinberger[46] offers a political reading of this text: Bacon couldn't finish *New Atlantis* because he had not experienced a perfect government. But Rawley's explanation is not only nearer the source but also less mentalistic and more literary in its analysis. The lengthy process of "Collecting" material for *Sylva Sylvarum*, writes Rawley, simply diverted Bacon. Why? Because Bacon "preferred [by] many degrees" the subject of science to that of the remaining and purportedly lengthy segment of *New Atlantis*, which was to be on law. Having spent a lifetime in the practice of law, and given the dreadful events of his criminal conviction in 1621, Bacon apparently did not relish laying out the details of the legal system in Bensalem. But Rawley proceeds to say that, nevertheless, *New Atlantis* has a "neare affinity (in one Part of it) with the preceding *Naturall History*."[47] Not only are they physically bound together, then, but the two works belong that way by virtue of their "affinity," namely, their material concern for the aims or effects of scientific inquiry. Rawley sees science as presenting the world untrammeled by "Imagination," as God made it. Thus, in *New Atlantis*, Bacon presents an imaginary world—a "Fable"—which chronicles the history of a college of creation. It is a fiction "devised" as an institutional hexameron: "This *Fable* my *Lord* devised, to the end that He might exhibit therein, a *Modell* or *Description* of a *Colledge*, instituted for the *Interpreting* of *Nature*, and *Marvelous Works* for the *Benefit* of *Men*; Under the Name of *Solamons Hous*, or the *Colledge of the Six Dayes Works*."[48]

On the surface, Bensalem would appear to be a society in which Imagination plays only a minor role if any role at all. The society represented is far advanced along scientific lines, and there appear to be no poets and no "fic-

tion" anywhere. Here, "man's estate" has already been relieved, and so we might presume that a plan much like that laid out in *The Advancement of Learning* has already worked its beneficent effects. And yet the unique success of this idealized, scientific world is not based on empirical evidence, nor on a perfect melding of observation and reason. The "secular salvation" that many find incipient in Bacon's thought is not in fact derived from the Book of God's Works at all, but from the Bible—from "revelation." This island utopia has, in a strange epiphany (an ark mysteriously appears in a "great pillar of light"), received the divine "gift of tongues" along with the Old and New Testaments, which event explains why the inhabitants of Bensalem are Christians, but not why they are so much *more* Christian than their European visitors. That question is answered later, when the governor of Stranger's House explains how "*Salomon's House*" came into being. When we consider that including *New Atlantis* with *Sylva Sylvarum* was one of Bacon's last acts as the "Father of Scientific Philosophy," this explanation, especially in light of Bacon's sensitivity toward biblical exegesis when linked to statements about the world, is important. It turns out that the institute for scientific research on this fictive island is based on a book of the Bible omitted—nobody knows why—from Hebrew Scripture. That is, we have all the other Solomonic books mentioned in Scripture, such as Proverbs and the Canticles ("And he spake three thousand proverbs: and his songs were a thousand and five" [I Kings 4:32]), but the Bible has until now lacked the scientific description of creation, this notwithstanding that, in the same context, the Hebrew Scriptures clearly indicate that Solomon had also completed a comprehensive of the natural sciences: "And he spake of trees, from the cedar tree that is in Lebanon even unto the hyssop that springeth out of the wall: he spake also of beasts, and of fowl, and of creeping things, and of fishes" (I Kings 4:33). Although this catalogue suggests the wide range of subjects treated in Solomon's scientific writings, knowledge of this one book of the Bible had for centuries prior to the birth of Jesus of Nazareth provided this island with the means of sustaining a self-sufficient commonwealth.

We can see, then, that *New Atlantis* is Bacon's contribution to the sacred text. Science does not compete with, nor is it complementary to, God's Word. Rather, its existence derives from a recuperation of the sacred Hebrew texts, parts of which, somehow, through the ages, were lost. In his fictional addendum to Scripture, Bacon portrays "the Father of Salomon's House" as "comely of person" and possessed of "an aspect as if he pitied men." It is clear that his compassion is the key to the difference between Bensalem and the "Christian" society from which the Europeans have come. That is, Bacon's critique of Christian society (it is "the Jew" who brings the Father's invitation to a "private conference" and, hence, insight into the completed Hebrew Scriptures) devolves into a program of secular change guided by the principle of human compassion.

We know that Nietzsche admired Bacon (for reasons that will concern us in the next section), and yet their views on the value of compassion present a marked contrast. Nietzsche does not plead for the "relief of man's estate": that is the hunchback's theme. Rather, Nietzsche's biblical fiction and magnum opus, *Thus Spoke Zarathustra*, moves in an opposite direction. Although Nietzsche and Bacon share misgivings about their contemporaries's understanding of the Bible, for Nietzsche, the biblical texts and its interpreters were already *too* successful in imbuing man with pity, which—akin to the "spirit of gravity"—was a symptom of human contempt for life, and so, part of the history of nihilism.

Idolatry as Philosophic Occasion: The Case of Bacon

Although the most obvious connection between Nietzsche and Bacon is evident in *Twilight of the Idols*, remarks in *Ecce Homo* may show even more vividly how Nietzsche represented Bacon as a type of himself: first, he portrays himself as something of a mystery—the enigmatic author of "Why I am So Clever," of "Why I Write Such Good Books," and, above all, of *Zarathustra*, "A Book for Everyone and No One." And, then, as we discover in his discussion of Bacon, he is also the author pacing up and down with his own book in hand after "looking into [his] *Zarathustra*, . . . unable to master an unbearable fit of sobbing" (*EH* "WIASC" 4). With this dramatic statement, Nietzsche interrupts his discussion of Shakespeare:

> When I seek my ultimate formula for *Shakespeare*, I always find only this: he conceived of the type of Caesar. That sort of thing cannot be guessed: one either is it, or one is not. The great poet dips *only* from his own reality—up to the point where afterward he cannot endure his work any longer. (*EH* "WIASC" 4)

The comparison between the two authors—dual instances of the same cleverness—is borne out by the reaction the author reports on dipping into his own text. Although overwhelmed by his own "reality," even Nietzsche is constrained to admit that the most "heart-rending reading" is Shakespeare, especially *Hamlet*. For, since it is certainty that "drives one insane," and since it has already been established that Shakespeare is great because he "dips *only* from his own reality," it follows that, to have so mastered the absurdity of Hamlet's character, Shakespeare was "profound, an abyss, a philosopher." This is so because Shakespeare overcame the ordinary impulse to retreat in the face of truth.

Rhetorically, this juxtaposition of great philosopher-poets posits an unargued thesis. In praising Shakespeare, Nietzsche purports to express admiration of "Lord Bacon," but by doing so he also draws attention to his own taste and discernment. Only the living realist—the genealogist of real*ism*— knows the philosophical ascents and/or declines that emanated from Bacon's thought. For Lord Bacon was "the first realist in every great sense of that word, to know everything he did, wanted, and experienced in himself" (*EH* "WIASC" 4). For Nietzsche, it is Shakespeare's achievement as a poet that matters most. It is less important to know that Nietzsche believed Shakespeare and Bacon were one and the same person ("I feel instinctively sure and certain that Lord Bacon was the originator, the self-tormentor of this uncanniest kind of literature") than to appreciate *why* he thought so. It was the predecessor's willingness to risk all, to experience all, to "be profound, an abyss, a philosopher" despite his "all-too-human" fear that made him a "great poet." In order to write *Hamlet*, Bacon, the great realist, experienced everything that he wrote of that character, including insanity. Bacon overcame himself ("We are all *afraid* of the truth," which made him, as it had the author, a great philosopher and a "great poet"). Not only does Nietzsche suggest that he, like Bacon, is a realist, but he shows himself willing to go beyond Bacon in unfolding the truth by permitting the public figure of philosopher and poet—the author of fiction, of *Zarathustra*, a "Book for Everyone and No One," author of "Why I Write Such Good Books," and of "Why I am So Clever"—to appear as one and the same:

> And damn it, my dear critics! Suppose I had published my *Zarathustra* under another name—for example, that of Richard Wagner—the acuteness of two thousand years would not have been sufficient for anyone to guess that the author of *Human, All-too-Human* is the visionary of *Zarathustra*. (*EH* "WIASC" 4)

We are suggesting, then, that Nietzsche admired Shakespeare for qualities of mind which he represents himself as cultivating. For instance, in *Human, All Too Human*, he argues that, like Homer and Aristophanes, Shakespeare was "deeply irreligious." Nietzsche poses a rationale for this remarkable, ahistorical assertion: Shakespeare was so much at home with the gods that, like all great artists, he had no need to worship them. Accordingly, Nietzsche admires Shakespeare for his philosophic mind, which seems, perhaps, surprisingly like Nietzsche's. Again, in *The Gay Science*, Nietzsche writes "*In praise of Shakespeare*," and singling out Shakespeare's sublime characterization of Caesar. What he admires most about *Julius Caesar* (here, Shakespeare's greatest play) is its steadfast representation of Brutus, whose "awesome quintessence of a lofty morality" was only enhanced by the fact of Caesar's greatness: "The height at which he places Caesar is the finest honor that he could bestow on Brutus: that is how he raises beyond measure Brutus's inner problem as well as the spiritual strength that was able to cut *this knot*" (*GS* II 98). Even though Shakespeare didn't get the title of the play quite right—it should have been called *"Brutus"*—the sacrifice made by Shakespeare's protagonist transcends all others in its "Independence of soul": "No sacrifice can be too great for that: one must be capable of sacrificing one's dearest friend for it, even if he should also be the most glorious human being, an ornament of the world, a genius without peer—if one loves freedom as the freedom of great souls and he threatens this kind of freedom" (*GS* II 98).

It would distort Nietzsche's argument here to imagine that he advances *Julius Caesar* as a parable of political liberation. It is possible, for him, to think of the play as void of political consequences. The political theme of the play, the author muses (as if thinking aloud), might only present "a symbol of something inexpressible." And this possibility, posed as a question, leads to another question, which leads to another, and finally to engagement of the possible interior landscape of Shakespeare's mind:

> Could it be that we confront some unknown dark event and adventure in the poet's own soul of which he speaks only in signs? What is all of Hamlet's melancholy compared to that of Brutus? And perhaps Shakespeare knew both from firsthand experience. Perhaps he, too, had his gloomy hour and his evil angel, like Brutus. (*GS* II 98)

So whether the greatest play of the moment is *Hamlet* or *"Brutus,"* the relative merit of Shakespeare's art depends on the degree with which the text stimulates an imagined authorial engagement with "inexpressible" philosophical anguish: self-awareness as "self-torment." In this context, Brutus suffers more than Hamlet because he endures the horrible recognition that he must execute his best friend, who is also the most glorious human being on the face of the earth. In contrast, Hamlet, who has expressed misgivings about the value of life at various times throughout the play, kills himself, not Horatio. Indeed, in *Hamlet*, friendship is the key to the ultimate unfolding of the truth as history: the narrative of a faithful survivor.

Probably Nietzsche has in mind here the soliloquy in Act 2, delivered just before the conspirators call to firm up plans for the assassination, and just prior to Portia's complaint about her husband's bizarre behavior. Thus, the issue of political freedom in conflict with the value of friendship is not isolated from its marital opposite. Portia comes on stage to remind Brutus that he does not eat or sleep, that he avoids their bed, and that she is genuinely worried about him. She tries to pry out of him the nature of his conference with the half-dozen or so men who have just left the household, and, in fact, to persuade him to reveal the "cause of [his] grief[49]": "It will not let you eat, nor talk, nor sleep; / And could it work so much upon your shape / As it hath much prevail'd on your condition, / I should not know you, Brutus"[50]

But by then the decision has been made, and Brutus has already separated himself from the demands and rewards of both friendship and marriage. In accomplishing this heroic triumph over the pedestrian morality of Roman (and Elizabethan) commoners, Brutus exposes the weakness of the legal system, which is based on the unhelpful logic of the past, which leads only to this antinomy:

> Caesar has committed no offense.
> Caesar must be executed.

In the ordinary world of common morality, this logical impasse would seem to provide no room for the requisite action. Necessity requires execution, but Caesar has committed no offense; which is only to reiterate the problem: that the system of justice speaks only to the past, which no longer exists. Without action, the future prospects for individual freedom change enormously. Thus, Brutus must create the future by transcending "the rule of law":

> It must be by his death; and for my part,
> I know no personal cause to spurn at him,
> But for the general. He would be crowned:
> How that might change his nature, there's the question.
> It is the bright day that brings forth the adder,
> And that craves wary walking. Crown him that,
> And then I grant we put a sting in him
> That at his will he may do danger with.
> Th' abuse of greatness is when it disjoins
> Remorse from power; and to speak truth of Caesar,
> I have not known when his affections sway'd
> More than his reason. But 'tis a common proof
> That lowliness is young ambition's ladder,
> Whereto the climber-upward turns his face;
> But when he once attains the upmost round,
> He then unto the ladder turns his back,
> Looks in the clouds, scorning the base degrees
> By which he did ascend. So Caesar may;
> Then lest he may, prevent. And since the quarrel
> Will bear no color for the thing he is,
> Fashion it thus: that what he is, augumented,
> Would run to these and these extremities;
> And therefore think him as a serpent's egg,
> Which, hatch'd, would as his kind grow mischievous,
> And kill him in the shell.[51]

Nietzsche is fascinated, not by Brutus's line of argument, but by its absence. For Brutus perforce concedes that he has seen, in Caesar's character, no evidence of ambition. Indeed, there is no hint that he challenges Casca's narrative in Act 1 of Caesar's dramatic declination—three times—of Antony's offer, supported by the cries of "the rabblement," of the crown. Brutus finds the motive for action, not in Caesar's weakness, but in human weakness. It is not unusual malice, but "all-too-human" nature to desire power, which desire, in every case but Caesar's, is restrained by absence of opportunity. For the common good, such power must be restrained. Here, Brutus's motives are pure—or at least they appear to be so in contrast to those of Cassius and the other conspirators, who hate Caesar if for no other reason than that the plebeians love him (the conspirators being incipient versions of characters fleshed out as Tribunes in *Coriolanus*). Brutus loves Caesar just as the plebeians do, which makes his resolve, in Nietzsche's mind, heroic rather than base. He is willing to surrender Caesar's life for the greater good of freedom, while "the rabblement" would invest him with unlimited power, thus, using him to their shameful end: the banishment of individual freedom. Brutus sacrifices his love for Caesar—conquers his "all-too-human" affections and beliefs (the values of friendship and family) for the superior value of freedom. Thus, because Caesar is human and inclined to take advantage of power should he have the opportunity, that opportunity must be denied him: "So Caesar may." That is, Brutus imagines a possibility, which is the sole ground of Caesar's doom. But, for Nietzsche, what may appear to others a hasty and even unfair leap to action (finessing, as it were, the question of the likelihood of Caesar's corruption by power) emerges as affirmation of the self, combined with a critique of received morality. Brutus overcomes conventional morality, which imposes sanctions only after the fact of criminal action. Ordinary justice reacts only in relation to published "law." But, let matters slide, and Caesar, crowned, becomes the lawmaker in absolute control of Rome's destiny. Brutus arrogates to himself the godlike power to shape the future, but the means of so doing and the cost are the same: he must separate himself from the "all-too-human," namely, from the abiding place of those he loves.

But we have said that Nietzsche entertains the possibility that *Julius Caesar*, the greatest of Bacon/Shakespeare's tragedies, has little or nothing at all to do with politics. Rather, the political conflict laid out on stage represents an inner turmoil "inexpressible" in the ordinary scheme of things, and perhaps even unutterable except through the medium of the "sign." Perhaps Shakespeare/Bacon engaged the most inexpressible of thoughts, as if a demon had approached him in his loneliest loneliness, with the terrible, heroic notion that, for all time and eternity, he and he alone (like the Brutus he creates) was responsible for the future—his own, and because the two were ultimately inextricably intertwined, that of the city and the nation as well. In this reading of *Julius Caesar*, Nietzsche imagines Bacon, the "realist," transcending the philosophical limitations of his systematic empiricism of "second causes." Bacon/Shakespeare, by looking within himself, becomes a forerunner of Nietzsche: the asystematic, *psychological* realist.

Although in notes published in *The Will to Power* Nietzsche places Bacon among the four great methodologists in history (the others being Aristotle,

Descartes, and Comte), *Twilight of the Idols* is probably his most explicit philosophical response—as we ordinarily think of such responses—to Bacon's thought. Even the title of the work seems to answer Bacon's *Novum Organum*, with its analysis of the four "Idols of the Mind" functioning as an important part of a critique aimed at sweeping away all impediments to a "new instauration" of knowledge. Indeed, by comparing Nietzsche's "Four Great Errors" with Bacon's four Idols of the Mind, we see how completely Nietzsche rejects the assumptions of Bacon's inductive perspective, how much Bacon is part of the history of "scientism" that must be overcome. That is, Bacon's rhetoric is that of the innovative builder and restorer. His theme is Pelagian; he would make science the handmaiden of Judaeo-Christian values in an apocalyptic transformation of knowledge, establishing a new ground of certainty: the "new instauration," "the advancement of learning," "new mercies," "New Atlantis." In contrast, Nietzsche's figure ("Twilight of the Idols") suggests the subtle fading of day's light. The musician's tuning fork betrays what lies beneath the surface of the idols idolized. Even if, at some level, the figure of the hammer with which the speaker "philosophizes" incorporates the violent possibility of destroying the idols (leaving them in pieces, like the "Old Tablets" in *Zarathustra*), the dominant figure is temporal. The day of the "Four Great Errors"—modern analogues to the older "Four Idols of the Mind—is nearing its end.

Superficially, we may perceive marked similarities between Bacon's project and Nietzsche's. For instance, we might think of Bacon's attack on the ancient belief that "man is the measure of all things" as quite like the latter's frequent assaults on egoism, when projected in the form of cosmic narratives. In discussing the "Idols of the Tribe," Bacon argues that the senses "are according to the measure of the individual and not according to the measure of the universe."[52] Thus, rather than measuring actuality, the human understanding "distorts the nature of things by mingling its own nature with it." The tendency is to generalize on the basis of limited experience, to favor those instances which fit one's preconceived notions of order in the world. Thus, Bacon's insistence that the "negative instance" was more helpful to the inductive process than the positive.

With the "Idols of the Cave" and "Idols of the Market-place," Bacon moves from general impediments derived from "human nature itself"[53] to those derived from individual idiosyncrasy and bias, to those derived from the individual in association with others. The best example of the first of these is Aristotle's bias toward logic. Such predilections are individualized versions of the "Idols of the Tribe," since certain systems of thought rather than others appeal to individual philosophers, whose understandings, then, are marked by expressions of these preferences. Certain minds are adept at observing similarities, while others are keen to mark differences: "For that school is so busied with the particles that it hardly attends to the structure; while the others are so lost in admiration of the structure that they do not penetrate to the simplicity of nature."[54] Similarly, clarity of perception can be impaired by the individual's association with others, which is subject to the vagaries of language as it is used by the common man. Of course, it would be a mistake to think of Bacon as an early exponent of views held by Wittgenstein or G. E. Moore. For Bacon, language in ordinary usage was more apt to corrupt than to enlighten philosophic discourse. Hence, the "Idols of the Market-place are the most troublesome of all,"[55] in that they involve the tendency of the vulgar to believe that for every noun an object can be found in nature: "Fortune, the Prime Mover, Planetary Orbits, Element of Fire, and like fictions."[56] Or, language can slide into acceptance of "faulty and unskillful abstraction," with similarly pernicious results for science.

Lisa Jardine[57] argues that Bacon thinks of the "Idols of the Theatre" as less pernicious than the other Idols. But consider: in his earliest formulation of the "Idols" in *The Advancement of Learning*, Bacon describes only three classes of impediments to scientific thought. He adds the "Idols of the Theatre" in his treatment in *Novum Organum*, placing the new category fourth in the series. That sequence, we will recall, moves in the same manner as scientific discovery itself from the more particular to the more general. This placement would seem, if anything, to impose the greatest emphasis on the added category of mental hindrances to scientific progress. The sequence, as we find it in *Novum Organum*, moves from human nature as inhering in the individual, to the individual in society, to the individual in society with a range of systems designed to explain the workings of nature. In describing the "Idols of the Market-place" Bacon avers that some of the categories of meaning thus derived were "like fictions." "Idols of the Theatre" differ from these in that they *are* fictions: "And in the plays of this philosophical theatre you may observe the same thing which is found in the theatre of the poets, that stories invented for the stage are more compact and elegant, and more as one would wish them to be, than true stories out of history."[58] Thus, Bacon envisions an interior "heterotopia," a place where the mental analogue of those public disorders at London playhouses that so troubled Stephen Gosson and others appear: a "School of Abuse" of the mind.

And yet it turns out that systems are just like their makers—inclined to excess of one kind or another. One scaffolds a system on a few particulars by wrenching the explanation to fit them in. Another blithely skims over the surfaces of a variety of experiments and leaves the work of finding coherence to others. But it is the "third class" that may explain why Bacon chose to finesse discussion of these Idols twenty years earlier (*The Advancement* was published in 1605). Those philosophers "mix their philosophy with theology and traditions,"[59] the most egregious offenders being thinkers like Plato and Pythagoras, who invented fanciful, abstract terms based on religion and custom to describe the world. Even more problematic for Bacon was the fact that leading thinkers of his own time (Bacon probably had in mind the syncretism of such authors as Pico della Mirandola and Robert Fludd) were repeating the same error:

> Yet in this vanity some of the moderns have with extreme levity indulged so far as to attempt to found a system of natural philosophy on the first chapter of Genesis, on the book of Job, and other parts of sacred writings; seeking for the dead among the living: which also makes the inhibition and repression of it the more important, because from this unwholesome mixture of things human and divine there arises not only a fantastic philosophy but also an heretical religion. Very meet it is therefore that we be sober-minded, and give to faith that only which is faith's.[60]

Jardine is right in pointing out that Bacon accords to the interpretation of nature the highest value in his utopia.[61] And, we would add, he also explains the establishment and preservation of that Christian society as grounded on a revised text of the Bible. Pico, Fludd, and other imaginative hermeneuts of Scripture might be wrong in conjoining their interpretations of the text with science, but as Bacon imagines the hegemony of science, he finds its source, not in interpretation of the Bible, but in the revision and perfection of its text. Thus, as we suggested in the preceding section, Rawley's assertion that Bacon's project banished "Imagination" must be regarded skeptically. Rawley himself construes *Sylva Sylvarum* in terms of religious metaphor and purpose. And he imputes a thematic connection between Bacon's *Naturall History* and his science-fiction "Fable."

If we think of *New Atlantis* as taking away much that Bacon implies about the pernicious influence of "fictions" on science, we might find ourselves supporting Charles Whitney's recent attempt to rescue Bacon's thought from the charge of "visionary materialism."[62] But Whitney's effort is vitiated by a bias toward modernity: "We know, for instance, as Bacon did not, that the Bible in its glorification of God suppresses its enormous debt to prior religions' beliefs, practices, and revelations."[63] That is, Whitney gives the impression of uncritical acceptance of knowledge claims affirmed in more recent history, this with an accompanying and perhaps licit sense of faith and satisfaction in the intrinsic superiority of current opinion. (We stand, not on the shoulders, but on the faces, of giants.) Temporal xenophobia has its attractions, of course, and, in the spirit of pluralism, we offer no objections. But historical ethnocentrism can becloud the reading of a text. Whitney writes, for instance, that readers ought not overlook the "religious and reformative ideals in Bacon's 'new' ideas of discovery,"[64] a view which seems safely to accord with many Bacon utterances. But when in his zeal to fit Bacon into a more Nietzschean project Whitney turns to *New Atlantis*, he surprisingly finds that Bensalem had escaped the horrible consequences of European history "through luck"[65] compounded by a proto-Marxist (earnest) "revolutionary urge . . . to achieve liberation."[66] Thus, Bacon's blindness in predicating his utopia on predatory economic values should caution us against neocolonial industrial development today."[67]

We do not aim to defend Bacon's thinking in its Renaissance context.[68] We wish only to suggest that what Bacon thought he knew and what he believed were the best means of advancing human understanding may represent one historical viewpoint in a manner quite like our own claims to "know" (as in the locution: "We know, for instance, as Bacon did not . . .")[69] that a text (in this case, "the Bible") caused such and such a psychological or historical effect ("suppresses its enormous debt to prior religions' beliefs, practices, and revelations"). To enlarge on this point it might be helpful to turn to Nietzsche's own rejoinder to Bacon's "Idols of the Mind" as a means of comparing the two approaches to knowledge, and of seeing how Nietzsche's critique of Bacon may be applied, not just to assertions such as Whitney's, but to "fictions" of knowledge in general.

Although on the face of it the two philosophers agree that problems in thinking arise from the mental "habits of mankind," Bacon urges a sweeping away of those individual propensities which incline toward imaginative constructs, while Nietzsche insists that such a purpose leads only to frustration. Consider the first "Great Error," which appears in religion and morality, namely, the all-but-ubiquitous tendency to confuse cause with effects. This phenomenon is especially evident in the chronic harm inflicted by popular beliefs, for instance, those surrounding the Bible, the most pernicious of known texts. (In *New Atlantis*, Bacon improves the sacred text by revision; in *Twilight of the Idols*, Nietzsche improves it by deletion.) Nor is this a particular new or old mistake, but a habitual and therefore universally corrupting fact of human consciousness. Religion and morality—the ascetic ideal—are twin expressions of humankind's confusion of effects with causes. Nietzsche places the harm done by "the famous Cornaro," author of a contemporary fad diet, almost on a par with that done by the Bible. Nietzsche objects to the idea that a diet of certain foods in certain portions produces a long and happy life in that it entails the erroneous assumption that the intake of a diet—any diet— precedes the body's capacity to assimilate food in ways other than in fact it does. Thus, Cornaro's metabolism caused his slender diet rather than the other way round. The argument that Cornaro was "free to eat little *or* much" is as erroneous as attributing praise or blame to a physical condition which could not have been otherwise: "he became sick when he ate more" (TI "FGE" 1). Similarly, happiness and long life are not rewards of virtue, but preconditions to the explanatory narratives which embody their valuations. What moralists call virtue results from "that slowing down of the metabolism" which is not in one's physiological control. Moralists declare that generations are destroyed by licentious behavior, as if the one caused the other, whereas exactly the opposite is true. Physiological degeneration causes the desire for stimulation, which, when satisfied, religionists designate as licentious behavior, cause of the prior need, and so on.

What, then, causes the error in judgment about causes? Nietzsche's "*higher politics*" (*TI* "FGE" 2) posits error as a distancing of the errant party—corporate or individual—from instinct: nature minus self-dignifying explanation. But we know from already developed sections of *Twilight* that nature minus explanation is the one thing humankind cannot tolerate. So "degeneration of instinct" and "disintegration of the will" are coexistent expressions of life in decline, which moralists erroneously explain along lines of the Cornarist non sequitur. Instinct is good, necessary, easy, and free. Hence, all that is corrupt, extraneous, awkward, disposable, and encumbered is anti-instinct, anti-nature, anti-life. Effort ("laboriousness") is a sign of life in decline, of mankind out of touch with instinct. Hence, Nietzsche's stunning juxtaposition of god and hero. One is admired for cleaning stables fast, while the other moves on winged feet.

The second "Great Error" derives from the false attribution of causation itself. Custom extrapolates from "the famous 'inner facts'" of consciousness to predicate an "act of willing," which is causality incarnate: "with that we have knowledge of motives" (section 3). Conveniently, freedom and its twin, responsibility, require dependence of thought upon a prior condition ("the act of willing"), which, in turn, prepares the way for a causative agent of that prior agent, "the ego." Thus, belief in three supposed "'inward facts'" became established as "*empirical*": (1) of the will as cause; (2) of consciousness as cause; and (3) of the ego as cause.

According to Nietzsche, modernity has undermined the foundation of all three supposed facts. For instance, we now know that actions need not follow motives, but may in fact precede, be coterminous with, follow, or be absent from specific actions. Further, we know that, with respect to causative functions, the ego is a "fable" or "fiction," not a fact. Nietzsche wonders, "What follows from this?" The answer is that a nullity necessarily follows from all projections leading from false attributions of cause. There is no warrant for belief in mental causation of anything, and yet belief in such a "fiction" stands behind the abuse of a world of imagined causes. Happily, this belief has "gone to the devil" because, like the "true world," such fantasms were a source of suffering. We created a world replete with willing subjects and a myriad of effects of these subjects willing. Doers multiplied under will's direction, and the process—the idea of substantial being ("the thing itself")—was projected to the cosmic level as a counterpart of the ego. Thus, the world in itself reflected belief in the ego as cause. No area of inquiry—not even physics (here, Nietzsche begins to shape his response to Bacon's "new instauration"), with its atom-in-itself—has escaped the same error in metaphysics: the attribution of cause to spirit, with its being plus cause, namely, God.

We can see the connection between the first two errors, for they alike lend themselves to the same teleological understanding of the world: the uncaused doer *par excellence*. The movement is from error to hypostatization of error, so that the two particular errors cause the same effect, namely, attribution of the ultimate causation to an uncaused deity. And the same is true of the third "*error of imaginary causes*" (section 4). Humankind, creator of narratives for all events, feels, therefore it feels for some reason, moved by some will or spirit called "motive." Nietzsche presents the dream state as a case in point: "To begin with dreams: *ex post facto*, a cause is slipped under a particular sensation (for example, one following a far-off cannon shot)." In the sleeping state a feeling occurs as one reacts to the sound. A narrative ("often a whole little novel") unfolds with the dreamer as hero, as the plot or "meaning" of the sensation unfolds. The cannon shot is not a chance occurrence unrelated to the sleeper's existence, but one in which the hero's reaction is the operative mode of its explanation. The sensation which followed now precedes the cannon shot, with the net residue of meaning replacing the random sound within a world ordered by feelings it—the cannon shot—in fact aroused.

If sleeping states differed substantially from waking ones perhaps this error might not be "Great," but in fact the same slip occurs when we are awake. All feelings must have causes. Inner events, like outer ones, require narrative significance: "we want to have a reason for feeling this way or that" (section 4). Even the memory is pressed into the service of explanation, as events are arranged, as in the dream state, with all sensations represented as part of a larger narrative scheme accompanied by an exponentially greater number of feelings attached to meaningful explanations. Since the self is the protagonist of this ever-expanding, "any-explanation-is-better-than-none" novel, the narrator takes on the comfort of familiar stimuli and responses. The memory inscribes every feeling (say, of fear) in a situation with which one has coped effectively before. The tendency toward formulaic narratives derives from the comfort individuals derive from successful resolution of such sequences. The unfamiliar is banished, as it does not explain away but rather exacerbates fear. Each protagonist will have particular stories of causation, but they share this common motif of familiarity.

Again, the third error devolves toward the same end as the first two: belief in God's intimate workings in the explanatory narrative. Since all feelings have explanations, with the self as hero, the cause of bad feelings must be laid to such notions as retributive justice. If we feel badly we feel badly for some reason, which must mean—if we are to have meaning—that these feelings are part of a retributive system, and so deserved (here, in section 6, Nietzsche specifically responds to Schopenhauer's argument that all pain, "whether physical or spiritual, declares what we deserve"). Likewise, good feelings are caused, not by good digestion, but by "trust in God," the mover of the retributive system of narrations. But, Nietzsche insists, once again we have put the cart before the horse. Religions proffer a reverse system which alienates the protagonists of the corporate narrative from the psychology behind their own story. We do not experience hope as a reward for trust in God, but, rather, "one trusts in God *because* the feeling of fullness and strength gives a sense of rest" (section 6). Faith, hope, and charity are physiological conditions which religions falsely attribute to imaginary causes. In their right temporal order, sensations of fullness and ease (faithfulness, hopefulness, charitableness) precede novelistic interpretations, precede reasons. Religionists insist that motives or ends "cause" the conditions, whereas in fact the conditions thus explained are *pre*-conditions of the explanations.

The third error, which is a miniature poetics of fiction, points the way to the fourth (section 7). It is clear that the confusion of states of consciousness with their causes are entangled in the moralists' narrative of rewards and punishments. The aim of such a narrative is to impose a retributive system on the world. The ultimate narrative cannot be left without a cause, and, again, "any explanation is better than none" (section 5). It is important that such a retributive scheme appear just. Hence, the rhetorical function within the system of the concept of "free will." The vituperative tone emerging here emphasizes the analysis of the motives of those who employ the cosmic narrative, and the idea of the ego as cause, to self-serving ends. For this concept is "the foulest of all theological artifices, aimed at making mankind 'responsible' in their sense, that is, *dependent upon them*" (section 7).

This exuberant passage precedes Nietzsche's famous one-liner: "Christianity is a metaphysics of the hangman." The indefinite article is important here, for Nietzsche's tirade encapsulates a brief excursus on the priestly class from ancient times on. Thus, the fourth "Great Error" purports to be, so to speak, a "culture-free" observation. Whenever and wherever they appear the priestly classes seek to gain power by advancing an artifice, that is, an explanatory narrative or fable, which is the supporting ground of their power: guilt, which cannot exist without free will. So God is now projected as the cause (or Judge) in a narrative of retributive justice. For Nietzsche, the fabulous origins of the concept cannot be separated from the social strivings of the priestly class. Nietzsche does not argue the merits of "free will" as a concept, say, in contrast to that of determinism—not in the manner of the debate between Luther and Erasmus. Rather, he vigorously addresses the use to which the doctrine has been and is being put. The earlier three errors dealt with humankind's proclivity to explain events, including inner ones (or states of consciousness), by inventing narratives with causation as the basis of coherence. Nietzsche advances a coherent perspective on the narrative-creating habits of the race, which ascribes meanings as causes where none exist, or confuses cause with effect, or attributes the wrong causes to effects. The fourth "Great Error" situates humankind as the protagonist in a narrative of crime and punishment. In this world narrative, humankind is the central character—responsible for everything, good or bad, that has ever happened, including all individual good and bad feelings, virtues, and vices.

Taken together, "The Four Great Errors" provide a narrative in which humanity is provided with an explanation for everything. But it is a narrative in which the artifice empowers the fashioners of the narrative embodying "The Four Great Errors." The aim of error is, for Nietzsche, rhetorical. First, it aims to convince humankind that it lives in a world of causes. Causes provide meaning and design, which are, in turn, regarded as properties. Since spirit and will infuse all things, thoughts and feelings, also, are part of an unfolding story of causation, will, and meaning. Explanations of order exfoliate, encompassing every sensation ever experienced in a cosmic fable of virtues rewarded and vices punished. The ego places humankind at the center of this novelistic enterprise. But since only a responsible agent can be controlled through guilt, the concept of free will functions as the instrumental basis of the erroneous encoding of all "Four Great Errors." But what makes this idea erroneous in and of itself is its use. For to hang someone who is *not* guilty would violate the inner coherence of the retributive system of justice on which the narrative depends.

Although Nietzsche divides his discussion of the first and third "Great Errors" into numbered parts, the section on *"The error of a false causality"* is likewise divided into parts by a rhetorical question and the sense of dialectical progression from question to answer. We could say that section 8 of "The Four Great Errors" marks a similar division in the discussion of *"The error of free will."* But, we suggest, this section functions as a denouement to the entire section, as it draws to closure the exposition of the single enabling error: belief in a teleology of cause and effect. In tandem, all four errors comprise a narrative in which the individual is handed the role of responsible protagonist, a story in which everything that one does matters in relation to a given accord between the self and God's interlocutors: the priests.

But in fact the world has no order, no narrative plot, no meaning. The world just is. Feelings just are. Events just happen, whether within or without the sleeping state. The world precedes all explanatory narrative. Why? Because the narrative is unfolding, not told. We are here and nobody knows why, because design is the product of artifice: "neither God, nor society, nor his parents and ancestors, nor he himself" is responsible for the way we are. The narrative of "The Four Great Errors" makes humankind the end of a plot, which is the underlying motif of error itself:

Man is not the effect of some special purpose, of a will, and goal; nor is he the object of an attempt to attain an "ideal of humanity" or an "ideal of happiness" or an "ideal of morality." It is absurd to wish to devolve one essence in some goal or other. We have invented the concept of "goal": in reality there is no goal. (*TI* "FGE" 8)

The peroration to "The Four Great Errors" draws the entire section into a single indictment, namely, that humankind is prone to direct the apparently natural impulse to create narratives toward seriously punitive ends. By creating narratives with good and bad endings, the protagonist is misguided into self-alienating, unrealistic fantasy. But since humans are fabulizing creatures, determined to accept any explanation rather than none at all, then it follows that some narrative must be accepted, and the author does not present himself as an exception. The difference is that, in *Twilight*, Nietzsche creates, not a narrative with an ending, but an anti-narrative without one: an alternative definition of the protagonist's place in an unfinished story which no one is writing, about characters with no specifiable or necessary traits, whose destiny cannot be known.

Just as the other three sections closed with demonstrations of how the error in question led to the concept of God, so this summary passage ends with an alternative exposition of the individual's place in the world:

> One is necessary, one is a piece of fatefulness, one belongs to the whole, one is in the whole; there is nothing which could judge, measure, compare, or sentence our being, for that would mean judging, measuring, comparing, or sentencing the whole. But there is nothing besides the whole. That nobody is held responsible any longer, that the mode of being may not be traced back to a *causa prima*, that the world does not form a unity either as a sensorium or as "spirit"—that alone is the great liberation; with this alone is the innocence of becoming restored. The concept of "God" was until now the greatest objection to existence. We deny God, we deny the responsibility in God: only thereby do we redeem the world. (Section 8)

This closing paragraph, with its marvelous periodic sentences, serves not only as a meditation of the speaker's objections to the concept of free will, as it is punitively promulgated by the priestly class, but also to elicit a sense of the interdependence of "The Four Great Errors" in a single, end-oriented narrative of a "*causa prima*." All four errors lead from the common ascription of an uncaused cause, who designed the world in such a way as to cast everyone in precisely the same role in a psychomachia of the virtues and vices. The great liberation derives from a different narrative perspective: to be free of all four errors at once, to be free of the artifice and artificer—the narrative of design and designer—all at once. That liberation comes in the form of an affirmation or creed. St. Paul writes, "For in him we live, and move, and have our being; as certain also of your own poets have said, For we are also his offspring" (Acts 17.28). And the author answers that the individual could not be otherwise, is part of everything that is, was, or ever shall be. In the world as it is we live and move and have our being. Judgment is therefore erroneous because it entails knowing and sentencing the totality of being, an absurd notion. It is not so much that this passage implies a radical determinism in which individuals are fateful parts of a process, but rather that the speaker pronounces the "end" of end-oriented narratives of being. In so doing, the philosopher answers Bacon's "new instauration" with a new "new instauration." The reason for denying individual responsibility is, we might add, emphatically rhetorical, for by this means the author asserts that we finesse anyone's capacity to construct a trail of cause and effect "*back to causa prima*," which was, at least from Nietzsche's perspective, an underlying motive of Bacon's project.

Our analytic comparison has shown how vigorously Nietzsche rejects the underlying obsession of his predecessor, Bacon, who sought to prepare the world for a "new instauration" by exposing the four "Idols of the Mind," and thus to make way for an empirical inquiry into "second causes." For, he insisted, "God worketh nothing in nature except by second causes." In fact, Nietzsche answers, God worketh nothing in nature. The problem was that Bacon's critique of idolatry focused on everything but the issue in question, for the "first realist" wanted to sweep away the "Idols of the Mind" in order to more clearly perceive the non-existent wonderful workmanship of God in creating the world. For Nietzsche, there can be no *Novum Organum* to relieve man's estate, for such a narrative of cause and effect, Fall and Redemption, has "gone to the devil" and good riddance. Science will not, could not, and should not provide for the "relief of man's estate." Nor will empiricism provide the "new instauration" on which a "New Atlantis" can be built. The problem with Bacon's critique is that it omits the narrative-creating aspect of the critic— that aspect of himself that shows so brilliantly in *Hamlet* and in *Julius Caesar*: the self as creator, not of induction as a process, but, as a poet, a creator of values.

As for utopian fantasies—expressions of "the incarnate desire to be different, to be in a different place" (*GM* III 13)—they belong to art, to imaginative states of mind. Nietzsche's treatment of Zarathustra's experience with perfection is revealing in more than its parodic tone. Tired of running, Zarathustra comes to a tree covered by a grapevine. It is around noon, and he feels "the desire to quench a slight thirst" (*Z* IV "At Noon"), which prompts him "to break off a grape." But between the desire and the action taken that might satisfy it—Zarathustra reaches out his arm—the desire is overtaken by "a still greater desire for something else." It is noon, "the perfect noon hour," and Zarathustra's thirst is overcome by an even stronger desire to lie down under the tree and go to sleep. But, again, just as he is ready to drift off to sleep, his mind is captivated by the waking possibilities of observing the grapevine as it lovingly embraces the tree. It is in this context of a diversion of desires that Zarathustra, in a half-waking state, experiences perfection. Utopia. Stillness. To be neither awake nor asleep: "Still! Still! Did not the world become perfect just now?" Morpheus dances on Zarathustra, touches him with conquering, "caressing hands," and yet Zarathustra neither sleeps nor dreams. It is as if his soul were stretched "out, long, long—longer." And this sense of expansiveness is neither spatial nor temporal, but rather ecstatic and amorphous. Afterward, Zarathustra rises "from his resting place at the tree as from a strange drunkenness" (Z IV "At Noon").

The relevant tableau is probably from the mystical writings surrounding the text of the Song of Songs. For centuries, the wine pressed from the fruit in the shade of the tree inebriated the souls of the faithful: "I sat down under his shadow with great delight, and his fruit was sweet to my taste"; "Stay me with flagons and comfort me with apples, for I am sick with love."[70] The figures were construed analogically, with the emphasis on a mystical, "experimental" meaning to the sexual and sensual language of the text. Accordingly, the soul expands in the shade of this divine tree, luxuriating in mystical union with the Deity: "When will you drink this drop of dew which has fallen upon all earthly things? When will you drink this strange soul? When, well of eternity? Cheerful, dreadful abyss of noon! When will you drink my soul back into yourself?"

In this rhapsodic parody of mystical experience, Nietzsche wryly depicts a tired Zarathustra, who has been chasing disciples hither and yon, fetching disciples to his cave for last supper, giving Sermons on Mounts, spreading the gospel. But even Zarathustra is vulnerable to "the incarnate desire to be different, to be in a different place, and indeed [to] this desire in its greatest extreme" (GM III 13): to the irrepressible lure of the ascetic ideal. As Nietzsche's fiction insinuates, one can desire to desire that desire not be fulfilled even at the moment of its being fulfilled. Zarathustra thirsts until the moment of its slaking is at hand; he wants to sleep until sleep is upon him. His desire to be elsewhere is elusive and subtle, for it needs no geographic longing to enliven it. He wishes only that the moment of desire both be and not be, that the moment of its feeling both end and be extended. That is, his desire to be elsewhere has a temporal aspect. The "strange soul" from which he steals a drink is a well of timelessness: "well of eternity . . . dreadful abyss of noon." But the author's tone suggests that this desire, like those antecedent to it in Zarathustra's momentary straying from his quest, only masks another expression of world-weariness and asceticism. To wish to be in another time is, if anything, even more ludicrous than the desire to be in a different place. But to desire to sleep and yet not sleep is a desire just beyond desiring to quench thirst, with the grape just within reach. What good is desire if it can be satisfied? And, again, the rhetorical question: "Did not the world become perfect just now? Round and ripe? Oh, the golden round ring—where may it fly? Shall I run after it? Quick! Still!" And, as the narrator tells us, it is just at this moment when Zarathustra, who in his revere has been speaking to his heart, "felt that he was asleep."

For Nietzsche, the idea of a "great instauration," which would cleanse the human mind from its sullying penchant for fictions, establishing a scientific mechanism for a perfect social order, is not only absurd, but a waste. Bacon was on the right track, the hegemony of the divines in the academy had to be overturned. But he looked away from the part of himself that was, in the end, the most important philosophically. Bacon's project—attempting to overcome the human mind in order to see the world in such a way as to render a utopian dream feasible—was, in the end, predicated on a Pelagian version of Fall and Redemption. For Nietzsche, such a narrative lacks the merit of candor. Further, Bacon sought to begin his work by altering the human mind, which is—more than absurd—unworthy of a poet. For, at his best, in the creation of such magnificent dramatic portraitures as those found in *Hamlet* and *Julius Caesar*, Bacon experienced, firsthand, a reality far more interesting and complex than would ever by "discovered" by the Royal Society: the self.

The Philosopher as Evangelist:
The Quest for Audience

The idea that philosophers and poets are special people is an ancient one, but the question of identifying either species has never been easy. Philosophers must be unusual in some way, or why would their sayings have any special claim to attention? And even if one knows that one is a philosopher, a problem of linking vocational identity to action often remains. Early in his career, Bacon writes that he knew almost from the beginning of his life that he "was born for the service of mankind," but this knowledge did not deter him from preparing himself for an ordinary career in the hope that this might better his chances of reaching a sympathetic audience. When Milton's "great Proclaimer with a voice/ More awful than the sound of Trumpet, cried/ Repentance,"[71] "the Son of *Joseph*"[72] arrives at the Jordan, "obscure/ Unmarkt, unknown,"[73] and he emerges from anonymity to be baptized, "Heaven open'd, and in likeness of a Dove / The Spirit descended."[74] At this moment of Epiphany it seems that the Son's private life has ended. Now, his "Godlike office" is "mature," and "the Great Proclaimer" offers to surrender to him his "Heavenly Office." But after this spectacular episode, the protagonist withdraws from public exposure as suddenly as he appeared, uncertain of his vocation: "How best the mighty work he might begin / Of Savior to mankind, and which way first / Publish his Godlike office now mature."[75] The Son knows who he is, and in a personal sense of the dedication required of him as distinct from others, knows what it means to be the "Savior to mankind." But the public meaning of his identity is not clear. If the Son is not to continue the work of John the

Baptist, then what *is* he to do. The question is how ("which way first") to begin a "mighty work" the features of which remain unknown.

On reflection, the Son's retirement is explicitly paradoxical, for now it transpires just when the narrator has announced the immediate propriety of public service. His "Godlike office" is "mature"; now, "the Great Proclaimer" has passed the mantle to him, as Elijah had to Elisha. And yet the Son marches away into the wilderness, as if this were the "way first / [to] Publish his Godlike office now mature." And this seems a strange step in becoming "Savior to mankind." But, again, the issue cannot be one merely of identity.[76] The Son knows he is the promised Messiah, that "The time prefixt"[77] has come, that his long-awaited Epiphany as "Savior to mankind"[78] has been accomplished. He demurs, knowing who he is, as if the time for him to act (as, in epic, heroes do) has come, and yet not in the public sense inferred by John the Baptist. That is, his actions as Savior are characterized, first, by negation: He has not been called to replace John as the "great baptizer." But, if not that, what then? As he recalls the episode at the Jordan, the Son does recognize that he was, to use Bacon's figure, "born for public service":

> The Spirit descended on me like a Dove;
> And last the sum of all, my Father's voice,
> Audibly heard from Heav'n, pronounc'd me his,
> Mee his beloved Son, in whom alone
> He was well pleas'd; by which I knew the time
> Now full, that I no more should live obscure,
> But openly begin, as best becomes
> The Authority which I deriv'd from Heaven.[79]

The question concerns the nature of public service. In "His holy Meditations," the Son considers various possibilities: rescuing "*Israel* from the *Roman* yoke,"[80] ending war, freeing "truth," conquering "willing hearts,"[81] (by mastering the art of rhetoric). But rather than taking up a military career or turning to the study of Cicero, the Son, after acknowledging his readiness to leave the quiet, obscure life, walks into "A pathless Desert."[82]

The narrator's theme is quietistic. The Son doesn't "will" his itinerary. Led by "some strong motion,"[83] he no more understands the purpose of his solitude than he knows "How best the mighty work he might begin / Of Savior to mankind." He does seem instinctively to know that, regardless of his vocational choice—warrior or rhetorician—he must know not only who he is but what he is to do. One kind of knowledge works here: because the Son knows the Scriptures, he knows that he is the Messiah. But this knowledge is incomplete in that it does not answer the specific of public service: How can he decline the offer to replace John the Baptist unless, in some way, he is led toward an alternative career? For the moment, the Son contents himself with the possibility that more knowledge—that is, knowledge supplemental to the Scripture that he has learned—will be provided, this, in his "Solitude" when it is needed: "And now by some strong motion I am led / Into this Wilderness, to what intent / I learn not yet, perhaps I need not know, / For what concerns my knowledge God reveals."[84] From the outset, then, knowledge—never an end in itself—assumes value only at propitious moments, which may seem to be at hand and yet not be so.

It turns out that solitude is not without its own distractions; it is here in the wilderness that Satan tempts the Son—with money, power, knowledge, but above all with occasions to act, though in obscurity, out of public sight. The fact that Satan presents the Son with the mastery of Athenian culture after the attractions of wealth and power have been rejected suggests Milton's aware-ness of the seductive power of Renaissance humanism. Here was the contem-porary equivalent of Satan's seductive promise to Eve: "That ye should be as Gods."[85] Thus Satan, who begins and ends his project with direct challenges to the Son to prove his identity, attempts to trivialize the conflict as a semantic quibble:

> The Son of God, which bears no single sense;
> The Son of God I also am, or was,
> And if I was, I am; relation stands;
> All men are Sons of God. . . .[86]

Although he admits that he must resort to "Another Method,"[87] Satan has pre-sented the Son with many variations on the theme of the uncertain limits of his knowledge. Set aside the testimony of others (including John the Baptist), set aside the astral display of the Epiphany, set aside all reinforcement of belief emanating outside of himself, and what does the Son know? The implication of the Son's faith prior to his encounter with Satan ("For what concerns my knowledge God reveals") is not made clear until Book IV. In his "holy Medi-tations," as he imagined possible forms his redemptive ministry might take, the Son came last to the achievement of rhetoric: "Yet held it more humane, more heavenly, first / By winning words to conquer willing hearts, / And make persuasion do the work of fear."[88] It is a sign of Satan's mastery of "persuasive Rhetoric"[89] that he proffers Athenian culture after "The Kingdoms of the world,"[90] as he seems to accede to the Son's peaceful intentions while answer-ing the underlying question of "how" the work of redemption is to come about: "And with the *Gentiles* much thou must converse, / Ruling them by per-suasion as thou mean'st, / Without thir learning how wilt thou with them, / Or they with thee hold conversation meet?"[91]

The Son's response to Satan's offer of "*Athens*, the eye of *Greece*, Mother of Arts / And Eloquence,"[92] with "sage Philosophy" of Socrates, is often cited as a reversal of the humanism found in Milton's *Of Education* and *Areopagitica* for its seeming rejection of learning. It is true that the Son holds steadfastly to the priority of Scripture, and in doing so seems to deprecate humane letters:

> However, many books
> Wise men have said are wearisome; who reads
> Incessantly, and to his reading brings not
> A spirit and judgment equal or superior
> (And what he brings, what needs he elsewhere seek)
> Uncertain and unsettl'd still remains,
> Deep verst in books and shallow in himself,
> Crude or intoxicate, collecting toys,
> And trifles for choice matters, worth a sponge;
> As Children gathering pebbles on the shore.
> Or if I would delight my private hours
> With Music or with Poem, where so soon
> As in our native Language can I find
> That solace? All our Law and Story strew'd
> With Hymns, our Psalms with artful terms inscrib'd
> Our Hebrew Songs and Harps in *Babylon*,
> That pleas'd so well our Victors' ear, declare
> That rather *Greece* from us these Arts derivd;
> Ill imitated, while they loudest sing
> The vices of thir Deities, and thir own
> In Fable, Hymn, or Song, so personating
> Thir Gods ridiculous, and themselves past shame.[93]

It isn't quite fair to say that the Son repudiates worldly knowledge. Rather, he criticizes its employment to any but proper ends, which are truth and understanding. The Son could not propound the historical influence of Hebrew law and art on the Greeks without a knowledge of both cultures. Nor does he claim that reading is intrinsically "wearisome," but only that it can become so when pursued by an undiscerning mind, which "reads / Incessantly" without bringing to that activity an independent and "superior" judgment. Further, he sets forward the view of that learning unrelated to values external to the text read is unhelpful, in that it does not settle the mind or lend substance to the character. Accordingly, the Son does not distance himself from Greek culture because it lacks value, but because the value that it does have is already embodied in his own Hebrew Scriptures, and because such value as it does have is vitiated by its expression in degenerate form of the Hebrew original. The Son answers Satan's rhetoric with his own divine poetics: The Greek fables are "ridiculous" because Greek Gods themselves are so. It is on the basis of comparison—that is, of experience (which makes clear that the Son has indeed read far beyond the Hebrew Scriptures)—that he knows the superiority of "*Sion's* songs." Why do the Psalms excel "all true tastes"? Because in the Psalms "God is prais'd aright."[94]

Although the Son undergoes a solitary initiation throughout which his public role remains undefined, the narrative states that the Son will give to "*Adam* and his chosen Sons" "A fairer Paradise"[95] than the race had lost in Eden. But even though the narrator exults over the Son's present and future triumph, the theme of the Son's "Heavenly Office" is never reasserted in the text. The epic ends with a sense of a beginning ("Now enter, and begin to save mankind")[96] as the Son—privately—returns to private life: "he unobserv'd / Home to his Mother's house private return'd."[97] Thus, from the public moment of Epiphany at the Jordan, the narrative moves from private experience to private experience, ending with the Son's return to the privacy of family life.

For all that Nietzsche's *magnum opus* is also based on the narrative of the life of Jesus, this return of the Son to private life marks an interesting contrast in emphasis between Milton's protagonist and Zarathustra. Both the Son and Zarathustra feel that they have important work to do; both know that, although the way may be unclear, they must play a role in humanity's redemption. But Zarathustra is drawn away from private life, even while repeatedly returning to his mountain retreat. As he seems to recognize at the close of Book IV, his "ruling passion" (as the eighteenth century might have described it) is his "work," and his work is both a vocation (teaching) and a doctrine (subject) conveyed by that vocational enterprise. Zarathustra must be what he can and must do. But the pervasive sense of urgency in his sermons emanates from his unusual doctrine. For one cannot teach or promulgate any "doctrine," much less an innovative one, without an audience. The function of the teacher requires the existence of a less initiated congregation of potential learners. Teachers may use as well as generate texts, but they instruct students, and they do so from a necessarily privileged perspective. Zarathustra "descends" from a height to society because of his desire. "Zarathustra wants to become man again" (Z "Prologue" 1) in order that he might teach the future "meaning of the earth": "*I teach you the Übermensch.* Man is something that shall be overcome. . . . Behold, I teach you the *Übermensch*" (Z "Prologue" 3).

From a rhetorical point of view, Nietzsche's theme of *amor fati* emerges in a hortatory context within which an alternative perspective—imbued with *ressentiment*—is not only possible but unhappily probable. Novitiates, potential disciples, anyone able to hear—all must attend to this strange, new doctrine. The sense of urgency in Zarathustra's evangelistic style is not unfamiliar to readers of other Nietzschean texts: *Toward the Genealogy of Morals, Beyond Good and Evil, Twilight of the Idols, The Antichrist.* Evangelism is an optimistic mode, predicated on the assumption that, under the right conditions, something useful can come of the Preacher's homiletics. Even when he excoriates his audience in the manner of Jeremiah, the Preacher assumes that his message can make a beneficial difference in the world. Even if the message is that history moves in a settled, cyclic course, the audience must be—at least potentially— better off believing than not believing the proffered "truth." Indeed, belief and unbelief in the here and now must make an all-important difference.

As Kathleen Higgins argues,[98] Nietzsche's attitude toward the past affects our understanding of his critique of morality as well as of his idea of eternal recurrence. Nietzsche often separates himself from romanticism, and he seems also to distinguish his creative doctrine of values ("revaluation of all values") from easy categorization as a species of internal utopianism. And yet his recurring emphasis on the "higher man"—on the potentialities of that responsive reaction to his hortatory prose—not only fits the evangelical tone familiar in many of his writings, but it also suggests an evolutionary theme. In the next chapter, we will be discussing the views of Northrop Frye and others on the subject of Nietzsche's supposed pessimism. For now, suffice it to say that, for him, God is *not* in his heaven, and all is *not* right with the world. And yet we must not omit the evangelical assertion that, at the same time, all *could* be right with the world, supposing only that the right audience appears, ready to listen to the "truth." Humankind, the problem-creature, must and will be overcome. Even Zarathustra, for all that he recognizes the shortcomings of his disciples, seems at times sure that the day of the "higher man" is at hand: "But for all these the day is now at hand"; "my hour has come: this is *my* morning, *my* day is breaking " [Z III "OTE" 2; IV "Sign").

Thus, "every day in every way" humankind *could* if it chose get better and better. A belief in progress is the theme connecting Nietzsche to his great Renaissance forebear, Bacon. Spengler and others may think of Nietzsche as a pessimist, but for Nietzsche pessimism was (like pity) a human problem to be overcome. In his "Attempt at Self-Criticism," Nietzsche ridicules his own youthful pessimism. We think of ridicule as a literary symptom of hope. Although Nietzsche does not see in the advance of science evidence of an upward evolutionary movement, he does adopt evolutionary figures to his own literary and philosophical perspective.

In 1887, Nietzsche entered several brief sentences in his notebook, all of which have analogues in *Twilight of the Idols*. In one, he observes that, for Comte, the "history of scientific method" and philosophy were virtually identical, which may explain why Comte is the only modern whom Nietzsche lists among "the great methodologists: Aristotle, Bacon, Descartes, Auguste Comte" (*WP* III 468). Interestingly, two of the four great methodologists are Renaissance contemporaries. Like Nietzsche, Bacon and Descartes were also energetic critics of received attitudes toward knowledge, and both were theoreticians of methods for conceptual renewal. For Nietzsche, half of the great innovators in philosophical method are Renaissance thinkers: like many *fin de siecle* Europeans (notably, Pater, Ruskin, and Burckhardt), Nietzsche was fascinated by this epoch of Western civilization.

Tracy Strong[99] argues that Burckhardt's *The Civilization of the Renaissance in Italy* (1883) was a shaping influence on Nietzsche, especially in the period immediately prior to his mental collapse. Strong notes in particular that the first section of Burckhardt's great work treats "The State as a Work of Art." He is

probably right in thinking that Nietzsche would have found this part of Burckhardt's monumental work interesting, but the historian's attribution of the invention of warfare as a work of art to the Italian Renaissance might have
seemed to Nietzsche an even more fascinating development. In the interne-
cine struggles among the principalities of Italy, individuality emerged along
with the rise of a new kind of social power, the *condottieri*: mercenaries who,
though largely illiterate, made themselves absolute rulers by dint of their own
achievements in battle. They hired sculptors to fashion statuary in their image: "The result of these combats was no longer regarded as a Divine judgment, but as a triumph of personal merit. . . ."[100]

In his penetrating analysis of Nietzsche's political aestheticism, Tracy Strong
(acknowledging his debt to Alexander Nehamas) claims that "we can never
start or end by claiming to know what they [Nietzsche's texts] mean": "He
[Nietzsche] wants us to encounter these texts as we would encounter another
person, with the assurance of his presence."[101] But, Strong argues, this acquaintance is not like the ascertaining of Nietzsche's meaning. Citing Stanley
Fish's essay on "Affective Stylistics" for support, Strong writes: "We learn from
them [Nietzsche's texts] by finding ourselves in them. . . ." For Strong, this contention touches the issue of the rhetorical analysis of Nietzsche's speakers and
their audiences:

> It is in *Ecce Homo* that Nietzsche explores what it means for an author to explore these
> topics. *Ecce Homo*, that is, is about writing itself and is thus, in this mode, an autobiogra-
> phy. And here, necessarily, he must allow others to find themselves in him. He must warn
> them away from finding a message. That is why he separates himself from his writings
> at the beginning of the section "Why I Write Such Good Books" and when he suggests
> that he will be born posthumously, that is, in his readers: "Ultimately, nobody can get
> more out of things, including books, than he already knows. For what one lacks access to
> from experience one will have no ear."[102]

We quote this paragraph at length because it seems to us problematic. First,
if Nietzsche proposes that, in reading this text, we "encounter another person,
with the assurance of his presence," why in the same section does Strong claim
that Nietzsche doesn't "want to be confounded with others—not even by [him-
self]"? Does Strong suggest that in reading a text—any text—we find "ourselves" *re*-presented therein? And does our "finding ourselves in them" constitute a conflict of interest? Suppose we wish to affirm or deny that we have
found ourselves in another's text? Must we demonstrate (to whom?) that we
have or have not heretofore been, in some manner of speaking, lost? Do we
find the same "ourselves" whether we are reading *Ecce Homo* or *The Civilization
of the Renaissance in Italy*? Do genres matter? Do we find the same ourselves *re*-
presented regardless of whether we are reading *Ecce Homo* or *The Life of St.
Teresa* or Browne's *Religio Medici* or Bunyan's *Grace Abounding*?

It is possible to think of such autobiographies as convenient sources of authorial self-representations, so it is not surprising that discussions of the historical "Nietzsche" often focus on *Ecce Homo*. For instance, Tracy Strong thinks of Nietzsche's observation that "some are born posthumously" as an invitation to an exercise in reader-response self-discovery. And yet the opening of *Ecce Homo* does not seem to be about "us" as readers at all, but about the first person "I" in a typical pose of the author explaining special characteristics of his work:

> I am one thing, my writings are another matter.—Before I discuss them, one by one, let me touch on the question of their being understood or *not* understood. I'll do it as casually as decency permits; for the time for this question certainly hasn't come yet. The time for me hasn't come yet: some are born posthumously. (*EH* "WIWSGB" 1)

The problem addressed concerns the philosopher-poet's quest for an audience. For the prophetic voice, the question of the readiness of the contemporary audience to listen persists. As he proceeds, adverting to the possibility that chairs in philosophy might someday be established for the study of his writings, Nietzsche unfolds the "facts" of his own experience. But the experience of an author, especially that of the prophetic, philosopher-poet, is shaped by those who, like Bacon, have preceded him. Not every utterance that the author makes will be understood. In order to have an appreciable, appreciative audience, the author must expand the temporal opportunity for communication with potential members of the audience. The remedy to misunderstanding (readers who ignore the evangelical text betray one species of misunderstanding) is time, which is always on the side of apocalyptic thinkers. If an author associates his teaching with the future, if he implies that only the subtle and enlightened few are capable of understanding and of aligning themselves with the futuristic wisdom of his gospel text, he not only challenges readers to attend to his work sympathetically, but at the same time provides editorial assistance toward that end by imaginatively rewarding them for their esoteric perceptions.

We realize that the issue of "authorship" is not a simple one, especially in light of the brilliant analyses of Walter Benjamin[103] of the emerging impact of modern technology on the process of text formation. But the concepts of generic and social change presuppose the existence of forms to change. We see at least three aspects to the question of "authorial selves" as it appears in most literary contexts: first, we find ourselves in all texts; we find the not/ourselves in all texts. Since the two formulations of the consequences of reading are equally valid, they are equally uninformative; neither differentiates between the selves or not/selves that we find as we read *n* number of texts. Neither would help differentiate genres, periods, styles, texts, and so on. This leads us to the second aspect of the problem: What becomes of the quest for audience if we find, not ourselves, but someone else, in every text that we read (other than those produced by our own hands)? Suppose the act of reading were actually an encounter with someone else. Would we not necessarily encounter at the same time the possibility of misunderstanding the text? Is the remedy of correction the same when we misunderstand our own voice and when we misunderstand the voice of another? In critical discussions, misunderstanding is the country-cousin of correction. Ben Jonson writes "To the Reader": "Pray thee take care, that tak'st my book in hand,/ To read it well; that is, to understand." [104] But how, if we encounter ourselves in Jonson's text, can we ever experience misunderstanding? To whom does Jonson "Pray" for understanding? When we read Nietzsche or Luther do we say to ourselves, "I agree," or, "I disagree with myself"?

The third aspect of the problem is more difficult: To what extent, in our efforts to reconstruct an authorial self—the canonical "Bacon" or "Milton" or "Nietzsche"—do we chase an uncatchable will-o'-the wisp? Consider the changes that Milton's thinking underwent from the time he wrote his Prelatical tracts to the spring of 1660 when he wrote and then revised *The Readie and Easie Way to Establish a Free Commonwealth.* Given the evidence of individual change in many cases, it is not surprising that the concept of authorial integrity—the coherence of authorial selves—is now considered controversial. But as Wittgenstein wryly observes, "philosophical problems arise when our language *goes on holiday.*" [105] The theme is a familiar one: along with God, authors have expired. "It is obviously insufficient to repeat empty slogans," writes Foucault, elaborating on a line from Nietzsche: "the author has disappeared; God and man died a common death." [106] Having asserted this disappearance, Foucault adds that "we should reexamine the empty space left by the author's disappearance." Although the symptoms of bereavement are not hard to document, the coroner's report is not unequivocal in its implications. Or, to put the same point another way, sometimes deaths can be as elusive to eager observers as resurrections. So critics still refer to "the author" of a text under discussion, as if there existed some ontological connection between the incantation of that name and the sounds or signs designated as the text. They are, if a strict construction of Foucault's metaphor holds, like the old man in the "Prologue" of *Zarathustra*: "Could it be possible? This old saint in the forest has not yet heard anything of this, that *God is dead*?"

On this analysis, then, authors have been banished from the privilege of critically-affirmed "existence" of literary integrity. Instead of immortality ("That last infirmity of Noble mind"), their inscriptions earn them no more than membership in the null set: "absence." Thus, it is an offense to suppose that a human voice remains constant from work to work, or even from sentence to sentence within a work, for to support such a conceptual travesty entails hypostatization of a fictive, unchanging being, whose character we extrapolate from a myriad of conflicting attitudes, actions, and beliefs. And if this argument stands, it must be equally foolish to talk about a changing authorial self, for such a concept merely presents the same structure in temporally segmented form: the unified self as divisible into *n* number of separate but equal unified selves.

And yet this guise is hard to sustain. As Foucault's text purports to deconstruct the concept of the unified authorial voice, the footnotes tell a different story, citing other works by Foucault, prodding the reader to perceive in the apparent chaos of "*différance*" a Platonic voice, unerringly confident, unerringly "true": "Foucault's purpose, concerned with determining the 'codes' of discourse, is explicitly stated in the Preface to *The Order of Things*."[107] That is, here and throughout the sequence, Foucault expresses ideas identical to those encoded elsewhere: "This statement is the polemical ground of Foucault's dissociation from phenomenology . . ."; "This is a particularly important point and brings together a great many of Foucault's insights . . . ."[108] It could be objected, of course, that these notes represent only reifications derived from Foucault's editor, whose efforts to make a point carry him, perhaps unwittingly, into apparent but unintended affirmation of the coherence of the "Foucault" who composed the various texts. But then it could be objected to that objection that Foucault himself appears to hypostatize a unified, authorial Nietzsche: "at least on those occasions when he [that is, Nietzsche] is truly a genealogist"[109]; again, "In numerous instances, Nietzsche associates the terms . . . "[110]; and "In fact, Nietzsche's criticism, beginning with the second of the *Untimely Meditations*, always questioned the form of history. . . ."[111]

We do not doubt that certain ideas find repeated expression in Nietzsche's writings, although perhaps Foucault's dependence on *The Will to Power* to support his thesis is a bit like relying on *The Garden of Eden* for a definitive commentary on the work of Ernest Hemingway. But we cannot even say that attitudes change without in some fashion "reifying" attitudes prior to and after the supposed change. Authors and genres do change, but we recognize these changes by discriminating among features, which we recognize by their particular differences: *A* becomes *B*. Rhetorical flourishes may be recognizable generic features: the prophetic voice declares that it is misunderstood by the Philistine multitude. But the figurative expressions with which that rhetorical voice is set out must be seen within the context of other generic features. That is, Nietzsche's figure of the philosopher-poet who might be "born posthumously" is apposite to many such declarations through the ages: the prophet lives an exile in his own land; the time of the prophetic word is not yet come.

The prophet's quest for an audience is predicated on the difference between—even the tension between—the anointed and the comparatively unenlightened, which explains the frequently affirmed need for a period of quiescence or deathlike hiatus between utterance and acceptance. The quest for audience requires time, perhaps centuries, even epochs and dispensations.

Within this context, the philosopher-poet not only puts his gospel forward, but he also proclaims its ultimate value. He triumphs over recalcitrant members of the audience by envisioning the outcome of the issue in question. This strategy may help explain the apparent function of figures of rebirth in *Ecce Homo* and *Areopagitica*, for in the former work Nietzsche draws attention to the potential "liveliness" of his prophetic word in a manner reminiscent of Milton's famous affirmation in *Areopagitica*:

> For books are not absolutely dead things, but do contain a potency of life in them to be as active as that soul was whose progeny they are; nay, they do preserve as in a vial the purest efficacy and extraction of that living intellect that bred them. I know they are as lively and as vigorously productive as those fabulous dragon's teeth; and being sown up and down, may chance to spring up armed men. And yet, on the other hand, unless wariness be used, as good almost kill a man as kill a good book: who kills a man kills a reasonable creature, God's image; but he who destroys a good book, kills reason itself, kills the image of God, as it were, in the eye. Many a man lives a burden to the earth; but a good book is the precious lifeblood of a master spirit, embalmed and treasured up on purpose to a life beyond life.[112]

There are noticeable differences, of course. For Milton, the word is like a seed (the Parable of the Sower) in that, as it moves through time, it may seem to be inert or dead, out of sight in the ground. But the liveliness of the literary text appears as in the fable, in action. The author's words change the behavior of *future* readers. By its rhetorical power, the word transforms readers into warriors; the vicarious becomes actual. For Milton, the word presents the "soul" of an author ("God's image"), which suggests that the text bestows a "life beyond life" (the claim of the Renaissance poet that his lines bestow immortality upon the favored subject), that the word, like a seed in its "potency of life," conveys the essence—"the purest efficacy and extraction"—of the "living intellect that bred them."[113]

Milton's generative figures (they are far from unique, as Milton follows Bacon here) in apposition to those of death, suggest that censorship is worse than murder. Nietzsche's utterance insinuates that unsympathetic reading is rather like the consequences of "licensing" in *Areopagitica*. If a text is misunderstood, it loses its liveliness. It's "potency of life," placed there by the author, remains, but it remains in a closed-up, seed-like state. Wanting the vividness of a sympathetic reading, the voice or spirit or self of the author exists only potentially. The act of perceptive reading transforms the inactive word into its "lively" expressiveness. Communication transpires, as the variable possibilities of change come into being, as the once-silent voice of the speaker is heard by the intended audience. The alternative to communication in both Miltonic and Nietzschean figurations is death—that is, silence.

We are touching here on the question of the power of reading to affect behavior, or what some critics refer to as the influence of "strong authors." Suppose we hold with Milton and T. S. Eliot that reading—at least reading of the texts of "strong authors"—changes readers by bringing them to share the attitudes and values of the text's author. Such a perspective has the immediate value of affirming the importance of literature, which may be dangerous, but may also, for the same reason, be socially productive. Unless we allow for some bearing of the reading act upon behavior, it is hard to see why society ought to insist (at great expense) that its citizens learn how to read, and then dedicate at least part of their reading to a preferred canon. Reading changes readers in the process of "education." T. S. Eliot writes:

> The common ground between religion and fiction is behaviour. Our religion imposes our ethics, our judgement and criticism of ourselves, and our behaviour toward our fellow men. The fiction that we read affects our behaviour towards our fellow men, affects our patterns of ourselves. When we read of human beings behaving in certain ways, with the approval of the author, who gives his benediction to this behaviour by his attitude toward the result of the behaviour arranged by himself, we can be influenced towards behaving the same way.[114]

Eliot thinks that in conceding that fiction can be a cause of behavior that he may appear to give aid and comfort to the proponents of censorship, but he argues, instead, that the narrow range of perspectives in modern fiction, the whole of which is "corrupted by . . . secularism,"[115] approximates an assault on individuality. For him, as for Milton and Nietzsche, reading has important consequences in the so-called "real" world, and therefore may be taken seriously as symptomatic of cultural conditions and also as a primary shaper of those conditions. Nietzsche complains about the quality of books available as early as *Philosophy in the Tragic Age of the Greeks* and as late as *Zarathustra*; the implication is that the entire culture suffers when philosophy and poetry are in a low estate. Not surprisingly, Eliot's view of the power of fiction was a familiar one in the Renaissance. This explains why Milton's conception of the power of the word is similar to Eliot's in conceding the dangers posed by serious reading: "I deny not but that it is of the greatest concernment in the church and commonwealth to have a vigilant eye how books demean themselves as well as men,"[116] but this must be conceded if reading is to be allowed any salutary benefit. The change in readers is one evidence that the word gives life; and it is further evidence of the importance of the creative artist.

Figuratively, it follows that literary utterance constitutes a species of resurrection. It is interesting that Nietzsche singles out *Zarathustra* as the text in such special need of interpretation—interesting because Nietzsche now dramatizes himself in a role similar to Zarathustra's. Finding an audience properly equipped to hear his "truths" is not easy for Zarathustra, and, as the recursive structure of the work seems to imply, his fictive life ends where it began, with Zarathustra ready to descend the mountain as teacher of a new gospel in search of an audience. But perceptive interpretation presupposes a demanding text, with a "potency of life" in it. In 1886, in a retrospective glance at *The Birth of Tragedy* ("Attempt at a Self-Criticism"), Nietzsche expresses gratitude for the fact that even his first book, with all of its faults, is a *"proven* book" in that, after all, it communicated "as in a dialogue" with its intended audience, Richard Wagner (*BT* "Attempt" 2). Nietzsche claims that "after sixteen years" he has changed in certain ways. In order to create different texts for alternative audiences, time is required, not only for interpreters, but also for authors. Although in certain respects "more demanding" as a writer, Nietzsche finds himself less given to excesses of length and "storm and stress" than was the younger "artist" of *The Birth of Tragedy*.

And yet, unlike many of his predecessors in the history of prose style, Nietzsche declines the opportunity to revise the early work in any significant way. Rather, his "Attempt at a Self-Criticism" engages a retrospective glance at a youthful treatment of a theme which was to preoccupy the author throughout his creative life. Now, hindsight allows him to see that the task of unmasking "the problem of science" was "uncongenial to youth." But the older man has learned the art of condensation. He is also less moody, less "defiantly self-reliant," and in being so he is able to accept the faults of his younger "self"—in fact, to separate himself from it by criticizing the earlier achievement.

The older writer's affirmation of the text written so long ago not only follows from his statement of philosophical continuity ("science considered . . . as problematic") and the genealogy of Western metaphysics as a history of decline (Socratism). Science and philosophy alike expressed the same disquiet, the same withdrawal from "the best, the strongest, the most courageous period." While tolerating the younger author's stylistic self-indulgence, the mature artist reaffirms the view that art and science alike are expressions—or symptoms—of life, which became, after the tragic, pre-Socratic epoch, a dishonest effort to evade the inescapable onslaught of pessimism: "O Socrates, Socrates, was that perhaps *your* secret? O enigmatic ironist, was that perhaps your—irony?" (*BT* "Attempt" 1).

This perspectival shift from exposition to direct address suggests that the younger Nietzsche had perhaps not mastered the ironic mode, that, perhaps, neither had he fully appreciated Socrates as a thinker. Could it be that Socrates understood, long before the author of *The Birth of Tragedy*, the "truth" of the young man's thesis? Perhaps he sensed the emerging malaise of which his own thought was only one "sign of decline, of weariness, of infection, of the anarchical dissolution of the instincts" (*BT* "Attempt" 1). The warmth with which the older author addresses Socrates is in accord with his tolerant acceptance of his earlier "self." Nietzsche commentators, especially his detractors, do not often remark upon, much less appreciate, this congenial aspect of perspectivism. The elder author, affirming certain aspects of the younger Nietzsche's work, reminds us of Sir Thomas Browne's recognition in *Religio Medici* of tolerance as an expression—in his case prospective rather than retrospective tolerance—of the possibility of personal growth: "I COULD never divide my selfe from any man upon the difference of an opinion, or be angry with his judgement for not agreeing with mee in that, from which perhaps within a few days I should dissent my selfe . . . ."[117]

And yet the mature Nietzsche is stringent in his judgment of *The Birth of Tragedy*. While ignoring the option of rewriting the work, he nevertheless pronounces the work to be "impossible," lacking in irony, and—most devastatingly—"romantic." The younger writer dramatized his isolation, his fury, his independence, his romanticism. But, as he "sought to exclude from the beginning the *profundum vulgus* of the educated even more than 'the mass' or 'folk,'" he simultaneously concealed himself behind a mask of the scholar whose abiding confidence in the present condition of German music (read Wagner) hid from himself the terrible truth of his own "resignationism" (*BT* 7). Why, then, not do as Montaigne, Bacon, and others had done successfully before him: rewrite? Implicitly, the older author indicates that, since the world already has *Thus Spoke Zarathustra*, it does not need a revised version of *The Birth of Tragedy*. The young scholar, with all his philosophical and stylistic faults, has been replaced by the author of a peerless fiction. Thus, the earnest, humorless, romantic pessimist, with his longing for other-worldly comfort, has become the author and practitioner of "the art of *this-worldly* comfort" (*BT* 7). The implication seems to be that, had Nietzsche not matured, not learned to laugh—had he not mastered the way to engage an audience other than Richard Wagner—he could not have written so profound, so satisfying, so complete a work as *Zarathustra*.

Nietzsche's figure of authorial rebirth is apposite to this easy affirmation of *The Birth of Tragedy*, and is relevant, also, to Nietzsche's theory of time as well as to his ideas of the power of writing. Consider Nietzsche's remark that one learns no more from a book than one already knows. As we have seen, Milton's Son in *Paradise Regained* makes the same observation. But does this theory of learning apply to composition? When, in this ostensibly anti-pedagogical diatribe, does "already" begin? Are we to assume that, as the author and audience change, no improvement in either reading or writing is possible? Is the very character of Zarathustra—teacher, evangelist, philosopher—absurd. Is the hortatory spirit of works like *Toward the Genealogy of Morals* and *The Antichrist* similarly wasted? Why preach forever if, eternally, nobody who can hear—supposing for the moment that an audience of some shape and size possesses efficacious ears—is able or willing to change?

It is not surprising that when Wittgenstein thought of Nietzsche he thought of eternal recurrence, an idea that he found a not very useful instance of confusion between the uses of two auxiliary verbs. Because someone "has" accomplished a certain feat in the past, we say that he "can" do so in the future. The presumption is that the locution expresses an expectation or belief concerning a possible future state of affairs. It would make no sense to say, just as one completes a task, that he "can" complete it. Wittgenstein perceives an equivocation here: "The use which is made of the word 'can'—the expression of possibility in 49)—can throw a light upon the idea that what can happen must have happened before (Nietzsche)."[118] This observation is typical of Wittgenstein's skepticism regarding the use of spatial metaphor in elucidating concepts of time.[119] In the passage above (from *The Blue and Brown Books*), Wittgenstein stresses the psychological "reality" of the reaction entailed as the mind leaps from what might happen in the future to hypostatization of what must have happened in the past. Typically, he offers no final critique of the notion itself, nor does he suggest a better formulation of the idea that the mind recognizes in the occurrence of certain events a distinct sense of repetition. But the parenthetical identification makes the name function metonymically as a sign of the assumptions and attitudes that Wittgenstein associates with Nietzsche's idea of eternal recurrence. In this context, we recall the passage preceding the quotation from *Zarathustra* toward the close of *Twilight of the Idols*. The author writes in retrospect:

> And herewith I again touch that point from which I once went forth: *The Birth of Tragedy* was my first revaluation of all values. Herewith I again stand on the soil out of which my intention, my *ability* grows—I, the last disciple of the philosopher Dionysus—I, the teacher of the eternal recurrence. (*TI* "WIOA" 5)

As he returns to the "point" at which he began to recreate values—in touching this point of earliest departure—the author recognizes and affirms this beginning as the "soil" that nurtured his talent. The underlying figure here is that of organic growth. The author's "intention" and "ability" grew, but apparently only by repeated recursion to this native soil. For the imagined "self" of the speaker is an instance of repeated renewal, a figure *re*-presenting as well as teaching the doctrine of eternal recurrence. Thus, first and last utterances conjoin as expressions of a single identity, which is that of a dual function as disciple and teacher of the source behind the source of both intention and ability: "the philosopher Dionysus." The fact that the close of *Twilight* is drawn from Part III of *Zarathustra* (from "On Old and New Tablets") doubles the recursive motif. One teacher refers to his fictional characterization of another, and both—creations of Nietzsche—are remembered for their insistence on the common theme of eternal recurrence.

The best-known instance of Nietzsche's melding of part of one composition with a similar expression of eternal recurrence in another is probably the section in *The Gay Science* called *"The greatest stress."* Here, Nietzsche's earliest enunciation of the doctrine precedes two paragraphs which roughly approximate the opening "Prologue" of *Thus Spoke Zarathustra*; and, as we have just seen, parts of *Zarathustra* form sections of *Twilight of the Idols*. Segments of the "non-fictional" work become parts of "fictional" ones, thus blurring a common sense distinction while focusing attention on the one unquestionably "fictional" member of the trio, *Zarathustra*.

What follows "*The greatest stress*" is, of course, the beginning of Zarathustra's literary existence: "*Incipit tragoedia*." The key motif linking the two passages concerns one's readiness to affirm life on the only basis one knows, namely, that of one's own experience—all of it: "every pain and every joy and every thought and sigh and everything unutterably small or great in [one's] life . . . all in the same succession and sequence . . ." (*GS* IV 341). Does the idea of such irrepressible and invariable recurrence instill nausea or joy? To what extent does the answer to this question indicate the direction of the respondent's life, whether toward fulfillment or despair? If the author knows what he is talking about—if the author is, in fact, telling the "truth"—then, at the close of *Twilight*, in his affirmation, he "experiences" with joy something akin to the overabundance that might accompany saying "yes" to the eternal recurrence of the same. That is, the author offers neither revision nor regret for his first creative effort, flawed though he admits it is. And yet, in this playing with "authority," he is not only taking advantage of the reader by suggesting that he has come back from the dead. He has come back from the dead for a reason: "*Incipit tragoedia*" (*GS* "Preface" 1). The message is: "Beware! Something downright wicked and malicious is announced here: *incipit parodia*, no doubt" (*GS* "Preface" 1). Walter Kaufmann suggests that Nietzsche is announcing in advance that *Zarathustra*, his next book, will be "something of a parody." [120]

The foregoing remarks are not meant to deny that Nietzsche draws attention to the author's special character: "But let us leave Herr Nietzsche: what is it to us that Herr Nietzsche has become well again?" (*EH*) Indeed, it is important that the author has been, in past times, both well and ill. He is an author who is strong enough to wonder aloud if it makes any difference to the readership if he is well enough to write or not. His illness is the "*nausea*" endemic to poetry in the present time, in his case a "*nausea*" unto death. Only the figuratively dead can be figuratively resurrected. In the next chapter, we return to consider in greater detail the literary convention of the poet's descent into the underworld and subsequent return. For now we wish only to isolate Nietzsche's metaphoric strategy as part of his critique of philosophy. Of course, that critique is couched in a hyperbolic presentation of the author's credentials. The problem with run-of-the-mill philosophers is that their pronouncements are uttered with an appalling lack of conviction, which is the *sine qua non* of creative power. Traditionally, that power is bestowed on privileged authors in conversations with the honored dead. But the speaker goes tradition one better by providing direct communication with, not an interlocutor to the dead, but with the once dead, now resurrected, author of *The Gay Science*. The text requires the author's interpretive assistance, which elucidates the figures of death and transfiguration:

> This whole book is nothing but a bit of merry-making after long privation and powerlessness, the rejoicing of strength that is returning, of a reawakened faith in a tomorrow and the day after tomorrow, of a sudden sense and anticipation of a future, of impending adventures, of seas that are open again, of goals that are permitted again, believed again. (*GS* "Preface" 1)

Returning to the issue suggested by Wittgenstein's remark, here we find that Nietzsche presents a truncated narrative of past, present, and future, in a brief account of the making of the book. In one periodic sentence the author provides a theory of composition. The sentence unfolds from a statement in the present tense describing the artifact, which "may need more than one preface," as "it seems to be written in the language of the wind that thaws ice and snow . . . ." That is, the style embodies the force of nature, which is marked by change: "high spirits, unrest, contradiction, and April weather are present in it, and one is instantly reminded no less of the proximity of winter than of the triumph over the winter that is coming, and perhaps has already come" (*GS* "Preface" 1).

Here, the author does more than offer guidance to readers of the work that he intends to write. He explains the "authority" behind the malice, not only of *Thus Spoke Zarathustra*, but of *The Gay Science*, *Twilight of the Idols*, and *The Antichrist*. This author has been "resurrected" (*GS* "Preface" 1) for a purpose: "to vent his sarcasm." Why? As an antidote to "the *nausea* that had gradually developed out of an incautious and pampering spiritual diet called romanticism." Of course, there is parody even in this critical discussion of parody. Nor do we think the remark about being "the resurrected author" should be taken any more literally than Nietzsche's aside that "Some are born posthumously." (Why should we take any literary expression literally?) Rather, we wish to point out how Nietzsche represents his return to writing after a season of quiescence in figures of temporal change—the seasons—and of life and death. His persistence is one evidence of willing return to the place of his beginning: "Alas, it is not only the poets and their beautiful 'lyrical sentiments' on whom the resurrected author has come to vent his sarcasm: who knows what victim he is looking for, what monster of material for parody will soon attract him?" (*GS* "Preface" 1).

3

New New Testaments:
Writing in Blood

For the longest time philosophy would not have been *possible at all* on earth without ascetic wraps and cloak, without an ascetic self-misunderstanding. To put it vividly: the *ascetic priest* provided until the most modern times the repulsive and gloomy caterpillar form in which alone the philosopher could live and creep about. —GM (III, 10)

If every second of our lives recurs an infinite number of times, we are nailed to eternity as Jesus Christ was nailed to the cross. It is a terrifying prospect. In the world of eternal return the weight of unbearable responsibility lies heavy on every move we make. That is why Nietzsche called the idea of eternal return the heaviest of burdens. If eternal return is the heaviest of burdens, then our lives can stand out against it in all their splendid lightness. But is heaviness truly deplorable and lightness splendid? —Milan Kundera, *The Unbearable Lightness of Being*

Contemptus Mundi: The World as Disciple

Nietzsche was not alone in thinking of eternal recurrence as the epitome of his "doctrine" as it is that of his fictional hero, Zarathustra. Philosophers, historians of ideas, and literary critics of a wide range of outlooks have come to the same conclusion. We have discussed Wittgenstein's rather wry expression of this view, and both Northrop Frye[1] and Miguel de Unamuno,[2] who see Nietzsche as something of the *bête noir* of modern malaise, more or less identify Nietzsche with that one idea. For Frye, Nietzsche's Romanticism, as represented in his idea of eternal recurrence, veers radically from attitudes grounded on an encyclopedic understanding of the biblical narrative of Fall and Redemption which had dominated Western thought for two millennia. Accordingly, Nietzsche's "glumly cheerful acceptance of a cosmology of identical recurrence [sic]"[3] marks the onset of an age of irony. Frye finds in Nietzsche the emerging voice of Darwinism (the struggle for existence defined as "will to power"), with marked affinities between his "Dionysianism" and

Freud's "unconscious." Further, he perceives a peculiarly modern drift in Nietzsche's new spirit of intoxication with change, in his expansive sense of an external and immovable order in which the tragic hero is not killed or eaten (as in the liturgy) but in which the hero (Unamuno joins Frye here) perceives man's tragic place in the scheme of things.[4]

Although Nietzsche would probably have balked at Frye's tidy, structural system, he would surely have agreed with Frye's underlying thesis that the Bible was a formative text—if not *the* formative text—of Western culture. Nietzsche could not bluster about the Bible as the most pernicious text, nor fashion his antitext of *Zarathustra* as his gospel to end all gospels (including itself), were the Bible not, in his genealogical scheme of things, singularly powerful in scope and influence. As the source of the life of Jesus, the line of whose career Zarathustra retraces, the Bible sets out the narrative of a public existence which has more in common with Zarathustra's "life" than Frye's reductionist placement of Nietzsche allows. Because of his transcendent interest in the future, Karl Jaspers argues, even when his surface argument "turns into a radical negation of all belief in God, even then Nietzsche shows a remarkable proximity to Christianity."[5] But surely we may think of Nietzsche's project, however much its interest in "becoming" may invite comparison with Christianity's transcendence, as not at all at odds with, but rather a vehicle of, a coherent anti-ascetic, anti-Socratic insistence that the "apparent world" is the only one we have. True, it doesn't stay put: hence, the emphasis on the future and "becoming." On the other hand, we could take Jaspers' assertion in a different sense, and consider "Christianity" as a literary term designating beliefs and attitudes encoded in the narrative of the life of Jesus, however drastically revised. In this context, we perceive in *Zarathustra* the shaping figures and cadences of the New Testament account. It is not only that, like Jesus, Zarathustra takes up his public calling at the age of thirty (Z I "Prologue" 1), but, like him, too, he does so immediately after a period of withdrawal from the world. And this appearance is accompanied by wonders: preaching, like that of its New Testament original, confounds the people, overturns the law, and so on. It is all very familiar, and all very Christian, but the aim of Nietzsche's narrative is, as Frye argues, not toward "transcendental" renewal within a historical metanarrative of corporate redemption at the end of time.

And yet, like Jaspers, Frye places too much emphasis on Nietzsche's dramatic critique of metaphysics, and in so doing overlooks the fact that, like other poets and critics before him—and not withstanding his revolutionary protestations—Nietzsche is a captive of generic limitations as much as he is of history. The figurative claim that the poet "moves in the Zodiac of his own wit" is central to Sidney's poetic theory. But as we have seen,[6] one defends only what is under attack. The poet cannot be a "poet" unless readers find their way *into* his "Zodiac."

Early in his career Nietzsche employed a similar cosmic figure to represent the hard "self-sufficiency" of the philosopher (*PTAG* 8). The single-minded commitment of the philosopher, which is actually an expression of "*personality*" (*PTAG* "Preface"), is so complete that its residue in an articulated philosophy seems like a world apart:

> Such men live inside their own solar system; only there can we look for them. A Pythagoras, an Empedocles too, treated himself with an almost super-human esteem, almost with religious reverence, but the great conviction of metempsychoses and of the unity of life led him back to other human beings, for their salvation and redemption. (*PTAG* 8)

In *Philosophy in the Tragic Age of the Greeks*, the philosopher is more than an expression of the spirit of the age; Heraclitus, for example, is a world unto himself. In this sense, Nietzsche presents a theory of the comprehensive soul of the philosopher, who "is a contemplative-perceptive like the artist, compassionate like the religious, a seeker of purposes and causalities like the scientist, even while he feels himself swelling into a macrocosm, he all the while retains a certain self-possession, a way of viewing himself coldly as a mirror of the world" (*PTAG* 3). In the post-Eleatic period this creative inwardness of the philosopher is necessary because the social and political environment is inhospitable to the art: "Mankind so rarely produces a good book, one which with bold freedom sounds the battle-cry of truth, the song of philosophic heroism" (*PTAG* 2). The philosopher's self-esteem is a necessary part of the creative process, which in the post-Eleatic era, pits the inheritor of a lost tradition against a world of post-Platonic ("mixed") minds. Self-esteem protects the creator from the world, but in order to share the valued "macrocosm" with "mankind," which the philosopher is compelled to do, he must find a means of communication. Hence, the ambivalent striving of the artist toward solitude and the private stage. The often-noted tension between Milton's "L'Allegro" and "Il Penseroso" derives, at least in part, from this paradoxical wish of the poet to enjoy public recognition and solitude at the same time. The poet yearns for the peace and quiet of the cloister, and for a reliving of "the tale of *Troy* divine."[7] Mirth and Melancholy alike summon the soul of "*Orpheus'* self," and if the poet loves the "the dim religious light" of the hermit's "mossy Cell," he also hopes for the declamatory public voice that commands attention: "something like Prophetic strain."

In a similar way, Zarathustra is drawn from just as he is drawn to his cave, into and out of the succor of half-sleep (*Z* IV "At Noon"). As he tells his disciples, he is, after all, a poet as well as a teacher. He cannot be what he is without leaving his cave and accepting the quotidian discomforts of mundane office. This makes Zarathustra in many ways like all the other heirs of Orpheus, before and after him. And Zarathustra bears the further burden of the "Prophetic strain" of his message. Although he may be unlike Jesus in "doctrine," he teaches in a manner strongly reminiscent of Jesus, and, in fact, is like him in so many ways that his story prompts our ever-renewed awareness of the other's life and death. The one narrative intertwines with its original in such a way as to require the presence of the past existence in order to shape and define the present character and situation.

We see, then, that Zarathustra presents himself to the world as a poet, but also as Christ's replacement. Just as Jesus came from heaven to fulfill and set aside "Mosaic Law," so Zarathustra descends from the mountains to undermine the claims of all "laws," new *or* old. By focusing on the motives of lawmakers (the ascetic ideal), Zarathustra "overcomes" his predecessor. Accordingly, in "On the Teachers of Virtue" (and in a revisionist approach repeated and amplified in "The Voluntary Beggar"), Zarathustra replaces the "Beatitudes" with declamatory sequences of his own. But Zarathustra's rhetorical flair depends upon audience recollection of the eloquent Sermon on the Mount. As the apposite hortatory situation emerges and many of the same words echo in Zarathustra's speech, differences—in diction, character, and tone—define by powerful contrast a new and revolutionary gospel. Even so, Zarathustra himself concedes that his gospel and his rhetorical triumph over his predecessor depend on the fact of the crucifixion:

> Verily, that Hebrew died too early whom the preachers of slow death honor; and for many it has become a calamity that he died too early. As yet he knew only tears and the melancholy of the Hebrew, and hatred of the good and the just—the Hebrew Jesus: then the longing for death overcame him. Would that he had remained in the wilderness and far from the good and the just! Perhaps he would have learned to live and to love the earth—and laughter too. (Z I "OFD")

The rhetorical point is not that Zarathustra praises "that Hebrew's" nobility of spirit. Being younger than Zarathustra, Jesus can be forgiven his immature "hatred of man and earth": "He died too early; he himself would have recanted his teaching, had he reached my age," says Zarathustra.

In delineating a radically anti-dialectical Nietzsche, Gilles Deleuze provocatively asks in response to this passage, "who is more suitable than Christ to play the role of antichrist . . . and of Zarathustra himself?"[8] But Zarathustra's momentary concession to "that Hebrew" propounds an even more interesting literary question: Does Zarathustra live long enough to separate himself from ambivalence toward "man and earth"? And this question suggests another: Does Zarathustra's survival, in contrast to the ignominious execution of the "sermonizer on the mount" (Z IV "VB"), indicate that he is the superior teacher of the two?

Neither question leads to easy answers. Not that Nietzsche fails to emphasize important differences between Zarathustra and "the Redeemer." We meet Zarathustra as a contemplative recluse who has spent ten years in the fastness of his mountain retreat. Unlike Jesus or the Son of Milton's *Paradise Regained*,

Zarathustra does not appear suddenly on the scene (the Epiphany at the Jordan), his uniqueness on earth heralded by a voice from heaven, nor emerge from the wilderness to amaze believers and unbelievers alike with miracles, such as bringing the dead to life. In the "Prologue," Zarathustra has a hard time disposing of a dead body, much less bringing it back to life. As a miracle-worker, he is not even a good grave digger. Although he preaches the values of the higher man, Zarathustra earns the contempt of the lowliest: grave diggers laugh at him. On the other hand, just as Zarathustra's age is defined in apposition to the "Redeemer's" youth, so his teaching, Deleuze's engaging anti-dialectical thesis notwithstanding, is in dramatic conflict with established canons of the New Testament. And yet, although the message seems to change, the shared medium of the prophet's voice continues with surprising clarity, as the two narratives recount the intimate relationships between two preachers and their audiences. Both men are aloof from disciples, and that aloofness marks not only their uniqueness but that of their gospel. And yet, although almost haughty, both teachers are poignantly interested in the lives and characters of their companions. Both see acceptance of their respective friendships as nothing short of spiritual conversion, and yet both seem free to leave their disciples at will and without provocation. For both, discipleship is a species of test, with no specified rules nor end.

Thus, the relationships between these "redeemers" and their disciples is similarly ambivalent. The two prophets conduct their friendships on an approach/avoidance basis, as they tease, cajole, and castigate disciples and ordinary folk who gather to hear their wisdom. Zarathustra's conflict of desires between pursuit of his worldly mission, on the one hand, and retreat to the bliss of his cave and solitude, on the other, persists in the narrative, and, as we shall see, may not be over at the close of Part IV. Satisfaction of the former impulse entails capture and retention of audience interest, which only begins a process to be completed when Zarathustra's teaching has been understood. It is no wonder that in his disenchantment he often reminds us of Jesus reproaching his disciples, who never seem quite able to grasp the full meaning of his parables. Zarathustra aims to overcome his predecessor, but to do so he may have to teach without being understood. If a teacher remains human—if he has yet to overcome the "all-too-human" within—and if, moreover, the centerpiece of the doctrine taught holds that the teacher must affirm his eternal return with the identical message for the same, eternally-obtuse congregation, then the act of teaching becomes an ostensive definition of courage in the face of suffering: the love of life that is the opposite of nihilism in all its elusive forms.

Zarathustra's rhetorical stance toward his various audiences is no simple matter, but one entangled with a myriad of aesthetic and philosophical themes. And yet it is in his relationship with others that Zarathustra's years of solitary reflection are aimed. Not only does he leave his sanctuary in the mountains to preach a new gospel, but every time he returns to his cave he does so only to leave it again for his quest.[9] Again, in "On the Pale Criminal," we find the intractable nature of the gospel writer's task represented in Zarathustra's disclaimer, as a teacher, of all responsibility for interpretations of his words by his audience: "let those who can, grasp me. Your crutch, however, I am not." Zarathustra's point is that he can both give and receive his "railing by the torrent." The tone of complaint concerns the inequity of roles here, with the preacher giving his all and the audience appearing to believe that he can fulfill its obligations, too. Zarathustra is adamant: he had done his part. The hearer must, in hearing, understand: "Man is something that must be overcome" (Z I "DB"). Clearly, the rhetorical situation is a difficult one, not only because Zarathustra is, as he admits, "railing" at his audience. But he often harangues his listeners with a message that is as unpleasant as his preacher's tone: "Verily, like preachers of repentance and fools, I raised a hue and cry of wrath over what among them is great and small, and that their best is still so small. And that their greatest evil too is still so small—at that I laughed" (Z III "ONT" 2).

Here again Zarathustra strikes the apocalyptic pose of the visionary St. John at Patmos: ""He that hath an ear, let him hear . . . I know thy works, that thou art neither cold nor hot: I would thou wert cold or hot. So then because thou art lukewarm, and neither cold nor hot, I will spue thee out of my mouth."[10] New sayings will not help. The trouble with his disciples—and with everyone who pretends to hear—is that they lack passion; their feigned love of life is bland and bloodless. Thus, in "On Old and New Tablets," Zarathustra finds all tablets, new as well as old, to be marked by two characteristics: they are "broken," and they are partially "covered with writing" (Section 1).[11] Similarly, Zarathustra's excursus on "Reading and Writing" imputes discredit to the tablets of "virtue" on the apparent ground of their formulaic character. Customary ways of thought cannot be creative because they are received from others: "On the Teachers of Virtue," "On the Afterworldly," "On the Despisers of the Body," "On the Pale Criminal," "On Reading and Writing." In the first of these chapters "a sage" reiterates an amalgam of the Ten Commandments and the Beatitudes: "Thou shalt nots" and "Blessed are they." But Zarathustra's gospel urges the virtues of wakefulness and life, which suggests that prior tidings—the Old and New Testaments—intoned the spurious values of formulaic imperatives and judgments, which mark the death of the self—or its surrogate, somnambulism. In a shrill voice, Zarathustra tells a new story, not of the afterworld, but of "a meaning for the earth" (Z I "OA"). He promises a narrative with a new meaning, but he cannot teach this novel story unless his listeners overcome their human (that is, long) ears. To hear with discriminating sense entails effort and virtuosity the equal of Zarathustra's. This is the demand no less than the promise of Zarathustra's *new* New Testament.

The contrast between old and new may seem brash at first, but in fact it is as subtle as it is daring. The old New Testament, with Christ as both shepherd and Paschal Lamb, linked humankind's redemption to blood, and so does Zarathustra's gospel. But under the two dispensations quite different notions of the Passion play out in different ways. In this apposition between Christ and antichrist, it is no coincidence that the sequence ("On the Pale Criminal," "On Reading and Writing") concerns blood and virtue, for Zarathustra has been trying to convince his audience that the blood of the New Testament is no longer relevant, now that God is dead. (This is the theme of "On the Teachers of Virtue" and the following chapters on the "ascetic ideal.") And yet, as we have already suggested, the new gospel does depend on blood. Blood—even the "bliss of the knife" which characterizes the enlivened moment of the criminal act (Z I "OPC")—is the newly-acknowledged sign of an authentic motive. In this context, blood is the outward sign of the inward grace: unadulterated feeling—the original passion for revenge that informs the act of robbery with meaning. Hence, the hidden motive, when exposed, reveals that the criminal, like his counterparts—teachers of virtue and the afterworld—are alike pale.

This is the gospel of the imminent, new dispensation. Zarathustra has come from the mountain to seek and to save humanity from deception, to redeem lost humanity from all that would separate it from its motives. The old order shields the human race from the truth that it and its spiritual guides are as dead to the world as the corpse that Zarathustra has until recently been carrying about: "He [the criminal] was equal to his deed when he did it; but he could not bear its image after it was done. Now he always saw himself as the doer of one deed" (Z I "OPC"). That is, the pale criminal collapses the whole of life into a single act, which must make sense to others. Again, the impulse to fabulize is turned against life. The end of all narratives must approximate a story that maximizes comfort to all who hear it. So the criminal and his accusers alike would have all actions, including his, make sense. The multitude wants a corporate version of the same plot: "No shepherd and one herd! Everybody wants the same, everybody is the same: whoever feels different goes voluntarily into a madhouse" (Z I "Prologue" 5).

Since everybody is the same, no exceptions need be made to the new order: Everyone must change. Everyone must repent. Zarathustra may preach the innovative gospel of "new values" (Z I "TM"), but he knows that his audience will recognize the form of his presentation: "Verily, like preachers of repentance and fools, I raised a hue and cry of wrath over what among them is great and small, and that their best is still so small" (Z "ONT" 2). Christ and antichrist alike bear the news of liberation from the Old Law, and both are met by the derision and hostility of a stubbornly complacent society. What Zarathustra says of reading and writing could already have been inferred from preceding events. The fact is: Zarathustra's career has not been going well. He teaches but nobody learns; he speaks, but nobody hears. The length of his listeners's ears militates against the desired end of his mission: "I will teach men the meaning of their existence" (Z "Prologue" 7), he says to his heart (after realizing that, instead of being a fisherman—or even a fisher of men— he has hauled in only a corpse), ". . . but I am still far from them, and my sense does not speak to their senses" (Z I "Prologue" 7).

Here, Nietzsche retells the story of Christ's sermon on "a grain of mustard seed."[12] Like Zarathustra, Jesus has been preaching (to the dismay of the Pharisees) on the subject of hypocrisy. Both narratives link the innovative tenor of innovative doctrine with mortal danger to the teacher: "The same day there came certain of the Pharisees, saying unto him, Get thee out, and depart hence: for Herod will kill thee."[13] In Nietzsche's narrative, it is "the jester from the tower" who tells Zarathustra that his message has not been well received:

> "Go away from this town Zarathustra," said he; "there are too many here who hate you. You are hated by the good and the just, and they call you their enemy and despiser; you are hated by the believers in the true faith, and they call you the danger of the multitude. It was your good fortune that you were laughed at; and verily, you talked like a jester. It was your good fortune that you stooped to the dead dog; when you lowered yourself so far, you saved your own life for today. But go away from this town, or tomorrow I shall leap over you, one living over one dead." (Z I "Prologue" 8)

Thus, Jesus and Zarathustra alike offend the faithful. Like Jesus, Zarathustra bears a gospel at odds with established law and "true faith." And like him, Zarathustra is an outsider, reviled for his message, which is reminiscent also of the precursor text: "Beware ye of the leaven of the Pharisees, which is hypocrisy. For there is nothing covered that shall not be revealed; neither hid, that shall not be known."[14]

But the gospels are far from identical, and their differences are as interesting as their similarities. In the New Testament, unnamed Pharisees threaten Jesus; in the "new" New Testament, "the jester from the tower" episode (in which the tightrope walker falls to his death) conveys an ominous message concerning the reactions of the townsfolk to his teaching. The many hate him; "the good and the just" consider him a danger. And the jester's message is no idle, objective analysis of audience reaction "in the market place" (Z I "Prologue" 3). His meaning is sinister, for if Zarathustra does not leave the village, he will jump over him ("one living over one dead") as he jumped over the tightrope walker. Thus, Zarathustra's integrity as a teacher will cost him his life.

And yet the jester's warning does depend on his analysis of Zarathustra's performance as a teacher, which Zarathustra himself recognizes as a failure: "They do not understand me; I am not the mouth for these ears" (Z I "Prologue" 5). Not that he contents himself with a species of dramatic criticism; the jester's critique goes deeper, touching Zarathustra's courage and determination. Oddly, the man suggests that Zarathustra survived the encounter with the townsfolk only because they did not take him seriously. They took Zarathustra to be—like *him*—a jester, trying to entertain, but annoying the audience with unintended substance. Because townsfolk do not distinguish between Zarathustra and the man now threatening him, Zarathustra escapes their retribution. Apparently, as a teacher, Zarathustra is a failed clown.[15] But we cannot miss the more telling implication of Zarathustra's implicit praise of "the Crucified": Had Zarathustra succeeded as a teacher, the townsfolk would have executed him.[16] Even now, he seems to be, for some unstated reason, responsible for the death of the acrobat, whose body he carries about. So either Zarathustra's poor teaching method, or the stupidity of the townsfolk (or the two in tandem) are all that keep the new anti-lawgiver alive. Not surprisingly, earth-affirming Zarathustra heeds the jester's warning by leaving town, but not before Nietzsche's ludic motif is amplified by an incident just prior to Zarathustra's departure. Thinking him an unworthy buffoon, grave diggers laugh at Zarathustra. Again, their derisive laughter indicates how lightly ordinary folk take Zarathustra's threat to the town. Unlike his gospel predecessor, Zarathustra is not worth executing.

There is a further difference between the narratives. After Zarathustra leaves town, disposes of the corpse, and has had a good night's sleep, he recognizes on reflection a germ of truth in the jester's whispered warning: He, Zarathustra, teacher of the *Übermensch* as "the meaning of the earth" (Z I "Prologue" 3), has saved his life by a ruse, albeit an unintended one. As he stooped to help the dying man he had in fact looked like a dog. Zarathustra felt pity, and in his pity he lowered himself, and in that lowering a fact of his consciousness had been exposed. Zarathustra identified with the lowest—the fallen, the dying, the dead—and by so doing he became like them, carrying the corpse away from town, earning the ridicule of the vulgar in the process. For they recognized in him a literal representation of their own espoused beliefs in the virtuous and just. But when he separates himself from the corpse, Zarathustra awakens to a new idea that the living make better companions than the dead. Concomitant with this insight is a new sense of his calling: he must not follow in the footsteps of the good shepherd, for to do so he must attach himself to the herd. Rather, he must teach a new gospel, not of law and virtue, but of their creative opposites. Instead of a sermon on the blessed poor, Zarathustra proffers a vision of a creator who shatters the old tablets, inscribing anew (in a parody of both the Ten Commandments and the Sermon on the Mount) the news that old virtues affirm only the pointlessness of waking up. Since he is newly-awakened, Zarathustra is the wellspring of a gospel, not of the kingdom of God, not of the afterworld, not of despisers of the body, but of a being yet to be created by Zarathustra's disciples, the *Übermensch*: "Man is something that must be overcome".

From the moment of his awakening, Zarathustra's sermons take on a vindictive ring. They concern blood and justice, yes, but they are also about the judge and judgment. Although the pale criminal seems to exist apart from the herd, in fact, he is the herd's truest symptom. As Zarathustra describes the symptoms of this wretched creature, he suddenly interrupts himself to turn his wrath directly on the criminal's submerged rage. Judges inherit their contemporary status as Pharisee:

> But your ears do not want to accept this: it harms your good people, you say to me. But what matter your good people to me? Much about your good people nauseates me; and verily, it is not their evil. Indeed, I wish they had a madness of which they might perish like this pale criminal. (Z I "OPC")

Here, Zarathustra not only links the faithful and just to the pale criminal, but he explicitly answers the jester's implied critique of his teaching style. He will no longer temporize. Rather than entertain, he rails "by the torrent." If his listeners think him harmless now—if they laugh at him now—then clearly, through no fault of the gospel's author and teacher, they have misunderstood. Only an audience separated from the herd will understand. And the newly-enlightened Zarathustra has discovered that this is the only audience and disciple he desires.

"On Reading and Writing" is Zarathustra's literary variation on the same theme: passion, courage, blood. Just as the virtuous huddle together in communal aversion to lawbreakers, so they recoil from the true creators of the world, namely, creators of new values. The virtuous reject Zarathustra, who rejects them, by creating a new and more demanding gospel requiring a more discriminating audience. Before holding forth on the subject of literacy, Zarathustra explains that reading and writing are interdependent functions in a process, which, as things stand, is pointless. The problem is that nothing of value can come from either reading or writing because modern readers and writers are as they are: timid, vapid, inattentive, weary, and wearying. Worst of all, they are numerous.

If we infer that Zarathustra is merely objecting to the current trend toward expanded literacy, we miss the point, which is not political, and only incidentally historical. Zarathustra might agree with the speaker of *Twilight* that "Our institutions are no good any more" (II "SUM" 39), and that "Learning to *think*" is dying out "in our schools" (II "WGL" 7), but he wants his listeners to accept, not shift, the highways and byways of responsibility. Why does he venture into regaling the multitude with sermons they are unable and unwilling to hear? The answer might be that, in the immediate context of Zarathustra's remarks in "On Reading and Writing," the disciple addressed misses the point, which is about fiction. Why believe Zarathustra, a poet, who on record has affirmed that all poets lie? If he were merely untrained, the disciple would not be troubled, since if Zarathustra is telling the truth it must follow that some poets tell the truth. But logic is out place then, in that Zarathustra perceives that a prior question of the disciple's character exists. For either the disciple does not hear correctly or, if he hears correctly, he does not believe what he hears. In the latter case, the disciple lodges his faith in one whose word he does not believe. With such a follower, truth has no bearing on belief.

It is no coincidence that "On Poets" precedes "On Great Events," a tale of Zarathustra's descent into the underworld. What better means have poets from the time of Orpheus devised to demonstrate their unique authority than a visit to the underworld? Zarathustra's adventure *should* establish him as an exception to the rule of mediocrity in the current literary world. But in fact, when he returns to his disciples with wisdom from a non-human source, his reception only reinforces his critique in the preceding section. His other-worldly wisdom ("*the heart of the earth is gold*") might as well be gibberish, for in a doubling of the motif of the unhearing disciples, the narrator describes Zarathustra's audience as doltish and distracted: "But his disciples barely listened, so great was their desire to tell him of the seamen, the rabbits, and the flying man." The authentic poet/prophet requires a more discriminating audience. Zarathustra's disciples cannot tell the difference between trivial and "great" events. Just as philosophers need good noses, disciples need good ears.

Zarathustra's problem, as we learn at the outset of his sojourn, is that he loves man; he gives up his solitary life to endure suffering in order to share what he knows with those who dwell in lower valleys and towns. But this topography of audiences is only one indication of the general malaise in society, which marks a decline from God to man to rabble. Paradoxically, Zarathustra is not dismayed by the fact that so few people know how or care to read, since the more people who learn to read the more there are who pretend to think, and the worse matters get. Readership has descended from Gnosticism to democracy. In the modern world, no spiritual requirements exist for initiation into an enlightened reader/discipleship. Today idlers project their own slovenly spirit into the texts they read.

And yet the failure of the educational system to come to terms with the question of values, and so to make way for its own replacement in the overcoming of those weaknesses endemic to the species, is not the problem, but only one of its symptoms. For suppose the existence of a different world in which people approached reading with a fullness of life—reading as "will to power." Unfortunately, the situation would not improve, for there would not be anything to read since there are no writers worth reading: "verily, all of yesterday and today smells foul of the writing rabble" (Z II "OR"). Judging from the ominous description given by Zarathustra's ape, the popular press makes even skillful reading irrelevant: "It vomits verbal swill. And they still make newspapers of this swill!" (Z III "PB"). Modern poetry has been demeaned to the level of prevailing interests in the twaddle of the mere event:

"They hound each other and know not where. They overheat each other and know not why. They tinkle with their tin, they jingle with their gold. They are cold and seek warmth from brandy; they are heated and seek coolness from frozen spirits, they are all diseased and sick with public opinions" (Z III "PB").

Zarathustra provides an alternative to this contemporary emptiness in contemporary poetry by imbuing his writing with true creativity, namely, the creation of new values. He overcomes the limitations of bloodless poets of trivial events—poets of the mere present—by combining the poet's role with that of the priest and prophet of the future. Just as Christ did not leave the world bereft of poetry, neither does Nietzsche leave the text of his poet/prophet without a perceptive reader. The only disciple fit to hear Zarathustra is one already redeemed by the truth his teachings espouse. By analogy, the only interpreter of *Zarathustra* must be as gifted as the prophet/poet himself. It is appropriate, then, that Nietzsche makes "On Reading and Writing" a test case by providing a model to be imitated. The evidence of effective interpretation of good writing is more good writing. Thus, the third essay of *Toward the Genealogy of Morals* ("WMAI") is Nietzsche's commentary on a single sentence from "On Reading and Writing": "Unconcerned, mocking, violent—thus wisdom wants *us*: she is a woman and always loves only a warrior." Nietzsche presents this essay as a gloss on his own text, which, in turn, is a text about texts and their interpreters.[17] To exert any authority, both functions must assert the values of the warrior: violence, blood, conviction. In "On Reading and Writing," Zarathustra asserts that it is asinine to write about life's burdens: "We are all of us fair beasts of burden, male and female asses." The true poet and the worthy disciple overcome "the spirit of gravity." And in the opening section of "What is the Meaning of Ascetic Ideals," Nietzsche asks, "Am I understood? . . . Have I been understood?" The answer, of course, is a resounding "No": "'*Not at all, my dear sir!*'" For if the author has been understood he has also been silenced: "Then let us start again from the beginning" (*GM* III "WMAI" 1). And Nietzsche starts the following section by repeating the title prefixed to Section 1, which, in turn, folds back into the text of Zarathustra's sermon, "On Reading and Writing."

Nietzsche critics have often noted his intertwining of texts. Here, Nietzsche does more than use a prior text as a tag or motto—the epigraph—which usually aims at little more than establishing the prior text as on a par with the classics from which such tags are typically drawn. This is a case of a living author in a dying world ("Another century of readers—and the spirit itself will stink" [Z I "RW"])—a world which, with the sole exception of Zarathustra, is devoid of worthy writers and readers. Zarathustra survives in order to provide both services: his own elaboration or explanation ("Am I understood?") and, conveniently, another to fill the near void of reading matter. So it is that Nietzsche ends the third essay with a similar repetition of an utterance from section 1: "And to repeat in conclusion what I said at the beginning: man would rather will *nothingness* than not will" (section 28).

Of course, we are using the term "interpretation" rather loosely, for the relation of text to text here is explanatory only in the sense that elaboration or amplification are so. The text from "On Reading and Writing" is set in the context of a poetic and cultural crisis: no writers, no readers. But the issue of present lack is joined as a philosophical reflection on aesthetic and cultural values, in that this nullity of worthy texts and worthy readers exists because the world is infested by an ever-increasing number of printed pages and of people taught the rudiments of reading. Poetry has become like humankind: small, enervated, bloodless. Hence, the bravado of the line from "On Reading and Writing" to be elaborated in "What is the Meaning of Ascetic Ideals?" How does one create a true poet like Zarathustra? How can such a wonder exist without cultivated readers? How can the human and banal in popular culture be overcome?

It is tempting to see in this speaker another version of Robert Burton's Democritus, Jr., who places himself in an ancient and honorable tradition: "I did sometime laugh and scoff with Lucian, and satirically tax with Menippus, lament with Heraclitus," and, above all, with "Democritus in his garden."[18] But Burton, writing in the person of Democritus, Jr., claims to laugh at the world in order to retain his own sanity. Zarathustra and the speaker of the *Genealogy* may share such a therapeutic aim to some degree, but they are also concerned with the origins of poetry and art. If Sophia loves only a warrior ("wisdom wants us: she is a woman and always loves only a warrior"), then the artist who desires her affection must *be* a warrior, not a physician anatomizing her corpse. Laughter has an important function, true, but that function works only for the living. The true, poetic combatant must laugh at all tragic seriousness, not to preserve his sanity, but to "write with his blood," for "blood is spirit." But how is it that writing and readings as "will to power" can exist and yet not exist at the same time? As the author moves to explain, he thinks, first, of artists and philosophers in general (of their sense of difference, saintliness, otherworldliness) as a problem: they cling to ascetic ideals. And then he elaborates further with the notable instance of the Wagner case. Here, the problem is unmasked as a conflict between opposites within the artist himself, the seeming opposition between sensuality and chastity.

How is it that a great artist creates an ignoble work? The aesthetic problem Zarathustra examines in "On Reading and Writing" reappears, but is examined from a slightly different, "non-fictive" perspective. Zarathustra teaches that the writer must learn to laugh at all tragic seriousness. The speaker in the *Genealogy* faults Wagner for not seeing that the great artist "knows how to *laugh* at himself" (*GM* III "WMAI" 3). *Parsifal* signals a decline in creative "will to power" by externalizing a spiritual and philosophical relapse from Feuerbach to Christianity, from "'healthy sensuality'" to "morbid Christian and obscurantist ideals" (section 3). With this energetic flourish Nietzsche deflects his meditation from poetics to philosophy, and he does so in a manner much like Zarathustra's: "Let us, first of all, eliminate artists: they do not stand nearly independently enough in the world and *against* the world for their changing valuations to deserve attention *in themselves!*" (section 5). Rather than warriors, modern artists are more like "valets of some morality, philosophy, or religion."

So the antithesis between artist and world replaces that between sensuality and chastity, which polarity helps explain the dearth of writers-as-warriors in the world. Wagner doesn't matter nearly as much as Schopenhauer, for "what does it mean when a genuine *philosopher* pays homage to the ascetic ideal. . . ?" (section 5). The victim of this warrior's arrow is, of course, Richard Wagner. Nietzsche pulls rank on him. Since philosophy is, in the end, more important than music, Wagner's relapse is not such a blow to the old atheist's pride as the musician might think. Now that Wagner has betrayed him, Nietzsche proclaims that the arts are hierarchically arranged, with philosophy above music. Indeed, the prestige of music that Wagner enjoys in fact flows from Schopenhauer's philosophy. In the end, Wagner has been reduced to uttering "metaphysics" (section 5). Having called Wagner an obscurantist, a metaphysician, and (worse still) a priest, Nietzsche moves on to the still more general issue of the role of priest and philosophers in propagating the ascetic ideal.

If we glance backward at "On Reading and Writing" with this section in mind, we see how Nietzsche fills Zarathustra's imagined void of qualified readers with a philosophical meditation on the artist and ascetic ideals. In this context, his remarks on creativity and Wagner are more than a digression rising at a tangent from the subject of the prior text. Rather, the author's reconsideration of the subject ferrets out the underlying reason for the dearth of good reading and writing in the world. The original diatribe against mediocritization of the literary world is also a hymn of praise to Zarathustra, the poet, the master of the axiom, who sees the world from a great height, who looks down upon thunderclouds, who laughs at "the spirit of gravity" (the underlying spirit of ascetic ideals) as well as at "all tragic plays." Deep within the historical phenomenon of cultural decline is the nemesis of anything creative or new: *ressentiment* toward and flight from the world as it is and could be. In laughter, the creative spirit triumphs over "the spirit of gravity," hence, over the rabble, over the world. Or, rather, the writer, who in Nietzsche becomes his own critic, preempts the pernicious importunities of a literary world not of his own making.

Eternal Recurrence of the Similar

We could argue that Wittgenstein's association of Nietzsche with the idea that if an event *had* occurred it *would* occur again understates the scope of the doctrine of eternal recurrence by focusing only on its imagined cosmological claim without challenging the validity of his underlying metonymy: the thought of Nietzsche equals "eternal recurrence." At the close of *Twilight of the Idols*, Nietzsche makes something like the same declaration. Similarly, citing the summation of the ideas in *Ecce Homo*, Heidegger argues that "Nietzsche's fundamental metaphysical position is captured in his doctrine of *the eternal recurrence of the same*."[19] Heidegger finds in this doctrine the Nietzschean twist of the central issue in Western history as expressed in the biblical tradition: of "being as a whole."[20] He sees the doctrine, not as an essentially cosmological theory, but as a modern confrontation of all that is entailed in "Platonic-Christian" modes of thought.[21] Accordingly, he considers the three published versions of eternal recurrence (in *The Gay Science*, *Thus Spoke Zarathustra*, and *Beyond Good and Evil*) in tandem with unpublished matter (from the *Nachlass*, including the earliest of Nietzsche's autobiographical writings and material included in *The Will to Power*) in something like an account of the "development" of Nietzsche's thought. Implicitly, the "idea" exists in its earlier formulations in more or less inchoate, incoherent, "poetic" form—unfinished, unexpressed, so to speak. Thus, Heidegger thinks of the passages in *The Gay Science* and *Thus Spoke Zarathustra* as somewhat vitiated by their "poetic" contexts, which suggests that later entries, including that in *Beyond Good and Evil*, reflect more mature reflection on the subject.

Setting the canonical problems of *The Will to Power* aside for the moment, it is hard to see how the entry in *Beyond Good and Evil* (III "The Religious Nature" 56) is less "poetic"—less rhetorically forceful, less imaginative, less metaphorical—than the relevant passage in *The Gay Science* (IV "The Greatest Stress" 341). True, the earlier passage unfolds from a rhetorical question depicting a "fictive" situation ("What, if some day or night a demon were to steal after you into your loneliest loneliness . . ."), while the speaker in *Beyond Good and Evil* presents himself as one who, having "endeavored to think pessimism through to the bottom and to redeem it from the half-Christian, half-German simplicity and narrowness with which it finally presented itself to this century" (*BGE* III "RN" 56), is qualified to speak in a less diffident, presumably "nonfictive" voice.

The speaker in *Beyond Good and Evil*, having thought the causes of pessimism through to an imagined bottom, posits an imagined causative agent made up equally of German and Christian constituents, an imagined final form of the effects of the combined agent, namely "Schopenhauerian philosophy." Further, this speaker elicits consent from the reader on the basis of the very special point of view enjoyed by one who sees the world as if from far above, beyond Buddha, beyond Schopenhauer, beyond "the spell and delusion of morality," beyond the "'philosophers of reality' or 'positivists'" (*BGE* VI, "WS" 204), beyond illusion, in short, beyond good and evil. We are suggesting that the voice of the speaker is, itself, a successful fiction. It insinuates a perspective which transcends the human, who

> may have his eyes opened to the opposite ideal: to the ideal of the most exuberant, most living and most world-affirming man, who has not only learned to get on great with all that was and is but who wants to have it again *as it was and is* to all eternity, insatiably calling out *da capo* not only to himself but to the whole piece and play, but fundamentally to him who needs precisely this play—and who makes it necessary: because he needs himself again and again—and makes himself necessary—What? And would this not be—*circulus vitiosus deus*? (*BGE* VI "RN" 56)

The final rhetorical turn suggests a flash of insight. This oracular vision of the ideal imagines a "fictive" character who, regardless of circumstances, "affirms" the world, and insatiably desires everything in it to be repeated.[22] Further, this imaginative description leads the oracular speaker to a stunning metaphor: this ideal human is like an orchestral conductor, shouting: "Once more, from the top!" Such a marvelously figurative description of a transcendent being subordinates all past performances—of composers, publishers, teachers, instrument-makers, architects, stage-managers, and musicians as well. The conductor stands above them all, like the supra-Buddha, supra-Schopenhauer philosopher-seer, controlling every aspect of the musical performance in the here and now.

Of course, the dominant "poetic" figure in the sequence is that of "Nietzsche" himself. Readers are asked to suspend the very critical sense that, in other contexts, Nietzsche energetically advocates and defends. (Heidegger suggests the same thing in noting Nietzsche's affirmation and denial of the existence of "truth.") For it would be hard to deny that, in the prophetic mode, we find a point of view that is not subject to error, an "immaculate perception," so to speak. And yet, just as we associate Nietzsche with "eternal recurrence," we think also of his "perspectivism." Are we to take the fiction inherent in an oracular tone to suggest that, after all, some perspectives are more immaculate than others? Or do we think of the "philosopher's voice," as we find it in *Beyond Good and Evil*, as somehow less "poetic" than, say, that of the unrequited lover of the sonnet cycles, and therefore immune to the limits imposed by a thoroughgoing "perspectivism"? Shifting to a purportedly "fictive" context, we recall that Zarathustra thinks of pretenders to "immaculate perception" unsullied by desire as ("sentimental hypocrites") the moral and intellectual equivalents of the Pharisees (*Z* II "IP"). They exhibit the "bad conscience" of those who refuse to recognize death as an absolute limit on the claims of individual perception. The trick is to undo the impulse to falsify the immediate, if limited, hold we have on experience: "And this is what the immaculate perception of all things shall mean to me: that I want nothing from them, except to be allowed to lie prostrate before them like a mirror with a hundred eyes." But for humans to desire not to desire, not to see as they do in fact see but only as a mirror with a hundred surfaces would see, is neither possible nor noble. For, even in desiring not to desire, the "hypocrites" imagine themselves innocently passive, "prostrate," inanimate (a mirror), unmoving and unmoved.

Zarathustra teaches that desire permeates all perception, and to remain "innocent," its infusion must not be falsified, but affirmed and enjoyed. Why desire not to desire? Why wish merely to reflect when one can create? Why remain passive and inactive as a world of Heraclitean flux whirls ceaselessly about? The pretender to immaculate perception is like one who prefers supine passivity to active lovemaking. In contrast, to one who sees with no illusions about "immaculate perception," tomorrow comes like the promise of sexual union to a desiring lover:

> Look there: how she approaches impatiently over the sea. Do you not feel the thirst and the hot breath of her love? She would suck at the sea and drink its depth into her heights; and the sea's desire rises toward her with a thousand breasts. It wants to be kissed and sucked by the thirst of the sun; it wants to become air and height and a footpath of light, and itself light. (Z II "IP")

In associating "bad conscience" with "immaculate perception" Zarathustra implies that the stasis of perception desired by the Pharisees is antithetical to "becoming," and indicates a wish to thwart the interests of the future. Clearly, this reflection is not far from the theme of eternal recurrence as we find it, soon, in "On the Vision and the Riddle." Here, in Zarathustra's exchange with the dwarf that he has been transporting on his back, the dominant figures elucidate a temporal motif: a landscape marked by a gateway inscribed "Moment." This image, moreover, occurs in a narrative of travel (Zarathustra tells of climbing alone up a mountain path) within another narrative of travel (Zarathustra takes ship for a sea-journey). Time is passing and Zarathustra passes the time telling a story about time in which, paradoxically, it seems that time, as it has been expressed by active verbs, pauses, and the focus shifts away from Zarathustra and the dwarf (they stop walking, climbing, striding) to the landscape, to an isolated structure in the landscape, which Zarathustra draws to the dwarf's attention. He points out that the gateway can be traversed in either direction. It occupies space, and so do the two paths that meet at the gateway. (The past and the future meet appearing—only at the gateway, "Moment"—to affront each other.) Further, Zarathustra emphasizes the sense that this pathway, which stretches forward and backward in time rather than in space:

> "This long lane stretches back for an eternity. And the long lane out there, that is another eternity. They contradict each other, these paths; they offend each other face to face; and it is here at this gateway that they come together. The name of the gateway is inscribed above: 'Moment.'" But whoever would follow one of them, on and on, farther

and farther—do you believe, dwarf, that these paths contradict each other eternally?" (Z III "VR" 2)

For critics who take eternal recurrence to be a cosmological theory which Nietzsche seriously propounds, the fact that the dwarf responds by saying that "time itself is a circle" presents an inconvenience. But if we consider the gateway as a threshold figure of becoming, much of what Gilles Deleuze says regarding the illusory opposition between chaos and circularity is applicable here.[23] And even here, although the conflict between the the dwarf and Zarathustra is dramatic, Zarathustra does not actually contradict the dwarf:

> "From this gateway, Moment, a long, eternal lane leads *backward*: behind us lies an eternity. Must not whatever *can* walk have walked on this lane before? Must not whatever *can* happen have happened, have been done, have passed by before? And if everything has been there before—what do you think, dwarf, of this moment? Must not this gateway too have been there before? And are not all things knotted together so firmly that this moment draws after if *all* that is to come? Must we not eternally return?"

The eeriness of the landscape ("Was I dreaming, then?"), with its almost lunar bareness and the spider and the dog howling and the haunting childhood memory of the full moon ("silent as death") lend credence to Zarathustra's promise as a storyteller—that he would give the sailors a "vision of the loneliest." In this dreamlike montage of scenes from past and present, Zarathustra describes the experience of a young shepherd into whose throat a black snake has crawled. This is Zarathustra's final "vision of the loneliest." For if it were not for Zarathustra's timely assistance, the shepherd might have expired. Instead, Zarathustra recalls, he leaped to his feet, "no longer human—one changed, radiant, *laughing*!"

The connection between the two movements of Zarathustra's story is, of course, made by the snake, a figure with well-established temporal associations from the Renaissance on, but especially evident in such popular forms as emblem books. In George Wither's *A Collection of Emblemes*,[24] for instance, several uses suggest the circled snake as an emblem of "The Revolution of all earthly things." Thus, in figure 1, we find a child, its left hand touching a skull, encircled by a snake. The poet explains: "The *Snake*, her Taile *devouring*, doth implie / The *Revolution*, of all Earthly things." Thus the accompanying poem is a meditation on mortality and the impermanence of creation: "All things wheele about; and each *Beginning*, / Made entrance to it[s] own *Destruction*, hath." (We might recall that Zarathustra's eagle wears the uroborus as a necklace "wound around his neck" [Z "Prologue" 10].) In another context, we see the ringed snake depicted with this text: "The *Circled-snake* ETERNITY declares."[25] Again, we think of Zarathustra: "Oh, how should I not lust after eternity and after the nuptial ring of rings, the ring of recurrence?" (Z III "SS" 2) Finally, a third engraving (figure 2) follows this telling motto, "*Through many spaces* Time

Figure 1   George Wither, *A Collection of Emblemes, Ancient and Moderne* (London, 1635), p. 45. Reproduced by permission of The Huntington Library, San Marino, California.

90

ILLVSTR. XL.

Book. 2

Figure 2 George Wither, *A Collection of Emblemes, Ancient and Moderne* (London, 1635), p. 157. Reproduced by permission of The Huntington Library, San Marino, California.

doth run, / *And*, endedth, *where it first* begun," and is accompanied by these lines:

> Old *Sages* by the Figure of the Snake
> Encircled thus . . . did of expression make
> of *Annuall-Revolutions*; and of things,
> Which wheele about in *everlasting-rings* . . . [26]

Figures of eternal recurrence are, then, not unusual, but Nietzsche seems to insist that the idea exercises powerful effects despite the obvious fact that, although its "truth" eternally returns, it is just as eternally forgotten. Only the god/man Zarathustra "knows," but he knows without pretending to remember a single incident of his future life, this notwithstanding that, if what he suggests to the dwarf were so, he has lived all such future incidents of his life an infinite number of times already. The question is: Why should anyone worry about unremembered experiences? What does the idea of eternal recurrence affirm, beyond the possibility that, in the here and now, one might invest the present experience with an imagined sense of *deja vu*?[27] In *The Gay Science*, Nietzsche braces the reader in a similar way, asking if the idea of eternal recurrence must not cause an emotional reaction: "Would you not throw yourself down and gnash your teeth and curse the demon who spoke thus?" (*GS* IV 341). Is it possible to remain unmoved—to be neither horrified nor overjoyed—to learn that "The eternal hourglass of existence is turned upside down again and again, and you with it, speck of dust!"

Unusual or not, in both *Thus Spoke Zarathustra* and *The Gay Science*, the idea of recurrence is insinuated rather than propounded, this despite the fact that neither Zarathustra nor Nietzsche himself may be described as reluctant to speak their minds. Nietzsche's notes indicate that, however briefly, he entertained eternal recurrence as a logical requirement of the law of conservation of energy (*WP* 1063), and that at one time he thought the idea a difficult one for humankind to fathom or accept without a thoroughgoing "revaluation of all values" (*WP* 1059). But in neither *The Gay Science* nor *Thus Spoke Zarathustra* is the idea of recurrence asserted as anything other than a fictive representation in which the threshold, "Moment," might be imaginatively traversed. Rhetorically, the questions propounded in both works insinuate that a bland or neutral response ("So who cares"?) is impossible. Both fictive representations exclude apathy as an option.[28] In *Zarathustra*, the idea almost slays the protagonist, and he enters a period of convalescence. In *The Gay Science*, the speaker asks the reader if the response to such a confrontation would not be an extreme of anguish or despair: "Would you not throw yourself down and gnash your teeth and curse the demon who spoke thus? Or have you once experienced a tremendous moment when you would have answered him: 'You are a god and never have I heard anything more divine'" (*GS* IV 341).

Elsewhere we consider the limited value of taking Zarathustra's teachings literally, especially when they are formulated in a series of provocative rhetorical questions. We know that the mathematics of eternal recurrence won't work out, but it isn't clear what difference it would make if it did. Suppose Zarathustra and the dwarf were repeating their experience for the nth time, or that they would continue doing so for an infinite number of times in the future. Or suppose, as Gary Shapiro suggests, that the formulation were extended to space, with an infinite number of enactments of the same experience were transpiring simultaneously.[29] It would still be unclear why Zarathustra, the dwarf, the shepherd, or anyone else should be, unaware as they are of the infinite number of coterminus, identical enactments, moved to any *particular* feelings at all, much less to intense nausea or joy. If all that is must have been and must again be repeated an infinite number of times, then this suggestion must be made to one who has heard the same suggestion myriads of times before without remembering a single instance of having been told this "truth."[30]

But suppose instead of a theory of repetition, that Nietzsche's prose pieces characterize and so delimit the possible attitudes that *could* arise in the context of serious reflection on the idea of recurrence in a lonely, moonlit setting. Suppose the emphasis were on the feelings one might have if, in surroundings far removed from hearth and home, one were to think of oneself as unimportant as an individual. The monolith "Moment" dominates this Chiricoesque landscape, and the speaker asks his audience to consider this possibility: That nothing one will ever do or think or say will, in the scheme of an infinite number of repetitions of things, make the slightest difference. As we argued in chapter 1, this crux presents enormous difficulties, especially for the critic who wishes to extract from it a specific outlook or one or another version of prescriptions or proscriptions by which to live or to avoid living. Perhaps this is the effect that the author elicits after all. For he confronts the reader with a series of questions. Yes, everything will be exactly as it is, namely, as it was and will be, an infinite number of times—exactly the same. But the questions are then propounded. Would not the effect be to elicit an extreme reaction? Anguish or exultation? As we suggested, the pathway back permits recollection of peak experiences, but it permits, also, reflection on the horrors of war and human indifference. The path leads in opposite directions into eternities, past and future, but the speakers in both *The Gay Science* and *Zarathustra* seem to preclude indifference or apathy as a possible imagined response to the gateway, "Moment."

We note erotic overtones in Nietzsche's figurative delineation of the future. Tomorrow comes like a woman hungry for love. "Yes," we read in *The Gay Science*, "life is a woman" (IV 339). The problem is that our feelings toward her are uncertain: "Life is hard to bear." It is no wonder, then, that fictions revel in the woe man suffers at the hands of woman, for she embodies all that is unsettling, uncompromising, and unaccountable in nature. She is the giving/ receiving capacity of renewal, of life, which explains our ambivalent feelings toward her. Woman represents the unleashed force of nature in process— violent and self-destructive—in a passion to create a new generation: "Do you not feel the thirst and the hot breath of her love? She would suck at the sea and drink its depth into her heights; and the sea's desire rises toward her with a thousand breasts": (Z II "IP"). To meet this lusty Amazon with anything approaching equal passion requires a lover atypically endowed with passion and endurance. To a great extent, having overcome much of the herd/man within, Zarathustra measures up; he loves life. So he whispers to the woman ("life"), presumably to promise that he'll be back, but they weep together after- wards, as if to acknowledge the bittersweet quality of their prospective re- union. Life knows, but ordinary folk do not, that she is faithful to those who are inconstant in their affections toward her. And although Zarathustra, like other gospellers, is not ordinary, even he is almost destroyed by the idea of eternal recurrence. As we read toward the end of *Twilight of the Idols*, there is something terrible about the power *behind* eternal recurrence:

> *Eternal* life, the eternal return of life; the future promised and hallowed in the past; the triumphant Yes to life beyond all death and change; *true* life as the over-all continuation of life through procreation, through the mysteries of sexuality. For the Greeks the *sexual* symbol was therefore the venerable symbol par excellence, the real profundity in the whole of ancient piety. Every single element in the act of procreation, of pregnancy, and of birth aroused the highest and most solemn feelings. In the doctrine of the mysteries, *pain* is pronounced holy: the pangs of the woman giving birth hallow all pain; all becom- ing and growing—all that guarantees a future—involves pain. That there may be the eternal joy of creating, that the will to life may eternally affirm itself, the agony of the woman giving birth *must* also be there eternally (*TI* "WIOA" 4)

It is, of course, risky to assume that we have anything like a Nietzschean figure of "Woman" used uniformly throughout his work. But this passage serves to remind us that even apparently misogynist utterances can say some- thing about attitudes toward the unmanageable wonder of life, with all its ag- ony. After all, "woman was God's *second* mistake" (*A* 48). If we hold that gender difference represents a fatal error, then perhaps the problem is that we need to overcome our world-weary *ressentiment* against life. For in this passage, "woman" is a metonym for life: the *sine qua non* of eternal recurrence. This is not so much a cosmological figure as (to use a Renaissance term) an "elemen- tal" one—one composed of physical elements. (Today we might prefer the locution "existential.") "Revaluation of all values" requires the present act of a valuing agency, not just the history of that agency (the record of past valua- tions), but the original generation, *in utero*, as well. For the revaluation is part of the natural process, which hasn't just occurred, but is occurring: the gate- way "Moment." For Nietzsche, sexuality is a mystery no less than a recurring theme. In its fullness, sexuality is as terrible as it is holy. Hence, a single word—that of a god—embodies a host of values which are, in a sense, both hidden and revealed by the god's appearance: "All this is meant by the word Dionysus."

If sexuality is a mystery it is so because it is the mechanism of eternal recurrence, which, again, explains our aversion to it. Sexuality reminds lovers that they are used in a process over which they exercise little if any control. This is why we see so close a connection between the threshold figure of the gateway "Moment" in *Thus Spoke Zarathustra* and childbirth in *Twilight of the Idols*. Dionysus both hides and reveals his human characteristics. "Moment" and childbirth are threshold figures which suggest, not eternal recurrence of the same, but eternal recurrence of the similar. Every moment is different; every birth is unique. Indeed, except in the imagination, how can we encounter a repetition of "this life as you now live it and have lived . . . every pain and every joy and every thought and sigh and everything immeasurably small or great in your life . . . all in the same succession and sequence?" Threshold experiences point toward the future: birth, sexual union, death, rebirth. This is the implacable way of nature. Tomorrow is the domain of woman as a lover, or, in the vernacular of myth, of Venus. In Spenser's *Faerie Queene*, votaries worship Venus in a temple hidden within "Delightful boweres" and "False Labyrinths,"[31] and the goddess, entwined with a snake, is veiled. Not even her priests know why this is so. The folk believe that in her body Venus possesses the power of the combined genders to reproduce: "She syre and mother is her selfe alone, / Begets and eke conceives, ne needeth other none."[32] And yet, as the figure of the snake in this context cleverly implies, this is just a rumor ("But for, they say"). The less prudish truth lies hidden from mortal eyes deep within *"The Gardin of Adonis,"* where Venus eternally enjoys the embrace of Adonis in "the first seminarie / Of all things, that are borne to live and die."[33]

In the figurations of Britomart, Spenser characterizes different aspects of the same "mystery."[34] A wonderful knight as her name implies, she is able to restore womanhood to its rightful place in the history of warfare. But we know that, like her armor, her name conceals her close affinity to Venus. For even her martial demeanor reveals as well as disguises her most intense desire for sexual union with Artegall. It could be argued that their romance is no more than an allegory of Tudor genealogy intended to flatter Queen Elizabeth. But Spenser's poetic genealogy leads backward into the mythological mists of Trojan ancestry, including Anchises's renowned copulation with Venus. In *The Faerie Queene*, the germinating power of nature lies hidden from mortal view. And the same is true of the birth canal—the threshold image, as Nietzsche might say, *par excellence*:

> It [the *Gardin* of *Adonis*] was in fruitful soyle of old,
> And girt in with two walles on either side;

The one of yron, the other of bright gold,
That none might thorough breake, nor over-stride:
And double gates it had, which opened wide,
By which both in and out men moten pas;
Th'one faire and fresh, the other old and dride:
Old *Genius* the porter of them was,
Old *Genius*, the which a double nature has.[35].

Citing the comparison of the birth canal to "the dores of [his] mother's womb" in Job (3.10) as one source of a traditional association, A. C. Hamilton notes that the threshold figure of "The gate is a natural image of birth."[36] "*Genius*" governs both access to and egress from the garden by not only tending the gates ("He letteth in, he letteth out"), but by dressing the creatures ("naked babes") in "fleshly weeds" in order that they might be prepared for their "eternal fate," namely, their inevitable return to the same garden. What seems "Miraculous" in the birth of Chrysogone's twins, Amoret and Belphoebe, is actually only a hidden sexual encounter between Chrysogone and Titan (Spenser's recounting of the myth of Danae and Jove). The hidden aspect of sexuality extends to the manner of specific encounters: "But reason teacheth that the fruitful seades / Of all things living, through impression / Of the sunbeams in moyst complexion, / Doe life conceive and quickened ar by kynd."[37] Thus, in "the middest of that Paradise," hidden from every other creature in the "*Gardin* of *Adonis*," is the Mount of Venus, topped by a grove of myrtle trees. There, in the "thickest covert of that shade," Venus and Adonis make love eternally: "There now he liveth in eternal blis, / Joying his goddesse, and of her enjoyed."[38] In Spenser, the sense of order, beauty, and satisfaction in these passages represent Nature's fullness, which exhibits an overall decorum. "*Genius*" dresses the forms created by the cosmic copulations of Venus and Adonis, but he does so with a mind to an orderly replacement of "kynd" by like "kynd." Like an everlasting "wheel around they [the forms emerging and returning] runne from old to new,"[39] but for all the seeming welter of activity, the amount of "substance" to be dressed for the world remains constant: "eterne in mutability."[40] Here, eternal recurrence is a natural process which may, from a human perspective, seem mysterious. Nietzsche likewise associates "the mysteries of sexuality" (*TI* 561) with eternal recurrence, but the differences between the two conceptions are more interesting than the similarities. Spenser poetically depicts a garden with a local god meticulously ordering all access and egress, with a mind to orchestrating a balance between the two. Sexuality is the hidden energy driving the process of germination through which the species are preserved, despite the vagaries of "Time." This unfolding story has an end, because it has a narrative plot that has been rehearsed over and over. What will be is what has been, namely, reproduction of the species as they are and have been all the way back to the beginning. In Nietzsche, the focus is not on reproduction of the various kinds in nature, but on the agony of childbirth itself. Here, the emphasis is not on orderly repetition. No *"Genius"* at the point of origin governs re-entry and egress. Nietzsche's threshold figure links the idea of becoming with pain. For him, the figure touches something deeply suicidal in Western thought: a world-weariness, a hatred of life which expresses itself in the man-woman relationship and in a revulsion toward sexuality. And yet, in his emphasis on spirituality of the physical, in his sense of the wholeness of life, and in his skepticism toward "scientism," Nietzsche looks back to Renaissance humanism as much as forward to the sexual romanticism of such post-Freudians as Wilhelm Reich and D. H. Lawrence—a psychologist and a novelist who sought to unmask the "mysteries of sexuality."

Two Types of Messianism: Nietzsche and Lawrence

It would be wrong, we think, to argue that Spenser represents a Renaissance perspective and Nietzsche a "modern" one, for in many respects Nietzsche represents his views as a recuperation of Renaissance values. And often he is closer in thought to a Renaissance poet like Spenser than he is to an author, such as D. H. Lawrence, with whom his name and literary reputation are often linked. We can see that this is so by pursuing, as we have with Spenser, a comparative analysis between figurative treatments of the two "proto-moderns." For instance, we have Nietzsche's playful use of the resurrection motif. Earlier, we noted that his playfulness with the figure, as is so often the case, involves deeply-held aspirations of his audience, religious beliefs included. When, in *Twilight*, Nietzsche rhapsodizes about the sacred mysteries of eternal return, he supposes the existence of a real mystery: of will to power. Neither Christ nor Dionysus appear in the flesh, and yet both are, metaphorically speaking, ever present, striving as the warrior and "pale criminal," male and female, good and evil within, struggle for dominance. But this is only to say that poetic language need not aim a mimetic precision. (Some would argue that all natural languages engage the mind with metaphysics.) Be that as it may, particular authors do emphasize a more literal vocabulary than we find in Nietzsche's prose. D. H. Lawrence, for instance, represents what Nietzsche calls "the mysteries of sexuality" as no mystery at all. For him, religious myth only masks sexual fantasies. The difference between the metaphoric strategy of Nietzsche and the literal reductionism of Lawrence can be seen in a comparison between the Christ figures of the two authors: Zarathustra and "the man who had died":[41] two types of resurrected gospellers.

There are obvious similarities. The protagonist of Lawrence's *The Escaped Cock* suffers "nausea"—profound revulsion toward life—after his death and resurrection. As in Nietzsche, here too, death is not simple; it isn't clear, for instance, that "the man who had died" has actually died, although he does rise on Easter morning. The problem is that Lawrence's fiction explains the resurrection naturalistically. So, later on, the man tells the peasant whom he meets not to be afraid, for all that he has heard about Golgotha is untrue. Nothing unusual has happened: "I am not dead. They took me down too soon. So I have risen up."[42]

In an interesting way this declaration both follows from and contradicts the omniscient narrator's description of events preceding the encounter. The naturalistic explanation of the crucifixion and resurrection is in some places borne out. For example, the man awakens "from a long sleep in which he was tied up."[43] With no undue subtlety, Lawrence has the burial cloth restrain "the man who had died" just as the cord restrains the peasant's cockerel: "He was tied by the leg, and he knew it. Body, soul and spirit were tied by that string."[44] And the analogy is developed throughout Part I of the narrative, which recounts a dual liberation. For "the man who had died"[45] and yet not died awakens also "tied up.". He can move if he wants to, but why should he want to? Why be resurrected? For resurrection as an act of senseless will entails affirmation of life: "Who would want to come back from the dead?"[46]

Readers of gospel narratives will of course find the account familiar. And yet the story of Easter morning is retold in such a way as to suggest that the resurrection, beyond being naturalistically explained, is also no cause for joy. That is, "the man who had died" awakens to a sense of death: he "lay dead, resting on the cold nullity of being dead."[47] Everything around him gives a feeling of lifelessness. He is full of nausea and revulsion toward life: "his breast lay cold and dead still"[48] and "his thin legs that had died"[49] remind him that "having died"[50] he is beyond caring, "even beyond loneliness."

So the protagonist feels a sense of revulsion against life. Like Zarathustra, he has gone under, and emerged—as if newly baptized—into an appalling distaste for all that preceded his burial. And yet in the midst of his nausea an awareness emerges of the burgeoning, irrepressible force of life abounding around him. This sense of an exterior world unlike that within him—all pervading and yet restrained within the agglomeration of his dead body parts (as if held by the winding sheet in which he had been buried)—contrasts vividly with the "wanness of the chill dawn"[51] of Easter morning. It seems to him as if this vital world were and would be forever the same: "The world, the same as ever, the natural world, thronging with greenness, a nightingale winsomely, wistfully, coaxingly calling from the bushes beside a runnel of water, in the world, the natural world of morning and evening, forever undying, from which he had died."[52] At the time of his encounter with the escaped cock "the man who had died" sees the world as if from a distance: a mere lapse of time, morning to evening, "forever undying," a world from which he had died. This is the man whom the peasant perceives as a corpse: "The peasant changed countenance, and stood transfixed, as he looked into the dead-white face of the man who had died. That dead-white face, so still, with the black beard growing on it as if in death; and those wide-open black sombre eyes, that had died! and those washed scars on the waxy forehead!"[53] The omniscient narrator does not clarify the matter of the man's death, but states that the man has died or been killed "from out of"[54] the world. Although it seems that the world is eternally resurrected, the man himself is like a walking corpse. No longer in the grave, he is nevertheless not part of the resurrected world. This sense of distance from the world is amplified by the man's rejection of the sexual advances of the peasant's wife, to whom (in a drastic revision of Christ's sermon on the "bread of life" [John 6.48 ff.]) he offers money given him by Madeleine: "'Take it!' he said. 'It buys bread, and bread brings life.'"[55] The reversal of the gospel text is hard to miss. In St. John's gospel, Jesus says:

> I am that bread of life.
> I am the living bread which came down from heaven: if any man eat of this bread, he shall live for ever: and the bread that I will give is my flesh, which I will give for the life of the world. (John 6.48, 51)

But here the Lawrentian text is not as strikingly familiar as that in Part II: "in the end I offered them only the corpse of my love. This is my body—take and eat—my corpse—"[56] Paradoxically, and in sharp contrast, "the man who had died" explicitly denies the peasant woman his "flesh" by refusing to satisfy her sexual desire. In a reversal of Eucharistic meaning, the woman comes to him with "wine and water, and sweetened cakes":

> The day was hot, and as she crouched to serve him, he saw her breasts sway from her humble body, under her smock. He knew she wished he would desire her, and she was youngish, and not unpleasant and he, who had never known a woman, would have desired her if he could. But he could not want her.[57]

Here, death and transfiguration are only partially accomplished. So "the man who had died" has no desire for the peasant's wife, but then he has never experienced desire for *any* women. Abstinence was and remains his way with Mary Madeleine (he asks *her* for money, which he gives to the peasant's wife in the place of his sexual favor). In a drastically altered version of the communion rite, the crucified but risen protagonist passes his first real opportunity to love a woman in a new, non-abstinent manner. Willing to pay to be left alone, he nevertheless recognizes his obstinate celibacy as a moral flaw: "But now he knew that virginity is a form of greed; and the body rises again to give and to take, to take and to give, ungreedily. Now he knew that he had risen for the woman, or women, who knew the greater life of the body, not greedy to give, not greedy to take, and with whom he could mingle his body. But having died, he was patient, knowing there was time, an eternity of time."[58] Oddly, the man's ersatz resurrection has prepared him for an sight into an eternal perspective on his own unleashed sexuality. Taking leave from the peasant's household, "the man who had died" returns to the garden on the third day. He had promised to meet Madeleine, who has brought with her the woman "who had been his mother" and a friend "called Joan."[59] But still the man draws back: "May I have this money? I shall need it.—I cannot speak to them, for I am not yet ascended to the Father. And I must leave you now."[60] The implication seems to be that they, like the peasant's wife, are women possessed of ungiving souls: "hard, and short-sighted, and grasping."[61]

Here, the fable departs from St. John's gospel, in which Mary Magdalene comes to the sepulchre with Peter, and remains to weep after he and the other disciples have gone. When she looks inside the tomb, two angels ask why she is weeping. As soon as she answers Jesus appears, but she does not recognize him. Thinking him the gardener (which, allegorical interpreters insisted through the ages, he was, though in a sense not understood at the time), Mary Magdalene inquires about the disposition of the body of Jesus. But when Jesus speaks, she recognizes him ("Rabboni"), whereupon he instructs her: "Touch me not; for I am not yet ascended to my Father."[62] He tells her, further, to take the news of his resurrection to the disciples, which she promptly does.

In Lawrence, resonances from the gospel take on a different tone in Part II. Derrida remarks on the emphatic division of Blanchot's novella, *Death Sentence*, a work in which the protagonist encounters what appears, superficially, to be two quite different women—indeed, two different *kinds* of woman—in the sharply divided segments of the narrative. Similarly, *The Escaped Cock* is divided into two parts (likewise, also, of almost equal length). The spatial division is marked by a virtually empty white leaf with only "Part II" printed in red, this leaf followed by a blank, white verso, white space, and a color print of the "woman who serves Isis." In contrast to the peasant's wife and Mary Madeleine (women whose sexual experience seems to render them in the man's eyes neither whole nor desirable), "the woman" induces in him a sense of life's enjoyment, especially in its sexual possibilities. But in their failure to evoke desire in the "man who had died," they are, like him, unfinished: parts only of an intended natural form. Like the cockerel, tied by a string, so the "man who had died" is restrained, first by a winding sheet, then by numbness to desire. Part I presents the male/female pair, but as partial, frustrated, and separate—unfinished and either promiscuous or virginal, which states of conduct—to "the man who had died"—come to represent the same greed.

Again, paradoxically, virginity is an essential pre-condition of nature's pristine pair: the god/man and the priestess/woman who serves Isis. Undifferentiated experience distracts and sullies, burying desire in the grave of nausea and disillusion. Like "the man who had died," the priestess lives apart from the world. A pagan, she has kept herself for a particular kind of man. Her mother provides the requisite reminder that the world is full of undiscerning women and of men ready to accommodate their indiscriminate impulses. All about her, copulation thrives, but because she is different "the woman who served Isis"[63] questions the need for men rather than her twenty-seven years of virginity: "'Are all women born to be given to men?'"[64] This question, put to "a philosopher," adduces a puzzling response:

> "Rare women wait for the re-born man. For the lotus, as you know, will not answer to all the bright heat of the sun. But she curves her dark, hidden head in the depths, and stirs not. Till, in the night, one of these rare invisible suns that have been killed and shine no more, rises among the stars in unseen purple, and like the violet, sends its rare, purple rays out into the night. To these the lotus stirs . . . and spreads her sharp rays of bliss, and offers her soft, gold depths such as no other flower possesses, to the penetration of the flooding, violet-dark sun that has died and risen and makes no show. But for the golden brief day-suns of show, such as Anthony, and for the hard winter suns of power, such as Caesar, the lotus stirs not, nor will ever stir. Those will only tear open the bud. Ah, I tell you, wait for the re-born, and wait for the bud to stir."[65]

Like "the man who had died" and been reborn, the woman cannot desire an ordinary lover. She is like the poet in the Coleridge poem who sees but does not feel the beauty around him; she apprehends the manliness of Anthony and Caesar, but male attractiveness does not stir desire. Her quest is for copulation of a magnitude to transcend the grave.

When the priestess discovers the wounded fugitive she insists that he end his desperate flight, enter her temple (be converted), and present himself before the statue of "Isis in Search." The man complies, but without much feeling. It is the woman who attributes religious significance to the moment. In contrast to Mary Madeleine ("she, believing him to be a gardener"), the priestess believes "the man who had died" to be "the lost Osiris,"[66] and the energy of her belief overcomes the man's impulse to withdraw (*Noli me tangere!*).[67] Despite his lifelong aversion to physical contact with the opposite sex, he is suddenly alive to the woman's touch, feeling her now to be "a tender flame of healing"[68] to one known as a "physician."

But the more the two lovers are drawn to each other the more the sullied world of soldiers, townsfolk, slaves, and the woman's mother seems to oppose their union. "The man who had died" is in flight from execution, and the woman fears retribution, too. And yet, paradoxically, it seems that the force of the cosmos compels their desire for each other toward coition: "Suns beyond suns had dipped her in mysterious fire, the mysterious fire of a potent woman, and to touch her was like touching the sun."[69] The woman, having tempted the man to worship Isis, completes her ablutions, undresses him, and, in a reenactment of the Maundy Thursday ritual, anoints his wounds and washes his feet with her tears:

> And, behold, a woman in the city, which was a sinner, when she knew that Jesus sat at meat in the Pharisee's house, brought an alabaster box of ointment,
> And stood at his feet behind him weeping, and began to wash his feet with tears, and did wipe them with the hairs of her head, and kissed his feet, and anointed them with the ointment.[70]

When the man recalls this loving act, the priestess asks if he had actually loved—that is, made love to—Mary Madeleine, his answer is evasive: "'I asked them all to serve me with the corpse of their love. And in the end I offered them only the corpse of my love. This is my body—take and eat—my corpse—.'"[71]

Lawrence's rhetoric is caustically reminiscent of the gospels and the liturgy. The man recalls his interference in the lives of others in a way quite different from his renunciation of women and the world in Part I. Then, his rejection of a religious vocation was only partially expressed, in that he fled not only from the soldiers but from the life abounding within and around him. Withholding himself from human touch had become a way of life with him. His stubborn renunciation of desire denied the resurrection of the body—the eternally returning body of Osiris, eternally returning because eternally desired. Having risen to view life as "Isis in Search," in a gesture reminiscent of his loosening of the string restraining the peasant's cockerel, the man unties the woman's tunic. The effect is cataclysmic and historical, largely because Lawrence's audience knew the relevant text: "And I say also unto thee, That thou art Peter, and upon this rock I will build my church, and the gates of hell shall not prevail against it."[72] With a narrative inflection more attuned to the thinking of Wilhelm Reich and Herbert Marcuse than to that of Augustine or Aquinas, Lawrence reinscribes the Passion story with a naturalistic turn: "And his death and his passion of sacrifice were all as nothing to him now, he knew only the crouching fulness of the woman there, the soft white rock of life . . . .'On this rock I built my life'—The deep-folded, penetrable rock of the living woman!"[73] As the quotation from Matthew suggests ("'Let not your heart be troubled'"),[74] "the man who had died" builds his life, not a church, on this rock, which, although rock, is compliant and penetrable. On this established structure, which exists now, as if in an instant already built (Lawrence echoes, too, Christ's promise to raise the Temple of Solomon in three days), the man places his hopes for a settled mind.

Like the progenitor text, Lawrence's gospel points to the future. The woman's soon-affirmed pregnancy requires the man's departure. Although he promises to return ("'sure as Spring'"),[75] and although the woman protests his leaving, his promise and her remonstrance are half-hearted. In fact, she has already made arrangement for his escape. Since eternal return is miraculous, danger and rescue are part of the unfolding pattern of the man/god's death and resurrection. Accordingly, the man's escape is accomplished through an advantage gained by an earlier act of voyeurism. The young slave whom he had watched at his illicit love-making provides the boat for his escape. As he rows out into the open waters "the man who had died" muses: "I have sowed the seed of my life and my resurrection, and put my touch forever upon the choice woman of this day, and I carry her perfume in my flesh like essence of roses."[76]

We can think of the Lawrence Passion as an interesting gloss on Nietzsche's theory that the self, waking or asleep, transforms events into comforting narratives with the author as hero. In *Twilight of the Idols* ("FGE" 4), Nietzsche posits a genetic theory of fiction which suggests that individuals create narratives—interpretations of "events"—which impute comforting causes to the surrounding world. But then these interpretations, in turn, become stimuli in the actual world, which must then be processed by n number of individual minds, and so on. The "apparent world," with its perils and suffering cannot be left, simply, as the "apparent world," with its perils and suffering. Minds replace this world with another, in which the unfamiliar and threatening give way to the familiar and comforting.

From this point of view, Lawrence's story of the Passion might appear as an evasion of the sense of mortality. Lawrence's reinscription proffers immortality. That is, this gospel writer turns the "apparent world" into the "true world" by the wonderful workings of the creative process, with the result that death is, as one gospel replaces another individuated with a new source of comfort, diminished if not indeed vanquished. In its place we have death modified by transfiguration of the man/god narrator. Again, with the fictive perspective of the third "Great Error" in mind, it is neither coincidental nor surprising to learn that Lawrence finished *The Escaped Cock* while on his deathbed, nor that Lawrence more than once painted Christ with his own face (in one instance, a face which exactly matches that, also, of the dancing Pan). From this viewpoint, *The Escaped Cock* is the narrative counterpart of Lawrence's "The Risen Lord." Both works see, in the Easter story an underlying "truth," albeit one whose metaphysical foundations lie in psychoanalytic theory of repressed motives:

> So it is, so it will be, for ever and ever.
> And still the great needs of men
> will clamor forth from the flesh, and never
> can denial deny them again.[77]

Lawrence's celebration of the flesh bears some resemblance to Nietzsche's Dionysianism, and might be considered an instance of Frye's thesis that the modern romantic movement departed from acceptance of the mythological system based on and emanating from the textual hegemony of the Bible. Beliefs change, but, as Nietzsche observes, the insistence on belief remains constant—ingrained—for humans will accept any condition in the world except one in which the underlying narrative lacks significance. So, as we would expect given such a point of view, changing beliefs and changing forms reflect shifting loci of the familiar and comforting. The myth-making capacity, with the hero as narrator, embodies new beliefs, for individual pasts elucidate new representations of the world with ever-exfoliating bases for an understanding of the "apparent world" as manageable and unthreatening. Lawrence's belief-system, for instance, exhibits a romantic "scientism" unimagined by Bacon, but more or less an established creed of Freud and his mildly deranged pupil, Wilhelm Reich. And yet, as Frye points out, in Nietzsche (and, we would add, in Lawrence), the central figure of the biblical tradition—cyclic return—is a dominant theme. Though both writers are vigorously "anti-Christian" in their pronounced attitudes, *Thus Spoke Zarathustra* and *The Escaped Cock* are firmly scaffolded on the New Testament narrative of the life of Christ.

We have lumped Lawrence with Nietzsche in this connection, not to suggest that the two are of equal importance, but rather to demonstrate how two anti-texts differ in the way in which they relate to their common textual progenitor. To be sure, Lawrence's revision of the Passion narrative whistles a different tune in the dark, but the theme of cyclic return is only doubled by his fusion of biblical and pagan mythologies. His fictional amalgam of Christ and Osiris represents eternal return in a manner reminiscent of Zarathustra's promise to the woman in his "dancing frenzy," and of the passage (already cited at greater length) toward the close of *Twilight of the Idols*: "*Eternal* life, the eternal return of life; the future promised and hallowed in the past; the triumphant Yes to life beyond all death and change; *true* life as the over-all continuation of life through procreation, through the mysteries of sexuality" (*TI* "WIOA" 4). The fictive treatments of eternal recurrence in Nietzsche and Lawrence are apposite, but the differences, which are striking, are never more evident than in the endings of *Zarathustra* and *The Escaped Cock*. For whatever one might think of Part IV of Nietzsche's *magnum opus* (we will be dealing with this question in greater detail later on), it seems to us that we cannot say that it fails so obviously as does the ending of *The Escaped Cock*.

And yet the weakness of the ending of Lawrence's short novel may tell us something about the paradoxical development of the sexual revolution: "Tomorrow is another day."[78] While amplifying the Passion motif of death and resurrection, this is how Lawrence ends the story: "Tomorrow is another day." Superficially, this closing sentence seems little more than a bland reminder of the Preacher's promise that, notwithstanding the passage of generations, "the earth abideth for ever."[79] The problem with the narrative's ending is its thematic irrelevance: "The earth abideth"—yes—but with or without the self-resurrecting narrator and artist in it? If he is not resurrected, what happens to "Isis in Search"? The Gospel according to Lawrence promises wonderful things to the woman who waits for his return. But it also punishes her with eternal virginity, should tomorrow come without the potent man/god/artist in it.

We can see the Lawrence narrative as an allegory of the eternal return of gospel writing, but it seems to demand a thematically more expansive reading, too. Lawrence does not merely celebrate the possibilities of a literary genre. The narrator himself must return. Failing that, the best woman of the next generation will be forced to live a celibate existence. Further, since *The Escaped Cock* is also an allegory of the ongoing life of the race, her celibacy entails the man's imagined retribution of genocide against the human race. Given the genetic and erotic figures of the narrative, what comforts the narrator may endanger others: townsfolk, soldiers, the world. Either the man/god returns or nobody does: "Tomorrow is another day." But if the novel ends in vacuity, allowing room for closure on a rhetorical question, has Lawrence not undermined the notion of the novelistic demand for hero and purpose? Tomorrow is another story, but who will write it? When the man/god has gone away, what gospel *can* be written?

Zarathustra's problem is that nobody who will listen is qualified to hear. As a teacher, he stays alive only because the townsfolk, misunderstanding his message, laugh at him, thinking him no more dangerous than the jester who leaps over the acrobat on the tightrope. Lawrence's protagonist has already suffered the consequences of a world offended by the innovative Word; his new gospel declares that the flesh, not the Word, is the true source of cyclic return. "The man who had died" hopes to be the son conceived of his own spectacular lovemaking. But that hope is like the hope Madeleine and his disciples have placed in *him*. "The man who had died" rests his faith in the woman. But, unhappily, the world is full of women—the woman's mother, for instance, and Madeleine—women whom the man regards as untouchable. And, after all (as Nietzsche elsewhere observes, "Woman was God's *second* mistake" [A 48]), the world is also full of men: Judas, Peter, slaves, Caesar, Anthony. The other side of the misogynist coin is misanthropy.

The problem of the novelistic ending here may reflect Lawrence's own misgivings about the fideism required by the doctrine of recurrence. As the post-Victorian threw off the shackles of repressive mores, it seemed that unrestrained sexuality would impart transcendent energy, and with it, effortlessly, a better world. Moreover, sexuality and art would give what in the imagination has been taken away: Christianity's promise of immortality. For only the crabbed inheritors of tradition die, because only they are so anesthetized to life and they sustain the death blows of a living creator. But is this faith sustaining? Does "the man who had died" row the stolen boat into the darkness with a strong sense that he will in fact return? Zarathustra whispers to the woman ("Life"), presumably, to promise that he will be—*wills* to be—back; but they weep together afterward. If he were to return, would that be cause for rejoicing? Again, Nietzsche's fiction provokes a question about the value of life. Christianity teaches an anti-life yearning for immortality in another, better world. But, then, does this yearning for another world render empty its simultaneous protestations of the hallowed origins of the "apparent world"? In Lawrence, the question seems to be more narrowly focused on cyclic return itself: What if hope in the resurrection, however refashioned by romantic "scientism," is unwarranted? What if the woman lies? What if faith in "Isis in Search" is no more efficacious that faith in "the Crucified"? What if "the man who had died" doesn't return?—is, in fact, not actually within the woman's quickened womb?

Oddly, Lawrence represents the hope of personal immortality in the woman's desire to give birth to her lover. But he hedges his bet, too. The man's love for the woman cannot overcome his prior contempt for women. The man holds out ("Don't touch me, Madeleine"; "I am not yet risen to the Father"; "Oh, don't touch me").[80] He prefers, as the Evelyn Waugh novel has it, his "resurrection now." But if the woman fails, well then—here is the good news— "Tomorrow is another day."

After comparison with Nietzschean and Miltonic texts, we say: bland, empty, not convincing. "The earth abideth forever," but who cares? Without an author and savior—without the speaking gospel-writer—the world has no comfort, no life, no regenerative power in it. When Nicodemus, the Pharisee, whose function in the progenitor texts resembles that of the hunchback in "On Redemption," avers that Jesus can do miracles, Jesus replies with a *non sequitur* in rebuke: "Jesus answered and said unto him, Verily, verily, I say unto thee, except a man be born again, he cannot see the kingdom of God."[81] Such an insistence on rebirth, we must remember, is precisely the woman's motive. The philosopher told her to wait for the reborn man, and she waited, and now she is pregnant. But in the end, as in front of the man who had died the sea waits—now that the woman has taken from him what she wanted—will she wait for him again? And even if she waits, the man must die—as an individual—in order to be reborn in nine months. Will it work? Can the woman's faith work such a miracle? Does she *have* such faith, or was it only a show to succeed where Madeleine and the peasant's wife had failed to seduce him?

Scaffolding a metaphysical system on belief in the transcendent, resurrecting power of the orgiastic moment is not without epistemological inconvenience. The man's impotence has been overcome by the woman's desire, but his lifetime of celibacy and introversion seems to fit the bleak seascape more surely than do those promises of withdrawal and return. Lawrence's orgiastic romanticism appears more at ease with twilight and temples, with lovers together and only incense burning between them, than with the lone figure rowing the stolen boat into the darkness. Does the sense of danger and thrill of desire, once suppressed and then aroused and satisfied, indicate a sure direction? The protagonist promises to return, but his promise is subject to the same uncertainty as the woman's promise to wait. He has sowed the seed of the next generation, but reassurance of rebirth exists now only as recollection, satisfying, perhaps, but not as exquisitely so as the orgiastic moment itself. And the darkness around "the man who had died" is like the darkness to which he awakened in the tomb. Already comfort in the form of woman, even in recollection, has slipped away: "The high coast was utterly dark against the starry sky. There was no glimmer from the peninsula: the priestess came no more at night."[82] It is not only that the lovers have parted, but as the man rows into night, the woman has already disappeared from all future landscapes. Tomorrow's dawn, likewise, exists only in the man's hopeful expectations, which are in conflict with imagined reprisals against the woman and the human race. His expectations proffer hope of immortality, but they cannot erase the gathering sense of personal mortality and defeat.

Perhaps this somber tone is the most telling departure from a "Nietzschean" perspective on eternal recurrence. Deleuze may exaggerate in suggesting that, for Nietzsche, philosophy produces sadness. Zarathustra returns to his cave—his solitude—and yet repeatedly descends to teach, which is his "destiny." But that teaching persistently invites anyone who will listen to surrender all pity, including self-pity, and to give up all semblance of romantic pessimism. We say that *Thus Spoke Zarathustra* is an "inverse gospel," a Menippian satire in the mold of Lucian's "Golden Ass"[83] narrative, a parody of the liturgy and of all sermons and sermonizing (including the Sermon on the Mount), and it is all of these, and more. It is also, like Burton's *Anatomy of Melancholy*, a medical treatise and self-help manual: How to recapture youthful joy and frenzy in only one lifetime of excruciatingly hard lessons. Zarathustra grows old, but the process of withdrawal and return continues to the very end, which, like the beginning recounted in the "Prologue," seems to herald a new time and a new gospel. It seems as if, in the end, the old man has become young again: "Thus spoke Zarathustra, and he left his cave, glowing and strong as a morning sun that comes out of dark mountains" (Z IV "The Sign"). Zarathustra's embrace of "Life," in a dance, is a powerful antidote against time. But, again, this figural representation suggests a link between philosophy and attitude.

In Zarathustra's love affair with "Life," Nietzsche represents the desideratum of total engagement: "will to power." But much less seems to be at stake in *The Escaped Cock*, no more, we are tempted to say, than the consequences of the sexual encounter itself. With Lawrence, the structure of the narrative juxtaposes tomb and Temple, death and sexual union. His gospel exalts an emerging sexual utopia. Zarathustra's gospel teaches an endless process of re-inscribing gospels which become in turn the tablets to be, by the same process, dashed to pieces. This gospel seems to make Zarathustra young again. That is, the energy of the gospeller is renewed because it is part of the process itself. Sexuality, here, is a sign of the process of making all things new, but Zarathustra is not himself subject to the process. He is a bridge. He is the prophet of his own incarnation. Thus, after being an old man, he becomes new, strong, ready, like a young lover prepared to match the embrace of that insatiable Amazon, "Life."

The recursive strategy of *Thus Spoke Zarathustra* militates against the providential "sense of an ending"—any ending—whether sad or joyful. The sense of a beginning better describes the affects of the closing paragraphs of "The Sign." This anti-gospel resists closure, just as, in *The Anitchrist*, history thus far avoids destiny. The problem, of course, is the Germans—Luther, Leibniz, Kant, "Wars of 'Liberation,'" the "*Reich*" (A 61). To paraphrase Shaw (and perhaps lending a perverse meaning to his figure), the world is not yet ready to receive saints. Look what Luther did to the Renaissance. Then, for a brief historical moment, the race stood on the threshold of a new creation. Christianity was almost dead when Luther descended on Rome. He found there a wonderful paganism, Christianity in shambles in the very seat of its greatest power. But, thanks to him, the Reformation ended all that. The German spirit triumphed over life.

We are suggesting that, in Nietzsche, sexuality is only one of many figurations of an attitude toward history. In *Twilight of the Idols*, Nietzsche employs the figure of woman in childbirth as a complex image of "becoming." Birthing is holy, for it represents the triumph of life as "becoming" in a moment of absolute agony and joy. It overcomes all duality. Zarathustra's good news, then, is that there is no good news. Or, to put the same point another way, his gospel affirms that once a gospel is inscribed in stone, it is not "becoming" but dead. Clearly, the drift of such future-oriented thought is toward immediate and temporary valuation with a concomitant, absolute individuation of valuing agencies. But, in this context, is it fair to say (with Frye) that Nietzsche's outlook is cheerless and glum? Would not any answer reflect the respondent's feelings about such absolute individuation, with its implied total responsibility in the here and now for everything that touches one's life?

Like the Renaissance values vitiated by Luther and the Reformation, the future is immanent in that, in the here and now, human consciousness is at the threshold "Moment." To say that the living *can* create or *do* create their own gospels understates the doctrine implicit in Zarathustra's "On Old and New Tablets" (Z III). We will recall that in this sequence Zarathustra has, once again, withdrawn only to return, "to go among men once more," this time to teach them to "break, break the old tablets!" In their place he would put the "will to create" (section 16). Hence, this is a gospel all but devoid of doctrine, in that its doctrinal form cannot be known, for it will be the cumulative effects of adherence to but one "new tablet": "This new tablet, O my brothers, I place over you: *become hard!*" (section 29) But is this a clear directive? Do we surrender Mosaic Law, the Christian reinscription, Kant, and all our other learned imperatives for this? And, supposing the answer is "Yes," what would a "hard" specimen of humanity be like? What would such a "being" think or do that one of a softer quality would not? Again, the figures of preparedness and of the future come to the fore, and they are the point as distinct from the doctrine:

> That I may one day be ready and ripe in the great noon: as ready and ripe as glowing bronze, clouds pregnant with lighting, and swelling milk udders—ready for myself and my most hidden will: a bow lusting for its arrow, and arrow lusting for its star—a star ready and ripe in its noon, glowing, pierced, enraptured by annihilating sun arrows—a sun itself and an inexorable solar will, ready annihilate in victory! (Z III "ONT" 30)

We are familiar, of course, with Nietzsche's use of this figure of noon. History unfolds toward that moment in the day's passage when the light of philosophy casts the briefest shadow. In his miniature genealogy of philosophical enlightenment, Nietzsche represents the darkness of Platonic/Christian metaphysics turning toward the "Gray morning," which announces itself in "The cock-crow of positivism" (*TI* "HTWBF"). The subtitle of this important sequence is: "*The History of an Error.*" Here, we suggest, the definite article stands out. Nietzsche is not thinking aloud, or offering possibly helpful animadversions to an ongoing philosophical discussion ("a history," "a genealogy," "an antichrist," "a meaning of ascetic ideals"). A particular end must be pronounced on this one error, and that end is in this one "*History.*" So this philosopher/genealogist reduces philosophy as metaphysics to a mere record of fault, and by this reduction propels history to that moment of creation which transcends history as error, namely, creation: "(Noon: moment of the briefest shadow; end of the longest error; high point of humanity; INCIPIT ZARATHUSTRA.)"

Significantly, "*The History of an Error*" ends with the insertion of a reference to Nietzsche's *Thus Spoke Zarathustra*. Hence, philosophical error is overcome by a new Genesis in the form of a miniature hexameron of "How the 'True World' Finally Became a Fable," this strategically situated at the end of an epoch of darkness. God took six days to create the world with humankind in it. Philosophy has droned on for over two thousand years, inscribing as wisdom a single error, making humankind miserable in the process. But in a mere six brief paragraphs, figuratively representing only a half-day, Nietzsche overcomes God by creating Zarathustra, prophet and forerunner of the race which will replace humankind. And while doing this, the author dispatches the problems of Western metaphysics as preserved in philosophy as well.

It is no coincidence that *Twilight of the Idols* also ends with another insertion from *Thus Spoke Zarathustra*: section 29 from "On Old and New Tablets." As in *Ecce Homo*, here Nietzsche turns back to earlier works, not only to accept and approve, but to re-create the earlier work as the later one as well. The issue here is not a particular doctrine to replace the desiccated corpse of Western philosophy. Nietzsche has but the one exhortation ("*Be hard*"), which is a far cry from Mosaic Law and the Sermon on the Mount. In its tone, the passage is a far cry, too, from the furtive flight of Lawrence's "man who had died." In Nietzsche, the energy of the speaker moves out from broad statement ("Creators are hard") to beatitude ("Blessedness to write on the will of millennia") to proclamation of a new law ("This new tablet, O my brothers, I place over you."). But, again, it is not the specific word or instruction or doctrine or motive that counts. Old and new are mingled together in the broken tablets of the past. And what emerges as "new" might actually be "old," but it makes no difference, so long as true creators affirm their own inscriptions in a way intended to last ("harder than bronze, nobler than bronze"). It is not likely that Nietzsche would here forget the progenitor covenant between God and Moses: "I call heaven and earth to record this day against you, that I have set before you life and death, blessing and cursing: therefore choose life."[84] To which Nietzsche, in agreement, answers: "*Da capo!*" "INCIPIT ZARATHUS-TRA." Once more, from the top.

The Philosophy of Composition
The Composition of Philosophy

A book is like a mirror. If an ape stares into it an angel won't stare back.
—Attributed to Lichtenberg

Philosophy as/and Literature

Nietzsche's influence on recent critical movements, including revisionism and deconstruction, is beyond question. Nietzsche's perspectivism provides the basis for Harold Bloom's famous dictum "There are no readings, only misreadings."[1] Zarathustra's rejection of discipleship appears to inspire Bloom's repeated protestations that he seeks no followers or converts; and Bloom's suggestion that all figuration involves an "urge to be elsewhere"[2] appears to reformulate Nietzsche's analysis of asceticism. Again, Paul de Man's deconstructionism is broadly indebted to the style and substance of Nietzsche's critique of the metaphysical tradition, and it owes something as well to Nietzsche's embryonic theories of rhetoric. Even a reaction against these movements, Daniel T. O'Hara's *The Romance of Interpretation*,[3] invokes the reasoning of "How the 'True World' Finally Became A Fable" in order to attack the "otherworldliness" of Bloom and de Man, along with Pater, Frye, and Hartman.

Of course, there is nothing new in literary critics borrowing terms and ideas, or even attitudes, from philosophy; but the application of techniques of literary analysis to philosophical texts is, if no longer surprising, at least newer; newer still is the recent interest of American philosophers in the value of critical theory and of literature itself in advancing discussion of "philosophical problems." In recent years, each of these activities has enjoyed notable successes that were simultaneously highly instructive failures.[4]

Paul de Man, for example, poses the question of the literature/philosophy relationship in a series of essays on Nietzsche in *Allegories of Reading*.[5] No one is more aware than Nietzsche of the origins of philosophy in rhetoric, of the way in which metaphysics unwittingly turns effects of language into philosophical "ideas." Yet de Man wonders if Nietzsche's awareness of this rhetoricity makes a real difference. How can it, when Nietzsche's demystifying critique depends on rhetorical reversals of earlier reversals—of truth back into lie, of good back into evil, and so on—which must paradoxically claim to undo the consequences of reversibility itself? How can rhetoric hope to "purify" philosophy of its rhetorical characteristic?

Does this mean, then, that philosophy should embrace its own literariness and imitate the artist in an unfettered exploitation of language's rhetorical possibilities? Nietzsche is too wise, de Man notes, to suggest this. How can the freedom to deceive make the artist less deceptive? And does the artist not also mistakenly believe in his own rhetoric? For that matter, de Man insinuates, are the philosophical rigor of Nietzsche's deconstruction of metaphysics and the trap into which the artist repeatedly falls not one and the same?

De Man implies that philosophy originates in literature—the most rhetorical form of language—but he does not seem to think that his critique has much to offer philosophy as such. On the other hand, some philosophers, Richard Rorty[6] and Alexander Nehamas, for instance, seem to think that literature has much to say in response to traditionally "philosophical" questions. In *Nietzsche: Life as Literature*[7]—one of the finest books on the subject in recent years—Nehamas argues that the literariness ("aestheticism" is Nehamas's term) of Nietzsche's writings is both the motivation for and the result of his perspectivism, and that this recognition helps provide answers to the difficulties presented to philosophers not just by perspectivism but by eternal recurrence, the *Übermensch*, and the will to power as well. Perspectivism is not a theory of knowledge so much as it is a condition of textualization, not just of making texts but of comprehending the world as if it were a text, as Nietzsche seems to think we do. "The will to power" is not a call to immoralism with inevitably nihilistic consequences but an ontology, Nehamas argues, based on the way in which the identity of the literary text (or the being of a character in the text) is not some essence but the sum of its effects.[8] "Eternal recurrence" is not a cosmology, nor does it define a moral imperative so much as a "therapeutic" fantasy or fiction by which the quality of one's own life can be measured by the same sense of inevitability that marks a well-constructed, satisfying piece of fiction. And the *Übermensch* is a character or one aspect of the character of the ideal human being, who exists within and because of the writings; such a being is no more real than the character that emerges from any body of fiction or poetry. Nor does Nietzsche urge us to become *Übermenschen* any more (or any less) than a novelist urges us to become like characters embodied in the work of fiction, much less like its author.

Yet for all the power of this approach, at times Nehamas's characterization of literature seems startlingly off the mark. He stages a meeting of philosophical ideas with a highly abstracted version of "the literary work," when neither the specificity of Nietzsche's own texts nor the complexity of the individual literary text is in evidence. There is a sense in which Nehamas's very choice of the term "aestheticism" betrays a desire to stay within the idealizing realm of aesthetics and to avoid crossing over into the domain of literary criticism, where virtually all recent theories (many inspired by Nietzsche) project a more fragmented and problematic image of the text.

Perhaps some examples will clarify this point. Introducing Nietzsche's aestheticism, Nehamas argues that Nietzsche

> looks at the world in general as if it were a sort of artwork; in particular, he looks at it as if it were a literary text. And he arrives at many of his views of the world and the things within it, including his views of human beings, by generalizing to them ideas and principles that apply almost intuitively to the literary situation, to the creation and interpretation of literary texts and characters. . . . The most obvious connection, of course, is supplied by our common view that literary texts can be interpreted equally well in vastly different and deeply incompatible ways. Nietzsche, to whom this currently popular idea can in fact be traced, also holds that exactly the same is true of the world itself and all the things within it. This view, as we shall see, motivates his perspectivism as well as aspects of his doctrine of the will to power, of the eternal recurrence, of the nature of the self, and of his objections to morality.[9]

Looking at "the world in general as if it were a sort of artwork" provides the double security of analogical distance ("as if") and of the formalist hypostatization of the literary text in particular as a discrete object of interpretation. By the end of the paragraph, Nehamas refers to the "world itself" in a way that suggests not only that "work" is still subordinate to "world" but that literature is the necessary digression by means of which we are returned once again to the world as the discrete object of our knowledge. It is this perspective that seems to us questionable. For Nietzsche seems to look on the world, not securely from without (as if it were a sort of artwork), but rather unassuredly as if from within an unfolding text whose alienness we must find a way to make our own. This is what happens when Nehamas characterizes the other essential aspect of Nietzsche's aestheticism:

> Nietzsche's positive thinking consists not so much in the specific ideas with which the individual chapters that follow are concerned (though it does certainly include such views) as, even more important, in the presentation, or exemplification, of a specific character, recognizably literary, who makes of these philosophical ideas a way of life that is uniquely his. The fact that this character is unique, that it is not described in the traditional sense, and that it is produced in a way that prevents it from ever being a model for direct imitation allows Nietzsche, as we will see, to persist in his perspectivism without being obliged to construct positions that are merely negative.[10]

Here and elsewhere, Nehamas starts out to explain why the literariness of Nietzsche's writings is essential to the work, but ends up talking as if it were merely instrumental—a means to more important ends. But, characterizing "the central claim of the interpretation of which this book consists," Nehamas soon asserts: "Nietzsche's effort to create an artwork out of himself, a literary character who is a philosopher, is then also his effort to offer a positive view without falling back into the dogmatic tradition he so distrusted and from which he may never have been sure he escaped."[11] Again, we are told that Nietzsche's "many styles are part of his effort to present views without presenting them as more than views of his own and are therefore part of his effort to distinguish his practice from what he considers the practice of philosophers so far."[12] In each case, Nietzsche's aestheticism appears as the instrument of a philosophical purpose, which may be described and detached and described in isolation after all.

Finally, Nehamas elaborates on earlier remarks about Nietzsche's self-fashioning:

> Nietzsche exemplifies through his own writings one way in which one individual may have succeeded in fashioning itself—an individual, moreover, who, though beyond morality, is not morally objectionable. This individual is none other than Nietzsche himself, who is a creature of his own texts. This character does not provide a model for imitation, since he consists essentially of the specific actions—that is, of the specific writings—that make him up, and which only he could write. To imitate him directly would produce a caricature, or at best a copy—something which in either case is not an individual. To imitate him properly would produce a creation which, making use of everything that properly belongs to oneself, would also be perfectly one's own—something which is no longer an imitation.[13]

Here, Nietzsche's literariness is subordinated to and justified by a project of self-fashioning. Yet Nehamas, for the most part unconcerned with Nietzsche's diaries, deals with the published works which, of course, solicit a readership. Implicitly, readers are invited to accept as exemplary a selfhood which refuses their efforts at imitation, and then turns around and thematizes those efforts and that refusal (*Thus Spoke Zarathustra*). It may be, as Nehamas asserts in his discussion of the will to power, that "literary objects, and in particular, literary characters, are constituted simply as sets of features or effects that belong to no independent subjects."[14] But readers will seek an author behind these character-effects, and although we do not expect characters to attend to us, we do expect the author who addresses us to do so.

In life, self-fashioning works sometimes against, sometimes in concert with, antecedent conditions of family, environment, personality, and so on. Writing involves antecedent conditions of its own, having to do with the nature of the activity, the experience, origins, and place in the world of the writer as writer. Nehamas's understanding of Nietzsche's "aestheticism" has the effect of making his writerliness transparent to the concerns of philosophy; but it might be more helpful to say that by taking Nietzsche's writerliness fully into account we actually "clarify" the problems posed by his ideas by showing that they are more deeply problematic than philosophers have yet recognized.

In his concluding pages, Nehamas argues that Nietzsche "does not describe his ideal character, but he still does produce a perfect instance of it";[15] that the writings "exemplify the perfect instance of his ideal character";[16] and that "The character exemplified in Nietzsche's writing is so specific and idiosyncratic that all attempts to imitate it have so far produced only caricatures."[17] In what sense, we must wonder, can the unique character created and existing only in the writings also be an instance of an ideal? Is "perfect" just another way of saying "only possible" instance? And how can an "example" that defies all imitation "exemplify" anything?

The way that Nietzsche's "character" arises out of and is precisely equivalent to the writings calls into question idealization as decisively as the literary uniqueness of this character undercuts exemplification. Yet both these modes—idealization and exemplification—do unearned labor here to assimilate literariness to the preoccupations and intellectual habits of professional philosophers. There may well be some temptations to dismiss our objections as merely "rhetorical"; but Nehamas's rhetoric is the means by which the literary text is silently appropriated to aesthetics, the creation of a literary character is equated with the moral project of literal self-fashioning, and acts of interpretation are made to respond to the preoccupations of epistemology.

All this is not to say that Nehamas's fundamental insight—that literature may provide the most telling response to certain philosophical questions—is mistaken. Far from it. In fact, we envision the argument that follows (and those in preceding chapters) more as a complement to than as a rebuttal of Nehamas. Yet it does seem clear, from the critics' point of view, that, as a philosopher, Nehamas draws up short of cashing out his own insight. He does make philosophically interesting use of literary materials—or of ideas of the literary—in a manner unsurprising to modern critics; but then his aim is not to add to what literary people already know about literature. By the same token, de Man brings sophisticated techniques of literary analysis to bear on Nietzsche's writings, but seems to have little to say that philosophers find interesting or useful. Painfully aware of this intransitivity, de Man bleakly concludes that neither criticism nor philosophy can answer the other's questions; rather, being the closest of disciplines, they are doomed to remain the farthest apart.

It is by no means clear that such a conclusion is not simply a self-limiting effect of de Man's particular conception of his identity as critic. Or, more precisely, that it does not flow from the tendency to treat generic differences as natural kinds that result from subordinating of oneself to the requirements of a genre in order to write. But if we think of philosophy and literature as genres (or meta-genres), it makes no more (and no less) inherent sense to agonize over their differences than over the differences between comedy and tragedy. These literary genres reflect very different conceptions of our condition in the world. From within a tragedy, for example, the tragic conception of our difference from the world is definitive, yet the generic awareness of its own conventions also bespeaks a recognition that it is what it is by virtue of an arbitary-but-responsible hypostasis of an aspect of or perspective on a larger and more confused field of experience. That we can be absorbed in a genre, that we can even regard it as somehow deeper, does not preclude access to other genres, nor does it obscure the partiality which it shares with those genres. More to the point, real differences between genres do not prevent us from mixing them in productive ways, ways that make dialogue and commentary of one on the other possible, without requiring that they be "reconciled" by reducing the terms of one to those of the other.[18]

The multiplicity of genres, each presenting itself as "true within the limits of its partiality," does suggest a fragmentation of experience, but this fragmentation is plastic and tractable. That philosophy (arising out of the possibilities of idealization) and literary criticism (based on the possibilities of textualization) tend to treat their generic differences as differences in natural kinds, and to harden these differences in the institutional transformation of genres into disciplines, is itself a sign of the powerful hold that the conventions of these genres have on the imaginations of their practitioners. That hold, we suggest, can only be loosened by self-conscious experiments in genre-mixing.[19] It may also be the sign of a deep anxiety that, for some, fragmentation means incoherence. Despite the difficulties, however, a genuine and fruitful dialogue should be possible, especially in the case of Nietzsche, where both disciplines—literature and philosophy—can stake legitimate claims to the same body of work. For an example of how this might be achieved, we return to Nehamas, and the perennial question of Nietzsche's style.

Hyperbole and the Case of Eternal Recurrence

Like many critics before him, Nehamas celebrates Nietzsche's style as an integral part of the substance of his thought.[20] Of course, he also notes that philosophers are divided over just how that style is to be characterized. Nehamas feels that most philosophical commentators have focused on the aphorism as the essential stylistic feature in order to evade the question of style altogether. The far more obvious choice, Nehamas argues, is hyperbole, the trope of excess or exaggeration, which has largely been ignored because it is too unphilosophical to fit into any previous commentator's conception of philosophy or of a properly philosophical text.[21] Nehamas makes hyperbole philosophically respectable by pointing out that it is Nietzsche's response to the characteristically Socratic trope of litotes, or ironic understatement.[22] Thus the style becomes a way of perpetually articulating his difference from and of reinforcing his critique of the metaphysical tradition.

This is a clever and enlightening argument but it is hard for a literary critic to miss the fact that style has been rendered philosophical by slipping into a manner of speaking that treats it as the supplemental expression of a pre-existing, anti-metaphysical conviction.[23] However, Nehamas's argument could just as easily lead in another direction: to the conclusion that the thought is a retrospective rationalization of Nietzsche's practices as a writer. We might ask, for instance, what else could someone who writes like this possibly think about metaphysical unities? Nehamas faces up to the question of how Nietzsche's style should be characterized only to evade the still more challenging question of what the mode of style's integration with substance might be.

The question of whether writing motivates thought or thought writing is central not because we can sensibly expect to answer it in any definitive fashion, but because it helps to formulate the tension between philosophical and literary-critical treatments of the same text—and because pursuing the idea of thought generated out of writing represents an alternative approach to vexed problems. Accordingly, we would press Nehamas to extend his inquiry into the nature of hyperbole and so, we think, to grasp its larger significance in Nietzsche's thoughtful prose. Hyperbole is, of course, inflated language, and since what goes up must come down, it follows from this, deflated language as well. But hyperbole is not just the language of heights aspired to and depths fallen to, it is also the language of detours, of errancy, extravagance, and even errantry.

Harold Bloom's readings of Romantic poetry suggest that litotes and hyperbole become virtually interchangeable as a consequence of the perspectivism that attends the internalization of the quest romance.[24] And this internalized quest romance is the self-descriptive hyperbolic expansion of trope into text that defines the Romantic project. Exaggeration, extravagance, errancy, quest—synonymous with want of due proportion as error—hyperbole is also the excess that leads to quality, sublimity, greatness. Whether the attitude is pro or con, characterizations of the hyperbolic tend to imply the existence, at least in theory, of some proper rhetorical degree, proportionate to the occasion, which serves to limit or restrain the capacity of rhetoric, of writing, to spin meanings out of itself, moralizing it and making it "responsible." Romantic internalization brings with it a perspectivism which frees hyperbole and its text-making capacities from these restraints. What happens in Romantic poetry is also intended, if only after the fact, in Nietzsche's writings. His perspectivism befalls him; it is also grasped and exploited as an opportunity to arrive at a deeper understanding of hyperbole, to recognize that the occasion of writing (another way of saying its "justification") has no existence apart from the variety of its tendentious representations. Here, there is no benchmark or zero-degree common to all.

As the text-producing trope, hyperbole has been variously (though largely unconsciously) characterized by contemporary theorists as errancy (de Man), transgression (Foucault), dissemination (Derrida), and daemonization (Bloom).[25] In this larger context, Nehamas's argument opens the way for a reading of Nietzsche which would grasp that the unconscious autobiography (that every philosophy is) is, in Nietzsche's case, an extended meditation on the hyperbole that makes his text and his philosophy possible—and that the central ideas of eternal recurrence, will to power, the *Übermensch*, and perspectivism are all characterizations of that hyperbole, hyperboles themselves. Because these ideas serve the same function, it becomes possible for a book like *Thus Spoke Zarathustra*—an incarnation piece if ever there was one—to serve as a kind of "last" evanescence not just of the Romantic plot of quest romance, but of our culture's pre-eminent model of the transformation of trope into text, the gospelizing journeys of the New Testament.[26]

Such a reading does not replace more conventionally philosophical readings, but rather supplements them at precisely those points where philosophical discourse fails to connect satisfactorily with what Nietzsche wrote. This is far from a case of literary criticism riding to the rescue of philosophy. For literary critics and theorists have yet to grasp sufficiently that in their various ways, they are all characterizing hyperbole as the origin of the texts they interpret and of their own critical projects as well. An account of Nietzsche's philosophy that brings its involvement with hyperbole to the fore would make it that much easier for the criticisms that he has influenced to grasp their own natures; it might also make it possible, as we have tried to suggest, to approach the phenomenon of Romanticism, central to literary studies, in new and interesting ways.[27]

Given the range of traditions and modes of reading, we think that the best way to start a rewarding dialogue and to tease out its implications for both disciplines—philosophy and literary criticism—is to exploit the timeless simultaneity of a library in order to put a philosophically important Nietzschean text like "The Greatest Stress" (*GS* IV 341), in which the idea of eternal recurrence is introduced, next to a theoretically significant work of literature like Browning's "Childe Roland to the Dark Tower Came," which seems to have deep if elusive affinities with its counterpart, despite the fact that it was written thirty years earlier.

We have already addressed some of the philosophical questions entailed by eternal recurrence.[28] Now we are concerned with the question of how Nietzsche's influence on a literary critic might return to elucidate his philosophy. Bloom's major thesis is that the strong poet is distinguished from others by a greater rebellion against the necessity of death. Nietzsche's critique of asceticism inspires Bloom to construe all figuration as an expression of an "urge to be elsewhere"—that is, as essentially hyperbolic. In this context, then, as a figure of the *Übermensch*'s reconciliation with or celebration of life, eternal recurrence appears as a way to reconcile the urge to be elsewhere with the willingness to remain where one is. It resolves the conflict between desire and the desire not to desire that is the chief source of human misery. But then eternal recurrence involves us in a paradox, for being content with what is— eternally, recurrently—is the greatest conceivable difference from what is. Hence, if we assume that Nietzsche is urging us to aspire to affirm eternal recurrence, we might ask: What are we to desire, to stay the same or to be different? This is not just a problem of what eternal recurrence means, but of what purpose a rhetoric of transformation can serve or what it should look like on this radically new Nietzschean ground.

Uncannily, it is precisely this ground over which Browning's young knight, Roland, seems to travel on his quest to the Dark Tower. And the story of this quest represents the poet's attempt to invent a genealogy of sorts, to imagine the circumstances under which so ambiguous an affirmation would be both necessary and triumphant. In "The Greatest Stress," Nietzsche similarly contextualizes eternal recurrence, only he reduces his narrative to its culmination in a primal scene of instruction: an ultimate test. He asks: What if a demon were to sneak into your "loneliest loneliness" and suggest that every detail of your present life must return over and over again exactly as it is now? Would this not be the greatest stress, the severest test of your actions? And what kind of person would it take not only to endure this notion but to affirm it, to actually desire it to be so? Browning's poem begins with its own "demon":

> My first thought was, he lied in every word,
> That hoary cripple, with malicious eye
> Askance to watch the working of his lie
> On mine, and mouth scarce able to afford
> Suppression of the glee, that pursed and scored
> Its edge, at one more victim gained thereby.
>
> What else should he be set for, with his staff?
> What, save to waylay with his lies, ensnare
> All travelers who might find him posted there,
> And ask the road? I guessed what skull-like laugh
> Would break, what crutch 'gin write my epitaph
> For pastime in the dusty thoroughfare,
>
> If at his counsel I should turn aside
> Into that ominous tract which, all agree,
> Hides the Dark Tower. Yet acquiescingly
> I did turn as he pointed: neither pride

> Nor hope rekindling at the end descried,
> So much as gladness that some end might be.
>
> For, what with my whole world-wide wandering,
> What with my search drawn out through years, my hope
> Dwindled into a ghost not fit to cope
> With that obstreperous joy success would bring,
> I hardly tried now to rebuke the spring
> My heart made, finding failure in its scope.[29]

These lines thrust us at once into a play of perspectives as dizzying as any imagined by Nietzsche. Roland's loathing for the cripple is first and foremost the self-hatred of the Romantic quester, who can never live up to the intensities of his own desire, who knows and despises the futility of his perpetual urge to be elsewhere. Second, the cripple is the bizarre muse of the poetic solipsist, directing him to the site of the absolute he seeks and of absolute self-destruction. And finally, he is the stunted sensibility of the resentful world, delighting in seeing the stronger, better man wander onto the path of apparent self-destruction. For all of this, as it turns out, the cripple is Roland's true muse as well, whose "lie" consists in telling him what he already knows: this way lies the Dark Tower and his true path—except that it is by now apparent that for Roland at least, all paths lead to the Dark Tower.

The ambiguous nature of Nietzsche's demon reappears even more strongly here: is he challenging us to find our true selves or seducing us to the pursue one more impossible and inhumane ideal? Is he directing us toward or away from our "true" path? Juxtaposing the Browning and Nietzsche texts, we think, suggests a reading of "The Greatest Stress" far more ambivalent—indeed suggests that Nietzsche himself was far more ambivalent—about eternal recurrence than "philosophical" discussions are inclined to acknowledge. For Browning's conclusion seems to speak directly and in greater detail to something in Nietzsche's text:

> Burningly it came on me all at once,
> This was the place! those two hills on the right,
> Crouched like two bulls locked horn in horn in fight;
> While to the left, a tall scalped mountain . . . Dunce,
> Dotard, a-dozing at the very nonce,
> After a life spent training for the sight!
>
> What in the midst lay but the Tower itself?
> The round squat turret, blind as the fool's heart,
> Built of brown stone, without a counterpart
> In the whole world. The tempest's mocking elf
> Points to the shipman thus the unseen shelf
> He strikes on, only when the timbers start.
>
> Not see? because of night perhaps?—why, day
> Came back again for that! before it left,

> The dying sunset kindled through a cleft:
> The hills, like giants at a hunting, lay,
> Chin upon hand, to see the game at bay—
> "Now stab and end the creature—to the heft!"
>
> Not hear? when noise was everywhere! it tolled
> Increasing like a bell. Names in my ears
> Of all the lost adventurers my peers—
> How such a one was strong, and such was bold,
> And such was fortunate, yet each of old
> Lost, lost! one moment knelled the woe of years.
>
> There they stood, ranged along the hillsides, met
> To view the last of me, a living frame
> For one more picture! in a sheet of flame
> I saw them and I knew them all. And yet
> Dauntless the slug-horn to my lips I set,
> And blew. "Childe Roland to the Dark Tower came."[30]

In the end, Roland's quest brings him to exactly where each of his precursors came and gives him up to the same ultimate defeat. The poetry aims to convey a sense of the revelatory force of a transformation which consists simply in seeing what is, what has by implication always been and ever will be. But Roland is not just seeing. He is also accepting, even embracing his membership in the band of "failures." This is not all. The difference between accepting and affirming, the difference that Nietzsche's demon stresses and which gives eternal recurrence its positive promise and seductive appeal, comes down to that single concluding utterance: "Childe Roland to the Dark Tower came."

A first, visceral response is that this is a heroic assertion of self in what little space fate leaves the individual. But that this utterance is the title of the poem suggests that the most Roland can do is now to assert what before he merely endured. Beyond even this, the title is not Browning's. It is a quotation from *King Lear*, another great work about what remains; and not even Roland's name is his own, it belongs to Edgar. Roland's victory, his difference, now comes down to the power to put this phrase, his poem, his quest within quotation marks. Each of these possibilities is less a potential interpretation of what eternal recurrence means than it is a mode in which it could conceivably be spoken. The last possibility is the most obscure but it also seems to correspond most closely to whatever it is that conceivably makes it worthwhile to assert the eternal sameness of things.

At this point, the notion of eternal recurrence becomes of particular interest to the critic because the power to put things in quotes is essentially the critic's power and challenge—always to find a way to speak through the words of others. Eternal recurrence begins from a critical perspective to look less like a prerequisite to the mastery of life than to the mastery of texts, suggesting in turn that this mastery is all that Nietzsche thinks we can expect to master of life.

Lest this seem overly fanciful, let us back-track to comment on one more element of Browning's concluding stanzas: Roland likens his sudden discovery that he has arrived at the Dark Tower to the way in which a trap is only noticed too late, when it is springing shut behind. In this moment, Roland also realizes that he has already been seeing and hearing for some time—maybe all along—what he only now notices. Nor is this the first such occurrence in the poem. When he first turns from the main road to follow the path pointed out by the cripple, Roland suddenly finds himself on a barren and seemingly endless plain. The path back has disappeared entirely. Similarly, he finds himself in the hills without ever seeing the end of the plain. One moment he is on its endless expanse, the next he is in the hills with no visible way to retrace his steps.

These sudden discontinuities, these radical shifts in perspective, describe the very sensation suggested when Nietzsche's demon infects his audience with the idea of eternal return. The immediate effect of the idea, perhaps its major function, is to bring about such a radical and vertiginous shift in perspective. As we have already noted, the plot of Browning's poem, the internalized quest romance, is fundamental to Romanticism. The wandering of the quester and the difficulty of distinguishing errantry from error make it the generating hyperbole behind Romantic poetry. In the case of Childe Roland, his quest after the name he desires is transformed in the end into a quest to desire the name he has already been given—not an inappropriate description of the challenge posed by eternal recurrence to inheritors, Nietzsche included, of the ascetic tradition.

In a more general sense, the discontinuities that figure so prominently in "Childe Roland to the Dark Tower Came" dramatize the discontinuous leaps, the hyperboles, by which tropes become texts, and by means of which the author and reader alike are entangled in the created text, committed to an unfolding project that may or may not be what either thinks or desires. In this context, eternal recurrence describes something like a definition of the ideal author as someone with the strength to affirm whatever that s/he has written, the strength, that is, to "intend" and even desire it after the fact.

Nehamas approaches this view when he says of "How One Becomes What One Is":

The creation of the self therefore appears to be the creation, or imposition, of a higher-order accord among our lower-level thoughts, desires, and actions. It is the development of the ability, or the willingness, to accept responsibility for everything that we have done and to admit what is in any case true: that everything that we have done actually constitutes who each of us is.[31]

For the Nietzsche of "The Greatest Stress," it is not enough to take responsibility for—to accept that we are the sum of—our actions. He is less concerned with the social virtue of responsibility than with the more intimate ("your loneliest loneliness") challenge of wanting unconditionally what is the case. Acceptance is not enough. The challenge posed by the idea of eternal recurrence can only be met by positive desire. The moralism implicit in the term "responsibility," the idea of instituting an internal hierarchy, the mature acceptance of what is in any case true—all point to the establishment of a sense of proportion as the sign of the self's necessary accession to the reality principle, almost as if reality and reason were one and the same. But the idea of eternal recurrence is not about proportion; its whole emphasis is on disproportionate acceptance, acceptance with a vengeance so extreme that the terrifying power of what is is subverted in a hyperbolic leap from resignation to desire, and an unexpected power is revealed ("You are a god, and never have I heard anything more godly").

Beyond this, there is another, more subtle difference between Nehamas's formulation and ours. In Browning's poem, the challenge of self-recognition and acceptance is posed and met in the specific context of his vocation as a poet struggling to write both in and against the Romantic tradition. It is as part of his vocation and of his tradition that Browning assumes that there is a special relationship between the activity of writing and the challenge of self-fashioning. Similarly, Nietzsche calls attention to his writing so consistently and, in *Thus Spoke Zarathustra*, explores the complexities of becoming what one is at such length and with such self-conscious literariness, precisely in order to question the relationship between what one is, does, and can do as a writer, and as a person. This kind of retrospective self-fashioning, achieving a sense of one's own inevitability ("I am a destiny") through an act of acceptance may well be more characteristic of the act of text-making than of literal "selfhood." Or, to put it more bluntly, what is essential to the author may be monstrous in the person—a suspicion reflected in a long tradition associating authorship with the daemonic, divine, or simply mad. The insistence with which Nietzsche calls attention to his writerliness—and, we might add, the conclusion to *Thus Spoke Zarathustra*—suggest his sense that the "life" derives its reality from the inevitability of the "work" rather than vice versa. Or, we might say, the relationship between what one is as a writer and what one is as a person remains uncertain.

Nietzsche's extravagant exploitation in *Thus Spoke Zarathustra* of the resources of fiction is significant in this regard. Fiction-making, as Socrates well knew in inveighing against myth, is inherently problematic; it can never be merely illustrative or exemplary. By making *Thus Spoke Zarathustra* a fiction, Nietzsche extends this problematic to writing, even "philosophical" writing, itself. One of the things that makes the book so difficult and distinctive is the way in which Nietzsche plays off and undercuts a biblical tradition of parable and story that "uses" the resources of fiction for illustrative purposes by means of a more modern, hyperbolic literary tradition, in which fictional worlds and characters achieve a kind of reality, a self-justifying self-sameness that resists reduction.[32] In consequence, Nietzsche continually tempts readers to see the message or meaning for which Zarathustra is merely the vehicle. And yet this meaning remains elusive, for Zarathustra, insisting on his uniqueness, refuses to be reduced to an exemplum. Nehamas argues that "Nietzsche" is a creation of the writings and is equal to the sum of these. Although he knows that Nietzsche does not assert a program for becoming what one is, he nevertheless seems to equate what happens in writing with a possibility of "life," in effect, to write as if lessons for life could be derived from the practices and achievements of writing.[33] Yet this is what is most problematical for Nietzsche, who knows and even exploits the fact that writing gives this appearance, but is far less certain than Nehamas appears to be about what this means, or how it can legitimately be used.

In contrast, we are suggesting that the "experience" on which Nietzsche draws in formulating his philosophy is, at least in part, the experience of writing and that it therefore deserves, as much as Socrates or Schopenhauer or the metaphysical tradition in general, to be studied by philosophers as "the origin" of Nietzsche's "ideas." What we are *not* doing is making the glib assertion that Nietzsche's philosophy refers *only* to its own textual condition. For one thing, Nietzsche conceived of himself as a philosopher, or at least an anti-philosopher, and even he was tempted at times to think that eternal recurrence might describe an actual cosmology.[34] We make, instead, the more modest claim that, in some cases at least, philosophy cannot answer its own questions within narrow disciplinary limits. Likewise, the literary critic cannot grasp the interrelation of reading and writing without at least taking into account the fantasy of escape from textuality which philosophy provides.

The (De)composition of Philosophy

In "On the Vision and the Riddle" and "The Convalescent," Nietzsche's most extended treatment of the theme of eternal recurrence—we find a veritable encyclopedia of Romantic representations of the hyperboles generating texts. Here we have the figure of the Romantic quester, who has come far and wants to go farther, who does not like to live without danger. Such a quester himself, Zarathustra addresses his vision to his fellow voyagers: "bold searchers, researchers, and whoever embarks with cunning sails on terrible seas . . ." (Z III "VR" 1). In the vision-quest, the outward movement of the voyage is complemented by the upward, transcending movement of the mountain climb. The would-be voyager is restrained by the fear of leaving home, of becoming lost, and above all of drowning; the would-be climber is shadowed by the fear of falling, which Nietzsche internalizes, á la Browning, in the form of the dwarf who embodies the "spirit of gravity," which threatens to draw him downward into an abyss.

The "leaden thoughts" with which the dwarf mocks him and which threaten to bring his climb to a halt are of the philosopher as a hyperbolist and as a hyperbole himself: a thrower of stones, a thrown stone, a self-thrown stone. As such, however high he throws or is thrown, he must fall, the higher, the farther and harder. Not only that, but insofar as the stone is also the creation or result of his hyperbole, he risks being crushed under its (his own) fall. This play of perspectives, reminiscent, now, of Childe Roland's dilemma, may (if our generic analogy holds) represent the demands of Nietzsche's philosophical task. We may imagine the hyperbole working in this way: the author must overcome the "spirit of gravity," in order to write. Hence, metaphorically, we might say that the "author" both throws and is thrown by philosophy as Nietzsche both writes and is written by his own unfolding text.

Wordsworth, out for his morning walk in "Resolution and Independence," also struggles to cope with a fear of falling: "But as it sometimes chanceth, from the might / Of joy in minds that can no farther go, / As high as we have mounted in delight / In our dejection do we sink as low."[35] Wordsworth frequently composed aloud on his walks, just as Nietzsche frequently wrote notes, later assembled into books, on his walks in the country. Not unlike "On the Vision and the Riddle" (itself a digressive-yet-central wandering from the main line of Zarathustra's story), Wordsworth's poem (an account of a walk) is an instance of hyperbolic wandering, and can likewise be understood as an attempt to come to terms with the anxieties that attend the act of composition.

Indeed, whether writing (the hyperbole of text-making) is seen as a voyage, a quest, a climb, or just a walk in the country, it seems to be attended by anxiety. But concerning what? Nietzsche, of course, emphasizes more dramatic and self-dramatizing images of hyperbole, implying more catastrophic dangers; but, we suggest, this device only intensifies awareness of the hyperbolic itself. And what of the lowly walk? Where is the risk there? Thoreau remarks: "If you are ready to leave father and mother, and brother and sister, and wife and child and friends, and never see them again—if you have paid your debts, and made your will, and settled all your affairs and are a free man, then you are ready for a walk."[36]

In Wordsworth's case, his sense of sharing in a natural enjoyment of life is shadowed and subverted by "fears and fancies thick," "Dim sadness—and blind thoughts" that slowly resolve themselves into the recognition that "there may come another day to me—/ Solitude, pain of heart, distress, and poverty."[37] Even worse, this possibility may be intimately related to his vocation:

> I thought of Chatterton, the marvellous Boy,
> The sleepless Soul that perished in his pride;
> Of him who walked in glory and in joy
> Following his plow, along the mountain-side:
> By our own spirits are we deified:
> We poets in our youth begin in gladness;
> But thereof come in the end despondency and madness.[38]

His fear that the sense of well-being that attends his enjoyment of the natural world is a dangerous illusion cloaks the even deeper fear that the satisfactions associated with writing—the "might" of poetry—are similarly illusions obscuring the remorseless degeneration of the writer's solitude into solipsism. Wordsworth reflects:

> My whole life I have lived in pleasant thought,
> As if life's business were a summer Mood;
> As if all needful things would come unsought
> To genial faith, still rich in genial good;
> But how can he expect that others should
> Build for him, sow for him, and at his call
> Love him, who for himself will take no heed at all?[39]

Here, the poet is alone and vulnerable. Even the solitude that writing/walking requires threatens to become impossible; and there is danger, too, that solitude, once achieved, may deepen into solipsism. Just as the climber fears a height from which descent is impossible, so here the walker/writer experiences an apposite fear of wandering so far that a path back to the world will be forever lost. And the poet fears that the world, whose necessary and sustaining work goes on all this while, is unconcerned about and unhelped by the poetic enterprise. The last three lines in particular express Wordsworth's sense of the poet as "free-loader"; we sense the anxiety that he will be noticed (like Chatterton) and found equally dispensable. There is the underlying figure of the tormented poet: alone, mad—rejected by the world. What, if any, relation can there be—or ought there be—between the poet's work and the world?

In this mood, Wordsworth encounters the leech-gatherer who, bent with age, pursues his lowly occupation alone and exposed to the harsh elements of the moor. Despite the "apt admonishment" provided by his example, Wordsworth tells us:

> My former thoughts returned: the fear that kills;
> And hope that is unwilling to be fed;
> Cold, pain, and labour, and all fleshly ills;
> And mighty poets in their misery dead.
> —Perplexed, and longing to be comforted,
> My question eagerly did I renew,
> "How is it that you live, and what is it you do?"

> He with a smile did then his words repeat;
> And said that, gathering leeches, far and wide
> He travelled; stirring thus about his feet
> The waters of the pools where they abide,
> "Once I could meet with them on every side;
> But they have dwindled long by slow decay;
> Yet still I persevere, and find them where I may."[40]

In other words, the old man doesn't understand the question! He answers a metaphysical question ("How do you live?") with literal precision. Not only do the poet and the leech-gatherer not speak the same language, they do not even occupy the same landscape: the poet's is imbued with visionary significance, while the old man's is hard and prosaic. In fact, the poet's landscape is discourse, writing, the text that throws up such questions. Similarly, the visionary landscape over which Zarathustra walks (and as we divine it in our hyperbolic leap, the answer to his riddle)[41] is that of literary composition. Indeed, we suggest, the corrosive strength of Nietzsche's skepticism—the thoroughness of his critique of philosophy, morality, religion and the thoroughness of his self-examination—depend on his ability to find his "reality" and to ground himself in that "reality" of writing. It is here, in the solitary voice and vice that he imagines the act and the sameness to difference from other acts that makes the imaginary creation/destruction moral, carrying it (and all with it) beyond good and evil.

In the end, the chasm that opens between Wordsworth's poet and the leech-gatherer is closed, or leapt over, fortuitously. The old man's last words, about the declining number of leeches and his perseverance in finding them where he may, touch on Wordsworth's own anxiety about the decline of his imaginative power and the increasingly elusive possibilities of imagination—a convergence that allows Wordsworth to see his anxiety and his burdened solitariness, not as unique conditions of his writerly vocation, but as common to humanity. This in turn reinstitutes the possibility of the turning away from the world required by composition.

Like the laugh of Nietzsche's shepherd, the imagined laugh of Wordsworth's "traveller" ("I could have laughed myself to scorn")[42] signals a reaction against fear, a return of confidence in the world out of which writing flows. In *Zarathustra*, the emphasis, more on "thrownness" than solitude, suggests a "fear of falling," of letdown or failure. The "spirit of gravity," antithetically characterized by the spirit of gaiety or laughter as dis/ease, is a down-dragging or holding back. The world in general, with its weight of the accumulated past (tradition, worn expectations) gives the stamp of objectivity to self-doubt and tempts the would-be quester to think that nothing worth doing remains to be done.

Zarathustra's protest ("Dwarf, it is you or I!") against the "spirit of gravity," which may also be a characterization of writing, is similarly hyperbolic; we see this aspect of the work in Zarathustra's awareness that "in every attack there is playing and brass" (Z III "VR" 1). In "Resolution and Independence," a sense that poetry lacks an authentic relationship to the world tempts the poet to an anxious flight from writing. Here, a sense of being ungrounded—unjustified, inauthentic—makes it possible to attack. Paradoxically, this sense of un-groundedness, which is a source of anxiety and guilt, is also a source of free-dom and transformation. Courage emerges, and this courage (as Zarathustra knows it) "slays even death itself." Implicitly, the death before which the imag-ination may otherwise stand helpless as before an absolute limit, with its cry ("Was that life? well then! once more!") functions in "On the Vision and the Riddle" in much the same way as the horn-blast in "Childe Roland" and, now, as the thought "of the leech-gatherer on the lonely moor!"[43] in Wordsworth's poem.

Returning to Nietzsche's presentation of eternal recurrence, we see, then, an apposite affirmation of what it takes—in writing—to lift the burden of the past. With a recognition quite like that shared by Childe Roland and Words-worth's poet, Zarathustra confronts the dwarf, and in so doing transcends the abyss itself of his "abysmal" thought. We might say that the idea of eternal recurrence inoculates in a "kill or cure" fashion against the disease of belated-ness. Zarathustra overcomes the overwhelming otherness of the world, with its legions of precursor poets and prophets, with a more-than-equal assertion of the unconditional nature of his own desire.

Zarathustra proceeds to describe a gateway with two faces, labeled "Mo-ment": "Two paths meet here; no one has yet followed either to its end. This long lane stretches back for an eternity. And the long lane out there, that is another eternity. They contradict each other, these paths; they offend each other face to face; and it is here at this gateway that they come together" (Z III "VR" 2). This face to face affronting parallels Zarathustra's confrontation with the dwarf (or conflicted consciousness). Like past and future, they are two faces of the same moment, eternally in contradiction and yet eternally the same:

> But whoever would follow one of them, on and on, farther and farther—do you believe, dwarf that these two paths contradict each other eternally?
> "All that is straight lies," the dwarf murmured contemptuously. "All truth is crooked; time itself is a circle."
> "You spirit of gravity," I said angrily, "do not make things too easy for yourself! Or I shall let you crouch where you are crouching, lamefoot and it was I that carried you to this height." (Z III "VR" 2)

The relationship between Zarathustra and his dwarf has been subtly al-tered; he is no longer the burden that Zarathustra carries but the eternal contradiction that Zarathustra must confront. To Zarathustra's "abysmal" idea the dwarf responds matter of factly; the earlier sense of momentousness is no more. "Of course," Zarathustra says, "truth is crooked; time itself is a circle," and now the dwarf is suddenly the obtuse one. It may be, too, that even maliciously reductive readers (including the reader within) exhibits, from the writer's point of view, the same obtuseness. Be that as it may (and there is plenty of room for interpretive variety here), we as readers might respond to the writer's hyperbole with his own litotes: an ironic, even parodic reduction. Zarathustra reacts angrily to the way the dwarf/reader takes for granted the heights to which he has been carried, calls him "lamefoot," reminding him and the reader of Oedipus, who as much as anyone ever born of the writer's pen carried the burden of the world-as-past. But this relationship between Zarathustra and his dwarf is even more fundamentally an internal one, in which past/reader and future/writer confront and contradict each other eternally in the moving moment of composition, in the perpetual face-off between a litotic shrinking from the world and a hyperbolic expansion toward it. This is the most abysmal thought of all, that Zarathustra's thought and the dwarf's abyss are one and the same, that the questing movement of writing—its pressing forward—implies no special resolution or goal, that writing and the disease it seeks to "cure" are identical.[44]

At this point, Zarathustra seems perilously close to throwing himself into the abyss to which the dwarf had failed to lure him: "Thus I spoke, more and more softly; for I was afraid of my own thoughts and the thoughts behind my thoughts." (Z III "VR" 2). At this moment, a dog's howling intrudes on Zarathustra's thoughts, drawing him back to childhood, tempting him to pity. Now, like Roland, Zarathustra finds himself on the verge of decision, confronted by yet another version of the "cry of distress.":

> A young shepherd I saw, writhing, gagging in spasms, his face distorted, and a heavy black snake hung out of his mouth. Had I ever seen such nausea and pale dread on one face? He seemed to have been asleep when the snake crawled into his throat, and there bit itself fast. My hand tore at the snake and tore in vain; it did not tear the snake out of his throat. Then it cried out of me: "Bite! Bite its head off! Bite!" Thus it cried out of me—my dread, my hatred, my nausea, my pity, all that is good and wicked in me cried out of me with a single cry. (Z III "VR" 2)

Again and again we fall asleep to awaken choking on life, choking on sameness, inevitability, limitation, the weight of "is," and, unless we are to acquiesce to the whine-without-surcease of self-pity, over and over again we must bite that bite. It will do no good to tear it out; we must bite into and through what most nauseates us.

In terms of the logic we have been developing in this chapter (construing Nietzsche's philosophy as, at least in part, one of composition) this biting is a trope for getting started. Something like this seems, indeed, acknowledged ("all that is good and wicked") in the ambiguity of the sequence. But here getting started is not a unique moment in which a decision is made once and never again. Rather, difficulties and complexities of composition recur at every moment of writing. When the shepherd does bite, he is transformed, no longer human, laughing as no one on earth has yet laughed.[45] This implies that this *über*sheperd is just that, an ideal or goal of the writer's desire, namely, freedom, a final release from the burden of composition. Yet to the very end of *Thus Spoke Zarathustra*, the *Übermensch* remains a distant possibility, a hope beyond the grasp even of Zarathustra, who is the shepherd only insofar as he displays the writer's capacity to write beyond intention, to say more and better than he means. This hyperbolic capacity of the writer goes hand in hand with a characteristic suspicion that this improved meaning perpetually recedes into the future, as we, with commensurate perseverance, pursue it.

Later, in "The Convalescent," Zarathustra is himself in the position of the shepherd and we now hear of his transformation "from within," as it were. If much of "On The Vision and the Riddle" is concerned with the fear of hyperbolic excess, "The Convalescent" seems to focus on the complementary fear of not wandering far enough. What if the hyperbolic cast of the philosopher's stone falls short? Hence, Zarathustra tells his animals:

> "The great disgust with man—*this* choked me and had crawled into my throat; and what the soothsayer said: 'All is the same, nothing is worth while, knowledge chokes.' . . . 'Eternally recurs the man of whom you are weary, the small man—. . .'
>
> "Naked I had once seen both, the greatest man and the smallest man: all-too-similar to each other, even the greatest all-too-human. All-too-small, the greatest!—that was my disgust with man. And the eternal recurrence even of the smallest—that was my disgust with all existence. Alas! Nausea! Nausea! Nausea!" (Z III "Convalescent" 2)

Now, all of his knowledge and acumen has led Zarathustra to this choking sense of appalling sameness. It seems that the difference between the greatest and the smallest, even the greatest and smallest in himself amounts to nothing. Besides, with all its human diminutiveness, humanity must recur eternally. In this crisis, Zarathustra comes face to face with the desire that drives him to cast beyond humanity's diminutive stature, to cast beyond himself. And yet this would not seem possible.

Self-recrimination sets in, and each accusation reinforces the notion that there is another, better ("true") humanity to replace the small ("apparent") forerunner: "The small man, especially the poet—how eagerly he accuses life with words! Hear him, but do not fail to hear the delight that is in all accusation. Such accusers of life—life overcomes with a wink. 'Do you love me?' she says impudently. 'Wait a little while, just yet I have no time for you!'" (Z III "Convalescent" 2). The small man (like "the great man," the poet, anyone who writes, perhaps?) accuses life with words. How can the choice to write not be a wish to be elsewhere and how can the wish to be elsewhere not accuse the life that is? But these accusations are expressions of desire. Life knows that small creatures accuse her in order to build themselves up to be worthy of her. She knows that their real complaint is not that life is unworthy of them but that she does not love them enough. And why should she?

It appears that Zarathustra's crisis turns on Nietzsche's doubts about the writerly vocation. How small a difference is there between Zarathustra and these accusers of life in words? But this concern is not just another accusation against life. Zarathustra recognizes a terrible truth: "Alas, my animals, only this have I learned so far, that man needs what is most evil in him for what is best in him—that whatever is most evil is his best power and the hardest stone for the highest creator; and that man must become better and more evil" (Z III "Convalescent" 2). The problem is not that our nature is mixed and contradictory, but that we are so small, our evils too petty to fuel a corresponding greatness. The hyperboles by which we accuse each other, ourselves, and "life," are too small.

But after awakening from his sleep of seven days, Zarathustra sees the situation differently. The difference between smallest and greatest has increased: "To every soul there belongs another world; for every soul, every other soul is an after world. Precisely between what is most similar, illusion lies most beautifully; for the smallest cleft is the hardest to bridge" (Z III "Convalescent 2). And furthermore, "How lovely it is that there are words and sounds! Are not words and sounds rainbows and illusive bridges between things which are eternally apart?" Does this mean that the essential sameness of smallest and greatest is itself an illusion of language? an illusion of the same kind as thinking that there is an "outside"?:

> For me—how should there be any outside-myself? There is no outside. But all sounds make us forget this; how lovely it is that we forget. Have not names and sounds been given to things that man might find things refreshing? Speaking is a beautiful folly: with that man dances over all things. How lovely is all talking, and all the deception of sounds! With sounds our love dances on many-hued rainbows. (Z III "Convalescent" 2)

In language, the outside rises from within, the difference an illusion that stems from the casting-away-from-the-self of utterance. The refreshing otherness and newness of the world is a creation of language, which dances over all things. The movement of writing is a dance, a glossing over the abysses, a movement which defies "the spirit of gravity." It is not aimed at anything so much as it performs itself. Indeed, only when it is aimed does it accuse, becoming the morass Zarathustra envisions in his despair.

In "Resolution and Independence," Wordsworth suffers from an anxiety that his poetic vocation is entirely unjustified in the terms of the world in which the poet must live. But the attitude behind Wordsworth's self accusation ("how can he expect that others should / Build for him, sow for him, and at his call / Love him, who for himself will take no heed at all?")[46] Zarathustra knows to be just one side of the coin whose reverse accuses life for not caring enough about "mighty poets in their misery dead."[47] Zarathustra's poet is more "philosophical" in blaming life for the failure of the project of knowledge that leaves his vocation unjustified. He misjudges what such a justification might look, or rather feel, like in the same kind of mistake he makes in playing the moralist when what is required is a lover, perhaps even a seducer. By contrast, the dancer's lightness depends implicitly on an aesthetic "justification" (if the word itself is not too moralistic) of the writer's work, which is to say on the values that arise from or attach themselves spontaneously to its performance.

Zarathustra's animals seem to "understand" instantly and, as it turns out, too easily, what he is saying:

> "O Zarathustra," the animals said, "to those who think as we do, all things themselves are dancing: they come and offer their hands and laugh and flee—and come back. Everything goes, everything comes back; eternally rolls the wheel of being. Everything dies, everything blossoms again; eternally runs the year of being. Everything breaks, everything is joined anew; eternally the same house of being is being built. Everything parts, everything greets every other thing again; eternally the ring of being remains faithful to itself. In every Now, being begins; round every Here rolls the sphere There. The center is everywhere. Bent is the path of eternity." (Z III "Convalescent" 2)

The animals treat eternal recurrence as true empirical description, as wisdom and cosmology, as the basis of confidence. Zarathustra's response is mixed:

> "O you buffoons and barrel organs!" Zarathustra replied and smiled again. "How well you know what had to be fulfilled in seven days, and how that monster crawled down my throat and suffocated me. But I bit off its head and spewed it out. And you, have you already made a hurdy-gurdy song of this?" (Z III "Convalescent" 2)

That is, this animal, healthy, sensible understanding is not what Zarathustra wants; it seems trivial and complacent, leaving out precisely the sense of struggle and crisis, precisely what it is to be Zarathustra, and to write. For "The Convalescent" does turn on the difference between speaking/singing/dancing and accusing life with words, between two aspects of writing as narrowly (and widely) separated as the smallest and the greatest human beings. There is a writing that dances over life, performing itself, and there is a writing that addresses life, falling willy nilly into accusation, that falls into the abysses that lie in wait. The animals urge Zarathustra to fashion a new lyre, which is to say they urge him to write in this other way, to teach eternal recurrence. But Zarathustra is turned inward upon himself, conversing with his soul; he turns away from his audience, allowing them their use of his words but evading the terms of their understanding and refusing their implicit claims of identity with him.

Thus Spoke Zarathustra:
The Envoi and the Problem of Being

From "The Greatest Stress," "On the Vision and the Riddle," and "The Convalescent," eternal recurrence emerges ambiguously both as concept and as enabling rhetoric, as self-descriptive and therapeutic. The connection between these functions seems related to a certain confidence that the writer's satisfying performance of the writerly task has salutary effects on readers, that the writer's withdrawal into the self and communication with others need not be perpetually at odds. On the contrary, by pleasing himself, Zarathustra can save others. Yet Zarathustra's indifference, even hostility, toward what others make of his speeches in their attempts to understand and put them to use calls this possibility into doubt and puts the question of the relationship between work and world at the center of Nietzsche's own project in *Thus Spoke Zarathustra*. Nietzsche challenges his auditors' grasp of eternal recurrence less in terms of concept than of sensation; that is, true understanding is indicated by the tenor of the emotional response. This emphasis on eternal recurrence as sensation is clearly related to Zarathustra's preference for "leapers," those whose interpretations display appropriate powers of divination.

In *The Marriage of Heaven and Hell*, his most "Nietzschean" work, Blake recounts the following "Memorable Fancy":

> The prophets Isaiah and Ezekiel dined with me, and I asked them how they dared so roundly to assert. that God spake to them; and whether they did not think at the time, that they would be misunderstood, and so be the cause of imposition.
>
> Isaiah answered. I saw no God. nor heard any, in a finite organical perception; but my senses discover'd the infinite in everything, and I was then perswaded. and remain confirm'd; that the voice of honest indignation is the voice of God, I cared not for consequences but wrote.
>
> Then I asked: does a firm perswasion that a thing is so. make it so?
>
> He replied. All poets believe that it does, and in ages of imagination this firm perswasion removed mountains; but many are not capable of a firm perswasion of anything.[48] (Plate 12)

At first, Blake's compound question seems epistemological (how could *one* know for sure?) and moral (one's words can be perverted into the oppressive Christianity that one is even now condemning?). But the end of the second paragraph ("I cared not for consequences but wrote") makes clear that these are also questions about writing prophetically, about what it takes to write and, specifically, about what doubts (legitimate to "normal" people) must be overcome in order to begin.

It is not that Isaiah saw anything in particular, certainly not a finite organical perception of God, but that he felt differently ("perswaded") on the basis of a new and intensified experience of his senses. ("My senses discover'd the infinite in everything.") Revelation comes not as an alternative to the senses (as in the blind Milton's "insight"),[49] as something "spiritual," but as their intensification, rising from within as much as entering from without. The prophet is persuaded that his own voice, the hyperbolic rise and expansion of honest indignation, is the voice of God. The prophet *feels*—and this is the sign of his election—that what he has to say is what God wants said.

Blake's next question focuses on the heart of Isaiah's speech and speaks for every frustrated reader of a divinatory interpreter: "does a firm perswasion that a thing is so make it so?" How can I tell prophecy (or divination) from fanaticism or delusion, how can I keep from being imposed on? Blake's pitiless answer is, of course, "you can't—except by becoming a prophet yourself (Moses's remark "Would to God that all the Lords people were prophets" is the epigraph to Blake's *Milton*). But to make "perswasion" answerable to the reader would be to make it other than it is, and render writing impossible. This "firm perswasion" brings with it the conviction that, appearances to the contrary, the prophet has never been truly persuaded of *anything* before. Writing in the voice of God, which is also the prophet's voice, makes Blake aware that he has never before spoken his own mind or meant what he said. The moment of this "firm perswasion" operates like one of those invisible thresholds that Childe Roland repeatedly crosses. In that moment, the prophet, recognizing that previous intentions were in some measure falsified, realizes that all previous moments of apparent conviction were actually shadowed by doubt, hesitation, and fear, that is, were marked by the uncertainty endemic to communication in everyday life. Blake links the power to mean what we say with poetry's dream of achieving a fundamental alliance with divine or natural power. The self-sameness expressed in the notion of "firm perswasion" not only refers to what is necessary to inception, it also speaks in its exclusivity to the dream of originality—the poet's desire for a satisfaction unique to him, answering to and confirming his innermost self.

We can argue, then, that this passage is self-referential for Blake's writing in something like the same sense that the passages on eternal recurrence are self-referential for Nietzsche's writing. Yet Nietzsche is not the visionary literalist that Blake is. For instance, even though Blake has Isaiah say that he does not literally see or hear God, Blake himself insisted on the literal reality of more than one conversation with the dead, such as the one he "records" here. For Blake, even his irony is enfolded in visionary literalism, and his conviction that only prophets are capable of truly meaning what they say poses a formidable challenge to readers without divinatory powers, those who might wish to read figuratively Blake's claim that an angel came down and sat in a tree in his garden at Felpham. But figural reading is, for Blake, a sign of our inner division, a consequence of *our* inability to mean what *we* say.

For Nietzsche, the "firm perswasion" necessary for beginning is not literal but hyperbolic—it can only be written not underwritten. The challenge he poses is not to our tendency to respond with interpretation where conviction is called for but to our desire to believe that *somewhere* intention accords with what a writer says. Blake may give the sometimes unpleasant feeling that he really means what he says; Nietzsche gives the sense that he *never* quite means what he says. This difference may stem from their very different treatments of asceticism. Blake's "firm perswasion" functions as a kind of alternative to asceticism as the origin of meaning and of belief in the reality of the desired. Blake's prophets practice asceticism not in order to create the possibility of their belief but as a visible extension of their persuasion. Asceticism is not a sign of their reaching after the spiritual so much as a consequence of its presence:

> I also asked Isaiah what made him go naked and barefoot three years? he answered, the same that made our friend Diogenes the Grecian.
> I then asked Ezekiel. why he eat dung, and lay so long on his right and left side? he answered. the desire of raising other men into a perception of the infinite this the North American tribes practise. and is he honest who resists his genius or conscience. only for the sake of present ease or gratification?[50]

For Blake, the ascetic behavior of the prophets is a proof that they mean what they say—the apparent ridiculousness and incomprehensibility of the inspired man's behavior is a measure of his self-acceptance that indicates the absence of the embarrassment that usually attends our inner uncertainty. For Nietzsche, asceticism—at least Christian asceticism—is a reaching after what (for the very reason of our reaching) we do not have, which must also serve as a confirmation of the fact that we have it (as a consequence of our willingness to give up the substance we do have in order to get it).

A writer who means exactly what he or she says is as unreadable as one who never means what he or she says. (What would such writing look like?) We cannot help but respond as if Blake and Nietzsche alike were playing a part, making a point with theatrical flourish. Finally, what emerges from Zarathustra's divinations as from Blake's vision is a certain space of reserve, a solipsism which turns away from the reader as if jealously to internalize the origin of writing. This solipsism is very much at issue in deciding exactly what is "meant" by *Thus Spoke Zarathustra*, a work in which the gap between the writer's and the reader's versions of the text may yawn widest at the beginning and at the end.

Commentators have found the subtitle of *Thus Spoke Zarathustra*, "A Book for All and None," a particular focus of contention. In her fine book *Nietzsche's*

Zarathustra, Kathleen Higgins reviews the debate and makes her own distinctive contribution. She begins by pointing out that Heidegger tries, in effect, to make both terms of the paradox mean "for a few"; that is, for everyone, but only at such times as his other "essential nature becomes . . . an object worthy of his thought," and for none except those who are not aiming merely to "intoxicate themselves with isolated fragments and particular aphorisms from his work."[51] On the contrary, Higgins argues that "the book is for all" in a "not deeply problematic" sense: "books written for publication address an unspecified general public. Nietzsche's book is 'for all' in the same sense that Zarathustra speaks 'to all' at the beginning of the Prologue."[52] The real problem comes in deciding in what sense the book is "for none." A possible answer, Higgins suggests, is provided by "Nietzsche's inclusion of sections that present Zarathustra's introspective meditations, sections which, like those that report Zarathustra's speeches, conclude with the refrain, 'Thus spoke Zarathustra.' Not all Zarathustra's speeches are for an audience. Sometimes Zarathustra's speeches are for himself."[53] Hence, Zarathustra's meditations are "for none" in the sense of not being addressed directly to the audience.

This line of argument calls to mind the dramatic character of the book as a whole and Zarathustra's status as a fictional hero: "While the book does attempt to communicate directly some of Nietzsche's insights about the human condition, it is also a gesture of an indirect sort. *Thus Spoke Zarathustra* is not only a series of speeches directed at us as an audience; it is also a narrative that has an internal integrity and is written *for* an audience only in an indirect way."[54]

Furthermore, as a fictional character, Zarathustra is speaking "for himself and for no one else" in that "through his speech he represents his own way of being. In this sense his speeches reveal the fictional person whose story we are reading, and in this sense they are not *for* us as readers."[55] Higgins posits a tension, then, "between Zarathustra as Nietzsche's mouthpiece, who speaks to us, and Zarathustra as a fictional character in his own story." Nietzsche represents the ambivalence of self-expression, with its solipsistic demands, and the writer's reach for a public audience:

> The subtitle indicates, therefore, that *Thus Spoke Zarathustra* will address the paradox involved in human communication, the paradox that communication must bridge the chasm between individual experience and communal understanding. The subtitle also indicates that *Thus Spoke Zarathustra* will not only address this paradox but instantiate it. Through Zarathustra, Nietzsche will simultaneously attempt the expression of his deepest insights and a kind of interpersonal communication.[56]

As probing as this analysis is, it could be argued that it does not really describes a book "for none"—perhaps "for Zarathustra," perhaps "for

Nietzsche," perhaps even "for those [as Alderman would have it][57] who can deal with its 'masks,' its dramatic indirection," but not "for none." We might also observe that it is "the ambivalence between the individual's effort to express himself and his effort to tailor his words to the understanding of the audience" that causes Nietzsche's commentators over and over again to reduce "for all and none" to some version (to borrow Milton's locution) of "fit though few." The element of self-expression, which carries with it some of the specificity and individuality of the author, guarantees that it cannot be "for *all*," any more than a person can be liked by *everyone*. Similarly, the effort to address an audience, and tailor words to their needs, prevents it from being "for *none*." In a sense, "for a few" is the audience concept that virtually defines what one means by a book (for reasons having much to do with the influence of The Book in shaping our culture, as Nietzsche well knows). This vague conception locates the audience indeterminately between those who should but will not, should not be able to but will, cannot and will not, and can and will comprehend. Again, one might ask whether Nietzsche (or any other author, at least since the Romantics) is "a nonsolipsistic speaker," in any but the philosophic sense of "solipsistic"? Our discussion of Blake indicated that the opacity-to-the reader at the center of writing, and the solipsistic self-regard underlying and motivating the act of writing, carry with them the subversive suggestion that the satisfactions of the writer and the reader are not only not the same, but that there may not be any relationship between them, or worse, that the apparent relationship may well be deceptive.

Of course, Higgins recognizes the problem, but, we think, attempts to foreclose it by appropriating both dramatic indirection and the attempt at self-expression to the inherent difficulties of communication, and thus obscuring the potential for willful perversity that lurks in the element of self-regarding solipsism in Nietzsche's writing. Our example of Blake suggests the possibility that what the writer holds back is the "best" part.

This potential split between the writerly and the readerly versions of the book will be central to our reading (in this chapter) of Book IV. For the moment, let it suffice to say that the subtitle links hyperbole (for all) with litotes (for none) in a book which is at once an expansive wandering in and through the literary and scriptural traditions, and an exclusive reduction to "my work" (*Werk*) in the end. It is possible—and may even help—to think of this, too, as another version of "a book for all and for Nietzsche" rather than as "a book for all and for none."

"None" could imply that the book wanders beyond Nietzsche himself, that its evasiveness and hyperbolic wandering exceeds the author and requires something like the *Übermensch* as the projected author of the work that *Thus Spoke Zarathustra* may become as it wanders on its way. This line of thought would suggest that "A book for all and none" is less a subtitle than an "*envoi*," an instance of what in English is sometimes called the "Go little book" topos. One well-known example from Spenser must suffice:

TO HIS BOOKE

Goe little booke: thy selfe present,
As child whose parent is unkent:
To him that is the president
Of noblesse and of chevalree,
As sure it will for succoure flee
    Under the shadow of his wing,
And asked, who thee forth did bring,
A shepheards swaine saye did thee sing,
All as his straying flocke he fedde:
And when his honor has thee redde,
Crave pardon for my hardyhedde.
    But if that any aske thy name,
Say thou wert base begot with blame:
For thy thereof thou takest shame.
And when thou art past jeopardee,
Come tell me, what was sayd of mee
And I will send more after thee.[58]

This example suggests, we think, that Higgins's thesis (that *Thus Spoke Zarathustra* is "a book for all" in an "unproblematic" sense) may require at least some qualification. From a writer's point of view, a book addressed to all is as complex a notion as the idea of an "unspecified general public." For, as we see in Spenser, the envoy pleads for the protection of the noble audience to which it is implicitly addressed (Sir Philip Sidney), who happens to be a famous poet and courtier. Moreover, as is often the case, the envoy serves to situate the work, heretofore the exclusive possession of its author, in the world. Today we know that author to be Spenser, but he appears in 1579 in the guise of an unknown. Thus, the signature, "Immeritô," doubles the theme of unworthiness articulated in the tone of deference to the great. The poem begins in an echo from Chaucer ("Go litel bok, go litel myn tragedye") and ends with a declaration of earned anonymity: a book from no one to someone. Like the poetic child being sent into the world, distinct from its "parent," the work represents (or perhaps misrepresents, for the text is accompanied by an immense explanatory apparatus of explanation) the unknown poet. The famous "E. K." states that he is, in Chaucer's term, "UNCOUTHE UNKISTE."[59] In Spenser's time, the dangers of appearing in print without a protector could exceed hurt feelings of a spurned author; but there were dangers, too, in an unknown author addressing a distinguished person. Spenser not only declares his anonymity, but he also implies, by associating the anonymous *Shepheardes Calender* with Chaucer and Sidney, that his talent deserves comparison with the best. For he has, if cheekily, chosen the best for his audience.[60]

And yet the envoy recounts the loss of control necessary as author separates from creation, and the process of production, distribution, and reception comes into being. It expresses not only Spenser's trepidation at the thought that the world can now do with the work as it pleases, but also an awareness that the literary artifact, like a living child, may hope for the intervention of a noble or accomplished dedicatee protector. In this latter way, the envoy also marks out a path for the author's return to the world from the private, imaginative space of writing. Here, as elsewhere (the reader can multiply examples), it expresses a sense of vulnerability, while specifying directly and indirectly the audience (Sidney, Harvey, and their circle) that will welcome the work and the poet, easing the way of that return.

In Spenser's envoy, we find the "Go little book" topos, but we find, too, an instance of the double-edged disclaimer of the author who is undeserving. But undeserving of what? Anonymity? Well, then, why the declamatory allusions to the great, present and past? Nietzsche's subtitle, "A book for all and none," likewise seems to claim for itself a status as a test of one's place in the public eye, and also of one's disposition toward the gift of life. Life too belongs equally to all but in the end to none. Life, for Zarathustra, may appear like this book, a gift at once extended and withheld. "How well disposed must you be," it seems to ask the poet, not to rebel against the necessity of your own death? "How well disposed must you be," it seems to say to the philosopher, not to take refuge from the arbitrariness, the capriciousness, with which life is given and taken away?

"A book for all" is a book without a writer, without a specific origin to interfere with its reception; "a book for none" is a book addressed to no one, a book without readers. In a sense, Nietzsche's subtitle/envoy parodies the secret and contradictory desires of writer and reader not to have to cope with one another's strangeness; it is also a way of withholding the subject or self, either as the "behind" or "beneath" toward which the reader aspires or as the basis of the writer's faith in the literary vocation. The book purports to offer neither writer nor reader the satisfactions of self as an antidote to or distraction from life.

Finally, the relationship between the hyperbole "all" and the litotes "none" is both that of antithesis and reversibility, as "head" and "tail" are sides of the same coin, opposable and interchangeable, for as Zarathustra himself observes in "The Higher Man," "I stood in the marketplace. And as I spoke to all, I spoke to none" (Z IV "OHM" 1). Similarly, the elaborate wanderings of Zarathustra can be reversed in an instant into "my work," as at the moment of "closure" at the end of "The Sign" (Z IV). All that is left out of Nietzsche's challenging claim (gift?) that his is "A book for all and none" is the few, the norm between hyperbole and litotes, the balance that makes the book. Nietzsche signals his awareness of and calls into question *authorship* itself. If the envoy tells us definitely of anything, it is that *Thus Spoke Zarathustra* is intended, by testing its limits, to function as a sustained meditation on author-ship, sometimes writerly, sometimes readerly, but finally questioning the very existence of a perspective or identity from which these perspectival claims can be decisively resolved or adjudicated. Indeed, so compelling is the question of writing for Nietzsche, that he casts the "problem" of being in its form.

Authorial Withholding and the Reader's Share

One of the most powerful and original aspects of Higgins's book is its defense of Part IV, too often seen as an excrescence by philosophical commentators, and her recognition of its origins in Menippean satire, specifically the "Golden Ass" stories of Apuleius and especially Lucian. Higgins quotes from Frye's *Anatomy of Criticism* in order to characterize the features of Menippean satire: "'This form,' according to Frye, 'deals less with people as such than with men-tal attitudes,' and these attitudes frequently stem from the particular charac-ter's occupational orientation toward life."[61] She goes on to quote directly from Frye:

> At its most concentrated the Menippean satire presents us with a vision of the world in terms of a single intellectual pattern. The intellectual structure built up from the story makes for violent dislocations in the customary logic of narrative, though the appear-ance of carelessness that results reflects only the carelessness of the reader or his ten-dency to judge by a novel-centered conception of fiction.[62]

A stock character in Menippean satire, Higgins observes, is the *philosophus gloriosus*, and she point out ways in which Zarathustra recognizes himself in this role. Perhaps because Higgins is a philosopher, or perhaps because she is judging by a novel-centered conception and focusing on Zarathustra, the character, she more or less ignores the possibility that the determining occu-pational attitude or backdrop may not be that of the philosopher at all. The source as well as the butt of the satire may well be Nietzsche, the author. This is not to say that "writing" or "authorship" provide the allegorical keys to *Thus Spoke Zarathustra*. We are suggesting, rather, that this category of fictive analy-sis is the domain of experience out of which conception and representation alike arise and to which they are answerable.

Earlier, in "The Convalescent," Zarathustra was tempted to give in to nausea at the thought of the eternal recurrence of the small man. Now, in "The Cry of Distress," the soothsayer returns to tempt him with the "sin" of pity. He brings with him a vision of the misery that gathers and laps ever higher at the base of Zarathustra's mountain, encouraging despair: "But all is the same, nothing is worth while, no seeking avails, nor are there any blessed isles any more" (Z IV "Cry"); or "All is the same, nothing is worth while, the world is without meaning, knowledge strangles." This despair, the shadow of his shadow, Zarathustra rejects, though the soothsayer assures him that when he returns, he and it will still be waiting for him. This initial rejection is beside the point because in responding to the cry of distress, Zarathustra has, in some measure, given in to the pity that leads to despair; his "error" is contained in his implicit assumption that the cry of distress is somehow *for him*. Like Blake, Nietzsche rejects pity as a turning aside from the proper work of the creative thinker/artist, a temptation to make the work *immediately* answerable to the needs of others and somehow responsible for their condition in the world.

Zarathustra's relationship with "the higher men"[63] is the heart of what might be termed Nietzsche's internalization of Menippean satire as a meditation on authorship's pitfalls and possibilities. At one level, the satire mocks the literal-mindedness of these readers and the ways in which they allow their own preoccupations to determine their contradictory understandings of Zarathustra's teachings. Their earnest attempts to imitate Zarathustra constitute the sincerest form of parody. (Imitation *is* the sincerest form of parody.) Yet for this very reason, the parody hits home, for what they "see" in Zarathustra is really there; despite themselves, they know *something* about Zarathustra and serve him as reflections, however, distorted, of himself. Thus their interpretations also serve as a catalogue of the pleasures and temptations associated with writing. "Reading" him inadvertently, they force on Zarathustra the author's discomfiture at "being read"—a sense that to be read is to be parodied, but parodied truly. Yet this parodic truth is at odds with or simply misses the basis of Zarathustra's authorship. The errors of the higher men allow Zarathustra to put off one-by-one his own mistaken notions about himself and so bring him in the end to a self-understanding, which excludes the higher men and, we suggest, may raise serious questions about the difference between the writerly and readerly versions of the book.

In his own way, each of the higher men reflects Zarathustra back at himself. The kings in Part IV, for instance, echo Zarathustra's condemnations of the emptiness of modern manners, of kingship, and of the rule of the mob. Though "obviously they were very peaceful kings with old and fine faces" (Z IV "CWK" 2), they assert their desire to fight, to return to their fathers' virtues of combat. The kings' absurdity is evident in their literality, in their failure to *see* themselves, and in their sense of having been especially "called" by Zarathustra. Nietzsche may implicate Zarathustra in their silliness, but we are left with the sense that the problem is accepted as "real," that, here as elsewhere, however similar to the higher men he may appear to be, Zarathustra *is* different. And the signal difference between them appears in his "work."

"The conscientious in spirit," bled by the leech of conscience comes next, boasting: "in matters of the spirit there may well be none stricter, narrower, and harder than I" (Z IV "Leech"). He will assert nothing that he does not *know*, however narrow the ground that leaves him. He hates the half-baked and vaporous (everything else); honesty is his law, and honesty is "hard, strict, narrow, cruel, and inexorable" (Z IV "Leech"). Confining himself, bleeding himself of life, "the conscientious in spirit" pursues an impossible purity which leaves no room for a warmer, gayer existence. Yet how indeed is "self-overcoming" to occur without some such self-curtailment, some such self-wounding? How else does one prove one's seriousness, distinguish knowledge from mere desire, except by some form of ascetic sacrifice? Of course, Nietzsche's emphasis on gaiety, the crucial role of laughter, especially laughter at oneself, helps to distinguish Zarathustra from "the conscientious in spirit." But this does not explain adequately how laughter can achieve what asceticism cannot or why laughter directed at oneself is not simply another, subtler form of asceticism.[64]

The magician speaks, perhaps most powerfully of all the higher men, to the reader's suspicion of Nietzsche and of the despair that his writing is capable of engendering (perhaps even in its author). The magician apes Zarathustra's rhetoric of spiritual struggle, fashioning himself an "ascetic of the spirit" struggling to break free of a "hangman god." He flatters Zarathustra in phrases belonging to Zarathustra himself. Despite his protestations, the magician is malicious; he wants to make others the victims of their own beliefs and utterances. Believing in the ultimate emptiness of everything (including himself), he gives way to the temptation to *make* this true. Rather than the unmasker of inauthenticity, he is its agent. Perhaps because he sees something of himself in this poseur, Zarathustra recognizes that the magician's protestations of falsehood are a cloak for residual sincerity; he *is* an ascetic of the spirit after all. Otherwise he would not be so driven: "your magic has enchanted everybody, but no lie or cunning is left to use against yourself: you are disenchanted for yourself. You have harvested nausea as your one truth. Not a word of yours is genuine any more, except your mouth—namely, the nausea that sticks in your mouth (Z IV "Magician" 2).

Zarathustra turns back this first challenge by demonstrating that the temptation to pity is at least partially the result of a too-hasty, superficial identification. The magician, also an author, has succumbed to contempt for his audience: those who *believe* in him. This is at bottom, as the magician confesses, self-loathing:

> my art nauseates me; I am not *great*—why do I dissemble? But you know it too: I sought greatness. I wanted to represent a great human being and I persuaded many; but this lie went beyond my strength. It is breaking me. O Zarathustra, everything about me is a lie, but that I am breaking—this, my breaking, is genuine. (Z IV "Magician" 2)

The magician's nihilism comes, in effect, from aspiring too high, from hyperbolizing or casting beyond himself and "breaking." But he wants to be an "author" for the wrong reason, or rather, lacking the right reason, namely, having something to say that he genuinely believes to be important. That Zarathustra is gloomily willing to accept this as a genuine moment suggests an element of his own recognition or anxiety, since the magician's false hyperbolizing is outwardly indistinguishable from that which every genuine author must perform—the casting beyond the self to address an audience.

Indeed, the magician's next utterance does call the sincerity of that moment into question: "I seek one who is genuine, right, simple, unequivocal, a man of all honesty, a vessel of wisdom, a saint of knowledge, a great human being. Do you not know it Zarathustra? *I seek Zarathustra*" (Z IV "Magician" 2). We see here a sly and destructive parody of Zarathustra's supposed "genuineness." The silence that follows Zarathustra's absorption and the "kindness and cunning" with which he replies ("I have not yet seen a great human being") suggest that Zarathustra too perceives a trap, which he avoids. Nevertheless, at this point it is not impossible to say with confidence whether Zarathustra denies his pretensions to genuineness, or merely avoids exposing them to the magician's malicious mockery.

The question of Nietzsche/Zarathustra's motives is raised, as well as the Socratic question about the corrosive power of art's feigning. What are the consequences of committing philosophy to writing, much less to the quasi-fictional space defined by Zarathustra? And what of Nietzsche's own extensive use in *Thus Spoke Zarathustra* of gospel materials? How can he immunize himself against his own relentless ironizing? The retired Pope, whom Zarathustra meets next, seeks him as the true anti-believer, who represents in an even severer form that "other world" lost with the death of God. He clearly dramatizes the danger of deconstructing metaphysics only in order to reinstantiate it in another form, and raises the possibility that Nietzsche's clearsightedness about religion and morals cloaks a search for another religion, another morality.

In his encounter with the ugliest man, Zarathustra makes his way into a dismal valley, "Snakes' Death," where he experiences a sense of *dejá vu* that surely directs us back to "On the Vision and the Riddle." In this valley, he encounters a man so ugly that it embarrasses Zarathustra to see him. The ugliest man causes Zarathustra to be all but engulfed by a pity that is also self-pity before he can collect himself. Zarathustra recognizes the ugliest man as the murderer of God, which act was his "revenge on the witness" who saw him as he truly was, in all his ugliness.[65] This first movement raises questions about Zarathustra's nausea and the biting-through of the snake that choked him—now the snake of Christianity, God himself choking him with a vision of his own smallness. Here, the biting-through is not the creation of a heroic discontinuity but a turning away from an unbearable truth. Even more fundamentally, this encounter calls into question Zarathustra's own rejection of pity. The ugliest man rejects pity as too slight a response to his ugliness, in which he takes a kind of pride, declaring himself "rich in what is great, in what is terrible, in what is ugliest, in what is most inexpressible" (Z IV "UM"). "Pity offends the sense of shame," the ugliest man says, but of what, then, is he ashamed? of his ugliness or of the fact that his ugliness is so small?

The figure of the ugliest man joins together inextricably a hyperbolic self-love with a litotic self-hatred. Each is the basis of the other and the excessiveness of each inevitably brings on the other. Not able to come to terms with man's smallness, he must be bigger than he is at all costs. He holds up the spectral possibility that all of Zarathustra's self-exaltations, including his rejection of pity, are at bottom merely compensatory. The ugliest man is looking to Zarathustra for someone who will take him at his own estimation. This Zarathustra seems to do; indeed, he takes him at *both* his face values, admiring the height of the ugliest man's self-love, and the depth of his self-hatred. Nevertheless, Zarathustra concludes, "Man . . . is something that must be overcome" (Z IV "UM").

The voluntary beggar threw away his riches and tried to give the poor "his fullness and his heart." But the poor would not accept his gift, so he had to go to the cows instead. As Zarathustra observes in a speech that takes us back to our own discussion of *l'envoi*: "right giving is harder than right receiving, and . . . to give presents well is an *art* and the ultimate and most cunning master-art of graciousness" (Z IV "VB"). This raises the question of how, given a readership defined by the extremes of the self-important mob and the all-accepting cows, *does* one give this gift, this book? The poor and the rich are equally unworthy. Zarathustra sees through the violence of the beggar's complaint, recognizing that what he really wants is not to awaken the rich and poor to his message, but an existence that answers to his own gentleness, "the happiness of animals." The exchange with the voluntary beggar raises forcefully the question of Zarathustra's own withdrawal and leaves suspended the question of how (or whether) to give this gift. Perhaps the only way to get people to accept it is to pretend that it is for others. At bottom, does Zarathustra prefer the ease of his own work to the pain of engagement?

Finally, Zarathustra encounters his own shadow, which naturally he cannot outrun, which has followed him everywhere, to the point of despair at his homelessness. Too free in his freedom, he no longer knows what pleases him. He is a wanderer rather than a quester: "With you I unlearned faith in words and values and great names. When the devil sheds his skin, does not his name fall off too? For that too is skin. The devil himself is perhaps skin" (Z "The Shadow"). But what is a human being with the skin stripped off? How would one live? Is this what Nietzsche really does, strip off the skin, leaving only this shadow? How does one live without illusions? We sense here a deep-seated anxiety and self-doubt, which laughter may not erase. And yet how is one to respond to the loss of a *goal*, Zarathustra says, but to jest at it? Zarathustra responds with a certain heroic élan, yet the whole situation is reminiscent of Ulysses's appearance in Dante's *Inferno* in the circle of the false counselors. His offense was to entice his friends to join him in a voice to seek out the isles of the blest, a voyage in which he and all his companions were killed.

At the heart of Zarathustra's "advice" to the higher men, then, are his speeches on self-overcoming, on cultivating the ability to "dance away over yourselves," "laugh away over yourselves." He calls on them to be willing to be overcome and superseded by the *Übermensch* who follows the death of God. Since higher types rarely succeed, their failure is all but inevitable. For precisely this reason, not guilt but the gambler's jest and laughter is the proper response. Zarathustra, of course, has already transformed himself into something like the higher higher man (the writer), pronouncing his own laughter holy, crowning himself. He is now "Zarathustra soothsayer, sooth-*laugher*, not impatient, not unconditional." What separates him from the higher men is, as he puts it, "you suffer from yourselves, you have not yet suffered *from man*" (Z IV "OHM" 6).

Zarathustra no longer confuses contingent, personal failings (about which guilt—or a measure of self-reproach—is appropriate) with the inherent limitations of what we are or have become in the course of our history. About these, we can only laugh (or dance). This is not quietism but the first step in genuinely opening ourselves to temporality, to futurity. For the higher men, suffering from themselves, self-overcoming means that the sickness must also be the cure; what they are is the only conceivable antidote to what they are. Unwittingly, the higher men treat themselves as the culmination or limit of possibility, rather than as a part of an ongoing process. Because of this limitation, they face a problem without a solution, endlessly divided against themselves, parsing and re-parsing the "bad" from the "good," alternately self-hating and self-loving.

Behind the plight of the higher men, Zarathustra knows, is the fear of death. He privileges dancing and laughter and rejects melancholy and the "spirit of gravity" because these are signs that the paralyzing fear of wasting one moment of precious time, of leaving undone the one thing that would transform and save us, has been lifted. Perhaps more than any other philosopher, Nietzsche discloses an understanding of the continuing power of "magical thinking" for our "rationality." The fear of death and its form, the desire for perfectibility, to enjoy a "more than mortal privilege" while still in our skins, links Nietzsche's analysis of the higher men with a tradition of crisis poetry that stretches at least from Milton's "Lycidas." Taking the form of the pastoral elegy, though sometimes disguised, it includes Gray's "Elegy Written in a Country Churchyard," Wordsworth's "Intimations of Immortality," Shelley's "Adonais," and Arnold's "Thyrsis." Over and over, these poems pose the question: "What good is poetry in a world of death?" How can we justify or even explain the turning away from the world and its pleasures involved in writing when life is so short and death inevitable? These poems erect a variety of defenses against the paralyzing fear of death that seems so intimately related to the self-consciousness that makes poets writers to begin with. In doing so, each gives an account of the thoughts and feelings that make it possible to write. In order to tear his or her gaze away from the specter of death, the author must accept in advance the imperfection of the proposed composition; in order to write at all, the poet must accept the probability-tending-toward-certainty that no poem as poem, no act of writing, will satisfactorily answer this question, will be adequate to the task it sets itself.

Thus Spoke Zarathustra, then, which announces the death of God, which makes such obtrusive use of images from the "pastoral" books of the Bible, and which exploits so thoroughly and ironically the role of pastor and all the cultural baggage associated with it, deserves consideration as one of the most complex and profound pastoral elegies we have. And especially in Book IV, it explores the partial transformation of the pastor into the writer that follows on the death of God, and explores its implications in the fluid relations between Zarathustra and his "readers," the higher men. Thus, during the final four chapters, Zarathustra's response to the higher men oscillates between irritation and encouragement, between a desire to get away from them and a desire to instruct and embrace them. For instance, at the beginning of "The Awakening," "overcome by a slight aversion and by scorn for his company" (Z IV "Awakening" 1), Zarathustra leaves the cave for one of his periodic breaths of "fresh air." With a little distance between himself and the higher men, their hilarity now seems a positive sign that they have learned to laugh and that "the spirit of gravity" is in retreat. Yet Zarathustra's speeches here have some peculiarities well worth remarking.

For example, he says at one point, "if they learned to laugh from me, it is still not *my* laughter that they have learned. But what does it matter? They are old people convalescing in their own way; my ears have suffered worse things without becoming grumpy" (Z IV "Awakening" 1). They are not laughing as *he* would laugh, but he is, generously, still willing to accept their laughter as a sign of genuine awakening and convalescence. At the same time, there is beneath this a certain hint of satisfaction that the unique difference/superiority of Zarathustra's laughter is still intact.

This ambiguity of tone and attitude is even more strongly marked in the succeeding paragraphs, when Zarathustra boasts:

> They are biting, my bait is working: from them too their enemy retreats, the spirit of gravity. Even now they have learned to laugh at themselves: do I hear right? My virile nourishment, the savor and strength of my words are taking effect; and verily, I did not feed them bloating vegetables, but warrior's nourishment, conqueror's nourishment: I wakened new desires. New hopes throb in their arms and legs; their hearts stretch out.

> They are finding new words, soon their spirit will breath prankishness. Such nourishment, to be sure, may not be suitable for children or for nostalgic old and young little females. Their entrails are persuaded in a different way; I am not their physician and teacher. (Z IV "Awakening" 1)

He boasts of his success as physician and teacher without accepting his patients and pupils as peers. Indeed, as we have already suggested, his condescension here is linked to an element of sneaking satisfaction at their limited success. And are the higher men fish wriggling on Zarathustra's hooks, warriors and conquerors to be admired, or patients and students to be cared for, instructed, and condescended to? Zarathustra's willingness to see himself in a pastoral role here is the first thing to go when he sees the higher men worshipping the ass: "all these higher men . . . were all kneeling like children and devout little old women." In other words, these fish are not his true patients and pupils; indeed, there is some question as to whether these even exist yet. And exactly what kind of "teacher," "physician," or "pastor" believes that no such thing exists as a worthy pupil or patient?

Not only does it not occur to Zarathustra that this prankishness might be turned on *him*, but he himself begins to look forward "nostalgically": "This I take to be the best sign: they become grateful. Not much longer, and they will think up festivals and put up monuments to their old friends. They are convalescing!" (Z IV "Awakening" 1), convalescing in the sense of learning to be grateful for and to celebrate life. But what "old friends" does Zarathustra imagine that they will want to monumentalize? His violent immediate reaction to the ass festival shows that "Jesus" was not his first choice. Not only do his pupils and patients seem to be regressing but he sees graphic proof that they would as soon worship an ass as Zarathustra. As Kathleen Higgin has pointed out, Zarathustra is an ass; he becomes the object of satire (which is also a Nietzschean self-satire), impaled on his own self-importance.[66]

Clearly, Zarathustra responds initially more to this abrupt undercutting of his pretensions than to the ass festival itself, because he fails to recognize it as a *parody* of New Testament virtues: on these terms, it is as easy to worship an ass as Jesus. Indeed, anyone, including Zarathustra, can be mocked by his own virtues. Each of the higher men, confronted with Zarathustra's accusation, teases and mocks him in his own Zarathustran fashion: the wanderer/shadow points out puckishly, "in the case of gods *death* is always a mere prejudice" (Z IV "AF" 1); the conscientious man suggests to him that "overabundance and wisdom could easily turn you too into an ass. Is not the perfect sage fond of walking on the most crooked ways?" (Z IV "AF" 1); and the ugliest man finally lets Zarathustra in on the "joke": "But one thing I do know; it was from you yourself that I learned it once, O Zarathustra: whoever would kill most thoroughly, *laughs*. 'Not by wrath does one kill, but by laughter'—thus you once spoke. O Zarathustra, you hidden one, you annihilator without wrath, you dangerous saint—you are a rogue." (Z IV "AF 1")

So, the ugliest man announces, the fish have caught the fisherman, the "hidden one" is finally flushed into the open. But what does it mean that the laughter that "killed" god is now being turned on Zarathustra? Is this the necessary drama by means of which the reader/student/patient comes into his or her own (perhaps not the master's equal but near enough at least so that earnestness and awe can give way to a little humanizing leg-pulling)? Or are the higher men (also) avenging themselves on Zarathustra for the loss of their faith? Are we seeing the necessary and self-respecting self-assertion of the truly convalescent, or is this the destructive cunning, the *ressentiment*, of the weaker men, unable to accept what Zarathustra has told them from the beginning: "It is not for you that I wait in these mountains" (Z IV "The Welcome").

In the speeches that open "The Awakening," it seems that Zarathustra is in danger of instantiating Nietzsche's claim that the philosopher "wants life for himself alone"; that there is a kind of trap hidden in the reaching out of the teacher/physician; that Zarathustra's deepest, truest motivation is the hunger for a personal sublimity that feeds on a hidden difference, even contempt. Even if true, *need* this concern the higher men, or, for that matter, Nietzsche's readers? Do they get something of value from his teachings, whatever their secret intent, whatever their private satisfactions? Are the higher men finally able to hold their own, from one point of view by legitimately using what Zarathustra has taught them, from another point of view by virtue of the cunning of the weaker reader/interpreter?

Zarathustra's response to the ugliest man's speech purports to see through the higher men's joke: "O you roguish fools, all of you, you jesters! Why do you dissemble and hide before me? How all your hearts wriggled with pleasure and malice that at last you had become again as little children, that is, pious; that at last you did again as children do, namely, prayed, folded your hands, and said, 'Dear God'" (Z IV "AF" 2). Their mockery of New Testament values hides, or rather fails to hide, their nostalgic satisfaction at returning even in parodic form to the complacencies of piety, as well as their vengeful malice toward Zarathustra, their better and source of their disillusionment. Yet this must also be in some sense a moment of self-recognition, in which the secret earnestness of the higher men's laughter leads Zarathustra to some realization of the secret predatoriness of his own teacherly/physicianly vocation. This implicit recognition supplies the bridge to the seemingly discontinuous speech that follows:

> "O my new friends," he said, "you strange higher men, how well I like you now since you have become gay again. Verily, you have all blossomed; it seems to me such flowers as you are require *new festivals*, a little brave nonsense, some divine service and ass festival, some old gay fool of a Zarathustra, a roaring wind that blows your souls bright.

"Do not forget this night and this ass festival, you higher men. *This* you invented when you were with me and I take that for a good sign: such things are invented only by convalescents.

"And when you celebrate it again, this ass festival, do it for your own sakes, and also do it for my sake. And in remembrance of *me*." (Z IV "AF" 3)

Here Zarathustra seems reconciled with the higher men, his readers, inviting them outside in a spirit of fellowship. And although it is certainly not what his vanity had envisioned, he even seems reconciled with the ass festival as the form of his commemoration, a somewhat rueful but genuine monument. Still, it is not entirely clear whether Zarathustra is exonerated or indicted in this sequence of events. Are we to understand that he has recognized and repudiated the predatory vanity, the condescension, at the heart of the pastoral role—that he is acting out Nietzsche's critique of the actual psychology of the tradition—or are these elements of Zarathustra's own psychology and perhaps of Nietzsche's as well? Are we reading a critique, a confession, or some combination of the two?

Outside the cave, in the dark of night, the higher men are "secretly amazed at feeling so well on earth" and Zarathustra thinks to himself, "How well I like them now, these higher men!" (Z IV "DS" 1) The reconciliation between Zarathustra and the higher men, the establishment of their peerage, seems complete when the ugliest man utters virtually the same affirmation of eternal recurrence that Zarathustra directs at his dwarf in "On the Vision and the Riddle": "For the sake of this day, *I* am for the first time satisfied that I have lived my whole life. . . . 'Was *that* life?' I want to say to death. 'Well then! Once More!'" (Z IV "DS" 1). Zarathustra's confidence seems like a sign that the higher men have arrived, a confirmation of his role as teacher. In response to the ugliest man's words, the other higher men "became conscious of how they had changed and convalesced and to whom they owed this" and they "jumped toward Zarathustra to thank, revere, caress him, and kiss his hands, each according to his own manner" (Z IV "DS" 1).

This moment of triumph is also the moment in which Zarathustra is literally overcome, and the moment—at least figuratively—of his "undergoing":

Zarathustra stood there like a drunkard: his eyes grew dim, his tongue failed, his feet stumbled. And who could guess what thoughts were then running over Zarathustra's soul? But his spirit fled visibly and flew ahead and was in remote distances and, as it were, "on a high ridge," as it is written, "between two seas, wandering like a heavy cloud between past and future." (Z IV "DS" 2)

This moment in which Zarathustra is overcome by joy is also a crisis that delivers him to the limits of his vocation as he has conceived and lived it. When the higher men attain the wisdom he has articulated, he is very nearly overcome in the self-consuming movement of the text. His readers have caught up with him and "consumed" him. There is no longer any reason to teach, to write. In his vision, he is "disembodied" and left wandering between past and future. It is interesting and perhaps troubling that precisely at this point the garrulity of the book gives way to the reticence of "who could guess?"

But Zarathustra does recover himself, and the vision that follows is at least arguably an unpacking of that complex and inarticulate moment of his over-coming. Zarathustra's becomes the voice of the midnight in a progressive rev-elation that culminates in the crucial assertion that "*joy is deeper yet than agony*" (Z IV "DS" 8). The possibility of making this affirmation is what is at stake in every major poem of English Romanticism; indeed, it is what is at stake in the secular romance in general. How, in the absence of a god to stand in surety for the fundamental goodness of things, can humankind arrive at a conviction that, on balance, life's joy outweighs its sorrow? The reason that Romantic poets seize on pastoral elegy as they do is that this genre puts this question specifically in the form of a question about their vocation as writers. If, as it so often appears, the deepest meaning and true profundity of life is suffering and the ultimate suffering of one's own extinction, then the turning away from the world's immediate pleasures involved in writing is deeply irrational, a fan-tasy sustaining a host of illusions about the value of fame, and originality. On the other hand, if joy is "deeper," not only is writing less irrational as an activ-ity, but it opens the way for writing—precisely because it is a turn from the world's immediate pleasures—to become the *sign* of the fact or conviction that joy exceeds pain.

More than that, writing does not articulate a conviction that exists apart from it; here the depth of joy emerges as part of the process, the momentum of writing itself, over the space of a gradually unfolding vision that gains mo-mentum over eleven sections of "The Drunken Song"—sections which self-consciously characterize the movement of the book as a whole as an attempt to take in everything, to swallow everything in order to arrive at this point where the depth of joy, the degree to which it exceeds pain, becomes manifest. This "moment" in the movement of writing, in which the measure of woe is taken and exceeded, is characterized with increasing explicitness as following on Zarathustra's "death." From his swoon on, he is in effect speaking with the voice and authority of the dead. The hyperbolic movement of writing is a cast-ing of life beyond death and the "rhetoric" of writing completes itself as text or book, achieves its formal coherence, by definition when this point is reached, the point of Zarathustra's "death." But, of course, the book exceeds this death, crossing a threshold where the reader, as it turns out, cannot follow in what is at once a coda and essential.

In a sense, the final two chapters of *Thus Spoke Zarathustra* belong not to this book but to the next book or the book after that. The hyperbole that makes this text plays beyond its limits in order to reinitiate the project of writing and avoid the disaster of having said all there is to say, of being contained in one's own text or, to put it another way, of undergoing reduction to the dead letter of one's own "wisdom." In order to see how all this works, let us turn to the details of Zarathustra's vision.

The bell that tolls the approach of midnight, like the bell that tolls for each of us in Donne's *Devotions*, whispers the secrets of midnight to Zarathustra, which he proposes to "whisper" in turn to the higher men with the same terrible cordiality. The voice of midnight, though perhaps like the moon always there in the sky, only now becomes distinct because the stillness and solitude of the night (the writer's solitude) mutes the clamor and confusion of the daylight world, the noisy static of normal, waking being. "Sooner would I die," Zarathustra says, "rather than tell you what my midnight heart thinks now." But of course, as we have already suggested, he is dead in a sense—a fact confirmed in the very next sentence, "now I have died," which prepares him to answer the question "What does the deep midnight declare?" (Z IV "DS" 4). From this vantage point, he poses to the higher men (and perhaps to himself) these questions:

> Have you flown high enough yet? You have danced: but a leg is no wing. You good dancers, now all pleasure is gone: wine has become lees, every cup has become brittle, the tombs stammer, "Redeem the dead! Why does the night last so long? Does not the moon make us drunken?"
> You higher men, redeem the tombs, awaken the corpses! Alas, why does the worm still burrow? The hour approaches, approaches; the bell hums, the heart still rattles, the death watch, the heart-worm still burrows. Alas! Alas! *The world is deep.* (Z IV "DS" 5)

Zarathustra writes as one in his cups; in fact he writes from the bottom of the cup, as one who has drained life's wine to the lees. And now he takes his flight of song from those depths. The higher men remain, by implication, dancers, fixated on death, whose ultimate form of desire is still redemption from death. This desire keeps the higher men from plumbing the world to its depths, from making the transition from dancing to flying. In Zarathustra's case, the dancing of his earlier speech gives way to flight as the result of his passage to the depths, the passage into the underworld which lies beneath the appearance that death presents to the living. Like Homer, Vergil, and Dante, he derives his particular identity and authority from his descent and return. This difference between Zarathustra, whose writing carries him beyond the end, beyond the imaginative limit of death, and the higher men, who remain at an impasse with that limit, is also the basis of the distinction between reader and writer that this final book of *Thus Spoke Zarathustra* seems to announce.

Approximately, in the next section, the bell becomes one with Zarathustra's lyre. The voice of midnight becomes his voice, embodying "every pain . . . father-pain, fathers' pain, fore-fathers' pain; your speech grew ripe—ripe as golden autumn and afternoon, as my hermit's heart; now you say: the world itself is grown ripe, the grape is turning brown, now it would die, die of happiness" (Z IV "DS" 6). The process of taking in (encompassing every pain, the maturing of speech in writing) and the growth of his hermit's (writer's) heart are one and the same, and issue forth in this sense that the world itself is "autumnal," reaching its point of maximum fullness, which only death can follow, but which seems nevertheless to cast beyond that limit: "the world is deep, *deeper than day had been aware*" (Z IV "DS" 6). And appropriately, too, Zarathustra begins the ensuing "Drunken Song" with a rejection of the day for which the dead of the higher men still pine ("Why does the night last so long?"): "Leave me! Leave me! I am too pure for you. Did not my world become perfect just now? My skin is too pure for your hands. Leave me, you stupid, boorish, dumb day!" (Z IV "DS" 7). Then, in a startling reversal, Zarathustra now sees himself as the object of *life's* desire. The dangerous coquette against which men rage and complain, the object of their desire, now wants *him*; even more startling, the vehicle of this reversal seems to be the higher men's anxious reaching after him, their pursuit of the redemptive sublimity he represents and appears to hold out to them, which is stunningly characterized from the writer's point of view:

O day, you grope for me? You seek my happiness? I seem rich to you, lonely, a treasure pit, a gold chamber? O world, you want me? Am I worldly to you? Am I spiritual to you? Am I godlike to you? But day and world, you are too ponderous; have cleverer hands, reach for deeper happiness, for deeper unhappiness, reach for any god, do not reach for me: my unhappiness, my happiness is deep, you strange day, but I am yet no god, no god's hell: *deep is its woe*. (Z IV "DS" 7)

Zarathustra fends off and refuses this groping after him of the day/world/ reader. Denying the effort to make a god of him, to use him as a god, he not only refuses divine sublimity in favor of a more human writerly sublimity, but he refuses to pay the price of divinity, the willingness to "die" for *them*. Deep is the world's woe because the answer to its reaching, its groping is not and cannot be present if Zarathustra is to overcome the lure of pity. If you want a god, pursue a god, Zarathustra cries. "God's woe is deeper" (Z IV "DS" 8), he asserts; which is to say, too deep for joy to overcome. "Reach for God's woe, not for me! What am I? a drunken sweet lyre—a midnight lyre, an ominous bell-frog that nobody understands but that *must* speak, before the deaf, you higher men. For you do not understand me!" (Z IV "DS" 8). The revelation that follows—joy is deeper yet than agony—depends on Zarathustra's setting aside the context of divinity, the hope of redemption as we are, which results in a woe too deep for joy to redeem. The context of divinity is set aside in favor of writing and of "authorship," which provide the context in which such a conviction can flourish. That "joy is deeper yet than agony" is not adduced as an absolute but as the product of a particular perspective from which "depth" emerges as the highest value (as opposed to weight, degree, distance, or some other metaphor for sublimity). "Depth" is the metaphor that receives privilege from the context provided by Nietzsche's own writing.

And yet it is here that we cannot help but recall that Zarathustra's sense of being desired by life is built on the higher men's pursuit of what he appears to offer, so that something of his own triumph still seems to depend on the pursuit of divinity from which he distinguishes himself—a point to which we will return shortly. For now it will suffice to note that Zarathustra responds to this ambiguity, to the guilt of his own position, when he begins the succeeding section with: "You vine! Why do you praise me? Did I not cut you? I am cruel, you bleed; what does your praise of my drunken cruelty mean? 'What has become perfect, all that is ripe—wants to die' thus you speak. Blessed, blessed be the vintager's knife! But all that is unripe wants to live: woe!" (Z IV "DS" 9). The vine seems to be at once the higher men, something within himself which is being superseded, and the world itself, against which he offends in his authorship. From his new perspective, Zarathustra recoils from discipleship, which appears as an endemic ripeness. Their ripeness (and perhaps the *readers*') is overripeness. What is being challenged here, we think, is Zarathustra's final willingness to risk the loss of self in order to be transformed (or not) into something rich and strange. Only the unripe resists this overcoming. The desire to live longer, wanting heirs, wanting "what is farther, higher, brighter" (Z IV "DS" 9) are all signs of the wish to be elsewhere, of the desire to be what one is not. Apparently, Zarathustra's desire for disciples, for readers, also qualifies as a sign of this unripeness, this need to be completed. The need for heirs links the fear of being overcome with a residual fear of death, which stands between the author and the overcoming that allows him to write beyond himself, beyond the present text in the direction of the next and the next. Without this overcoming, firstlings are indeed lastlings.

It must also be noted that here the joy that "wants itself, wants eternity, wants recurrence, wants everything eternally the same" (Z IV "DS" 9) corresponds to the wanting "myself" that recognizes and accepts itself in all its manifestations, regarding the most staggering and disorienting diversity as part of the self. Zarathustra rehearses his own diversity and, in doing so, asserts his own willingness to be overcome, when he soon issues this challenge to the higher men:

You higher men, what do you think? Am I a soothsayer? A dreamer? A drunkard? An interpreter of dreams? A midnight bell? A drop of dew? A haze and fragrance of eternity? Do you not hear it? Do you not smell it? Just now my world became perfect; midnight too is noon; pain too is a joy; curses too are a blessing; night too is a sun—go away or you will learn: a sage is also a fool. (Z IV "DS" 10)

Zarathustra celebrates the variety and ephemerality of his authorial incarnations and challenges the higher men to recognize the "him" in all of them as, by implication, he himself does. The moment in which his world becomes perfect is that in which the unrestrained reversibility of things *in rhetoric* ceases to be a threat of chaos to a death-haunted ego and becomes a proof of power, of the mobility and survivability of the self that writes. So Zarathustra continues:

> Have you ever said yes to a single joy? O my friends, then you said Yes to *all* woe. All things are entangled, ensnared, enamored; if you ever wanted one thing twice, if you ever said, "You please me, happiness! Abide, moment!" then you wanted *all* back. All anew, all eternally, all entangled, ensnared, enamored—oh, then you *loved* the world. Eternal ones, love it eternally and evermore; and to woe too, you say: go, but return! *For all joy wants—eternity.* (Z IV "DS" 10)

Joy emerges as an encompassing absolute, like Blake's "perswasion," the origin and context of writing. Joy wants itself even in the guise of woe or failure. Eternity is not the elsewhere where we want to be but the hereness that wants only itself, and accepts whatever comes with it and makes it possible. This is another way of saying that to embrace one Zarathustra is to embrace them all, to embrace one part is to embrace the whole book, one book, the whole corpus, because they are parts of a tangled whole—though it remains unclear whether anyone but Zarathustra, or the *Übermensch*, can actually grasp that whole. In the end, Zarathustra exhorts and challenges: "Have you learned my song? Have you guessed its intent? Well then, you higher men, sing me now my round. Now you yourselves sing me the song whose name is 'Once More' and whose meaning is 'into all eternity'—sing you higher men, Zarathustra's round" (Z IV "DS" 12). The song, summarizing into a whole the bits and pieces of Zarathustra's unfolding vision, follows. Whether the higher men actually do sing, and if so, how well, Nietzsche does not say.

The final chapter of *Thus Spoke Zarathustra*, "The Sign," chronicles Zarathustra's ultimate refusal of the higher men, the kinds of readers that his gospelizing teachings have thus far attracted to him. We have not yet made much of the fact that the "revelations" of the previous chapter are characterized as a "drunken song," but the final distinction between Zarathustra and the higher men turns on two very different senses in which this is the case. Quite simply, as "The Sign" begins, the higher men are hung over, still sleeping it off, whereas Zarathustra is invigorated. He jumps up, girds his loins, and comes "out of his cave glowing and strong as a morning sun that comes out of dark mountains" (Z IV "Sign"). Addressing the new sun, he wonders "what would your happiness be had you not those for whom you shone? And if they stayed in their chambers even after you had awakened and come and given and distributed, how angry would your proud shame be!" (Z IV "Sign"). Zarathustra seems to recognize his need for an audience, for readers, in the same breath in which he condemns the audience he has for its lack of responsiveness. By failing to do as he does, by sleeping when he is awake, these higher men prove to Zarathustra that

> "*these* are not my proper companions. It is not for them that I wait here in my mountains. I wait to go to my work, to my day: but they do not understand the signs of my morning; my stride for them is no summons to awaken. They still sleep in my cave, their dream still drinks of my drunken songs. The ear that listens for *me*, the *heedful* ear is lacking in their limbs." (Z IV "Sign")

For Zarathustra (*in vino veritas*), the drunken song is a kind of Dionysian celebration, the "meaning" of which is in its effect. For higher men, it has been a kind of emotional bender, for now, drunk on their own sublimity, they have in a sense been laid to sleep by the culminating "wisdom" contained in this revelation. In the form of sleep, the things of the night intrude on the day, drunkenness intrudes on sobriety. Part of the "truth" of the song is that "knowledge"—even ultimate knowledge—is curiously abstruse and ineffectual. Knowledge in the univocal, empirical sense will not "answer" the questions propounded by "life." Life is not "deep" in any final sense; that too is just a metaphor. Even the deepest knowledge returns us to the tension between Dionysian night and Apollonian day, between Zarathustra the prophet and Zarathustra the workman. Kathleen Higgins is right to characterize this as "tragic," but the sense of tragic inevitability is turned on Zarathustra, and on his relationship with the higher men.

For, despite his initial sense that he is incomplete without an audience (how can one be a writer without readers?), the conditions which Zarathustra imposes on his audience are extraordinary, even solipsistic. He looks for the ear that listens for *me*—not for his words, not for the context of his wisdom, but for *me*. This "heedful" ear is lacking "in their limbs"; that is, intellectual, even emotional assent is not enough. This heedfulness is a predisposition, a physiological predisposition, over which they lack control or awareness. So extreme is Zarathustra's demand that the very possibility of such readers must be questioned, and we must wonder if Zarathustra is not articulating a mystery religion for one, if he is not reversing the biblical situation to make of himself a Moses who enters the promised land, leaving the Israelites in the wilderness.

But the appearance of the sign, the laughing lion, is taken by Zarathustra as a sign that such readers, his *equals*, do exist: "My children are near, my children" (Z IV "Sign"). And yet it seems that the readers he has can never be a *blood* relation. We infer this from Zarathustra's decisive judgment against them, when the lion drives the higher men back into the cave. Just then Zarathustra grasps the danger he has been in, how he was tempted by pity to accept the higher men, to play the role demanded by their need: "Well then, *that* has had its time! My suffering and my pity for suffering—what does it matter? Am

I concerned with *happiness*? I am concerned with my *work*" (*Z* IV "Sign"). What would the end of Zarathustra's work be if not happiness for himself and possibly others? He seems to repudiate the salvific ambitions of religion, the redemptive promise of the roles of teacher and pastor, even the pretensions of philosophy to point the way to a better life by answering the question "how ought I to conduct my life?" All these are pushed aside, as he brings to the fore the decisive *my*-ness of his work. If this sense of vocation makes it possible to put aside the dream of happiness, where does that leave Nietzsche's readers? Is there a sense in which, having followed him this far, they, like the higher men, are decisively excluded from the reward, from whatever makes the game worth the candle? Are readers stranded feeling that they have been seduced only to be jilted?

At the risk of caricature, there are two basically conflicting kinds of readings of the end of *Thus Spoke Zarathustra* and of the general situation we have been discussing—readings that have a decisive effect on the orientation of commentators to Nietzsche's other works and to his work as a whole. The first of these might be termed the "good faith" reading, which holds that *these* readers, the higher men, are, as individuals and as a group, not good enough. *Somewhere* perfect readers do exist or will exist. There are laughing lions after all, and, at the end, Zarathustra turns away from aspirants who have merely proven inadequate to go once more in search of those who are adequate. In this sense, Nietzsche's "writer" is a complex and troubled but still continuous transformation of the pastoral, gospelizing traditions, as well as a reinscription of the internalized quest romance. Kathleen Higgins's is an example of such a good faith reading, in which the author implicitly sees herself as the reader that Zarathustra lacks among the higher men, and justifies this self-image in a reading that inevitably takes the form of a defense or apologia, in which Nietzsche is "humanized." This strategy may create difficulties. For instance, Higgins is too good a reader not to recognize that Zarathustra questions his own "wisdom":

> The end of *Zarathustra*, then, involves a mixed message. Zarathustra's final words show that in a sense he *has* learned his own lesson. His concern with his work [whatever that is] reveals his recognition that the value of his present activity does not derive from the eventual "happiness" it may produce but instead is a quality of the activity itself. To this extent, he succeeds in living out the tragic world view. But all the same, we have no reason to expect this recognition to be any more a bastion against future failure than any of Zarathustra's other insights.[67]

Notice how internally conflicted the rhetoric of this formulation is: Zarathustra learned his lesson and the lesson he has learned is that learning that lesson means none of the things he had hoped.[68] This is not to deny that Zarathustra undergoes "genuine development as a thinker and teacher,"[69] but only to say its—the lesson's—value pertains to Zarathustra's vocation. We must wonder if Zarathustra does not, after all, secretly hope for happiness, if only as a by-product. But there is little here for Nietzsche's (or even Higgins's) readers, so she is more or less forced in a concluding section, "The Gospel of Loving Life," to reinstitute the paradigm of achievable "wisdom":

> Zarathustra's perspective at the end of the book represents Nietzsche's view of what it is to be serious about life. To be serious about life is not to commit oneself to a goal or abstract ideal and to be concerned obsessively with its successful realization. Instead, it is to be fully engaged in one's present. Full engagement in the present, while it involves recognition of the ends toward which immediate activities are directed, involves an appreciation of the immediate contents of the present as well. The present moment, at any point in time, however distant from the attainment of some projected goal, affords an experiential richness that itself makes life meaningful.[70]

This formulation may, by making *Thus Spoke Zarathustra* accessible, prompt the only half-facetious question about this long and complex book: "why not send a telegram or even a greeting card instead?" Of course, Higgins is aware of the problem. She notes, for instance (in a "deceptively simple statement"), that "Our lives are meaningful when we love our lives," which view allows her to modulate the earlier formulation. Now, the proper relation to life is like, and has the complex variety of, a love relationship. But this complexity also reminds us that Zarathustra's love of life is also a desire and determination that life love *him*, and this insistence runs counter to the enlightened humanism of Higgins's formulation.

Our point is not that Higgins is mistaken—she isn't—but that we do not find in *Thus Spoke Zarathustra* any perspective from which the competing claims of Higgins's "good faith" reading and the "bad faith" reading we will shortly be discussing can be decisively adjudicated. This means that Higgins's "answer" to the questions posed by the conclusion to *Thus Spoke Zarathustra* is prompted by the requirements of her own writing, *her* vocation, as much if not more than by the Nietzschean text per se. In the end, her reading of the anti-philosopher, Nietzsche, has the effect of preserving the appeal and identity of philosophy.[71]

From the perspective of the "bad faith" reading of *Zarathustra*, no reader can be adequate to his demands. In the end, Zarathustra turns his back on the readers he has seduced in order to enjoy the solipsistic pleasures of authorship. He is not a pastor but a seducer. And the figure of the writer ultimately represents, from this perspective, a radical and destructive break with the pastoral tradition and with the writer's traditional responsibility to others. "Nihilism," then, names the despair of the reader who has invested everything in the wisdom and project which both Zarathustra and Nietzsche repudiate.

In its crudest form, this bad faith reading results in something like Allan Bloom's view of Nietzsche as a virulently infectious nihilist.[72] A more subtle and even-handed reading of this type is offered by Karsten Harries in his penetrating essay, "The Philosopher at Sea," in which Harries analyzes Zarathustra's "voyage" in terms of two literary analogues. The story of how Ariadne's thread allows Theseus to find his way out of the labyrinth allows Harries to characterize the profundity of Nietzsche's project as a descent out of the precarious and defensive daylight of Western cultural institutions back into the labyrinth of a confused and contradictory being (without, perhaps, due regard for the consequences). Harries explains his sense of Nietzsche's recklessness by invoking the passage in the *Inferno* in which Dante encounters Ulysses in the circle reserved for false friends and counselors. Harries derives this by extension from a reference to the Argonauts in Nietzsche's speech on "The Great Health" toward the close of *The Gay Science*. However, as we pointed out earlier, the reference is even more explicit, and Nietzsche's awareness of the issue of his own culpability is even clearer in "The Shadow" of *Thus Spoke Zarathustra*. As Harries puts it:

> neither tenderness to his son nor reverence for his father nor love of Penelope could keep him from sailing beyond the land-locked Mediterranean, through the warning markers Hercules had set up so that no man would pass beyond; longing to gain experience of the world, he sailed west with those few companions who had not deserted him, only to be shipwrecked before that dark, monstrous mountain which lies far west from Jerusalem.[73]

Harries goes on to argue: "As there is something inhuman about Socrates's ascent into the light of the forms, so there is something inhuman about Zarathustra's descent into himself: both threaten the individual in his being with others."[74] Consequently, "Both Socrates and Zarathustra insist on a compensatory countermovement that lets the thinker whose pursuit of wisdom leads him beyond all community rejoin those he has left behind." Socrates has the escaped prisoner in the "Allegory of the Cave" return and "similarly, Zarathustra must leave the privacy of his cave high upon his mountain."[75] Of course, Harries neglects to remind us that, in Socrates's case, the price of readmission to the community is death. And while it is true that *Thus Spoke Zarathustra* begins with and traces the progress of Zarathustra's *Untergang*, the double-meaning of the term is disquieting, and it is by no means apparent that after he turns his back on the higher men—the result of that "undergoing"—he will consent to still another descent, thus raising the question of just what the form of Zarathustra's return to the human community might take.

In descending from his mountain, Harries notes, "Zarathustra must do violence to his private wisdom, just as his attempts to give voice to this wisdom must do violence to ordinary language."[76] Letting pass for the moment Harries's assumption of a private wisdom apart from and prior to its expression (setting aside the work done by "ordinary" language), this means of course that the wisdom we receive as readers is always the watered down version: Our permanent inferiority is built into the situation, and nihilism is the result. In addition, the violence done to ordinary language in the impossible effort to convey such a "private wisdom"—in other words, Nietzsche's style—not only deprives us of these resources, but it involves, too, a "leaping over of common sense that threatens the shipwreck of all sense."[77]

In Harries's view, a notion like that of eternal recurrence, that "offers his readers the coincidence of time and eternity as a gate to a reality that is deeper than our reason," *intends* the "shipwreck of common sense."[78] Thus, Nietzsche is most like Ulysses in his willingness to pay—and for us to pay—any price in his solipsistic pursuit of a ground of being or existence.

> While the word "overman" gestures toward the new land that Nietzsche would have us discover, it names no more than an ill-defined hope that remains in the subjunctive. Nietzsche thus writes only *as if* he confronted that still undiscovered overrich country that lures him. . . . He *knows* [our italics] that he is no position to begin surveying its boundaries. He also *knows* [our italics] that, like those of Dante's Ulysses, his curiosity and craving will not be sated by any discovery. In the end, what lures him is not so much the promise of a new land as the depth of the sea, the whirlpool that means shipwreck. Like his Zarathustra, Nietzsche wants to go *zu Grunde*, to perish.[79]

This knowledge—that he can't be sure the promised new land is there, that his craving and curiosity, unlike those of his fellows, cannot be satisfied, that his rejection of what *is* is so strong as to amount to a death wish—this is what Nietzsche must hide from his readers as Ulysses must hide it from his crew. He must at all costs hide the fact that unlike them, as in Tennyson's version of Dante's story, he doesn't really care if they find the Isles of the Blest (to which Zarathustra sails and returns) or not.

Yet in light of such recent theories of poetry and the poet as Harold Bloom's theory of poetic influence,[80] Harries's argument seems less and less like an indictment of Nietzsche and more and more like an indictment of authorship, particularly Romantic authorship. And a defense of Nietzsche on these points might well resemble a defense of Romanticism, which could hinge on the naked power and exemplary value of the *writing* which results. Of course, Harries's indictment is a measured one. He knows that

> "*zu Grunde Gehen*" in Zarathustra means not just to perish but to descend to the *Grund*, to the ground of human existence. . . . But *what right* [our italics] does Nietzsche have to posit such an eternal ground, a ground furthermore that is also said to be a text—a text that has authority precisely because we are not its author? . . . *What justifies* [our italics] the thought that, once we remove all the misrepresentations of past thinking, something like a *Grundtext* will appear? Is the very word *Grundtext* not an oxymoron that on reflection plunges us into an abyss? *Grund* and *Text*—how do these belong together? Is not a text necessarily a human product, a conjecture that falsely claims the authority of a

Grund? Where can we find a *Grund* to speak to us as a text would, presenting our existence with a measure? When we try to descend beneath the surface created by our discourse, strip reality of our fictions, what remains? Something that deserves to be called a *Grundtext*? Will we not stare rather into an *Abgrund*, into an abyss?[81]

Here, we would suggest, even allowing for the limits imposed by a Nietzschean perspectivism, some adjustment may be helpful. Indeed, Harries's response may be an instance of the alternative nihilism/condemnation dyad: both a cause and product of a too-biased reading of Nietzsche. For instance, Harries criticizes the notion of *Grundtext*, derived from the "book of nature written by God,"[82] because its authority is based precisely on the fact that we are not its authors. Yet this seems less a characterization of Nietzsche's thought (or of his project of *Untergang*) than an accurate though parodic representation of the values and expectations that draw readers to Nietzsche. Readers, as Groucho might have put it, are like people who would refuse to attend a party that would have them as guests. Harries, the higher man, is, in effect, arguing against himself, not Nietzsche, when he asks: "Is not a text necessarily a human product, a conjecture that falsely claims the authority of a *Grund*?" Yes, a text is a human product—even when, as here, it takes the form of a reading— and authorship does involve a hyperbolic discontinuity and assertion that is perpetually open to the question, "by what right?" But Zarathustra warns the higher men repeatedly; he calls attention to the appearance of a *Grundtext* that makes a text a text and draws readers to it. Is it Zarathustra's (or Nietzsche's) fault that the higher men are deaf to his warnings?

It is not clear whether Harries condemns Nietzsche for concealing his authorship or for being an author; it is increasingly clear that authorship is unavoidable. In the migration of meanings among terms which mark the unfolding of this passage, *Grund* and text are variously used to distinguish different aspects of the reader's experience of the text: human product from natural revelation, human from demonic. "Where can we find a *Grund* to speak to us as a text would, presenting our existence with a measure?" is still a complaint against Nietzsche's *text*, now even more nakedly seen as the object of the *reader's* Ulyssean desire to get to its bottom, to plumb its depths. And the abyss into which readers peer beneath the surface of things is that of the readerly desire to plumb the text to its depths, as it is, too, the sign of Nietzsche's Ulyssean blandishments.

Tennyson's "Ulysses" offers an instructive contrast to Dante's original, and especially to Harries's reading of it. Like "Childe Roland to the Dark Tower Came," "Ulysses" explores the Victorian poet's ambivalence over the Romantic inheritance which, in the case of the second generation Romantics, combines extraordinary poetic power with early death in a volatile and threatening myth which—not surprisingly—evokes a protest on behalf of the natural self.

Tennyson's Ulysses is the Romantic quester, one of Zarathustra's voyager/

leapers, who would "follow knowledge like a sinking star, / Beyond the utmost bound of human thought";[83] he is also the Romantic solipsist who rebels against the limitations of his securely socialized and humane role as king of Ithaca, where "Matched with an aged wife, I mete and dole / Unequal laws unto a savage race, / That hoard, and sleep, and feed and know not me."[84] The phrase, "And know not *me*," is powerfully reminiscent of Zarathustra's final complaint against the higher men: the "ear that listens for *me*" is lacking. This personal sublimity, which Zarathustra describes not as a sense of loving life but of being loved by her, is the demand which drives Ulysses causing him to reject his subjects just as Zarathustra rejects the higher men.

There is clearly something demonic here, something which offends against the humane values of the community that Ulysses confidently leaves in the care of his son, Telemachus ("He works his work I mine").[85] As Ulysses points out, the world will go on perfectly well without him, full as it is with people competent and suited to conduct "This labor, by slow prudence to make mild / A rugged people, and through soft degrees / Subdue them to the useful and the good." [86] Indeed, this insight—that for every Ulysses there is at least one Telemachus—raises questions about Harries's claim that Nietzsche not only intends but actually threatens the "wreck of common sense." Is common sense so fragile, is the world's hold so tenuous, or is this accusation itself a case of blaming the messenger for the message, an indication that, as the result of "the death of God," the reader is no longer isolated from the responsibilities and anxieties of authorship? These include the awareness that what reassuringly appears to be given ("common sense," for instance) is in fact fabricated. The confusion of text with *Grund*—this is the readerly desire that Harries attributes to Nietzsche.

Yet if Ulysses is not the threat to the community that some would have us believe, what about his relationship with his companions—those he tempts by his promise and his need to see themselves as of his kind? Tennyson's poem takes the form of Ulysses's eloquent exhortation and appeal to this crew he must have:

> . . . Come my friends,
> Tis not too late to seek a newer world.
> Push off, and sitting well in order smite
> The sounding furrows; for my purpose holds
> To sail beyond the sunset, and the baths
> Of all the western stars, until I die.
> It may be that the gulfs will wash us down;
> It may be we shell touch the Happy Isles,
> And see the great Achilles, whom we knew.
> Though much is taken, much abides; and though
> We are not now that strength which in old days
> Moved earth and heaven, that which we are, we are—

One equal temper of heroic hearts,
Made weak by time and fate, but strong in will
To strive, to seek, to find, and not to yield. [87]

Is this also a seduction? Ulysses holds out to himself and to his mariners the possibility of defeating time and age itself, though what Ulysses says and what the crew hears may not be the same. Something inaccessibly private and absolute may motivate him. Interestingly, the introduction of the themes of age and loss of strength, the dream of seeing Achilles, the figure of youthful strength—these effect a kind of reconciliation between Romantic and Victorian, writerly and readerly, needs. Ulysses's defiance of personal age and limitation; his sense that "though much is taken, much abides," answers to the Victorian poet's determination, late though it may be, to follow the precursors, and make the most of the possibilities that remain. That what Ulysses says and what others hear may not be the same does not preclude a common purpose and value.

We might say, then, that Tennyson's poem dramatizes the reader's conversion into writer, suggesting that the writer's absolute commitment to the craft need not be seen as a betrayal of the reader's interests and faith. It suggests, however indirectly, that readers can escape the disappointment of their hopes and expectations, the nihilism into which their project leads, by becoming writers ("would to God that all the Lord's people were prophets"), by reading in the mode of writing—which is to say, by writing criticism.

"Like his Zarathustra," Harries tells us, "Nietzsche wants to go *zu Grund*, to perish," thus bringing to the forefront the question of Nietzsche's relation to Zarathustra. We have already noted that Zarathustra's *Untergang* or going under is not the same as Harries's going *zu Grunde*, not so much a desire to perish or to go to the ground of being in a religious/philosophical sense as it is the writer's descent into the underworld in search of a voice and an identity. This writerly project allows Nietzsche to exploit these others, which it resembles, without giving itself over entirely to them. To put it another way, Nietzsche creates the character Zarathustra not just to express himself but also in order to put parts of himself off on him, just as Zarathustra puts parts of himself off on the higher men. The identification between Zarathustra and Nietzsche is both very strong and ultimately broken. This break holds out the possibility of a similar break for the higher men, for a "metaphysical" readership, with its ever lurking resentment.

From this perspective, *Thus Spoke Zarathustra* "consumes" the traditional discourse of gospelizing and the roles of prophet, teacher, and pastor only in the sense of assimilating them to writing and the situation of Nietzsche, who strives to find some way to believe in his own creation. Zarathustra takes on many roles, and some of these remain, now to be put on and taken off, without being accepted literally, but still to advantage. Now, they derive their value from the text that speaks them, not vice versa. In a sense, both Higgins's and Harries's difficulties with Nietzsche stem instructively from the same source: from an unwillingness to remember that Nietzsche is not a sage, teacher, or pastor, any more than he is Theseus or Ulysses. He is a writer—and yet they themselves fail to write accordingly.

5

Reading Ascetic Reading:
Toward the Genealogy of Morals and the Path Back to the World

the ascetic ideal springs from the protective instinct of a degenerating life which tries by all means to sustain itself and to fight for its existence; . . . life wrestles in it and through it with death and against death; the ascetic ideal is an artifice for the preservation of life —GM (III, 13).

A Genealogy of Genealogy

At the end of *Thus Spoke Zarathustra*, Zarathustra turns away from the higher men to his "work," perhaps even to go in search of the "laughing lions" whose sign he has just seen. Yet it is not clear what this means or where Zarathustra can go from here, since the materials of quest, pastoral care, and gospelizing have already been used up as it were in order to yield their ultimate product, the higher men.[1] Zarathustra/Nietzsche's "work"[2] could be the writerly task of composition but it is still unclear what comes next when so much—almost a whole gospelizing and literary tradition—has been used to arrive where he is. "My work," in its vagueness bespeaks a certain solipsistic sublimity—but threatens a kind of impasse, too.

One of the more suggestive analogies one can invoke is with the conclusion of Wordsworth's *Prelude*. The final book begins with an ascent of Mount Snowdon, culminating in a revelation of the power of the imagination and of its fundamental affinity with natural power that confirms Wordsworth in his identity as poet, great poet, successor and even potentially superior to Milton. This revelation is followed by a recapitulation and addresses to his sister, Dorothy, and his friend, Coleridge, before the poem winds up with a vision of Wordsworth (and Coleridge) as "prophets of nature," ministering in a redemptive fashion to all humanity.

Nevertheless, one cannot help noticing that the perspective from which Wordsworth announces his new identification with humanity is still that of the mountaintop, as if that height were more than mere metaphor, as if it was still somehow necessary to sustain the sublimity of his stance. Wordsworth seems unable to reconcile the writerly sublimity of his hard-won position as "a being of more than mortal privilege" with his more readerly and humane protestations that he is merely "a man talking to men."

The Recluse, the grand, "philosophic" poem that was to follow and make good on the promise of *The Prelude*, was never written. The one part that did appear, *The Excursion*, is one of nineteenth-century English poetry's most instructive failures. In it, Wordsworth's hero, the Wanderer, has the virtues of the poet without being a poet—without writing. He is a kind of ideal reader, possessing the receptivity and power of insight of the poet without the poet's egotism or disruptive strength of imaginative demand. The Wanderer confronts a number of characters afflicted to the point of despair or even death by the strong disease of undisciplined, unhumanized imagination. This imagination leads them to the brink of rejecting life itself. It is the task of the Wanderer to persuade them—especially his chief interlocutor, the Solitary—to accept life and particularly the fact of death, to re-envision life in the image of a more muted imagination and more modest demands.

A striking feature of this situation, however, is that Wordsworth is a poet and casts his poem of the imagination against itself as a poem. Where the Wanderer's speeches are not flat and prosodic, that is, where they achieve real power and appeal, his rhetoric is most like that of the Solitary. Indeed, the poem's appeal is largely dependent on the quality of the Solitary's speeches. Wordsworth is hopelessly ensnared in the ambiguity of his simultaneous allegiance to a demonic poetic imagination and to a humanizing imagination associated with an enlightened and insightful readership.

It has been argued elsewhere[3] that what Wordsworth would have written had he been able is something like a work of criticism in the broadest sense, perhaps in the sense that the third essay of *Toward the Genealogy of Morals* is a work of criticism. It has also been argued that the evolving Anglo-American critical tradition originates in the failure of poetry to do what the Romantics had hoped. This critical tradition retains in its origins the same ambivalence concerning the imagination which prevented Wordsworth from making the transition from his poem on the genealogy of the poet ("the growth of a poet's mind") to the philosophic poem beyond poetry that he essayed to write under Coleridge's influence. Finally, it has also been pointed out[4] that it is these same literary-critical heirs of Wordsworth who have, in the last fifteen years or so, discovered and been deeply influenced by Nietzsche, directly or indirectly—perhaps for reasons that have as much to do with the requirements of their own tradition as with a sudden conversion to the style and substance of European philosophizing.

It is against this background that *Toward the Genealogy of Morals*—as the culmination of the movement down from Zarathustra's mountaintop begun with *Beyond Good and Evil*, and as the presumptive manifestation of his "work" (*Werk*)—assumes particular importance. That Nietzsche succeeds in finding his way back to the world (and in externalizing in some sense his concluding stance in *Thus Spoke Zarathustra*), and that this helps to explain Nietzsche's importance for his critical heirs, is our initial thesis here.

As a project of externalization, an attempt to define a path back to the world, *Toward the Genealogy of Morals* is also of particular importance for the argument we will be exploring here: that it is useful to read the significant context and immediate referend of Nietzsche's philosophy, in both its negative and positive aspects, as his own practice as a writer. It is one of the canards most frequently levelled at Nietzscheanizing literary critics—critics like Bloom and de Man (who see works of literature as commenting on their own origins and status as works of fiction)—that their emphasis on self-referentiality somehow undermines or excludes the very possibility of referentiality, of significant address to the world. In the case of Nietzsche, this accusation might well take the form of a complaint that the claim that Nietzsche is constantly referring to his own practices and identity as a writer undercuts, even makes impossible, readings that would see him as a philosopher, engaged with and attempting to make his own contribution to the philosophical tradition. This is not the case, either in general, or for Nietzsche.

We think that *Toward the Genealogy of Morals* shows not only that Nietzsche was aware of the problem but that he can usefully be read as rationalizing, if only implicitly, his dependence on his writer's self-experience as the origin/referend and necessary complement both of his parabolic fictionalizing in *Thus Spoke Zarathustra* and of his philosophizing. And it can be argued that it is precisely his success in forging this link between self and world, in demonstrating the general significance of internal self-experience that authorizes and releases the outpouring of (mock) autobiography and reflexive commentary that mark the final stage of Nietzsche's career.

To anticipate somewhat, these later works develop Nietzsche's interest—frequently expressed in *Toward the Genealogy of Morals*—in the physiological origins of moral evaluations and act out the supercession of the Romantic conception of writing/thinking as "expression" by what might be called "embodiment." Tracy Strong has remarked that Nietzsche

> wants us to encounter these texts as we would encounter another person, with the assurance of his presence. As with other people, we can never start or end by claiming to know what they mean—we do not mean the statement "I know John" to be equivalent to "I know what John means." We do not, therefore, if Nietzsche be correct, learn from them by determining what they mean, as if they were a container for his "message." We learn from them by finding ourselves in them.[5]

In contrast, our reading of *Thus Spoke Zarathustra* IV[6] suggests that the focus of Nietzsche's interest is not only in how this sense of "finding ourselves" in the text is frequently an illusion, but in how exploiting this illusion is the writer's stock in trade. And Strong's sense that Nietzschean embodiment also offers "the assurance of his [or any] presence" similarly strikes us as wide of the mark. Our point is not that the writer's embodiment of his or her ideas is a superior guarantee of genuineness; rather, embodiment represents a reconceiving which constitutes both a challenge and an addition to the philosophical tradition of how meaning happens. After all, actors also "embody," and few philosophers have been more alert to the variety of dramatic possibilities than Nietzsche, the theorist of tragedy and comedy alike. And, in this connection (on the subject of embodiment), it is often said that *Toward the Genealogy of Morals* is the most "digestible" of Nietzsche's major works, the one that looks most like an "argument." Perhaps for that very reason, it makes sense for us to pay more careful attention to the details of its unfolding than is frequently done.

"We are unknown to ourselves, we men of knowledge" (*GM* "NP" 1), Nietzsche begins, because we are concentrating too much on the object of our knowledge for self-knowledge to set in. Like critics intent on literature, Nietzsche's men of knowledge—and he does not exclude himself—are for the most part blind to the nature and origins of their own practices.[7] The comparison is particularly appropriate for a book culminating in a chapter that presents itself as a "commentary" on a few lines from *Thus Spoke Zarathustra*. The peculiar function of the genealogist, Nietzsche implies, is to alert us to the ground we stand on and which, for that very reason, we cannot normally see. Not that our "ground" is hidden from view, however; it hides in plain sight. As the ground we stand on, nothing is farther from us than our own practices, yet somehow, Nietzsche's stance gives him—and, through him, us—access.

The origins of the present attempt to examine the origins of our moral prejudices go back, we are told, to before the aphoristic work *Human, All Too Human*. In that book, Nietzsche tells us, he was able "to pause as a wanderer pauses and look back across the broad and dangerous country my spirit had traversed up to that time" (*GM* "NP" 2). The ideas contained here, however, are even older. But not only does Nietzsche still cling to them, "they have become in the meantime more and more firmly attached to one another, indeed entwined and interlaced with one another . . . arisen in me from the first not as isolated, capricious, or sporadic things but from a common root, from a *fundamental will* of knowledge, pointing imperiously into the depths, speaking more and more precisely, demanding greater and greater precision" (*GM* "NP" 2). Over time, largely in and through the medium of writing, an immanent intentionality or necessity has emerged, manifested in the way that diffuse ideas have revealed their underlying interrelatedness. The affinities between this "fundamental will of knowledge" and will to power are clear enough, and invite in the midst of this discussion of origins the speculation that the self-experience hyperbolically becomes the origin of the idea, without defining it sufficiently.

But the origins of this project go even farther back, to childhood, to,

Nietzsche writes, "a scruple peculiar to me that I am loth to admit to—for it is concerned with *morality*, with all that has hitherto been celebrated on earth as morality—a scruple that entered my life so early, so uninvited, so irresistibly, so much in conflict with my environment, age, precedents, and descent that I might almost have the right to call it my 'a priori'" (*GM* "NP" 3). What is this scruple that sets Nietzsche apart from all that one would expect from a bookish young German son of a clergyman? What is this early, uninvited, irresistible—this "already" or "before"—scruple that makes him the genealogist he is?

Paul Bové has commented on this very passage in his essay, "Mendacious Innocents, or, The Modern Genealogist as Conscientious Intellectual: Nietzsche, Foucault, Said." According to Bové, the Nietzschean genealogist is the type of the modern "oppositional critic," who here "identifies his difference from his age as the enabling factor of his insight and practice":

> Nietzsche gives us in this passage the scene of instruction of the conscientious intellectual. The violent penetration of consciousness by a "scruple" antagonistic to the shell of public sentiment is the initial weighing of Nietzsche's peculiarity. The cutting edge of this uninvited guest frees the intellectual's curiosity to examine a common phenomenon, morality, in an uncommon light, free of societal preconceptions. In fact, this irresistible scruple guides this curiosity in a struggle against family, nation, and religion—evils which must be overflown. The genealogist is "born" in a revolt against the given; the sharp edge of the liberating scruple which tears the obscuring veil of the hegemonic figures of morality becomes a pointed weapon not only goading the conscientious intellectual along in his process of research and individuation, but also fracturing the dynastic edifice against which the genealogist defines himself. This originary scruple, this "a priori" which enables genealogical research and individuation, is also a measure of success. . . .
> But this scruple exists nowhere but in the system of research, individuation, and liberation. It "enters," but from no "outside." Its "entrance" is merely a penetration pricking consciousness, announcing a "choice" of "identity" to be struggled for in the rhetorical and research struggle of the conscientious intellectual against the hegemonic mediation of meaning and value in his culture.[8]

In the end, Nietzsche's "a priori," which allows him to challenge the "hegemonic figures of morality" and fracture "the dynastic edifice" of his culture, comes down to "merely a penetration pricking consciousness." And this scruple "exists nowhere but in the system of research, individuation, and liberation." We have argued ourselves that it is in writing that Nietzsche's self-knowledge originates and emerges, that Bové's "nowhere but" is troubling, as is the vagueness of "a penetration pricking consciousness." Neither formulation quite seems adequate to the question that Bové shares with Nietzsche: "How *does* one get free of societal preconceptions?" Moreover, even this formulation leaves unclear its precise relationship with the far more specific story that Nietzsche claims to be telling: "How I became a genealogist / I have always been a genealogist."

And nothing in Bové's argument, which accommodates Nietzsche so neatly to the right-mindedness of Said and Foucault, gives even a hint as to why Nietzsche would be "loth to admit" to his scruple. Certainly no modern conscientious intellectual, no oppositional critic, hesitates for a second to do so. Make no mistake about it, there is much in Nietzsche that we do not approve of, much that makes us uneasy, much to make us doubt the ease of this accommodation.

Perhaps Bové does put his finger on something when he says that the "genealogist is 'born' in revolt." If we dispose of the quotation marks and take the figure seriously—this is, after all, what is at stake in one's genealogy—we begin to see that although the a priori emerges in the writing, the work, it is in relation to the work that it serves as a "before" or "already." In other words, what is at issue here is where and in what manner the project of writing, Nietzsche's work, touches the person, the life, the world—on what terms has self-experience been generalized, translated into concept and commentary. For instance, of the origins of "evil," Nietzsche writes:

> my curiosity as well as my suspicions were bound to halt quite soon at the question of where our good and evil really *originated*. In fact, the problem of the origin of evil pursued me even as a boy of thirteen: at an age in which you have "half childish trifles, half God in your heart," I devoted to it my first childish literary trifle, my first philosophical effort—as for the "solution" of the problem I posed at that time, well, I gave the honor to God, as was only fair, and made him the *father* of evil. (*GM* "NP" 3)

Here, Nietzsche's italics suggest that the father's death is connected with the scruple that entered Nietzsche's life "so early, so uninvited, so irresistibly" as to put him in conflict with "environment, age, precedents, and descent." "Fortunately," he "learned early to separate theological prejudice from moral prejudice and ceased to look for the origin of evil *behind* the world" (*GM* "NP" 3).

The separation that imparts the genealogist's perspective arises from this point of view, from the loss of the father. Nietzsche's first attempt to conceptualize that loss results in accusing the God, whose death he will later simply announce. That form allows him, by examining, questioning, and revising, to veer away from literal origins toward autonomous self-creation. Nevertheless, Nietzsche suggests, his writing, and therefore "Nietzsche" himself, are about the loss of the father. His externalization, conceptualization, and generalization are rational and justified insofar as the loss of the father and its consequences are of collective concern. Yet this origin, like the Freudian primal scene, is incurably ambiguous. Nietzsche cannot "know" that this narrative of origin is "true." He can only choose it or, perhaps to capture the quality of the thing more precisely, consent to be chosen by it.

To choose an origin or literality, to speak it, however indirectly, is to give up the would-be writer's dream, the illusion of originality as autochthony, or at least to mitigate it severely. Nietzsche recalls: "at length I had a country of my own, a soil of my own, an entire discrete, thriving, flourishing world, like a secret garden the existence of which no one suspected.—Oh! how fortunate we are, we men of knowledge, provided only that we know how to keep silent long enough!" (*GM* "NP" 3). This secret garden, this private, compensatory Eden in which the man of knowledge "rules" and dwells apart, playing at infinite potential, requires silence. It cannot survive formulation or exposure. In order to speak, to externalize, it is necessary to accept reduction, limitation, specificity—to accept the literal origin that is at one with a distinctive voice or style. But this still leaves us short of a satisfying explanation of why Nietzsche is "loth" to admit his scruple.

The fictional character, Zarathustra, who comes from nowhere in particular and goes nowhere in particular, is the center of a work addressed to everyone and no one. This infinite power of making, of evading, of feigning, of now being, now merely using Zarathustra—the same mobility and plasticity that moved Plato to banish poets from his Republic—Nietzsche is loth to forego. He is reluctant to remove the mask of Zarathustra, even though the Nietzsche behind it can only be a mask of Nietzsche. This is because the genealogy, which now accepts or emanates from an origin, is far from unambiguous—it is not even, contra Bové, unambiguously "oppositional." What Derrida will call "the name of Nietzsche," which must bear responsibility for what "the ear of the other"—including the Nazi ear—will make of it, which is the only conceivable recipient of the fame which the dead man himself cannot inherit, is given here.

Nietzsche names himself "fatherless" (or perhaps even better, since Wordsworth uses this same term to describe the imagination, "unfathered"). Whether this name is the end or origin of Nietzsche's quest is not clear. The writer's work of self-construction/discovery is irreducibly ambiguous, as uncertain as the literality of the Freudian primal scene or as obscure as the distinction between questing after the name one desires and questing to desire the name one has already been given, as in Browning's "Childe Roland to the Dark Tower Came." Nevertheless, the founding gesture of Nietzsche's genealogy can with profit, we think, be construed as this reaching out toward the world, toward "literal" origins, which sites and embodies the heretofore unembodied power of making and conceiving everywhere at play in *Thus Spoke Zarathustra*, which opens it to responsibility and guilt and above all, returns it to a world everywhere infected with the awareness of mortality.

Of course, not every fatherless child is a Nietzsche. While Nietzsche could not have named himself "fatherless" in this way without a real father who really died, this literal fact fails to help us much here. The denomination retains a connection with the fictional, asserts a mythic specialness, calling to mind as it does Oedipus, whose father's death is at once a contingent fact, an accident, and a structural necessity of his fatality—the central, exemplary figure of the tragic vision of the West. So if the literal fact of his father's death makes of the genealogy a history, or at least an interpretive history, the mythic dimension of his fatherlessness, its representation as self-presentation, also makes of the genealogy the story that requires Nietzsche as its authoritative commentator, the history that needs him as its last man or decadent as well as the avatar of its self-overcoming.

Nietzsche's immediate claim is that the fact of his fatherlessness freed him from the automatic investment in and identification with the received ideas and prejudices of his culture, deprived him of the automatic identification with received authority that is the patrimony of the fathered, and thus made possible the oppositional stance of the genealogist. But this singularity, this power of standing aside, is also a loss of patronymic, which is to say "natural," authority: authority that is never questioned because it is transmitted in the guise of biology, with mortality in the blood. Authority, wrapped in the awesome power of society and culture, fuses its own arrangements with the "natural," thus eliciting a tenuous sense of security. But such assurance (or "legitimacy," a term which resonates with the Socratic connection between the authority of the father, the claim of truth, and the activity of philosophy) can never be restored; its absence is the wound or limp that makes the genealogist and requires from Nietzsche the writer the assertiveness, the élan, the gaiety, the hyperbole that aim less at authority than at assurance. In this sense, then, "fatherless" names the lack that makes him a writer and that, furthermore, makes him the writer he is.

Much of this recalls Wordsworth in more than a casual way. The imagination is compared in *The Prelude* to the "unfathered" vapor that arises to confuse Wordsworth and his companion in the Simplon Pass. That episode leads directly to a revelation of pure, unsublimated imagination viewed as an apocalyptic power that portends the loss of the natural world. Furthermore, Nietzsche's originating "a priori," ambiguously found or created, recalls the "before" of Wordsworth's great "Intimations" ode, the imagined fore-life that becomes in him the means of detaching the sense of loss which haunts the individual from the Christian myth of original sin. That "before" creates the possibility that life is and must be its own compensation by radically shifting perspective away from the anticipation of a compensatory elsewhere, a life after death. In Wordsworth's case, that the strategy fails in its transumptive attempt to assuage his personal fear of death is indicated by the fact that the poem ends with those "thoughts that lie too deep for tears"—much less poetry—presumably, thoughts of his own death.

What is at stake early in *Toward the Genealogy of Morals* is less clear, although it would seem to bear on what, for want of a better term, we have here called embodiment—something at the intersection of mortal finitude, writing, and imagination/conceptualization. Perhaps of greater significance, however, is the comparison between a writer who names himself "unfathered" and one who, like the Wordsworth of *The Prelude*, is "unmothered" yet somehow refuses that ascription. Although Wordsworth adverts more or less in passing to the deaths of both of his parents, in *The Prelude*, it is clearly the death of his mother that is fundamental. The freedom to roam the hills of the Lake District and to discover himself as a child of nature, to which he attributes his special poetic powers, is also the result of the loss of maternal care and a compensation for that loss. The special sense that he is a "being of more than mortal privilege" makes him a poet, makes him the poet he is, and is bafflingly inseparable from a traumatic loss. The project of finding a principle of compensation for loss and death takes the form of a search for a sense of well-being ultimately associated with the security of the child in its mother's arms ("nature never did betray / The heart that loved her,"[9] he says hopefully).

In *The Prelude*, Wordsworth names himself a "child of nature," denying—as Nietzsche does not—that he is also, perhaps even more fundamentally, a child of death. The strength of Wordsworth's denial seems to tie him ever more strongly to the problem of death, commits him to the task of defining a compensation adequate to the terrifying intimacy of *my* death—or to evading the impossibility of doing so. For Wordsworth, the loss of the mother suggests the loss of a certain assurance in his relationship with nature; the deepening of thought and feeling that follows this loss must be our compensation. For Nietzsche, in contrast, the loss of the father signifies the loss of a certain assurance that is social rather than "natural": his compensation is not to imagine himself as "a power like one of nature's" but as the autonomous source of an assurance like (and the discontinuity of the figural is crucial here) that of society itself, which is to say the autonomous source of a power of feigning "nature," of self-transcending assertion. Yet this power can only be antithetical, originating as it does in loss, situated actorishly, indeterminately, somewhere between ironic self-awareness and auto-hypnosis.

Wordsworth's pursuit of a fundamental sense of well-being associated with nature leads ultimately to a politics of quietism, even conservatism. Nietzsche names the loss or lack at the origin and claims it as the source of his special socio/cultural power, his freedom from the moral prejudices within which others live unquestioningly. It is less clear what kind of politics, if any in particular, is implicit in such a stance, although Jacques Derrida has argued on the basis of subsequent events, perhaps more subtly than many, that there is something about Nietzsche that beckons compellingly to Naziism or to something like it.[10]

A Genealogy of Composition/Decomposition

He was first moved to publish his ideas on the origins of morality, Nietzsche tells us, by Paul Rée's *Origins of the Moral Sensations*, not as an instance of academic "hypothesis mongering" but as an opportunity to raise the question of "the *value* of morality"—a question all but unposed because the value of the phenomenon is simply assumed. In those rare instances where this has not been the case, as with Nietzsche's "great teacher," Schopenhauer, the value attributed to morality and particularly to pity, is the opposite of Nietzsche's estimation:

> What was especially at stake was the value of the "unegoistic," the instincts of pity, self-abnegation, self-sacrifice, which Schopenhauer had gilded, deified, and projected into a beyond for so long that at last they became for him "value-in-itself," on the basis of which he *said No* to life and to himself. But it was against precisely *these* instincts that there spoke from me an ever more fundamental mistrust, an ever more corrosive skepticism! It was precisely here that I saw the great danger to mankind, its sublimest enticement and seduction—but to what? to nothingness?—it was precisely here that I saw the beginning of the end, the dead stop, a retrospective weariness, the will turning *against* life, the tender and sorrowful signs of the ultimate illness: I understood the ever spreading morality of pity that had seized even on philosophers and made them ill, as the most sinister symptom of a European culture that had itself become sinister, perhaps as its by-pass to a new Buddhism? to a Buddhism for Europeans? to—*nihilism*? (*GM* "NP" 5)

"Pity" names the bad conscience infecting the individual's relationship with the gifts—beauty, strength, vitality—that life has bestowed. In a world filled with the sick, pity argues, how can the healthy help but feel guilty? Yet pity deprives us of the basis for a *positive* attachment to life, which makes no sense when appreciation of its compensations is repressed. Pity, Nietzsche implies, is the temptation to renounce (as opposed to valuing) the good because it is so unevenly distributed. The tainting of life's compensations with guilt creates the permanent imbalance between loss and compensation which constitutes nihilism, weariness: a turning against life arrested only by the invention of an imaginary existence elsewhere—that is, by Christian morality and eschatology.

The first problem with this account of pity and nihilism is the similarity it suggests between self-overcoming and pity, or even nihilism. How are they to be distinguished? Perhaps it can be argued that the self is overcome in the name of what is best in us, whereas in pity, what is best is overcome out of a loyalty to the condition of the majority. Such an analysis may cast light on structuralist and post-structuralist deconstructions of the self, which follow Nietzsche in the critique of a particular structure or ideology of selfhood, but diverge from him in an attack on the self in the name of a levelling politics, if not of pity then of equality. For Foucault and Derrida,[11] the deconstruction of the self takes the form of questioning the role of the author as the "sovereign" origin of his or her own text.

It is worth noting that Nietzsche's analysis of pity is first and foremost intertextual: as reader, he finds his own fate in Schopenhauer's. Part of the problem seems to be what Schopenhauer says, and part to be the position of reader itself. In one sense, Nietzsche's rejection of pity (somewhat like Blake's) is a rejection of the claims of a consumerist conception of the legitimacy of the reader's demands; still more precisely (and perhaps less "elitist") it might be seen as an argument against the author's preemptive capitulation to the imagined needs and demands of an absent readership. For an author, the audience is as much a fiction as author is for a reader. And if the "being" written is as unstable, as much a projection as the "sovereign" being who writes, then the benefits derived from renouncing authorial authority belong to the same imaginary space as the powers attributed to authorship.

As we have already noted, Nietzsche also seems to suggest that nihilism is the reader's disease. The reader, like Nietzsche—like Western civilization—is somehow "unfathered." Nietzsche knows—at least after *Thus Spoke Zarathustra* IV—that however much he is prepared to claim for himself as author in the face of the claims of the reader, his own "corrosive skepticism" as a reader undermines the author/father, drives a wedge between the two functions, and leaves the fatherless reader exposed to the nihilism, the sense of futility that attends this unlooked-for loss. As Nietzsche argues, God is not merely dead, we have killed him (*GS*, III "The Madman"). When he acknowledges his fatherlessness as the origin of his unusual perspective on morality, he not only acknowledges his father's antecedence, he *chooses* it. This positive choice of what is "true" allows him not only to judge but to kill this antecedence, and so to reduce it to "a being destined merely to pass by." Nietzsche's relationship to Schopenhauer here is equally instructive. Schopenhauer is his antecedent; in him, he discovers himself. Schopenhauer is also the prime example of the author who, in renouncing the predecessor's authority, exposes readers (including Nietzsche) to the nihilism of the unfathered. But how is Schopenhauer, whose pity unfathers the reader, any different from Nietzsche, whose corrosive commentary also undermines the author and unfathers the reader?

A crucial distinction seems to exist between commentary, in which authorship or writing is reinscribed within reading, and a readership which remains totally exposed to the death of the author as father. To put it differently, Nietzsche, the genealogist/commentator, chooses the identity "unfathered," whereas fatherlessness merely befalls the normal reader. It is no accident that this motif echoes Nietzsche's famous formulation at the end of *Toward the Genealogy of Morals*, "man would rather will *nothingness* than not *will*." That choosing fatherlessness is better then simply being fatherless accounts for the profound affinity that Nietzsche and commentary in general have for asceticism. At the same time, that fatherlessness and nothingness are not the same helps to account for his rejection of asceticism. In this context, the choice of "fatherlessness" is linked to the actual hyperbolic "What if?" that begins Nietzsche's project and defines its antithetical method:

One has taken the *value* of these "values" as given, as factual, as beyond all question; one has hitherto never doubted or hesitated in the slightest degree in supposing "the good man" to be of greater value than "the evil man," of greater value in the sense of further-ing the advancement and prosperity of man in general (the future of man included). But what if the reverse were true? What if a symptom of regression were inherent in the "good," likewise a danger, a seduction, a poison, a narcotic, through which the present was possibly living *at the expense of the future*? (*GM* "NP" 6)

There is nothing, Nietzsche tells us, more worth taking seriously than the problem of morality, and he marks this valuation by a dramatic reversal. Per-haps our valuations are the opposite of our true interests. Perhaps our malaise results from our mistaken valuations,

among the rewards for it being that some day one will perhaps be allowed to take them *cheerfully*. For cheerfulness—or in my own language *gay science*—is a reward: the reward of a long, brave, industrious, and subterranean seriousness, of which, to be sure, not everyone is capable. But on the day we can say with all our hearts, "Onwards! our old morality too is part of the comedy!" we shall have discovered a new complication and possibility for the Dionysian drama of "The Destiny of the Soul"—and one can wager that the grand old eternal comic poet of our existence will be quick to make use of it! (*GM* "NP" 8)

It is now the "eternal comic poet of our existence" and not the father or God the Father with whom we must deal. He is a comic poet in part because he mocks our tendency to see ourselves as the culmination and end—and to de-spair accordingly—instead of as a mere stage in the march of our kind. Even more, the unfolding spectacle of existence, seen from the genealogist's anti-thetical perspective, mocks all our solemn pretensions to knowing where we are or what we are actually doing. It is impossible to estimate the value of life or to justify it by aesthetic means—or by any others for that matter.[12]

Indeed, the "economic" imbalance that motivates *Toward the Genealogy of Morals* to begin with, challenges the totalizing claims of the aesthetic/tragic vi-sion of *The Birth of Tragedy*. The "tragic" apprehension of *Thus Spoke Zarathus-tra*, for example, is a sign of the limits of fictions, of their irreducible difference from the world and betrays a certain temptation to see this as a "thing-in-it-self." The cheerfulness, the gaiety of Nietzsche's new "science" stem from the fact that we no longer need to feel that everything depends on frail and inad-equate *us*. Again, the contrast is between a tragic vision, in which the author is doomed to fall short in his attempts to convey a message of urgent, even sal-vific, importance, and a comic one, in which the author recognizes that every-thing is not up to him, that there is plenty going on (perhaps even in his own text) to which he may be blind and over which he may have no control.

In this context, self-overcoming is more a self-affirmation of the authorial self in its finitude than a self-hating rejection of the self for its failures or imperfections. Kathleen Higgins argues that "The central, 'tragic' message of Zarathustra is that meaning in life is to be found in simply loving life for its own sake."[13] The "eternal comic poet" of *Genealogy* suggests that we can also love life for what it engenders and makes possible, even out of its errors. Whether we view life tragically or comically, we are doing something with life and to it, not just apprehending a "thing-in-itself." The problem posed by Nietzsche's comic vision, like that posed by his tragic vision, is, then, one of identification. In the former case, it is the capacity of a yearning, finite being to identify with a temporal extensiveness that is indifferent to its desires but, for that reason, liberating. In the latter case, it is the capacity of a being with unlimited desires to identify with a finite and therefore absolutely limited existence. The way toward the comic vision is blocked by the complexities and challenge of eternal recurrence; the way to the tragic vision is blocked by the logic of asceticism. Again, the analogy is literary: the book that we are writing must be good enough to justify it and us; on the other hand, we need no justification and it is only one book among many.

The importance of commentary is confirmed in the conclusion to Nietzsche's Preface, which not only calls attention to the fact that the third essay is an "exegesis" of a single aphorism, but recommends the aphorism as a form whose essence is that it requires exegesis. It draws the reader into an *askesis* fundamentally different from contemporary standards of "readability." Nietzsche makes demands on his readers, but these demands are anything but paternal. For instance, Nietzsche's first essay aims to show how the familiar distinction between "Good and Evil" actually overlays and intends to obscure a far more archaic and fundamental distinction between "Good and Bad" (like corpus over corpse, perhaps). Nietzsche derides "English psychologists" for an ahistorical method which merely imposes their own prejudices on the question of morality. The true origins of judgments of the good, he argues, were not with those benefited but with the "good" themselves. The noble called themselves "good," the lower orders "bad," not out of some utility but out of a "pathos" of distance—a distance somewhat reminiscent of the reader/writer relationship we have been discussing. Appropriately, the essay, an etymological investigation, reveals a consistent connection between words designating "'noble,' 'aristocratic' in the social sense" (*GM* I "GEGB" 3) and "'good,' in the sense of 'with aristocratic soul,' 'noble,' 'with a soul of a high order,' 'with a privileged soul'" (*GM* I "GEGB" 4). Indeed, "through the words and roots that designate 'good' shines the most important nuance by virtue of which the noble felt themselves to be men of a higher rank" (*GM* I "GEGB" 5). Typically, they refer to themselves as "the truthful," not in our conditional and moralistic sense, but in the sense of "one who *is*, who possesses reality, who is actual, who is true." By contrast, the common man "lies" in that he is at a greater distance from being (*GM* I "GEGB" 5).[14]

This redefinition of the truthful/lying distinction, like the argument of *Genealogy* as a whole, undercuts the authority of a readership inclined to measure a writer by the standards of its "reality." Revealing this reality to be constituted by fictions more egregious and less aware of themselves than those of many writers, Nietzsche not only puts readership at a disadvantage but projects the problem of authorship and the fictional onto the stage of morality and of society. But according to Nietzsche, this alternative system of valuation has been suppressed (though imperfectly, since its traces can still be read, by means of etymology, on the body of language). For Nietzsche, it is through etymology that language speaks for itself in a voice apart from conscious use, apart from the impositions of prejudice and ruling concept. In fact, Nietzsche's reading presents the moral point of view as the repression of what reappears (or persists) in the body of language like the symptoms of hysteria on the body of a patient. This link between hysteria and etymology as the symptom of a language which serves, at times unwillingly, as the body of thought is more than casual. In a long note to the concluding section of the first essay, Nietzsche calls for the interests of "philologists, historians, and philosophers" on the one hand, and "physiologists and doctors" on the other to converge on the question of the origin and evolution of moral concepts (*GM* I "GEGB" 17). And he closes the section itself emphatically:

> The well-being of the majority and the well-being of the few are opposite viewpoints of value: to consider the former *a priori* of higher value may be left to the naïveté of English biologists.—*All* the sciences have from now on to prepare the way for the future task of the philosophers: this task is understood as the solution of the *problem of value*, the determination of the *order of rank among values*. (*GM* I "GEGB" 17)

At the end of the twentieth century, we may well prefer the naïveté of English biologists to that of German philosophers, but what is striking is the convergence between this large clash of social (and even bio-social) values and the problematic of author/reader relations. The interests and authority of the one are pitted against the claims and demands of the many. And yet neither the archaic equivalence of "truth" and "proximity to being," nor the ideal of an order of rank among competing values, describes the actual evolution of moral concepts under the influence of religion in general and Christian asceticism in particular. The key figure in this evolution is the priest, whose appearance as part of the noble class does not necessarily contradict the rule that political superiority resolves itself into superiority of soul. The priestly opposition between "pure" and "impure" is initially taken quite literally by ancient folk whose notions were essentially unsymbolic. Nevertheless, though they still designate a difference in station, these concepts introduce something that is not entirely concerned with station—an abstract, qualitative distinction which creates the possibility of an alternative form of valuation. Despite the initial innocuousness of their appearance, these new concepts are pernicious:

> it is clear from the whole nature of an essentially priestly aristocracy why antithetical valuations could in precisely this instance soon become dangerously deepened, sharpened, and internalized; and indeed they finally tore chasms between man and man that a very Achilles of a free spirit would not venture to leap without a shudder. There is from the first something *unhealthy* in such priestly aristocracies and in the habits ruling in them which turn them away from action and alternate between brooding and emotional explosions, habits which seem to have as their almost invariable consequence that intestinal morbidity and neurasthenia which has afflicted priests at all times. (*GM* I "GEGB" 6)

Indeed, Nietzsche's treatment of the priest's "intestinal morbidity and neurasthenia" forcefully recalls Nietzsche's own chronic ailments, and the antithetical valuations of the priest are echoed and (perhaps) even parodied in Nietzsche's own antithetical method. By their bad health we shall know them. And could the author by his *askesis* to some degree be acknowledging his alignment with the valuations of the priests?

Be that as it may, on one point Nietzsche distinguishes himself. The priest, he says, sought to remedy this morbidity by means of asceticism, which "has ultimately proved itself a hundred times more dangerous in its effects than the sickness it was supposed to cure." And so the species goes on, but goes on, impaired:

> [it] is still ill with the effects of this priestly näiveté in medicine! Think, for example, of certain forms of diet (abstinence from meat), of fasting, of sexual continence, of flight "into the wilderness" (the Weir Mitchell[15] isolation cure—without, to be sure, the subsequent fattening and overfeeding which constitute the most effective remedy for the hysteria induced by the ascetic ideal): add to these the entire antisensualistic metaphysic of the priests that makes men indolent and overrefined, their autohypnosis in the manner of fakirs and Brahmins . . . and finally the only-too-comprehensible satiety with all this, together with the radical cure for it, *nothingness* . . . (*GM* I "GEGB" 6)

The suppression and paralysis of the senses and the consequent distance from being is explicitly characterized as an hysteria which even now we try to treat with more asceticism—an hysteria whose symptomology the etymologist finds apparent in the body of language, which is, in turn, confined and silenced in part by the tyranny of moral ideas. Still, Nietzsche adds, it is only "on the soil of this *essentially dangerous* form of human existence, the priestly form, that man first became *an interesting animal*, that only here did the human soul acquire *depth* and become *evil*—and these are the two basic respects in which man has hitherto been superior to the beasts!" (*GM* "GEGB" 6).

Nietzsche's intertwining of the state of language and the state of the body allows inspection of the pathology of conceptualization in the West, in which the suppression of the senses and devaluation of the body, on the one hand, are answered by the limitation and restraint of language, on the other hand. This asceticism of language and of the body makes conception possible by giving humanity *depth*. The relevance of this analysis to the philosopher as, in some sense, the priest of truth, should be apparent. Less obvious perhaps, but equally important, is that this discovery of depth also sets the stage for interpretation, for the hermeneutics of texts.

It was inevitable, Nietzsche maintains, that the priestly mode would branch off from and become antithetical to the knightly/aristocratic. And faced with their own relative impotence in the face of the knights' physical superiority, it was inevitable that priests, with their hatred of life, would grow to "monstrous and uncanny proportions" (*GM* I "GEGB" 7). For Nietzsche, the Jews of the Bible are the priestly people *par excellence*, whose thirst for spiritual revenge begins and sustains a "slave revolt in morality" culminating in the stunning victory of Christianity, in which hate triumphs by donning the antithetical guise of love:

> The slave revolt in morality begins when *ressentiment* itself becomes creative and gives birth to values: the *ressentiment* of natures that are denied the true reaction, that of deeds, and compensate themselves with an imaginary revenge. While every noble morality develops from a triumphant affirmation of itself, slave morality from the outset says No to what is "outside," what is "different," what is "not itself"; and *this* No is its creative deed. This inversion of the value-positing eye—this *need* to direct one's view outward instead of back to oneself—is the essence of *ressentiment*: in order to exist, slave morality always first needs a hostile external world; it needs, physiologically speaking, external stimuli in order to act at all—its action is fundamentally reaction. (*GM* I "GEGB" 10)

Here, the No to the "other" or "outside" and the "imaginary revenge" connected with it offer disturbing suggestions about the ambiguity of fiction-making, with its at least qualified rejection of what "is," its urge to be elsewhere, and its implied revenge on reality. The noble mode of evaluation, for which the reverse is true, may recall, too, the self-sufficiency of the authorial imagination. There is, Nietzsche points out, not hate but forbearance in the contempt of the masters; they are happy, present in themselves and not in relation to others. They are fully present in their own lives. Of course, as Nietzsche later admits, the behavior of nobles to those outside their groups was barbarous. But their "joy in destructiveness" can be seen as corresponding to the iconoclasm and insistence on the self, the necessary ruthlessness and indifference of an author to the claims of others.

And yet there is an ambiguity here. We can think of *ressentiment* as the "revenge of the reader," which Susan Sontag associates with interpretation grown arrogant, hateful, usurpatory.[16] Nietzsche links this revenge of the reader with a self-serving morality on the basis of which the reader tries to bend the author to the reader's needs and prejudices. The lesser instinctively desires to bring the greater, the luckier, down to its level. This levelling down is tantamount to a social disease. "Supposing that what is at any rate believed to be the 'truth' really is true," argues Nietzsche, then the meaning of culture is the domestication of the human beast. And *ressentiment* is one of its prime instruments, the resentful its prime bearers. Not only, he insists, is "the reverse not merely probable . . . today it is *palpable*." *Ressentiment* and the resentful are now regressive, restraining a new overcoming. Now we suffer from endemic malady: "we *suffer* from man" (*GM* I "GEGB" 11). Humanity is ill-constituted, sick, weary. This domesticated species—hopelessly "mediocre and insipid"—has been deluded into thinking itself the goal of history. But unlike the nobles they have displaced, the resentful cannot afford to take joy in the worthiness of their enemies; they seek to exclude all but themselves. They are amputees, who call up the specter of nihilism by their attempts to make their own incompleteness serve as the *ne plus ultra* of humanity.

Nietzsche thinks of this weariness in human consciousness as a symptom of nihilism. The mechanism at work here concerns "love" and "fear." In Nietzsche's account, it is humankind's sublimity, the "pathos of distance" between love and fear, that gives the project of humanization its impetus and underlying sense—but which also makes it deeply contradictory. For how can the sublime be rationalized and brought to heel by democracy? In effect, we have two versions of culture: domesticated, humanized; and demonic, sublime. These correspond to Thomas Weiskel's distinction between humane and sublime critics: those who subordinate themselves to the humane values they find immanent in the text and those who try to bring out and manifest a power, however problematical and ambiguous.[17] This is very much a difference about what people want and need, perhaps even about which values actually sustain and compensate the project of writing and the writer, as opposed to those values which make writing and writers acceptable to the mass of readers and, behind them, to society as a whole.

After all this, the question of "the *other* origin of the 'good,' of the good as conceived by the man of *ressentiment*" still remains to be answered (*GM* I "GEGB" 13). In a famous passage, Nietzsche likens resentful people to sheep, whose understandable dislike of birds of prey for bearing off little lambs leads them to condemn the birds and the characteristics associated with them as evil. The opposite of the bird of prey, the lamb, then becomes the embodiment of good. What is hurtful or disadvantageous to lambs is condemned and branded evil. This may be easy enough to comprehend. Less obvious is the intervention of "likeness," an abstracting figure of similitude by means of which predatory qualities are detached from the bird of prey. More fundamentally, "likeness" is a means of creating that aphasia, that discontinuity or gap, which once crossed, obscures from the sheep the origin of their judgment of evil in simple disadvantage *to them*.

Not even the fundamental judgments of value are above or beyond perspective. Clearly, the birds of prey not only see things differently. Since things are arranged very much to their advantage, they have no need of such an antithetical, "good-evil" morality; they are perfectly happy to regard tasty little lambs as "good." In fact, then, morality itself seems to belong to the particular perspective of the weak or disadvantaged. It must serve as their chief weapon against the strong. Implicitly, Nietzsche raises here the questions that will occupy all of the second essay: how are the strong subverted? How do they subvert *themselves*? By what means are they induced to play this game of morality? Implicitly, Nietzsche answers, the major source of human vulnerability is language. An underlying implication of the passage (the secret appropriateness of the bird of prey image) is that humans can be transported by words. And it is not just the moralist but the philosopher, Plato himself, who is "carried away" by language:

> For just as the popular mind separates the lightning from its flash and takes the latter for an *action*, for the operation of a subject called lightning, so popular morality also separates strength from expressions of strength, as if there were a neutral substratum behind the strong man, which was *free* to express strength or not to do so. But there is no such substratum; there is no "being" behind doing, effecting, becoming; "the doer" is merely a fiction added to the deed—the deed is everything. The popular mind in fact doubles the deed; when it sees the lightning flash, it is the deed of a deed: it posits the same event first as cause and then a second time as its effect. Scientists do no better when they say "force moves," "force causes," and the like—all its coolness, its freedom from emotion notwithstanding, our entire science still lies under the misleading influence of language and has not disposed of that little changeling, the "subject" (the atom, for example, is such a changeling, as is the Kantian "thing-in-itself"); no wonder if the submerged, darkly glowering emotions of vengefulness and hatred exploit this belief for their own ends and in fact maintain no belief more ardently than the belief that *the strong man is free* to be weak and the bird of prey to be a lamb—for thus they gain the right to make the bird of prey *accountable* for being a bird of prey. (*GM* I "GEGB" 13)

The "seduction of language (and of the fundamental errors of reason that are petrified in it)" points first to similitude as a principle of mobility that dissolves identities into qualities and makes differences equally accessible to judgment; second, it points to a hardening of language effects into identities, capable of being called to account and of receiving judgment. It is in language that all persons are created equal, in the sense of being rendered equally accessible to the law and its judgments. "The fundamental errors of reason petrified in language" are, in fact, the errors of philosophy and its epigone, science, whose founding gestures, Nietzsche implies, are to hypostasize effects of language.[18] The particular error that concerns him here is that of the "subject," a cause added to the effect in order to make this effect available to judgment (or analysis) by creating the illusion that it could have been otherwise if the subject had been otherwise ("*the strong man is free* to be weak and the bird of prey to be a lamb"). The view that "'The doer' is merely a fiction added to the deed" can be deployed in still another context than the standard philosophical one: that of authorship and of Nietzsche's own writing. Clearly, the author (or, as Foucault would have it, the "author-effect") is a kind of subject, constructed of "authorial" choices, which, in turn, open the work accessible to interpretation and judgment—by creating the illusion that it could have been otherwise.

But one has to wonder if the conviction that "it could have been otherwise" *is* an illusion. If so, in what sense? The scathing irony of Nietzsche's own "*the strong man is free* to be weak" seems to point to an "elsewhere" or "otherwise"— a language-effect that appears to open up the possibility of a choice. Also, Nietzsche's own "bird of prey" metaphor appears to exploit the abstracting power of similitude in the same way that moralists do. After all, is "the strong man" really like a bird of prey? In Nietzsche's analogy, the bird's "strength" manifests itself in a single way. Can the same be said of "man's"?

We are arguing, then, not that Nietzsche's logic is flawed, but that his central concerns can be read equally well as somewhat other than those expressly stated. We need not think of his attack on "the subject" as an attack on "the self" or "identity," as such. After all, the bird of prey has an identity that is completely expressed and comprehended in the act of predation. Even if the same could ever have been said of the strength of "the strong man," we have long since lost touch with the relevant sense of the word "strength" (perhaps as the result of the genealogy that Nietzsche describes).

But this *can* be said of an author: that one writes as one does because one cannot do otherwise and that the effects of that writing (that is, the texts) express and comprehend (or establish) a particular identity *as author*. And here is the problem. This self-sameness involves the reduction of an empirical to an immanent self, creating the possibility of the author who "writes" reading his or her own "authorship," and so of the reinscription of the "writer reading." The bird of prey suffers no such "residue." Disanalogy is also a "language effect," and there is no perspective from which the self-sameness of authorial identity is not also a language effect, seen from the opposite end of the reader-writer relationship. Authorial self-sameness, then, may be thought of as the complement of a readerly "otherwise" in a relationship that is portrayed here as a struggle for power and authority. And one of the stories that Nietzsche tells is of the subversion of authorial authority by readers (in a consumerist society); it is also the story of how authorship is infected by readership. *Ressentiment* is, in at least this sense, also the reader's disease, something directed against the author's apparent self-sameness. Inherent in this dynamic is the all-too-human impulse to disguise motives:

"we weak ones are, after all, weak; it would be good if we did nothing *for which we are not strong enough*"; but this dry matter of fact, this prudence of the lowest order which even the insects possess (posing as dead, when in great danger, so as not to do "too much"), has, thanks to the counterfeit and self-deception of impotence, clad itself in the ostentatious garb of the virtue of quiet, calm resignation, just as if the weakness of the weak— that is to say, their *essence*, their effects, their sole, ineluctable, irremovable reality—were a voluntary achievement, willed, chosen, a *deed*, a *meritorious* act. This type of man *needs* to believe in a neutral independent "subject," prompted by an instinct for self-preservation and self-affirmation in which every lie is sanctified. The subject (or, to use a more popular expression, the *soul*) has perhaps been believed in hitherto more firmly than anything else on earth because it makes possible to the majority of mortals, the weak and oppressed of every kind, the sublime self-deception that interprets weakness as freedom, and their being thus-and-thus as a *merit*. (*GM* I "GEGB" 13)

Creation of a "subject" that could be otherwise allows the resentful to represent what they must, in any case, be—quiet, calm, resigned—as virtue, "as if the weakness of the weak . . . were a voluntary achievement, willed, chosen, a *deed*, a *meritorious* act." There is an almost parodic relationship here between the representation of what is, as chosen, and Nietzsche's own descriptions of eternal recurrence as a kind of retrospective willing. From this perspective, the abstracting power, the mobility of similitude, allows the weak to act the role of strength, to embody falsely. Yet they do not so much embody strength as assume it as a cloak or dress-up, which fools even themselves. Perhaps the main difference is that the weak believe their morality and forget its interested origins in precisely the sense that Nietzsche, as we have argued, does not believe in eternal recurrence or present himself as its embodiment.[19] The resentful ones represent the hardening of the figural, and of the hyperbolic in particular, into the literal.

For writers like this, authorship, or fiction-making, is a kind of auto-illusion. As weak readers themselves, they mistake their incapacity to sustain the tensions and contradictions inherent in figuration for strength. Against an author's identification with the writing itself, weak readers offer a "judgment" based on the illusion that the "same author" could somehow have written "otherwise"—a judgment that sustains the illusion of a unified and stable self, a self, in principle, incapable of "authorship." Weak readers are simply unable to sustain the contradictions of an author's role. On the one hand, the author is identical with the text; on the other hand, the "self-same" writer is fragmented by that text, torn apart like Orpheus (or Pentheus) by the multiplication of authorial words. This scattering in language is a real Dionysian revel, corresponding to the self-disseminating movement of will to power, with the fragmentation of the aphoristic style, extending even to the body itself. In a sense, then, self-sameness of an author corresponds to the idea of eternal recurrence, corresponds to this lack of "otherwise" or "elsewhere"; however, its complement is the scattering in language that corresponds to the will to power, at once everywhere and nowhere. This ineluctable doubling-effect invites the resentful dream of creation without alienation. Coleridge's famous definitions of primary and secondary imagination speak to such a dream. His primary imagination internalizes the "eternal act of creation in the infinite I AM"[20]— the convergence of "I am" and "It is" in the single word that suffices for God to create and sustain the world in perpetuity. This divine will to power disseminates itself everywhere while subtracting nothing from itself, Coleridge suggests, a miracle reflected in the way that language as well emanates from and at the same time remains answerable to a single word.

But humankind is not God. So Nietzsche enacts a self-harrowing, or rather forces his reader, "Mr. Rash and Curious," to repeat it. Looking into "the secret of how *ideals are made* on earth," in a prosopopeia echoing that by means of which the poet speaks for the dead, Nietzsche speaks the original transvaluation of all values, putting noble names on weakness in the original antithetical criticism, devising figures that fail to recognize themselves as such, and holding his nose as we might expect to have to do among the dead and their decaying morality. Among the central mysteries addressed in *Toward the Genealogy of Morals* is an inversion of high and low, healthy and sick. It speaks to an even more fundamental sense of "economic" imbalance, of indebtedness that, try as he might, Nietzsche cannot entirely put off onto asceticism, with its vague sense that this debt can be redeemed, perhaps even at a profit, by scourging and sacrificing "this" life.

The first essay can be read as providing the what and why of the slave revolt in morality and its successful subversion of noble values. But the how of this subversion—how is it that the weak manage to overcome the better and stronger masters?—is left unanswered. How do the masters internalize the slave's unspeakable thirst for universality and neutrality—the slave's self-deceptive will-to-power—and in the process *become* weak, *become* slaves themselves? In the second essay, as Nietzsche attempts to answer these questions, his earlier account of slave morality as pathological begins to converge with a new account, in which this pathology is increasingly difficult to separate from "normal" socialization and from culture itself. By moving a sense of inversion, imbalance, and indebtedness from contingent pathology to aspect of civilization, Nietzsche begins to challenge in a fundamental way notions of balance, equilibrium that extend even to the body in the moral/intellectual tradition derived from Plato. But Nietzsche's sense of the fluid, idiosyncratic, and even indeterminate relationship between mind and body (which we have already begun to trace) is no less a challenge to the Christian ascetic's ideal of delicately balanced imbalance. The problem of reappropriating the body to the self through language is complicated by the way that language scatters the body— a complication echoed in and intertwined with the ambiguity of style.

Nietzsche begins his essay on "'Guilt,' 'Bad Conscience,' and the Like" by defining "the paradoxical task that nature has set itself in the case of man": "To breed an animal *with the right to make promises*" (*GM* II "GBC" 1). This project is opposed by an equally natural and necessary *forgetfulness*—an active faculty of "repression" or inhibition, determining that "what we experience and absorb enters our consciousness as little while we are digesting it . . . as does the thousandfold process, involved in physical nourishment" (*GM* II "GBC" 1). This active forgetfulness closes consciousness off, for example, from "the noise and struggle of our underworld of utility organs working with and against one another" (*GM* II "GBC" 1). For the "animal" in whom this capacity is damaged, there can be "no happiness, no cheerfulness, no hope, no pride, no *present*." Why? Because this creature has "bred in itself" a memory, which abrogates "robust health" in cases where promises are made:

> This involves no mere passive inability to rid oneself of an impression, no mere indigestion through a once-pledged word with which one cannot "have done," but an active *desire* not to rid oneself, a desire for the continuance of something desired once, a real *memory of the will*: so that between the original "I will," "I shall do this" and the actual discharge of the will, its *act*, a world of strange new things, circumstances, even acts of will may be interposed without breaking this long chain of will. (*GM* II "GBC" 1)

In order for this situation to occur, this "animal" "must first have learned to distinguish necessary events from chance ones, to think causally, to see and anticipate distant eventualities, to decide with certainty what is the goal and what is the means to it"; "Man himself must first of all have become *calculable*, *regular*, *necessary*, even in his own image of himself, if he is able to stand security for *his own future*, which is what one who promises does!" (*GM* II "GBC" 1).

This primitive capacity to make promises appears to be one of the necessary attributes of the author of books too. An author must be able to sustain a narrative or an argument, to fulfill a formal and creative "contract," to fulfill a "promise." But then the world of things can come between this promise and its fulfillment; by which we mean to say that, subject as it is to duration (say, of writing), it is necessarily open to intrusions from the outside. If all this is necessary to the *completion* of a project, a complementary forgetfulness is required to create the perpetual present which sustains writing from moment to moment. Otherwise, a dyspeptic inability to let go can fix the writer's gaze on the past; in retrospect, the writer frets and tinkers, anxiously recoiling from the expanse ahead. Dyspepsia is, for Nietzsche, a symptom of disorder in the body of the text as well as of disorder in the body as the physiologist thinks of it.

"Our organism," Nietzsche argues, "is an oligarchy," in which an "active" forgetfulness—"like a doorkeeper, a preserver of psychic order, repose, and etiquette"—makes room "above all for the nobler functions and functionaries, for regulation, foresight, premeditation" (*GM* II "GBC 1). He implies, too, that the organism of the text is an oligarchy. Such a characterization speaks to style as selectivity, continuity, an impression of harmony and unity typically based in a dominant key or keys. Yet "style" also rebounds upon oligarchy: the complement of this forgetfulness, the memory of will which may require cruelty, may base itself in indebtedness, may go beyond mere dyspepsia, and tends toward an illness indistinguishable from civilization itself. This points to style as idiosyncratic. Individual in a way testifying to the distorting power of the "memory of will" as character, it may testify to the distorting power of life. More pointedly, we may still be left to wonder whether Nietzsche's style is an expression of his *askesis*, or of his chronic illness.

The result of this project of calculability, Nietzsche claims, then, is the "sovereign individual," who (like the "sovereign author") possesses "free will," and has the "right" to make promises. For that reason emancipated and, so, imbued with value, this creature is "a proud consciousness, quivering in every muscle, of *what* has at length been achieved and become flesh in him, a consciousness of his own power and freedom, a sensation of mankind come to completion" (*GM* II "GBC" 2). The *"sovereign individual,"* "[t]his emancipated individual" embodies "what has at length been achieved" (*GM* II "GBC" 2). Indeed, this being sounds very much like the nobles of the First Essay—which may be the more remarkable considering what Nietzsche will have to say about the role of asceticism in creating memory and what he will imply about the continuity between conscience and the bad conscience exploited by slave morality:

> looking out upon others from himself, he honors or he despises; and just as he is bound to honor his peers, the strong and the reliable (those with the *right* to make promises)— that is, all those who promise like sovereigns, reluctantly, rarely, slowly, who are chary of trusting, whose trust is a mark of distinction, who give their word as something that can be relied on because they know themselves strong enough to maintain it in the face of accidents, even "in the face of fate"—he is bound to reserve a kick for the feeble windbags who promise without the right to do so, and a rod for the liar who breaks his word even at the moment he utters it. The proud awareness of the extraordinary privilege of *responsibility*, the consciousness of this rare freedom, this power over oneself and over fate, has in his case penetrated to the profoundest depths and become instinct, the dominating instinct. What will he call this dominating instinct, supposing he feels the need to give it a name? The answer is beyond doubt: this sovereign man calls it his *conscience*. (*GM* II "GBC" 2)

Above all, conscience carries with it the *"right to affirm oneself"* (*GM* II "GBC" 3). But what an ordeal of preparation was endured for this to be achieved! Extreme cruelty was required to create memory in a forgetful animal. Pain has proved to be the most powerful aid to mnemonics. "In a certain sense, the whole of asceticism belongs here" as "ascetic procedures and modes of life" are the means of freeing a few ideas "from the competition of all other ideas, so as to make them 'unforgettable'" (*GM* II "GBC" 3). The archaic codes of punishment used by the Germans testify to "the effort it costs on this earth to breed a 'nation of thinkers'" (*GM* II "GBC" 3)—and, through the connection with asceticism, to the violence of the psychodrama required to generate intellectual/creative activity. The odd leap here from "the right to make promises" to "a nation of thinkers" also tends to confirm the connection we have been pursuing between "genealogy" and Nietzsche's own work.

Conscience, created out of punishment and ascetic self-torture, is transformed through internalization into habit and made instinctual by a kind of forgetting. But can pain be forgotten in this way, and transformed into instinct? How great are the transformative powers of thinking and writing? It is a curious aspect of Nietzsche's discourse here that he insists on the "right" (*Recht*) to make promises, to affirm oneself, when it seems that the less moralistic/legalistic term, "capacity" (*Vermögen*) would have done just as well—better perhaps, since less suggestive of residual anxiety. Strictly speaking, Nietzsche is describing the origin and evolution of a capacity to keep promises more than of a "right to make them." The nobles assume their right; for them, it is not a question. They feel no need to establish or insist on their rights. The key question is "where does the 'right' to claim rights come from?" Nietzsche's answer is that it comes from pain—an answer that not only links pain indirectly to writing but also suggests that we write in order to establish rights, that is, to be "more" than others. Writing (at least of a certain kind) carries with it the burden of inequality, imbalance, disequilibrium, and distinction. It also requires and testifies to a pain that is never entirely subsumed or transformed into "instinct."

But how did the "consciousness of guilt," "bad conscience" come into the world? It evolved, not from some prior notion of the freedom of the will (a relatively late development in any case), but from the debtor/debtee relationship (in German, the word for "guilt" and "debt" is the same: *Schuld*). Furthermore, the injury of a broken contract could be compensated for by the pleasure of giving pain, as in the case of Shylock. In contrast, we moderns see pain and suffering as arguments against existence only because we have forgotten how powerful a seduction to life inflicting pain can be.[21] The pessimist's disgust at and weariness with life is not characteristic of the most "evil" epochs of what Nietzsche calls "the human race" (*GM* II "GBC" 2); instead, it arises from the "morbid" softening and moralization that occurs when humankind becomes ashamed of "all his instincts" (*GM* II "GBC" 7).

The "true"[22] object of humanity's indignation is not suffering but the senselessness of suffering. Gods were invented to make sense *out* of suffering. Hence, the Greeks represented both pleasure and pain as divine diversions: "What was at bottom the ultimate meaning of Trojan Wars and other such tragic terrors? . . . they were intended as festival plays for the gods; and, insofar as the poet is in these matters of a more "godlike" disposition than other men, no doubt also as festival plays for the poets" (*GM* II "GBC" 7). The invention of gods to bind suffering to sense—but also to express a positive enjoyment of cruelty—resonates strangely and yet inevitably with the relationship between poets and readers. Poets delight in cruelty attributed to the gods; they enjoy the unease that they cause their readers. Likewise, Nietzsche seems to revel in the disorienting effects of his iconoclasm. He delights in making readers squirm, in exposing and rejecting them. But this is not all. The gods, God, constituted a necessary audience:

> It was in the same way that the moral philosophers of Greece later imagined the eyes of God looking down upon the moral struggle, upon the heroism and self-torture of the virtuous: the "Herakles of duty" was on a stage and knew himself to be; virtue without a witness was unthinkable for this nation of actors. Surely, that philosophers's invention, so bold and so fateful, which was then first devised for Europe, the invention of "free will," of the absolute spontaneity of man in good and in evil, was devised above all to furnish a right to the idea that the interest of the gods in man, in human virtue, *could never be exhausted* . . . . The entire mankind of antiquity is full of tender regard for "the spectator," as an essentially public, essentially visible world which cannot imagine happiness apart from spectacles and festivals.—And, as aforesaid, even in great *punishment* there is so much that is festive! (*GM* II "GBC" 7)

Suddenly, in this unexpected reversal, the reader reappears in the position of the gods, without whose spectatorship being itself would seem empty of significance. But the modern author must make do with imagining a spectatorship composed of readers, not gods. The implicit contrast makes the point. The peculiar satisfaction of taking the gods for one's audience concerns their capacity to serve as spectators of internal struggles, to testify to a purely internal heroism; the European invention of free will decisively privileges this internal drama over all others, and provides a compensation for the suffering it involves.

Here, we might read "free will" as analogous to "artistic freedom" or "dramatic license," as the autonomy of art which frees creator and audience from determinism: i.e., from the certainty of boredom. At the same time, this autonomy frees art to serve as a vehicle for self-expression, the privileged mode of the inwardness comprehended (if not invented) in the notion of free will. But, again, readers are not gods. Above all, as spectators they lack the "aesthetic" detachment of the gods. Not only is the reader's insight less penetrating and less complete, but it stubbornly confuses its inwardness with that of the author. Unlike the emotionally involved reader, the gods are not frightened or revolted by suffering. There is no need to worry that they will turn away in disgust. The imposition inherent in authorship, which so concerns Derrida in his reading of Nietzsche,[23] cannot touch these gods; indeed, what makes them gods is the fact that they find us endlessly interesting and have all the time in the world to expend on the "festival" of existence.

Guilt, we have said, originates for Nietzsche in the creditor/debtor relationship. Punishment begins as one of the creditor's recourses, and the pleasure of inflicting pain is one means of reconciling both parties to life by making suffering meaningful, even pleasurable. Does this mean, then, that the phenomenon of punishment has been explained—are origins and purpose one and the same? Nietzsche thinks not. The explanatory narratives change, as do their interpreters, until previous notions of "'meaning' and 'purpose' are necessarily obscured or even obliterated" (*GM* II "GBC" 12). Beyond a disclaimer regarding the dynamism of punishment, this section on "will to power" also suggests an implicit account (or defense) of writing. In it, we suggest, Nietzsche approaches a philosophical poetics, a theory of reading, and a response to positivist nightmare-fantasies of an infinite regress of interpretation. Here, Nietzsche contrasts will to power with "adaptation" as active against merely reactive:

> indeed, life itself has been defined as a more and more efficient inner adaptation to external conditions (Herbert Spencer). Thus the essence of life, its *will to power*, is ignored; one overlooks the essential priority of the spontaneous, aggressive, expansive, form-giving forces that give new interpretations and directions, although "adaptation" follows only after this; the dominant role of the highest functionaries within the organism itself in which the will to life appears active and form-giving is denied. One should recall what Huxley reproached Spencer with—his "administrative nihilism": but it is a question of rather *more* than mere "administration." (*GM* II "GBC" 12)

Here, in one sense, we might construe will to power as the vital principle in life, an instinct for growth and durability; but in another, textual sense, will to power defends against a reduction to determined reactivity. In this sense, will to power is like style: not determined by (and therefore not reducible to) utility. It is not an "adaptation" to conception.

And here, too, Nietzsche distinguishes what is enduring in punishment—custom, act, drama, a sequence of procedures—from what is fluid—meaning, purpose, expectations—in a way that could be applied to the traditional fictions and tropes that he borrows, and the new meanings they acquire, in *Thus Spoke Zarathustra*. "Punishment" is for us a crystallized synthesis of meanings; it is now impossible to say exactly *why* people are punished, since "all concepts in which an entire process is semiotically concentrated elude definition; only that which has no history is definable" (*GM* II "GBC" 13). Overdetermined by utilities of all kinds, punishment cannot be specified as the origin of guilty conscience. No, Nietzsche argues, "bad conscience" actually originates as the "serious illness man was bound to contract under the stress of the most fundamental change he ever experienced . . . when he found himself enclosed within the walls of society and peace," when "instincts were disvalued and suspended" and his behavior could no longer be guided by his drives. Then, he had to seek "new and, as it were, subterranean gratifications" (*GM* II "GBC" 16). Accordingly, he concludes: "All instincts that do not discharge themselves outwardly *turn inward*—this is what I call the *internalization* of man: thus it was that man first developed what was later called his 'soul'" (*GM* II "GBC" 16). The inner world, "originally as thin as if it were stretched between two membranes," is enlarged and deepened by this inhibition and internalization (which can be read as commemorated and repeated in the inward turn of writing).

Deprived of an external theater of action and instinct, man "had to turn himself into an adventure, a torture chamber, an uncertain and dangerous wilderness." That man is now sick of himself is the result of this sundering from the animal instincts on which "his strength, joy, and terribleness had rested hitherto" (*GM* II "GBC" 16). The animal soul turned against itself. And this self-induced malady made humankind "among the most unexpected and exciting lucky throws in the dice game of Heraclitus' 'great child'" (*GM* II "GBC" 16). In other words, "the human race" *is* a "throw" or hyperbole; "hyperbole," as we are using the term, names not just a trope or element of style but the mode of our existence, the shape of our project as well. Here is a striking instance of the convergence of trope and world which is itself a trope for the whole of *Genealogy*.

If "the human race" is not a "goal" but a "great promise," it follows that the value of the inward turn (including Nietzsche's inward turn of writing)—can be construed in this "arena of instincts." This radical change in our mode of existence was not gradual or organic. Like the discontinuity which typically begins a book, it was a break, a leap, a disaster. It was a hyperbole made possible by violence, by the "blow" of the tyrant subduing. The originary violence of these ruler-organizers is explicitly equated with ("exemplifies," not "is exemplified by") "that terrible artist's egoism that has the look of bronze and knows itself justified to all eternity in its 'work,' like a mother in her child" (*GM* II "GBC" 17).

It was not *in* these archaic figures but *because* of them that bad conscience developed. The instinct to freedom was forced into latency; this turning-in-upon-itself of "will to power" Nietzsche calls "*bad conscience*" (*GM* II "GBC" 17). Now, out of the "secret self-ravishment," which is the literary analogue of this internal dynamic, comes the violent hyperbole representing the human estate, and with it the imaginary construct of its opposite, namely, "beauty and affirmation, and perhaps beauty itself" (*GM* II "GBC 18). As we can see, Nietzsche here equates "bad conscience" with that original malady afflicting the human animal. As a writerly illness ("as pregnancy is an illness" [*GM* II "GBC" 19]), ascetic self-torture involves a debt owed to ancestors, to parents, and to God. So the debt can never fully be requited, the guilt never fully expiated. The perfect text will never be finished. In Christianity, humanity's guilt before God—the creditor who sacrifices himself for his debtors—raises self-torture to its highest pitch. This God is the ultimate antithesis of instinct and his invention expresses a perversely hyperbolic *will* to be guilty beyond atonement: "what *bestiality of thought* erupts as soon as he is prevented just a little from being a *beast in deed!*" (*GM* II "GBC" 22). Even here, Nietzsche imagines the danger of a resurgent nihilism, that "*sickness*, beyond any doubt, the most terrible sickness that has ever raged in man" (*GM* II "GBC" 22).

What is "invincibly" horrifying here is the specter of the ultimate perversion of love. What if it is simply too late for divine love to be naturalized or humanized as that sensation of being loved *by life*? But the real abyss lies in the possibility that love—of our kind, of life—is irredeemably perverted by ascetic ideals, is so fraught with hidden conditions, so given over to compensating for self-hatred, as to be little more than the most seductive version of the ascetic desire to be somewhere else, to be someone else.[24] From this possibility, Nietzsche himself must draw back, lest he become frozen in place by an "unnerving sadness," reminiscent of Freud's account of melancholia. Indeed, Nietzsche suggests, nihilism is essentially a form of melancholia: humanity's unresolved grief at the loss of the primary object of its affection—the self.

And yet none of this, Nietzsche insists, had to be. The Greeks did not use their gods for self-torture. They used their gods to absolve themselves of evil, to characterize themselves as foolish rather than sinful. And when one of their "foolish" number did something terrible, they argued that the sublimity of evil was beyond them, that it could only come from the gods. The ascetic ideal and culture are not necessarily one and the same. But if this is so, how are we to extricate ourselves from "bad conscience"? From our present position within the culture and emotional economy of the ascetic ideal, any attempt to erect a new "temple" necessarily appears to be wantonly, if not apocalyptically destructive ("'What are you really doing, erecting an ideal or knocking one down?' I may perhaps be asked . . . If a temple is to be erected *a temple must be destroyed*" [*GM* II "GBC" 24]). Nietzsche's self-directed question might almost be taken as a reply-in-advance to such later commentators on the "end of philosophy" as Heidegger and Derrida.[25] Nietzsche's point is that from within a culture of millenial duration, any fundamental change assumes—for reasons having to do with our perspective—an apocalyptic aspect. We are no more able to judge the meaning (or "value") of such changes in advance than we are able to estimate the value of life. In the case of the ascetic ideal, we read:

> Man has all too long had an "evil eye" for his natural inclinations, so that they have finally become inseparable from his "bad conscience." An attempt at the reverse would *in itself* be possible—but who is strong enough for it?—that is, to wed the bad conscience to all the *unnatural* inclinations, all those aspirations to the beyond, to that which runs counter to sense, instinct, nature, animal, in short all ideals hitherto, which are one and all hostile to life and ideals that slander the world. To whom should one turn today with *such* hopes and demands? (*GM* II "GBC" 24)

Here, Nietzsche amplifies the interrogative mode: Who indeed—when these hopes and demands look so much like the ascetic wish to be elsewhere, when the hyperbolic "What if?" so closely resembles the ascetic rejection of what we are—is strong enough? How *are* we to take such an exhortation to overcome what we are in the name of what we are? Are we to choose between nature and culture, as if they were not one and the same?

Our own "decaying self-doubting present" is probably incapable of producing such a "*redeeming* man of love and contempt" who will "redeem us not only from the hitherto reigning ideal but also from that which was bound to grow out of it, the great nausea, the will to nothingness, nihilism; this bell-stroke of noon and of the great decision that liberates the will again and restores its goal to the earth and his hope to man; this Antichrist and antinihilist; this victor over God and nothingness—he must come one day." (*GM* II "GBC" 24) As often elsewhere, so here, Nietzsche echoes a biblical prophet, in this instance St. John at Patmos: "Even so, come quickly."[26] In fact, he very nearly transgresses this limit, failing to fall silent at the appointed moment: "But what am I saying? Enough! Enough! At this point it behooves me only to be silent; or I shall usurp that to which only one younger, 'heavier with future,' and stronger than I has a right—that to which only *Zarathustra* has a right, *Zarathustra the godless*" (*GM* II "GBC" 25)

We noted earlier in our discussion that, although Zarathustra "dies," this does not prevent him from speaking—before the end of the book.[27] What does it mean here, when Nietzsche "falls silent," with the Third Essay yet to come? Announcing the future and being part of it are not the same; the two may even be incompatible. But having announced the imminent pregnancy of the future, what remains but to wait silently for parturition?[28] Jonah discovered that announcement can alter the future, but announcing it and making it happen are still not the same. In the end, Nietzsche returns to the split between himself and Zarathustra. It seems that the individual of his own time, the one sufficiently of the temple to bring it down, cannot also be the emergent individual—no more than the Moses of the wilderness could become the "suburban" Moses in the promised land. At this limit, which is also the limit of what thinking and writing can in and of themselves do in the present, we come upon the discontinuity (Nietzsche/Zarathustra) at the heart of the "work." The "work" can be—must be—completed in the "other." So Nietzsche creates a Zarathustra to serve that purpose; Zarathustra imagines "laughing lions"— disciples unlike any disciple he has ever had, readers unlike any readers Nietzsche has or has had.

What, we might ask, is this "writing in the mode of silence"? In one sense, writing *is* a mode of silence, an inwardness which some mistake for solipsism (in the literary, not the philosophical sense). However, that mode is in fact, at least in the third essay, commentary, which Nietzsche treats not as a "safe" mode, a way of "hugging the shore" in Updike's metaphor,[29] but as a writing at the limit where thought and imagination recoil from the obduracy of the future. It is the ambiguous mode—Nietzsche and Zarathustra, speech and silence, writing and reading—a "play" at or about the limits. In this mode, hyperbolic "excess" finds expression in the paradoxical task of prophesying what has already been done, which is to say, of investing in the past our own prophetic awareness and of attributing to the past an efficacy with regard to a desperately desired future. In the context of this analysis, Nietzsche's commentary can be seen as a commentary on himself, on himself as Zarathustra, one which internalizes a complex relationship. Nietzsche attributes to that earlier work a prophetic awareness of what is to come in *Genealogy*. At the same time, his commentary marks the limits of that work: its need for the supplement of *Genealogy* to advance and fulfill its prophetic promise.

Figures of Figuration Figuring: Asceticism and Commentary

"What is the Meaning of Ascetic Ideals?"—the final essay in *Toward the Genealogy of Morals*—offers itself as a commentary on this passage from the "On Reading and Writing" chapter of *Thus Spoke Zarathustra*: "Unconcerned, mocking, violent—thus wisdom wants *us*: . . . she is a woman and always loves only a warrior" (*GM* III, "WMAI" Epigraph).[30] We do not want wisdom. She wants us, but only on the condition that we are "unconcerned, mocking, and violent," which is to say, that we cast off concern, seriousness, and restraint in a gesture which seems at least to be the opposite of ascetic denial, a kind of Nietzschean sublime. But what does *this* mean? The initial problem in determining the meaning of ascetic ideals is that they have meant so many things:

> In the case of artists they mean nothing or too many things; in the case of philosophers and scholars something like a sense and instinct for the most favorable preconditions of higher spirituality; in the case of women at best one *more* seductive charm, a touch of *morbidezza* in fair flesh, the angelic look of a plump pretty animal; in the physiologically deformed and deranged (the *majority* of mortals) an attempt to see themselves as "too good" for this world, a saintly form of debauch, their chief weapon in the struggle against slow pain and boredom; in the case of priests, the distinctly priestly faith, their best instrument of power, also the "supreme" license for power; in the case of saints, finally, a pretext for hibernation, their *novissima gloriae cupido*, their repose in nothingness ("God"), their form of madness. (*GM* III "WMAI" 1)

This variety of manifestations is "an expression of the basic fact of the human will, its *horror vacui*: *it needs a goal*—and it will rather will *nothingness* than not will" (*GM* III "WMAI" 1). The assertiveness of the will, like an errant hyperbole, wanders in so many directions that we are forced to wonder what the difference between not willing and willing nothingness actually is.[31] "Not willing" cannot merely name a quietism, the most pervasive mask the ascetic ideal wears, for this is no more than the nihilism of an unmitigated human condition. For Nietzsche thinks of this, too, as a mask: nothingness in disguise. Perhaps "not willing" is in this context the litotes to the hyperbole of willing "nothingness." As we argued elsewhere,[32] litotes and hyperbole mark perspectival differences at best, and, at worst, mark a distinction that makes no difference. Is the contrast then to be understood as a pure play of perspectives perhaps, like the difference between merely being the fool and laughing at *oneself*, only in this case emptied of all contents—a simple but saving shift in point of view? Will is represented by Nietzsche as a movement that leaves itself open to interpretation as an ascetic transformation, a sublimation: this for that, this into that, flesh into spirit, lower into higher, here into there.

Nietzsche is particularly concerned with the artist, for whom ascetic ideals mean "nothing or too many things," and the philosopher or scholar, for whom they are "a sense and instinct for the most favorable conditions of higher spirituality" (*GM* III "WMAI" 1). His exemplary artist (at least early on) is, of course, Wagner, who "pays homage to chastity in his old age," prompting Nietzsche to ask, why this unnecessary antithesis between chastity and sensuality? and why the failure of *Parsifal* to laugh at itself, to transcend Wagner's own art and overcome the ascetic ideal in self-directed laughter? This "secret laughter of superiority at himself" would have marked the "triumph of his ultimate artist's freedom and artist's transcendence" (*GM* III "WMAI" 3). As we see here, Nietzsche's own tendency is to separate the artist from the art work; he is, after all, "the womb, the soil, sometimes the dung and manure on which, out of which, it grows" (*GM* III "WMAI" 4). This origin must be forgotten "if one is to enjoy the work itself. Insight into the origin of a work concerns the physiologists and vivisectionists of the spirit; never the aesthetic man, the artist!" (*GM* III "WMAI" 4) But, one might ask, who is who here? Earlier, Nietzsche presented himself as a "physiologist" of the spirit. And what is a genealogist but an investigator of origins? But here he seems to be siding with the "aesthetic man" or "artist," who refuses to be concerned with such things and focuses instead on the work like a good (later) formalist. In these terms, however, Wagner is no artist; moreover, his failure is "typical." What are we to make of this?

Literality, the impulse to "real-*ize*" the work through some kind of reduction to world, might usefully be read as a key. Accordingly, the physiologist, like those historians who insist (mistakenly, we would say) that past origins define the present utility of customs and practices, becomes the critical equivalent of a vivisectionist by asserting a literal equivalence of origins and work. The aesthetic individual (one who perceives the world in such and such a way as distinct from one who produces such and such a "thing") becomes a "mere" artist by literalizing the product, that is, by identifying it with the consciousness (or "quality of perception") which produced it. This was Wagner's error:

> The poet and creator of *Parsifal* could no more be spared a deep, thorough, even fright-ful identification with and descent into medieval soul conflicts, a hostile separation from all spiritual height, severity, and discipline, a kind of intellectual *perversity* (if I may be pardoned the word), than can a pregnant woman be spared the repellent and bizarre aspects of pregnancy—which, as aforesaid, must be *forgotten* if one is to enjoy the child. (*GM* III "WMAI" 4)

Wagner mistakenly identifies with himself, and so literalizes the asceticism he must think and feel in order to write *Parsifal*. For that reason he cannot enjoy the work. He suffers from it, and identifies that suffering with the art he thinks of as its cause. Similarly, the pregnant woman may identify the misery attend-ing pregnancy with the child and consequently be unable to enjoy it. In this way, as Nietzsche sees it, the work is at once a source of the creator's suffering and of its audience's joy. It suggests why almost anyone is better qualified than the creator to appreciate the art work. But does the metaphor work? Is, then, almost anyone better qualified than its mother to enjoy the child?

This metaphor, we suggest, calls attention to its own pregnancy; it casts the whole question of the conception of bodies into the realm of the aesthetic. The child is "taken away" from the mother and appropriated to the "aesthetic man" who confuses it with nothing outside itself. What is at stake here is au-tochthony—freedom—a growing away from origins sufficient to cancel their authority. More radically, the figure points to the *potentially* autochthonous, self-creating nature of an author, a capacity that extends even to the creation of the artist's body (*the distinct body of the work*), since even the mature sense of one's own body is a creation of sorts.[33] But in Nietzsche's account the artist fails to realize this potential independence. Having created a freedom he is unable to exploit, Wagner chooses (through a fatality the dynamics of which we will discuss momentarily) to recreate his own enslavement. The artist recreates, in other words, the body of ascetic suffering. What we have in these remarks on Wagner, we think, is a truncated version of Nietzsche's critique of Romantic ascetics/aesthetics—his account of its power and failure, including, we would add, his own *Thus Spoke Zarathustra*.

Generalizing, then, the artist is only prone to confuse the creation with the self that created it, and so to forget what *fiction* is: "if he were it, he would not represent, conceive, and express it: a Homer would not have created an Achilles nor a Goethe a Faust if Homer had been an Achilles or Goethe a Faust" (*GM* III "WMAI" 4). For the artist above all, fiction is not enough, for no one knows better than the artist how alienating, how self-defeating it can be: "one can understand how he may sometimes weary to the point of desper-ation of the eternal 'unreality' and falsity of his innermost existence—and that he may well attempt what is most forbidden to him, to lay hold of actuality, for once actually to *be*." Such is "the typical velleity of the artist" (*GM* III "WMAI" 4). And yet, for Nietzsche, there seems to be a loophole: "Whoever is *completely* and *wholly* an artist [our italics] is to all eternity separated from the 'real,' the actual" (*GM* III "WMAI" 4). Is this to say that whoever is ambiguously, partially, and with reservations an artist may achieve contact with the real *and* preserve some elements of the artist's unrealized freedom of self-creation? Even as Nietzsche seems to envision the possibility of being a physiologist with regard to origins and an "aesthetic man" with regard to present practices and customs, a gap opens up that the genealogy crosses and recrosses by means of the "leap" of hyperbole/litotes. A bridge is provided, and hyperbole and litotes are prevented from cancelling each other out. By means of asceticism, they become part of the same structure, which is at once a "historical" origin and the structure of the aesthetic: the figure of figuration figuring.

Why then, in the case of artists, do ascetic ideals mean nothing or so much that it amounts to nothing? Either their identification with them is false, based on a desire to evade the fictional (as in the case of Wagner), or it is a fiction. Such beings as artists cannot stand "independently enough in the world and *against* the world for their changing valuations to deserve attention *in themselves*!" (*GM* III "WMAI" 5). They need some kind of prop, something outside their relationship with fictions. For Wagner, this prop was Schopenhauer, whose influence raises the more serious question of what it means "when a genuine *philosopher* pays homage to the ascetic ideal?" For it was Schopenhauer—"a man and knight of steely eye who had the courage to be himself, who knew how to stand alone" (*GM* III "WMAI" 5)—whose elevation of music moved Wagner to value it over drama, to see the musician as the mouthpiece of a metaphysical "in itself," until finally, inevitably, he offered ascetic ideals as the (dis)embodiment of this transcendent otherness.

In Nietzsche's account, "Kant, like all philosophers, instead of envisaging the aesthetic problem from the point of view of the artist (creator), considered art and the beautiful purely from that of the 'spectator,' and unconsciously introduced the 'spectator' into the concept 'beautiful'" (*GM* III "WMAI" 6). Kant's spectator was no enthusiast devoted to the immediacy of "vivid, authentic experiences, desires, surprises, and delights in the realm of the beautiful," but one above all disinterested, an observer with nothing at stake (Kant defined the beautiful as that "which gives us pleasure *without interest*" (*GM* III "WMAI" 6). In contrast, Stendahl (and Nietzsche) argue that there is no beauty without interestedness. By interpreting the words "without interest" in an extremely "personal" way, on the basis of "one of his most regular experiences" (*GM* III "WMAI" 6), Schopenhauer becomes an important revisionist of Kant. For him, aesthetic experience counteracts "*sexual* interestedness" and so provides liberation from the "will." Schopenhauer's famous conceptions of will and representation, Nietzsche suggests, were generalizations from his sexual experience:

> Schopenhauer described *one* effect of the beautiful, its calming effect on the will—but is this a regular effect? Stendahl, as we have seen, a no less sensual but more happily con-

stituted person than Schopenhauer, emphasizes another effect of the beautiful: "the beautiful *promises* happiness"; to him the fact seems to be precisely that the beautiful *arouses the will* ("interestedness"). And could one not finally urge against Schopenhauer himself that he was quite wrong in thinking himself a Kantian in this matter, that he by no means understood the Kantian definition of the beautiful in a Kantian sense—that he, too, was pleased by the beautiful from an "interested" viewpoint, even from the very strongest, most personal interest: that of a tortured man who gains release from his torture?—And, to return to our first question, "what does it mean when a philosopher pays homage to the ascetic ideal?"—here we get at any rate a first indication: he wants *to gain release from a torture.* (GM III "WMAI" 6)

Nietzsche's view of Schopenhauer's generalization from his sexual experience may indirectly pose the question of his own dependence on the immediacy of the writing experience, and, by analogy, the still more obscure question of the link between writing and sexuality. Kant's definition of the beautiful, with its stress on the pleasures of the spectator, empties life of personal meaning in precisely the same movement in which it renders it most available to philosophical scrutiny. From a writerly point of view, this disinterested spectatorship seems to correspond to the philosopher's assumption of the transparent or disposable nature of the stylistic "supplement" of ideas, what Frege was (more than a century later) in the habit of calling "[mere] coloration" (*Farbung*). Kant's focus on the spectator's point of view to the exclusion of the creator's, inclines toward a devaluing of the creative act, which is not only excluded as a criterion of "meaning," but virtually removed from Kant's scheme.

On the other hand, Schopenhauer's "interested" disinterestedness raises a fundamental question about the accessibility of personal experience to general statement. What does Schopenhauer say about the beautiful? Is he, in the end, just talking about Schopenhauer? For the moment, Nietzsche leaves the question unanswered. But, as in the case of Wagner, Nietzsche's identification with and critique of Schopenhauer begins to forge a path back to the world from "mere" expressionism. This point is twofold: the philosopher's "objective" contemplation/reading is always interested, is always sited, even when this interestedness corresponds with the partialities of philosophy itself; and, there is no automatic convergence (or divergence) of self-experience and the general or typical. That relationship must be worked out and worked over. But "interest" is no simple matter. If Schopenhauer *is* any indication, when a philosopher pays homage to the ascetic ideal it means that he wants to gain release from torture. No one, Nietzsche insists, needs to become "gloomy" at the word "torture." Rather, Schopenhauer needed enemies, for all that he deplored them: Hegel, woman, sensuality. Without them, "Schopenhauer would not have persisted, one may wager on that; he would have run away: but his enemies held him fast, his enemies seduced him ever again to existence; his anger was, just as in the case of the Cynics of antiquity, his balm, his refreshment, his reward, his specific against disgust, his *happiness*" (GM III "WMAI" 7).

So much for the "personal" Schopenhauer. Nietzsche thinks that his "irritation at and rancor against sensuality" is typical in philosophy: "Schopenhauer is merely its most eloquent and, if one has ears for this, most ravishing and delightful expression" (*GM* III "WMAI" 7). But this pose Nietzsche suggests, masks the underlying meaning of this prejudice and affection for the ascetic ideal: "Every animal—*la bête philosophe*, too—instinctively strives for an optimum of favorable conditions under which it can expend all its strength and achieve its maximal feeling of power" (*GM* III "WMAI" 7). For the philosopher, marriage and other forms of sensuality are impediments. Ascetic ideals reveal to the philosopher "bridges to *independence*," the "optimum condition for the highest and boldest spirituality . . . he does not deny 'existence,' he rather affirms *his* existence and *only* his existence" (*GM* III "WMAI" 7). In Schopenhauer's case (and in Nietzsche's case, too), this solipsism is the means of converting asceticism into a mode of strenuous self-affirmation or egotistical sublime, not an "ideal" but an aspect of being.

Similarly, the ascetic ideals of poverty, humility, and chastity are characteristic of "great, fruitful, inventive spirits" not as virtues!—but as the "most appropriate and natural conditions of their *best* existence" (*GM* III "WMAI" 8). That *desert*, "where the strong, independent spirits withdraw and become lonely" is not as commonly imagined:

> A voluntary obscurity perhaps; an avoidance of oneself; a dislike of noise, honor, newspapers, influence; a modest job, an everyday job, something that conceals rather than exposes one; an occasional association with harmless, cheerful beasts and birds whose sight is refreshing; mountains for company, but not dead ones, mountains with *eyes* (that is, with lakes); perhaps even a room in a full, utterly commonplace hotel, where one is certain to go unrecognized and can talk to anyone with impunity—that is what "desert" means here. (*GM* III "WMAI" 8)

This "desert" is, of course, the life out of which, like John, like Christ, Nietzsche now prosaically emerges. That is the point. This is the desert, not of the extravagances of fiction, but of commonplaces. It is not writing, but fiction, that conspires with the distractions of sensuality. It is the urge to be elsewhere implicit in the fictional, with its irreducible difference from the real, that prevents Nietzsche from affirming his and only his existence, and yet which answers to its own narcissistic discipline:

> One should listen to how a spirit sounds when it speaks: every spirit has its own sound and loves its own sound. That one, over there, for example, must be an agitator, that is to say, a hollow head, a hollow pot: whatever goes into him comes back out of him dull and thick, heavy with the echo of great emptiness. This fellow usually speaks hoarsely: has he perhaps *thought* himself hoarse? That might be possible—ask any physiologist— but whoever thinks in *words* thinks as an orator and not as a thinker (it shows that fundamentally he does not think facts, nor factually, but only in relation to facts; that he is really thinking of *himself* and his listeners). A third person speaks importunately, he

comes too close to us, he breathes on us—involuntarily we close our mouths, although it is a book through which he is speaking to us: the sound of his style betrays the reason: he has no time to waste, he has little faith in himself, he must speak today or never. A spirit that is sure of itself, however, speaks softly; it seeks concealment, it keeps people waiting. (*GM* III "WMAI" 8)

There are several things happening and happening to each other in this passage. First, there is the emphasis not on *what* but on *how* something is said as a guide to the inner imperatives that constitute meaning by giving it impetus. There is also the reversal of the immediacy of speech and distance of writing. The orator's "closeness" is aimed at disguising but nevertheless expresses separation from fact; it tells us that everything is mediated by the orator's awareness of the audience, and of the self before that audience. In the third example, not even the distance of reading can disguise the writer's fervent closeness. Here, there is thought without words—a thinking *before* words, Nietzsche seems to imply—a thinking in "facts." All is not "mere" language and the distinction between "words" and "facts" remains useful, not just because one can think closer or farther from fact, but because "words" and "thoughts" are both aspects of language. Furthermore, to insist on a thinking before words, in facts, is to insist on the continuing possibility of distinguishing between ambiguity and confusion. On the other hand, it is the "sound of [the] style" that betrays the quality of that thinking, even of thinking in facts. Style brings out the texture, the "interestedness," of the thought.

A philosopher, in Nietzsche's caricature based on Schopenhauer, shuns fame, princes, and women; they do not need to avoid him. His "humility" is an expression of his "maternal" instinct, "the secret love of that which is growing in him," which "directs him toward situations in which he is relieved of the necessity of thinking of *himself*; in the same sense in which the instinct of the *mother* in woman has hitherto generally kept woman in a dependent situation" (*GM* III "WMAI" 8). This is simple enough: a recurrence of the pregnancy figure. What the philosopher carries within himself, his project and preoccupation, preempts his participation in the things of the world and places him at a disadvantage like that of the pregnant woman:

They ask for little enough, these philosophers: their motto is "he who possesses is possessed"—*not*, as I must say again and again, from virtue, from a laudable will to contentment and simplicity, but because their supreme lord demands this of them, prudently and inexorably: he is concerned with one thing alone, and assembles and saves up everything—time energy, love, and interest—only for that one thing. (*GM* III "WMAI" 8)

So now the matter is not so simple. Who is this "supreme lord" who sounds so much like the "lord and master," father, husband, and husbander of "time, energy, love, and interest"? It would seem that he is, at once, the child being carried, the cherished object loved by life herself, and the begetter of himself on himself. In short, Nietzsche's philosopher makes *himself* pregnant. But how? We might helpfully ask the generative question in rhetorical terms: Is it dominance or subjection that matters here, hyperbole or litotes?

> This kind of man does not like to be disturbed by enmities, nor by friendships; he easily forgets and easily despises. He thinks it in bad taste to play the martyr; "to *suffer* for truth"—he leaves that to the ambitious and the stage heroes of the spirit and to anyone else who has the time for it (the philosophers themselves have something to *do* for the truth). They use big words sparingly; it is said that they dislike the very word "truth": it sounds too grandiloquent. (*GM* III "WMAI" 8)

It would appear, Nietzsche argues, that the philosopher is not merely aping, play-acting at female pregnancy, but actually competing with it in a serious way. We take the sign of this seriousness to be his restraint. But is this, Nietzsche's poker-faced protestations aside, a species of self-dramatization? Is "pregnant with truth" less "grandiloquent" than "suffering for truth?" For Nietzsche, the philosopher's "restraint" will seldom appear as an unequivocal value:

> As for the "chastity" of philosophers, finally, this type of spirit clearly has its fruitfulness somewhere else than in children; perhaps it also has the survival of its name elsewhere, its little immortality (philosophers in India expressed themselves even more immodestly: "why should he desire progeny whose soul is the world?"). There is nothing in this of chastity from any kind of ascetic scruple or hatred of the senses, just as it is not chastity when an athlete or jockey abstains from women ["No sex before a fight?"]: it is rather the will of their dominating instinct, at least during their periods of great pregnancy. Every artist knows what a harmful effect intercourse has on states of great spiritual tension and preparation; those with the greatest power and surest instincts do not need to learn this by experience, by unfortunate experience [?!]—their "maternal" instinct ruthlessly disposes of all other stores and accumulations of energy, of animal vigor, for the benefit of the evolving work: the greater energy then *uses up* the lesser. (*GM* III "WMAI" 8)

Here, withholding and propagation appear as false opposites. Restraint is a practical means of accumulating energy for the moment of ruthless and total discharge in giving life. Hence, Nietzsche interprets Schopenhauer's aestheticism as an explosion of sexual energy:

> the sight of the beautiful obviously had upon him the effect of releasing the chief energy of his nature (the energy of contemplation and penetration), so that this exploded and all at once became the master of his consciousness. This should by no means preclude the possibility that the sweetness and plenitude peculiar to the aesthetic state might be derived precisely from the ingredient of "sensuality" (just as the "idealism" of adolescent girls derives from that source)—so that sensuality is not overcome by the appearance of the aesthetic condition, as Schopenhauer believed, but only transfigured and no longer enters consciousness as sexual excitement. (*GM* III "WMAI" 8)

So it could be said that the "saving up" of the "supreme lord" nevertheless culminates in this ejaculatory "explosion" by means of which the energy of "contemplation and penetration" masters Schopenhauer's consciousness. Indeed, not only are the woman-hating Schopenhauer's powers of penetration exposed, but, Nietzsche implicitly represents him as an adolescent girl and pregnant mother. Perhaps our impulse may be either to look askance at this extraordinary passage or (defensively) to make clear what Nietzsche is "really" saying, to, in effect, rescue him from hyperbolic excess. Neither response seems quite right, however; for although the passage is violently parodic, it is also quite serious. Nietzsche succeeds in breaking through to the "fantasia" of a certain kind of philosophy that underlies its "style." The ambiguity of Nietzsche's figurative treatment allows, even demands, that, while abstaining from women does make a difference, it is nonetheless not asceticism because philosophers are not abstaining from what they really want. And what *do* they want? And what *is* this progeny whose birth must be indefinitely postponed by refusing to beget it on woman (who is, in any case, already pregnant)? Nietzsche's description of sexuality seems to be dominated by a sense that there is only so much, not enough to go around, that only by storing up and accumulating can "time, energy, love, and interest" somehow exceed itself, be more by being saved than spent.[34] "Enough" is enough to complete a circuit, a system of self-begetting, self-conception, an economy of perpetual dissemination, both of which point to a fundamental unwillingness to accept the limits of bodies, the limits that sexual differentiation imposes even on "conception."

If this way of reading Nietzsche presents his discourse as an usurpatory metaphorics of maternity, one might ask what a metaphorics of paternity would look like. As we have already seen from our discussions of "fatherlessness," Nietzsche came to see his project at least partially in this light. In *Toward the Genealogy of Morals*, commentary as begetting is opposed to conceiving (as he did in the fictional *Thus Spoke Zarathustra*); indeed, it appears that he "begets" this essay parthogenetically in the form of commentary on his own work. Here, Nietzsche is ambiguously one of the philosophers—an ascetic—and a commentator upon them at the same time: a, so to speak, fertile and fecund hermaphrodite of the spirit. That "a certain asceticism, a serene and cheerful continence with the best will, belongs to the most favorable conditions of supreme spirituality, and is also among its most natural consequences" helps to explain why "philosophers have always discussed the ascetic ideal with a certain fondness" (*GM* III "WMAI" 9). However, further investigation reveals that, for historical reasons, this bond is even closer than this passage would suggest: "it was only on the leading-strings of this ideal that philosophy learned to take its first steps on earth" (*GM* III "WMAI" 9). Without such a disguise, Nietzsche argues, the philosopher would have been unable to be himself; his objectivity and neutrality would have contravened the demands of morality and conscience. What we value today is, in a sense, the reverse of what was valued before: "All good things were formerly bad things; every original sin has turned into an original virtue" (*GM* III "WMAI" 9). For most of human history, under the sway of the "morality of mores," values were different, even antithetical.

Contemplation, Nietzsche argues, had to disguise itself to avoid being either feared or despised; it had to appear in ambiguous form "with an evil heart and often an anxious head" (*GM* III "WMAI" 10). The contemplatives of the "frightful ages" understood that by controlling pain, even as it was inflicted upon themselves, they could turn even the social stigma against them to their advantage, finally arrogating to themselves powers that once belonged only to the gods: "As men of frightful ages, they did this by using frightful means: cruelty toward themselves, inventive self-castigation—this was the principal means these power-hungry hermits and innovators of ideas required to overcome the gods and traditions in themselves, so as to be able to *believe* in their own innovations" (*GM* III "WMAI" 10). Thus, on this view, asceticism was a means of securing a belief in oneself by stimulating awe in others. Belief in one's own innovations is always blocked by internalized contemporary mores and values. How can our creations, our "innovations," be promoted and valorized as the verities we receive from without. How can they be "naturalized?" Ascetic self-punishment, so much at odds with the typical attachment to ease and sensual pleasure, is understood as a sign of "possession" by a higher power or force, of "inspiration" in a literal sense. If the philosopher uses asceticism as a means to an end without *really* being ascetic, the case of the genuine priest is quite different. For him the question of asceticism is deadly serious; his very existence depends upon it. The key to priestly asceticism is the valuation placed on life. The priest opposes life—nature, the world, becoming—to something else that opposes life, and demands that life oppose or deny itself. He treats life as the wrong road and wherever he can, he "compels acceptance of *his* evaluation of existence" (*GM* III "WMAI" 11).

What does such a "monstrous" mode of evaluation mean? According to Nietzsche, since the ascetic priest is anti-propagative yet repeatedly crops up throughout history, it can only mean that asceticism is, all appearances to the contrary notwithstanding, somehow in the *interest of life itself*:

> For an ascetic life is a self-contradiction: here rules a *ressentiment* without equal, that of an insatiable instinct and power-will that wants to become master not over something in life but over life itself, over its most profound, powerful, and basic conditions; here an attempt is made to employ force to block up the wells of force; here physiological well-being itself is viewed askance, and especially the outward expression of this well-being, beauty and joy; while pleasure is felt and sought in ill-constitutedness, decay, pain, mischance, ugliness, voluntary deprivation, self-mortification, self-flagellation, self-sacrifice. All this is in the highest degree paradoxical: we stand before a discord that

wants to be discordant, that *enjoys* itself in this suffering and even becomes more self-confident and triumphant the more its own presupposition, its physiological capacity for life *decreases.* "Triumph in the ultimate agony": the ascetic ideal has always fought under this hyperbolic sign; in this enigma of seduction, in this image of torment and delight, it recognized its brightest light, its salvation, its ultimate victory. (*GM* III "WMAI" 11)

This passage might call to mind Harold Bloom's adaptation of Nietzsche's thought to the task of describing the poetical character.[35] Bloom holds that the poet is distinguishable from other people by a greater rebellion against the necessity of death. Here, we suggest, the origin of the ascetic negation of life seems apposite to the poet's obstinate denial of death's final dominion. If the poet is denied this one thing (that is, exception to the rule of death), then the ascetic, by rejecting all else, forces the surrender of what is withheld. In this context, the "ultimate" agony of deprivation is the "hyperbolic sign" that the "ultimate victory" of satisfaction is at hand. On this view, ultimacy is radical, is absolute, is the essence of sublimity, in which ultimate dearth and ultimate plenitude are essentially the same. It is here, at the heart of ascetic psychology and practice, that hyperbole and litotes are linked and become rhetorically interchangeable.

The ascetic refuses the "gift" of life until a certain condition is met. Perhaps this stance invites characterization as "regressive." It may be reminiscent of the child who, by refusing substitute satisfactions, tries to coerce its parent into meeting a particular desire. The child tries to seduce authority into a contract. But who, in the case of the adult ascetic, is the authority to be seduced? Perhaps, Nietzsche suggests, God (the cosmic "cause"), who appears at times to be seduced into covenants by—not in spite of—the excesses of humankind. And in at least one of its aspects, the ascetic "contract" resembles the "agreement" imposed by the writer on the unseen, unconsenting reader.

Perhaps the foregoing discussion may help to explain Nietzsche's interest in distinguishing the priest's ascetic attempt to master *life* itself from the philosopher's more comprehensible attempt to master something *in* life. For one, "mastery" of life means changing the rules; for the other, it means learning to accept them as one's own. The priestly ascetic seeks, by embodying a sublimity based on a capacity to endure pain and suffering, to make them the locus of value. Why, Nietzsche asks, should sublimity not be based on a superior capacity to accept and affirm—even revel—in pleasure as well as in suffering?

Previously established religious types of the ascetic ideal—sorcerer, soothsayer, priest—served as the necessary masks of the philosopher, as the very precondition of his existence. His withdrawn and world-denying pose is the result of the conditions of philosophy's emergence, of a necessary "ascetic self-misunderstanding." But it is by no means clear that the butterfly philosophy is yet ready to emerge fully from the priestly/ascetic caterpillar it has long occupied. Indeed, if philosophy is tied to asceticism both by a disposition to higher spirituality and by history, it is not easy to imagine what a non-ascetic philosophy would look like; nor is it apparent, even if we could find some other way to believe in what we ourselves have made, that we would be inclined to call it "philosophy."

We have tried to suggest that the litotes/hyperbole connection made here may provide a helpful basis for considering the reversibility of perspectives, including the inside-outside of Romantic internalization. In this connection, it is significant that the next section of *Genealogy* is on internalization. What, Nietzsche wonders here, if such a will to contradiction, to the anti-natural, is moved to philosophize? It looks for error where the will to life posits truth; it renounces the senses, even reason, in order to conclude that "There is a realm of truth and being, but reason is excluded from it" (*GM* III "WMAI" 12). This recognition of ascetic reversals should not, however, be taken as an opportunity to achieve an impossible "contemplation without interest." Rather, the future "objectivity" of the intellect will reside in the "ability to control one's Pro and Con and to dispose of them, so that one knows how to employ a variety of perspectives and affective interpretations in the service of knowledge":

> Henceforth, my dear philosophers, let us be on guard against the dangerous old conceptual fiction that posited a "pure, will-less, painless, timeless knowing subject"; let us guard against the snares of such contradictory concepts as "pure reason," "absolute spirituality," "knowledge in itself": these always demand that we should think of an eye that is completely unthinkable, an eye turned in no particular direction, in which the active and interpreting forces, through which alone seeing becomes seeing *something*, are supposed to be lacking; these always demand of the eye an absurdity and a nonsense. There is *only* a perspective seeing, *only* a perspective "knowing"; and the *more* affects we allow to speak about one thing, the *more* eyes, different eyes, we can use to observe one thing, the more complete will our "concept" of this thing, our "objectivity," be. But to eliminate the will altogether, to suspend each and every affect, supposing we were capable of this— what would that mean but to *castrate* the intellect? (*GM* III "WMAI" 12)

It has been observed repeatedly that Nietzsche is not claiming that the accumulation of perspectives adds up to a definitive picture of "the thing in itself."[36] He is still pleading for partiality, sitedness, interestedness as valuable and necessary components of knowledge. There is, he argues, no individual insight, observation, or formulation that escapes the limits of perspective. Nevertheless, certain aspects of the formulation suggest the same kind of underlying certainty of reference, buried in a discourse of perspectivism, for which we challenged Nehamas.[37] In this passage we find something evasive in its dependence on eye/object terminology; that is, on its own perspective. Sight is a sense intrinsically dependent on perspective, and invoking it lends strong support to a perspectival view of knowledge; but sight is hardly the only sited sense. Other senses might well support different conceptions of knowledge.[38] Even more fundamental, the perspective of the passage is that of surveying an object from without. This serves the purpose of forestalling the otherwise very difficult question, "how do we know how or even that various perspectives are related?" The answer is so simple that the question need not arise: "with reference to the same object." Perspectives, in this self-consuming rhetoric, are always *of* something, are always views directed toward an object independent of perspectives—the very thesis perspectivism contests, displaces, or seeks to set aside.

But Nietzsche is also moving here toward a further consideration of the relationship between philosophy, asceticism, and the body for which the question of perspectivism is potentially very important. The privileged, will-less, external perspective of philosophy's "old conceptual fictions" was designed to secure a certain idea, image, or "experience" of the body as quasi-object. If, rather than a spatial and external perspective, one were to adopt a temporal or internal perspective (whatever that might mean),[39] as one views from within, for instance, the unfolding work of literature, the unity of the body as object is challenged, and with it the dependence of classical philosophy (for its own coherence in disposing of that body in a certain way). The multiplicity of perspectives that specify an object may fragment the self thought to have all of them. The nature of the control that we exercise over the play of perspectives, and its relationship to the nature of our perception and control over the body, emerges, we think, at this point.

For the moment, however, Nietzsche is content to explain how it is that a non-propagative asceticism can appear over and over again in the course of history. The appearance in asceticism of "life against life" can only be that, an appearance. In fact, "*the ascetic ideal springs from the protective instinct of a degenerating life*"; it points to a "partial physiological obstruction and exhaustion against which the deepest instincts of life, which have remained intact, continually struggle with new expedients and devices" (*GM* III "WMAI" 13). The ascetic ideal is one of these: "the case is therefore the opposite of what those who reverence this ideal believe: life wrestles in it and through it with death and *against* death; the ascetic ideal is an artifice for the preservation of life" (*GM* III "WMAI" 13) against disgust, exhaustion, the desire for the end. Like Bloom's poet, the ascetic priest incarnates the "desire to be different, to be in a different place" (*GM* III "WMAI" 13). The strength and intensity of this desire "is the chain that holds him captive so that he becomes the tool for the creation of more favorable conditions for being here and being man" (*GM* III "WMAI" 13). This power enables him "to persuade to existence the whole herd of the ill-constituted, disgruntled, underprivileged, unfortunate, and all who suffer of themselves" (*GM* III "WMAI" 13). It is not clear whether it is the ascetic priest's self-understanding or our complacent expectations that get overturned here.[40] Nietzsche's readers, including the higher men, are drawn on by his "promise," "persuaded to existence" by the appearance of a new, iconoclastic "gospel."

"Man," Nietzsche tells us, "is *the* sick animal" (*GM* III "WMAI" 13). "Man" is at once the most daring and the sickliest of animals, vexing himself so that his "own restless energies never leave him in peace, so that his future digs like a spur into the flesh of every present" (*GM* III "WMAI" 13). Sickliness has become the norm, Nietzsche insists, and he emphasizes the need to honor and protect from infection those few who are still healthy. It is not the fear of man, of "evil" (which is to say, of strength, health, and confidence), that is the greatest danger. It is *nausea* that threatens the species (a nausea which, interestingly enough, has been identified by Sontag and others with interpretation, that most modern of writerly activities). In Nietzsche's account, if nausea and pity were to unite, it would beget a "last will," or nihilism. "Where," he laments, "does one not encounter that veiled glance which burdens one with a profound sadness, that inward-turned glance of the born failure which betrays how such a man speaks to himself—that glance which is a sigh! 'If only I were someone else,' sighs this glance: 'but there is no hope of that. I am who I am: how could I ever get free of myself? And yet—I *am sick of myself*!'" (*GM* III "WMAI" 14). Here, nausea, figuration and the urge to originality (which so often masquerades as a desire to be fully oneself) are all knotted together. But now, not even the urge to be elsewhere can sustain itself; for even that requires a measure of faith in oneself.

These sufferers, bearers of *ressentiment* and "physiologically unfortunate," hate the well-constituted and desire revenge; they try to poison the consciences of the fortunate with their misery by making them feel shame. Nor should the well-constituted allow themselves to be seduced by the lure of pity into becoming nurses and physicians to the sickly. The higher should not be reduced to an instrument of the lower. Indeed, Nietzsche suggests, the situation requires doctors who are themselves sick: the priests. "Dominion over suffering" is his; he too must be sick of himself, profoundly related to the sick. He despises rather than hates; he knows how to feign superiority, to make fear look like restraint. He makes the healthy sick and the sickly tame. In addition to protecting the herd against the healthy, he protects the herd against itself. It is natural to seek a cause for suffering in order to vent affect on the "guilty"; this effort aims to establish a cause and effect relation. But the priest answers: "you yourself are to blame," and thus alters the direction of *ressentiment* (*GM* III "WMAI" 15). In Nietzsche's view, then, sinfulness is not a "fact," but rather an "interpretation of a fact—namely of physiological depression" (*GM* III "WMAI" 16). That someone feels guilty is no more proof of guilt than feeling good is proof of health:

> When someone cannot get over a "psychological pain," that is *not* the fault of his "psyche" but, to speak crudely, more probably even that of his belly (speaking crudely, to repeat, which does not mean that I want to be heard crudely or understood crudely)—A strong and well-constituted man digests his experiences (his deeds and misdeeds included) as he digests his meals, even when he has to swallow some tough morsels. If he cannot get

over an experience and have done with it, this kind of indigestion is as much physiological as is the other—and often in fact, merely a consequence of the other. (*GM* III "WMAI" 16)

Just how "crudely" should Nietzsche be understood here? Is he suggesting that perhaps we cannot so simply reduce psychology to physiology, after all, that they are complementary as well as antithetical? And if we can attribute psychological pain to the belly, it is indeed in part as a corrective; it is not a "materialism" (Nietzsche's cryptic aside: "With such a conception one can . . . still be the sternest opponent of all materialism"), because this "physiology" is actually a "textualism" or a "tropology" or a "style."

In any case, the priest is not a true physician because he treats only the discomfort and not the cause. His gift for the alleviation of suffering, his refinement and subtlety, is in guessing what stimulant affects will, at least for a time, overcome depression, exhaustion, and melancholy. The main concern of religion has been to fight an epidemic weariness. The priest combats the "physiological inhibition" (*GM* III "WMAI" 17) affecting his flock first, by reducing life to its lowest point, bereft of love or hate, to a selflessness akin to self-hypnosis. Renouncers of life may actually free themselves from physiological depression, but the crucial point is that this state is not attained by moral means: "For the man of knowledge has no duties" (*GM* III "WMAI" 17).

A more common means for dealing with displeasure is mechanical activity, or petty pleasure, including, in some cases, the pleasure of giving pleasure: "good deeds." The priests' "love they neighbor" is a small dose of will to power, allowing a slight, compensatory sense of superiority (*GM* III "WMAI" 18). These are the priest's "innocent" means of dealing with displeasure; his "guilty" ones all involve some kind of "orgy of feeling," or enthusiasm, achieved by exploiting the sense of guilt. Thus the invention of sin was the greatest event in the history of the "sick soul" and the most dangerous artifice of priestly interpretation. The sufferer must see that he causes his own suffering, and "he must understand his suffering as a *punishment*" (*GM* III "WMAI" 20). This will to misunderstanding (to misreading) makes life interesting again, creates a hunger for the pain of contrition, for conscience. Later, such orgies of feeling make the sick sicker. They lead to physiological and mental disturbances. We know that the priestly treatment has not worked because the sickness, not just spiritual sickness but physiological debility—hysteria, epilepsy, and venereal disease—continue to spread (*GM* III "WMAI" 21): "The ascetic priest has ruined psychical health (which is also physiological health) wherever he has come to power; consequently he has also ruined taste *in artibus et litteris*" (*GM* III "WMAI" 22). Nietzsche complains of the vanity of the early Christians, who said "we have no need of the classical tradition, we have our own book"—one which Nietzsche sneeringly describes as a book of "legends, letters of apostles, and apologetic tracts" (*GM* III "WMAI" 22). The bumptiousness of Christianity is typified by Luther, whom Nietzsche thinks of as a "lout" with no comprehension of good manners. Despite its apparent digressiveness, the point being made is an important one, for it makes the leap from physiology to a "body of books" or canon, and implies a connection between the Christian ascetic's disregard of the body and his lack of appreciation for the canon or body of culture.

The ascetic ideal, then, is a totalizing interpretation, a closed system which not even science can counter, indeed, of which "science" is itself an instance. Yet, Nietzsche insists, science is the noblest form of the ascetic ideal. Where it is not, it is self-narcosis (*GM* III "WMAI" 23). Even those unbelievers among philosophers and scholars, the would-be counteridealists who fancy themselves the enemies of the ascetic ideal, are merely the ascetics of "truth." Their faith and strength of self-denial remains absolute: *they still have faith in truth* (*GM* III "WMAI" 24).[41] No European has yet confronted and known from experience the Minotaur represented by the idea that "Nothing is true, everything is permitted" (*GM* III "WMAI" 24). Like science, modern scholarship, viewed in this light, is renunciation, refusing as it does to affirm or deny, to interpret; this turning away is also a mode of sensual denial. Scholars and philosophers alike are constrained by their faith in truth as a metaphysical value; the question of how to "justify" truth does not arise[42] because ascetic religion will not allow it any more than it will allow the question of how to "justify" God. Deny God, however, and the problem of "truth" is called—at least experimentally—into question. Asceticism and science rest, then, on the same foundation: the overestimation of truth, the belief that its value is inestimable, that it can be universally and objectively attached to states of "the self" and "the world."

Art, on the other hand, in which "the *lie* is sanctified and the *will to deception* has a good conscience" (*GM* III "WMAI" 25), is, as Plato recognized, much more opposed to the ascetic ideal than science. Putting oneself at the disposal of the ascetic ideal is the greatest corruption for an artist but, as we saw in the case of Wagner, it is common, for no one is more corruptible than the artist. "Physiologically" speaking, science requires the same "impoverishment of life" as does asceticism. Science belittles humankind; it holds up this self-contempt as its most serious claim to self-respect. The only *real* enemies of the ascetic ideal today are its "comedians," who "arouse mistrust of it" (*GM* III "WMAI" 27). Even atheism contains a remnant of the will to truth; in fact, it is the culmination of two thousand years of asceticism that denies itself the lie involved in a belief in God. For atheism emerges out of the privileging of "truth" and "truthfulness," which the Judaeo-Christian tradition sponsored. Therefore, it could be said that Christian morality has conquered the Christian God. Nietzsche attributes this apparent paradox to "the confessional subtlety of the Christian conscience translated and sublimated into the scientific conscience, into intellectual cleanliness at any price" (*GM* III "WMAI" 27). This has been Europe's "longest and bravest self-overcoming".

Now, however, it remains for Christian morality to be overcome, which can only happen when it finally comes to pose for itself the question, "'what is the meaning of all will to truth'" (*GM* III "WMAI" 27). It may well be that Nietzsche's uncanny suggestion is that "truth" once understood (i.e., "conscious of itself as a *problem*" [*GM* III "WMAI" 27]) will not only undermine morality itself over the next two hundred years, but that this prospect is both terrible *and* hopeful:

> As the will to truth thus gains self-consciousness—there can be no doubt of that—morality will gradually *perish* now: this is the great spectacle in a hundred acts reserved for the next two centuries in Europe—the most terrible, most questionable, and perhaps the most hopeful of all spectacles.—(*GM* III "WMAI" 27)

It may well be that this perspective prefigures the shape of "moral philosophy" after the Holocaust. For increasingly, philosophers as diverse as Bernard Williams and Michel Foucault, Martha Nussbaum and Jean-Francois Lyotard, Walter Benjamin and Richard Rorty, are beginning to suspect that "the moral point of view" *simpliciter* may be *the* problem rather than a solution. It is not merely that morality—conceived as the search for action-guiding principles— is too "thin" to do any useful work. Rather, the suspicion is now emerging that *immorality* may well be morality's Siamese twin, just as the irrational may be the flip side of rationality. The suspicion (i.e., the "truth") is now dawning that we cannot have the one without the other. The horrific insight is dawning that whatever gave us the electric light bulb *necessarily* also gave us the electric chair! Our will to truth virtually assures that—as we are beginning to learn from fetal viability technology—whatever *can* be thought *will* be thought, that whatever *can* be tried *will* be tried, that whatever *can* be done, *will* be done. For "someday, if there is a someday, we will have to learn that evil thinks of itself as good, that it could not have made such progress in the world unless people planned and performed it in all conscience."[43]

All of this is captured quintessentially in the image of that man in the glass booth in a courtroom in Jerusalem in 1961, who appealed—and we mean *thoughtfully*—to Kant's *Critique of Practical Reason* to justify his actions: Adolf Eichmann explaining his *duty* to carry out "the final solution to the Jewish question."

Nietzsche's claim that "morality will *perish* now" through "a hundred acts reserved for the next two centuries in Europe" is "terrible," of course, for those who think that without the moral point of view there is no defense against encroaching madness, no defense against nihilism. However, for those who have come to see "through those hundred acts" that morality itself has been invoked, necessarily, for the slaughter of millions of innocents, for them liberation from the moral point of view may well be "the most hopeful of spectacles." Indeed, as Milton passionately argued two centuries before Nietzsche, "good" and "evil" cannot be separated by edict, but rather only through the most excruciating and painstaking exertion of all that we are:

> Good and evil we know in the field of this world grow up together almost inseparably; and the knowledge of good is so involved and interwoven with the knowledge of evil, and in so many cunning resemblances hardly to be discerned, that those confused seeds which were imposed on Psyche as an incessant labor to cull out and sort asunder, were not more intermixed. It was out of the rind of one apple tasted, that knowledge of good and evil, as two twins cleaving together, leaped forth into the world.[44]

Nietzsche addresses his "readers," as yet unknown (perhaps yet to be born), in order to say that in us, "will to truth" becomes conscious of itself as a problem. However, "will to truth" also names Nietzsche's desire to find a path back to the world from the fictions of *Thus Spoke Zarathustra*. *Toward the Genealogy of Morals* is the process in and by which that desire is problematized and embodied as self-questioning—problematized as an aspect of his own project that answers to the will to truth.

In his conclusion, Nietzsche argues that "Apart from the ascetic ideal, man, the human *animal*, had no meaning so far" (*GM* III "WMAI" 28). He suffered from this lack of meaning, the absence of an answer to the question "Why man?" But humanity found meaning in suffering by inventing guilt to answer the question "Why do we suffer?" Humankind created meaning, and hence a capacity to will, thus closing the door on suicidal nihilism. Despite the fact that the species suffered even more deeply from guilt, the will itself was saved; humankind could at least will *something*:

> We can no longer conceal from ourselves *what* is expressed by all that willing which has taken its direction from the ascetic ideal: this hatred of the human, and even more of the animal, and more still of the material, this horror of the senses, of reason itself, this fear of happiness and beauty, this longing to get away from all appearance, change, becoming, death, wishing, from longing itself—all this means—let us dare to grasp it— *a will to nothingness*, an aversion to life, a rebellion against the most fundamental presuppositions of life; but it is and remains a *will*! . . . And, to repeat in conclusion what I said at the beginning: man would rather will *nothingness* than *not* will.—(*GM* III "WMAI" 28)

We see the circularity of *Toward the Genealogy of Morals* in this final observation, which suggests, among other things, the repetitive nature of commentary, its nature as a rebounding from limits. Indeed, we would say, it suggests a will to write against a silent void, to write over rather than to write nothing at all. For silence is the literary equivalent of death, an acquiescence to nothingness. In this context, the invention of guilt involves many things, many of which concern the philosopher/writer. It necessarily involves an "otherwise" or "elsewhere" and implies a someone or something that punishes and with whom a contract or bargain or act of identification can be made. Death in particular and suffering in general are understood as punishment and, as a corollary, asceticism is understood as a means of identifying with the punisher.[45] Will springs up as the measure of a human excess beyond life, the hyperbolic complement of the litotic "elsewhere" of death.

Viewed in this way, asceticism exhibits a hyperbolic inherent in mimesis. It is not just an attempt to imitate, but to exceed the punisher in harshness—and Nietzsche's project in *Toward the Genealogy of Morals* is as much a critique of mimesis as a definition of our mode of contact with the world as it is, by implication, a critique of philosophy (which it purports to be as well). "Metaphysics" can be viewed as acting or speaking or thinking as if there were someone or something out there with whom or with which the author might strike a bargain. Nietzsche persistently explores this "blind" relationship, using all means at his command of the reader/writer relations. Writing for "no one," or for friends as yet "unknown," he denies that there is anyone out there whose assent can be purchased by a self-imposed limitation. However, in writing as he does, he willingly risks becoming the avatar of nihilism, since the moment in which we are stripped of our traditional defenses, however injurious they have become, is also the moment in which the chances of our succumbing is greatest.

6

Post(pre)face:
The Body of Thought Redux

Literature is like phosphorous: it shines with its maximum brilliance at the moment when it attempts to die. —Roland Barthes, *Writing Degree Zero*

Concerning *Twilight of the Idols*, Walter Kaufmann remarks: "none of his other works contains an equally comprehensive summary of his later philosophy and psychology . . . the book furnishes a fine epitome of Nietzsche" (*TI* "EP"). In the essay that will provide our point of departure here, Bernd Magnus argues that the book may be read "as summarizing [Nietzsche's] philosophical intention not only in substance but in form as well. *Twilight of the Idols* is Nietzsche's alembic in the double sense that one finds here Nietzsche's philosophy as such, distilled, purified, while finding it expressed in aphoristic alembic at the same time."[1] Elsewhere in "The Deification of the Commonplace" Magnus refers to *Twilight* as a "synopticon" of Nietzsche's views—a metaphor that forcefully captures the perspectival problem lurking in all these characterizations of the relationship between *Twilight* and the rest of Nietzsche's canon. It might be asked, we think, whether such a "summary," "synthesis," "synopsis," "epitome," "distillation," or "synopticon" is outside of or a part of the "corpus" it purports to represent.

The convergence of canon and "corpus" here is scarcely accidental, nor do we intend it as forced in any way. The thought of perspectivism is profoundly shaped by the experience of a being whose dominant sense is sight, whose eyes are sited in a very specific place in a body never totally available to vision, who experiences vision ambiguously as looking out from inside the body and, at least in part, as surveying the body as an object from without; a being which has consistently striven to overcome these and other limitations of its defining sense by means technological, artistic, conceptual, and—as Nietzsche recognized—moral. This powerful coincidence of idea and physiology makes perspectivism a particularly appropriate vehicle for raising and exploring the question, central to *Twilight* and to Nietzsche's work in general, of whether, when we speak of ideas, we are ever talking about something wholly other than the body (that we can and do speak in this way is one feature of the ascetic "ideal"). Beginning with the title *Twilight of the Idols*, ideals are inseparable from and are known by the hollow idols in which they are embodied. But the problem of perspectivism—or rather, the very fact that it is "problematic"—also indicates that the dominance of sight and the metaphorics it engenders are *so* great that they render plausible the notion of a singly dominant, decisive, legitimating point of view; and precisely this has had a profound, anti-perspectivist influence on morality, religion, and philosophy.

We have claimed that the coincidence of corpus and canon is intended by us neither as accidental nor forced. If the very form of *Twilight* raises the question of its relationship to the rest of Nietzsche's writing in a way that refers us constantly to the problem of perspectivism, the "body" of the book is so thoroughly pervaded by corporeal metaphors that virtually no moral disposition, philosophical position, or historical development is allowed to go unshadowed by a "physiological" or "humorous" explanation or origin. Some of these physiological "figures" reflect the dominance of sight, as in Nietzsche's discussion of Socrates's ugliness; others seek to provide a corrective for sight's dominance, as in his emphasis on the invisible processes of digestion, or in his contrast between long asses's ears and his own tiny, finely tuned ears, or his acute sense of smell or, more generally, in Nietzsche's emphasis on the balance or lack of balance of elements implicit in the ideas of "health" and "sickness." In short, the aim of *Twilight* is to "represent" Nietzsche's other writings in order to create and shape a "body of thought" or "body of works," a canon or corpus. Yet it does this in a way that seems both to assert and to call into question the possibility of doing any such thing. Magnus points out:

> Nietzsche referred to *Twilight of the Idols* as a "Zusammenfassung wesentlichen philosophischen Heterodoxien" [a "summary of (my) essential philosophical heterodoxies"] in letters to Peter Gast on September 12 and to Franz Overbeck on September 16, 1888. In his notes he simultaneously refers to it as an *Auszug*, a point of departure, a starting point.[2]

All of which is to say that *Twilight* is a recapitulation of and a new addition to the canon, that it is a part of the canon and stands apart from it, that the fragmenting metaphor of perspectivism and the ultimately unifying metaphor of the body *both* apply and fail as well. For Magnus, the importance of aphorism, for *Twilight* and for Nietzsche's writing in general, reflects the pervasiveness of his perspectivist concerns:

> Thus this book begins, just as one would expect, with aphorisms which Nietzsche calls "maxims and arrows" (*Sprüche und Pfeile*). For, indeed, Nietzsche has often been called

the archetypal aphorist—and these pithy forty-four aphorisms remind us that aphorisms are meant to atomize rather than provide unity, connection, totality, and closure. Aphorisms divide, mark-off. Or, put differently, the aphorism, epigram, or maxim requires a special effort on the reader's part to provide the connective tissue, the logical ligature, which transforms glistening shards into a single organic whole which subtends them. And this too is an exercise in perspectivism, one in which the reader is the unindicted co-conspirator who blames or praises Nietzsche for his own results.[3]

Here, it is suggested that the aphorisms represent the form not only of *Twilight* as a whole but also Nietzsche's method in general. Indeed, if we extend Magnus's point but slightly, "maxims and arrows" represents the paradoxical atomization/unity of Nietzsche's canon of works:

> having abandoned traditional discursive philosophical procedures . . . Nietzsche favors an accumulation of self-sufficient insights, epigrams, maxims, aphorisms, fragments, and notes, which require of the reader that he *himself* [or she *herself*] provide the missing ligature which unifies his books. In consequence, the reader's constructed ligature both establishes and, paradoxically, dissolves authorial identity and intention. "Nietzsche" becomes "Nietzsche-as-read-by-*x*-on-occasion-*y*.[4]

These quoted passages seem to us to register the fractures or fault lines defined by the aphoristic form, not only between the atomizing effects of perspectivism and the unifying work of the reader but also between a corresponding inorganic and organic metaphorics ("glistening shards" versus "connective tissue"). Moreover, the conclusion also registers Nietzsche's transposition of the tension between perspectival and physiological metaphorics into the complexities of the reader/writer relationship. And here a crucial point surfaces: if the unifying ligature that bestows an organic body on the otherwise glistening shards belongs to the reader's share, what are we to make of Nietzsche's recurrent claims that *his* readers (and hence, he himself in a sense) have not yet been born? What happens to the work, the canon, the body of thought, if Nietzsche's maxims, instead of being "arrows which are perfectly poised to strike their target"[5] are actually "arrows shot into the air to fall he knows not where?" What if the readers who are to provide this connective tissue, including Nietzsche himself—who, after all, stands in the position of commentator or reflector on his own work—is capable only of constructing a bizarre body, a kind of Frankenstein's monster out of these fragments and assorted body parts? Where is the reader (or even the author as his own reader) capable of restoring to wholeness the Dionysian/Orphic dismemberment of the author-committed-to-language? The atomistic effects of aphorism, combined with the absence of a capable reader, has implications for the very possibility of a body of thought or canon. At the very least, a canon (or body of thought) can only be partial, with wholeness indefinitely deferred. Perhaps less obvious is the fact that the figure "body of thought" cuts in two ways; it has a fertility all its own and, like all metaphors, generates consequences and conditions quite apart from its immediately intended ones. The fragmentation or dismemberment of the body of thought is not just a problem for canon or conception, a threat to hermeneutics; it is a "physiological" problem, with consequences for the body enlisted in metaphorical support of the intellectual project. Nietzsche's pervasive example of how this works shows the way that ascetic ideals have made a sick animal even sicker.

Above all, there is the extensiveness of Nietzsche's writing, which imposes on reader and writer alike limitations akin to those attending the particular sitedness, the partiality of the eye. And to this partiality, writing adds a temporal dimension. Furthermore, the turning inward away from the world involved in writing corresponds to the eye's capacity to turn away, even inward in voluntary closure—an inward turn that is at once the antithesis of sight and merely one of its possibilities. Not just an ascetic metaphorics of corporeal sight and spiritual insight is built on this ambiguity, the romantic discourse of imagination depends upon it as well.

Because of the location of our eyes, our experience of our own bodies is diverse and partial. Some parts are routinely available to sight, others require the aid of a mirror and, even then, the effort required, odd angles, and relative novelty of the sight create a qualitative difference. Some parts of our bodies we know primarily by touch, others by a combination of sight and touch—and all this quite apart from functional differences. This partiality, this incompleteness and diversity, also characterizes the body of the text—so difficult to take in and hold, never present except in parts that continually pass into and out of the focus of consciousness. From a writer's point of view, there is the very difficulty of sustaining a theme or argument, of remembering what s/he was trying to say throughout. Indeed, the very fact of having a purpose or interest corresponds to the sitedness of the eye and prevents the writer from keeping all aspects of the text and language in view at once (De Man calls this "rhetoricity" and argues that it determines the blindness that attends all insight).[6] Insofar as this visual metaphor holds, it also suggests certain irreducible differences between the reader's and writer's experience of the same text. To invoke an analogy, certain parts of the body, the back, for instance, are only sporadically a part of the visual image of ourselves, which may be routine, perhaps even central, to someone else's image of us. It is by no means certain that we would immediately recognize ourselves going away; it is far more likely that a friend or loved one would. It is said that some people, when confronted by video tapes of themselves dancing, skiing or playing tennis strenuously deny they are the performers captured on film—even when the exercise was for the express purpose of constructive critique. Reader and writer seem similarly divided in their perceptions of what, in the literary context, we call style, which recommends itself as an attitude or impression that emerges from a diversity of parts. The status of this impression of style is a central concern of *Twilight* and of this chapter, as it was in chapter 1.

To be sure, there are also senses in which writing seems to diverge from a metaphorics of visual perspectivism in ways that suggest a non-visual metaphorics of the body, and even beckon beyond it. For example, the "go little book" topos[7] points beyond itself toward the possibility of a shared body, in which the author's transition to readership or a commentator's relation to his or her own work corresponds to the reader's hermeneutical possession of what is ambiguously the same and a different "body" of text. More immediately, Nietzsche's persistent appeals to "gaiety" and animal sensuality point to a mode of being, a system of physical organization, that functions with an efficiency which self-consciously guided behavior typically cannot even approximate. In fact, the difficulty of shaping a body of thought, of establishing a canon, does not seem to create in Nietzsche any anxiety over whether he is being "himself," in *Twilight* or elsewhere; and this performative assurance seems to find its counterpart in the hermeneut's presumption that the myriad details of the text are in some way assimilable to an "intention" or authorial "identity." Style, it seems, belongs to both these metaphoric systems, with their rather different implications. What can this mean and what implications does this have for the value of the notion of "style" in literature and philosophy?

Before continuing a more detailed discussion of "style," it is worth noting that by thematizing and exploiting the perspectival difference between reader and writer, Nietzsche's perspectivism generates a source of infinite self-regeneration—an interpretive sublime answering to fears, dating from the late seventeenth century, that the end of the literary tradition was at hand. Such fears are a natural consequence of perceiving the tradition as a unified, discrete "body," subject to "exhaustion." A new, perspectival hermeneutic forestalls an organic metaphorics of completion and decay but installs instead a competing anxiety over the endless, repetitive generation of interpretations which never form a body or canon. This question of the nature and possibility of a unified or unifying perception of an aphoristic thought, canon, body, can in the end be viewed as question of style: the bulk of Nietzsche's conclusion in *Twilight of the Idols* takes up this question. In concluding his discussion of Goethe, "the last German for whom I feel any reverence," Nietzsche writes *so* hyperbolically that the reader wonders if s/he is not *supposed* to question his self-characterization:

> I am often asked why, after all, I write in German: nowhere am I read worse than in the fatherland. But who knows in the end whether I even wish to be read today? To create things on which time tests its teeth in vain; in form, in substance, to strive for a *little* immortality—I have never yet been modest enough to demand less of myself. The aphorism, the apothegm, in which I am the first among the Germans to be a master, are

the forms of "eternity"; it is my ambition to say in ten sentences what everyone else says in a book—what everyone else does *not* say in a book.

I have given mankind the most profound book it possesses, my *Zarathustra*; shortly I shall give it the most independent. (*TI* "SUM" 51)

Nietzsche writes in German, one might surmise, because he is unique, possibly so unique that he neither expects nor wishes to be read today. To write aphoristically for an audience that does not yet exist, to practice archery without a target, obscures the distinction between litotic and hyperbolic. Rhetorically, this tension is evident everywhere in Nietzsche's text, in the interplay between statements and the prevalence of intensifiers and superlatives, positive and negative—a tension typified in the phrase "a little immortality." What exactly is a *little* immortality?

This striving after immortality, so studiedly offhand, combined with the pitch of Nietzsche's rhetoric elsewhere, may be construed as betraying a certain anxiety about the current and future state of his body of work. Moreover, it may be that this anxiety is intimately connected with the asceticism inherent in the aphoristic style, which reminds us that for Nietzsche, asceticism— whether it is the natural predisposition of the philosopher, the self-conscious ideal of the priest, or the variety of things to the artist—*is* anxiety about the body, whatever else Nietzsche has made of it. The reader may perceive something of this concern in "What I Owe the Ancients," in that celebration of the Roman style which Nietzsche embraces as his own:

My sense of style, for the epigram as a style, was awakened almost instantly when I came into contact with Sallust. I have not forgotten the surprise of my honored teacher, Corsen, when he had to give his worst Latin pupil the best grade: I had finished with one stroke. Compact, severe, with as much substance as possible, a cold sarcasm against beautiful words" and "beautiful statements"—here I found myself. And even in my *Zarathustra* one will recognize a very serious ambition for a Roman style, for the *aere perennius* in style.

Nor was my experience any different in my first contact with Horace. To this day, no other poet has given me the same artistic delight that a Horatian ode gave me from the first. In certain languages that which has been achieved here could not even be attempted. This mosaic of words, in which every word—as sound, as place, as concept— pours out its strength right and left and over the whole, this *minimum* in the extent and number of signs, and the maximum thereby attained in the energy of the signs—all that is Roman and, if one will believe me, *noble* par excellence. All the rest of poetry becomes, in contrast, something too popular—a mere garrulity of feelings. (*TI* "WIOA" 1)

This passage is quoted at length because it purports to state the foundation for Nietzsche's style. If the reader takes this reminiscence at face value, Nietzsche credits his epigrammatic turn to a "taste" which "does not like to say Yes; rather even No; but best of all nothing" about "whole cultures," "books," even "places and landscapes" (*TI* "WIOA" 1). This suggests that epigrammatic writing comes as close to silence as writing can. For Nietzsche, it appears, it is important to avoid garrulity. Hence, he admired, first, and then developed a mode of expression as narrowly removed as possible from, silence. Above all, however, this Roman style that Nietzsche here admires corresponds to a physical ideal. It is compact, severe. Just so the "man of bronze": exuding much energy contained in little space—strong and "silent"—he seems to be proof against time itself. However, one obvious difficulty in this privileging admiration is that it is hardly a description of Nietzsche's own wracked body, any more than it is only a partial description of his style, one which strikes the reader as more typically marked by hyperbole than by metallic restraint. To return to a perspectivist metaphor, it is not that Nietzsche's self-description is *mistaken* so much as that it is partial. We are tempted to say, pursuing our reflection-in-the-mirror analogy, that Nietzsche's epigrammatic style, with the body and body of work that it implies is, in effect, the partial aspect that Nietzsche sees in the mirror, not the whole (or at least, greater sum of parts) that we, his readers, see. Indeed, Nietzsche concedes that his debt to the Romans is more than balanced (as one section to four) by the power of the Greeks, which is at its heart, hyperbolic. He begins by protesting that "To the Greeks I do not by any means owe similarly strong impressions." How could he, when "their manner is too foreign, and too fluid, to have an imperative, a 'classical' effect"? (*TI* "WIOA" 2) Imperative, impetus, direction—these are the keys, derived from Roman compression. The Hellenic, hyperbolic thrust may well be more fundamental to the greater portion of his writing, even to certain aspects of its aphoristic style, whose hallmark is the paradoxical ability to spread itself abroad without loss of "substance." As Nietzsche puts it: "Who could ever have learned to write from a Greek? Who could ever have learned it *without* the Romans?" (*TI* "WIOA" 2).

Nietzsche rejects the then-prevailing scholarly admiration for the artistry of Plato—"a first-rate decadent in style," who "throws all stylistic forms together" [as does Nietzsche himself in some accounts?] (*TI* "WIOA" 2). And Plato's "idealism"—by implication intimately related to stylistic eclecticism—is in any case an aberration from the true Hellenic spirit. If he has to choose, Nietzsche says, the Greek he prefers and the "cure for all Platonism" is Thucydides, whom Nietzsche sees as "most closely related to [him]self by the unconditional will not to gull oneself and to see reason in reality—not in 'reason,' still less in 'morality'" (*TI* "WIOA" 2). The refusal to confuse reason and reality involves the recognition that there are limits to the conceptual reduction/distillation of experience, limits to idealization. Thucydides is offered, then as the complement of the Roman achievement in stylistic compression:

One must follow him line by line and read no less clearly between the lines: there are few thinkers who say so much between the lines. With him the culture of the Sophists, by which I mean the culture of the realists,[8] reaches its perfect expression—this inestimable movement amid the moralistic and idealistic swindle set loose on all sides by the Socratic schools. (*TI* "WIOA" 2)

Language—Nietzsche seems to say—exceeds itself, casts beyond itself, spilling over into the space between the lines, as experience exceeds ideal/moralistic attempts to confine it within the conceptual limits of "reason." On this view, the compactness or restraint of Thucydides resides in his matter-of-factness rather than in epigrammatic effects. For Nietzsche, he is "the great sum" and "last revelation" of a "strong, severe, hard factuality, which was instinctive with the older Hellenes. In the end, it is *courage* in the face of reality that distinguishes a man like Thucydides from Plato: Plato is a coward before reality, consequently he flees into the ideal; Thucydides has control of *himself*, consequently he also maintains control of things" (*TI* "WIOA" 2). Here one finds reassertion of a familiar Nietzschean emphasis on courage to *sustain* a style, the claim that the writer must, in the face of reality, exercise poise—self-control—in order to avoid the temptation of flitting from style to style. It is almost as if the contrary, equivocal mode of composition were an avoidance of what, carried far enough, a concentrated style would imply. The intensity, the anger and intemperance implicit in the passage—Plato is a "coward before reality"—is not like Thucydides, who, after all, is distinguished by the fact that he does not expect people to be reasonable, to be any better than they are. Hence, he has no more reason to be angry and rant than he does to run away. In contrast, Nietzsche's diction is often angry; it sounds as if the spectacle of human morality, of human behavior, were a constant source of nausea. But this reaction suggests the character of one who expects—or at least hopes for—something more. This is yet another perspective in the mirror. From this angle, in this light, Nietzsche looks less like Sallust or Horace, not at all like Plato, and more like Thucydides; and yet he is recognizably the same man who, looked at from still another angle, looks like Horace and Sallust.

Nietzsche's style, then, begins as a specific epigrammatic or aphoristic mode of writing, but develops a quality of "conception" or "gaze," even an attitude, which, in turn (in Nietzsche's discussion of the Dionysian heart of Hellenism) becomes more like a mode of "being," a defining stylistic disposition. Style, like the body itself, like a body's disposition, appears as a heterocosm whose dominant extremes are litotes and hyperbole, contraction and control, expansion and release.

Nietzsche boasts: "I was the first to take seriously, for the understanding of the older, the still rich and overflowing Hellenic instinct, that wonderful phenomenon which bears the name of Dionysus: it is explicable only in terms of an *excess* of force" (*TI* I "WIOA" 4). Dionysus, like this passage itself perhaps, is hyperbolic not in the sense of violating a norm ("exceeding the proper"), but in the sense of "having it to burn." This hyperbolic "element out of which Dionysian art grows" (*TI* "WIOA" 4) Nietzsche terms the "orgiastic"—"an overflowing feeling of life and strength, where even pain still has the effect of a stimulus . . . Saying Yes to life even in its strangest and hardest problems, the will to life rejoicing over its own inexhaustibility even in the very sacrifice of its highest types" (*TI* "WIOA" 5)—which is to say, in tragedy. This insightful leap, Nietzsche tells us, led him beyond Aristotle to the true goal of the tragic poet: "to be *oneself* the eternal joy of becoming, beyond all terror and pity—that joy which included even joy in destroying" (*TI* "WIOA" 5). The tragic poet is not *impinged on* by terror and pity; rather, the poet embodies them, and in so doing represents individual joy as a joy *before* differentiations. This is the "soil out of which my intention, my *ability* grows" (*TI* "WIOA" 5). This, too, is an aspect or perspective, a partial, occluded view, a self-image seen in a mirror, the mirror provided by *The Birth of Tragedy*. The fact that it seems to be an aspect Nietzsche wants to privilege does not negate its partiality. Writing in these final pages of *Twilight* about the Dionysian mysteries, Nietzsche gives us a fine example not only of that partiality, but of his hyperbolic style:

> it is only in the Dionysian mysteries, in the psychology of the Dionysian state, that the *basic fact* of the Hellenic instinct finds expression—its "will to life." What was it that the Hellene guaranteed himself by means of these mysteries? *Eternal life*, the eternal return of life; the future promised and hallowed in the past; the triumphant Yes to life beyond all death and change; *true life* as the overall continuation of life through procreation, through the mysteries of sexuality. . . . It was Christianity, with its *ressentiment* against life at the bottom of its heart, which first made something unclean of sexuality: it threw *filth* on the origin, on the presupposition of our life. (*TI* "WIOA" 5)

As Nietzsche reminded us earlier, the Greeks are irreducibly foreign; no one can learn to write from them, he insists, but that does not mean that we cannot discover the Greeks *in writing*, as he claims to have done in *The Birth of Tragedy* and thereafter. From this perspective, the Dionysian mode of being from which Christianity exiled Western civilization (with an "assist" from Plato) is recuperated as an aspect of writing or "style." Just as there may be no procreation without differentiation, there may be no style without it either. Thus, Nietzsche sees the Christian rejection of "*sexuality*" as a rejection of difference, a refusal to see and accept the limited partiality of a view, discourse, conception, or morality—a refusal to accept the irreducibility of difference. But what does this mean for style to spring from and embody difference? Perhaps a look at the structure of *Twilight* may shed light on this question.

The body of *Twilight* is framed by the aphoristic "Maxims and Arrows" and the hyperbolic "The Hammer Speaks." The litotic understatement of the former is linked to the hyperbolic overstatement of the latter as parts of the same body, like back and front, which can never be seen and taken in all at once. It makes as little sense to ask which is the "real" Nietzsche as to ask whether one's back or front is one's "real" body. Moreover, the metaphorical comparison with the body, which is apprehended in parts but functions as a whole, raises the question of whether litotic or hyperbolic, or any other specific characterization of style is not, by virtue of the specificity that is a consequence of perspective, "the style," or indeed, of whether "style" is a synecdoche for "styles," which may, depending on circumstances, be a convenience or a hindrance in advancing critical discussion. (What, after all, is the purpose of figurative language?)

At this point, we are broaching one topic of Derrida's discussion of Nietzsche's styles in *Spurs*,[9] which proceeds from Nietzsche's remarks about women to the relationship between sexual differentiation and style(s). In terms of the foregoing discussion of style, we might wonder whether the appearance of the plural ("styles") is a function of the limitations of our characterizations. But if this is the case, how are we to approach "style"—the singular form of the noun out of which the plural form may be said to be composed? Don't "styles" presuppose "style," in some sense of "presuppose"? How are we even infer "its" existence? And does this mean that "style" is more superficial or more fundamental than "argument," for instance?

In his collection of "clinical tales," *The Man Who Mistook His Wife for a Hat*,[10] neurologist Oliver Sacks records a case that could almost be a parable of the problem under discussion. The body in question—we could say radically, bizarrely in question—is that of Christina, a young woman who, apparently as the result of a reaction to medication, lost all sense of proprioception: "that continuous but unconscious sensory flow from the movable parts of our body (muscles, tendons, and joints), by which their position and tone and motion are continually monitored and adjusted, but in a way which is hidden from us because it is automatic and unconscious."[11] Proprioception is essential to our sense of ourselves "for it is only by courtesy of proprioception, so to speak, that we feel our bodies as proper to us, as our 'property,' as our own."[12] Interestingly, the same Weir Mitchell whose work with hysterics Nietzsche knew of and inveighed against in *Toward the Genealogy of Morals* was one of the pioneers of proprioception in his "work with amputees and nerve-damaged patients during the American Civil War."[13]

With her proprioceptive sense disrupted, Christina was unable to recognize her own leg, despite the "obvious fact" that it is "attached" to "her." There is a sense in which circumstances of such a case call the terminology of the previous sentence into question (hence, the scare-quotes). Happily, cases of total proprioceptive deficiency are rare, so rare in fact, that Christina's condition was initially misdiagnosed as "anxiety hysteria." From without, Christina was "as floppy as a rag doll."[14] From within, she describes herself as "pithed," "disembodied,"[15] and Sacks continues that in an all but unimaginable sense, she is "bodiless," "a sort of wraith."[16]

Such a loss of the proprioceptive body image, Sacks informs us, can only be compensated-for imperfectly, mechanically—by a kind of "visual automatism."[17] Instead of effecting a simple task like picking up a spoon and raising it to her mouth by "feeling it from within," she must monitor her own movements from without by watching the movement and progress of her limbs and making corrections. Eventually, she is able to approximate her former control over her body, but its relevance *to her* is gone forever. And whenever she closes her eyes, she is still liable to collapse in a heap.

For Sacks, the intellectual context of Christina's story is Wittgensteinian:

> This unquestionability of the body, its certainty, is, for Wittgenstein, the start and basis for all certainty. Thus, in his last book (*On Certainty*), he opens by saying: "If you do know that *here is one hand*, we'll grant you all the rest." But then, in the same breath, on the same opening page: "What we can ask is whether it can make sense to doubt it . . ."; and, a little later, "Can I doubt it? Grounds for *doubt* are lacking."[18]

Sacks goes on to remark that the possibility of doubting the body, of "losing one's entire body in total doubt . . . seems to haunt his last book like a nightmare."[19] And Sacks's epigraph—also quoted from Wittgenstein—about how the hardest things to see are those that are always before our eyes and how "the real foundations of his enquiry do not strike a man at all" could just as easily have been taken from the preface to *Toward the Genealogy of Morals*.

For Nietzsche, the loss or at least questionability of the body is not only the nightmarish catastrophe that haunts epistemology, any more than it is a mere contingent medical accident. For him, anxiety about the body is fundamental to religion, morality, philosophy, perhaps intellectual activity in general in the culture of asceticism. His genealogy can therefore be usefully read as an account of how putting the body itself in question is created, cultivated, confirmed, and replicated as a precondition of philosophical reflection. Therefore, the visual automatism that allows Christina a partially effective but parodic restoration of her own body as instrument has strong affinities with Nietzsche's genealogical account of the lost assurance which is only mechanically and imperfectly recreated by means of a contrived "gaiety," an assurance for which morality and religion have failed to fabricate a replacement.

The dramatic difference between proprioception and the clumsy, alienating body sense that vision is able to provide suggests the limits of a visual sense of the body which, Nietzsche suggests, dominates metaphorically and intellectually even more decisively than it dominates physiologically. It also suggests that perspectivism is itself a perspective, that its authority is as paradoxically partial and pervasive as that of the visual sense and its attendant metaphorics.

Interestingly, not just Christina but her doctors as well are taken aback and baffled by her loss of proprioception. How does the medical profession—or anyone—deal with a "thing" (a set of symptoms, a "disease") known by its loss. The situation was so rare as to be all but unimaginable. That we know proprioception only by its catastrophic loss suggests an analogy with "style" in its perspectival embodiments. This doubleness may mark one way in which human intellectual productions echo the organization and coherence of bodies, while also serving as signs of the degree to which they fall short and signal a loss—the loss that Nietzsche "chronicles" in *Toward the Genealogy of Morals*.

For some time now, we have been playing about the edges of Derrida's central discussion of the "styles" of Nietzsche in *Spurs*. Our discussion so far, then, helps to highlight and to distinguish our analysis from the particular emphases of Derrida's essay: (1) his tendency to emphasize the ways in which men and women differ as contrasted with those in which they are alike, his emphasis on sexual differentiation over shared visual and proprioceptive senses, for example; and (2) Derrida's tendency to explore the question of Nietzsche's representations of "woman" to the exclusion of the slightly different but arguably at least equally relevant question of the self-representation of "men" through their representations of "women." Of course, strictly speaking, Derrida's target is less Nietzsche than Heidegger's reading of Nietzsche; the priority Heidegger grants the question of Being, his related privileging of the "grand style" and the hermeneutical confidence underlying it. In Derrida's reading, more fundamental even than the question of Being is that of sexual differentiation, manifested in Nietzsche's text by a diversity of characterizations of "woman" that defy unification and prevent the multiplicity of his "styles" from coalescing into a single "grand style": "A joyful wisdom [*fröhliche Wissenschaft*] shows it well: there never has been *the* style, *the* simulacrum, *the* woman, there never has been *the* sexual difference. If the simulacrum is ever going to occur, its writing must be in the interval between several styles. And the insinuation of the woman (of) Nietzsche is that, if there is going to be style, there can only be more than one."[20]

Derrida's primary point of departure and differentiation is Heidegger's famous reading of "How the 'True World' Finally Became a Fable" in *Twilight*. Derrida points out that Heidegger analyzes in detail "all the elements of Nietzsche's text with the sole exception of the idea's becoming female"[21] in the second of Nietzsche's six epochs: "The true world—unattainable for now, but promised for the sage, the pious, the virtuous ('for the sinner who repents'). (Progress of the idea: it becomes more subtle, insidious, incomprehensible—*it becomes female*, it becomes Christian.)" (*TI* "HTWBF") "Surely," Derrida insists, the "necessity" of this "inscription of the woman . . . is not one of a conceptless metaphorical or allegorical illustration. Nor could it be that of a pure concept bare of any fantastic designs":

Indeed it is clear from the context that it is the idea that becomes woman. The becoming-female is a "progress of the idea" (*Fortschritt der Idee*) and the idea a form of truth's self-presentation. Thus the truth has not always been a woman nor is the woman always truth. They both have a history; together they both form a history. And perhaps, if history's strict sense has always been so presented in the movement of truth, their history is history itself, a history which philosophy alone, inasmuch as it is included therein, is unable to decode. In the age before this progress in the history of true-world, the idea was Platonic. And in this, the idea's inaugural movement, the *Umschreibung*, the transcription, the paraphrase of the Platonic statement, was "Ich, Plato, *bin* die Wahrheit," "I, Plato, *am* the truth."

But once this inaugural movement has given way to the second age, here where the becoming-female of the idea is the presence or presentation of truth, Plato can no more say "I am truth." For here the philosopher is no longer the truth. Severed from himself, he has been severed from the truth.[22]

For Derrida, this "severing" is the castration that Nietzsche refers to in the very next section of *Twilight*—"Morality as Anti-Nature"—when he argues that "The Church fights passion with excision in every sense: its practice, its 'cure', is *castratism*" (*TI* "MAN" 2). Such is the centrifugal pull of Freud and now Lacan in some contemporary theorizing in a psychoanalytic vein, that woman and only woman—as if "naturally"—presents herself as the figure of this castration. And here is a danger—a danger of which Derrida is acutely aware but which he does not, we think, *entirely* escape. Having "exposed" the underlying, metaphysical work done by Heidegger's question of Being and the idea of a "grand style," how is it helpful now to grant, as Derrida appears to do, the same privilege to differentiation or difference and the question of woman? Having recognized that the inscription of woman cannot be merely illustrative or purely conceptual, does it follow that it is *necessary*? But if there is no such danger, how, then, can Derrida claim that: "the question of style must be measured against the larger question of the interpretation of Nietzsche's text, of the interpretation of interpretation—in short against the question of interpretation itself. In such a confrontation either the question of style will be resolved, or its very statement will be disqualified."[23] Given the limitations of philosophy and interpretation that Derrida identifies in connection with the question of woman, from what perspective and in what discourse can the very statement of "the question of style" be decisively disqualified?

We would observe that one of the major concerns in "How the 'True World' Finally Became a Fable" is the fantastic—fabulation, or the making of fables. The sequence could just as easily be called "How the 'True World' Finally Became A Fable Became A Fable," since Nietzsche's mocking self-consciousness will not allow him to pretend that he can evade the radicalizing uncertainty that comes with representation—an uncertainty that suggests the absence of any perspective from which the competing claims of unifying and differentiating accounts can ultimately be adjudicated, which is another way of saying that the perspective is lacking from which we can say decisively whether the body that men and women share is more decisive than the body that separates them. And here, perhaps, the partiality of Derrida's account emerges. For, given his targets, not only do his claims tend to promote the authority of difference over similarity; even within the realm of sexual difference he shows little interest in the story that Nietzsche is telling in and through his many remarks on the question of woman, which is, after all, a fantasy of "man," and of "heterosexual man" at that. As a supplement, we would argue that Nietzsche is *also* telling the story of the loss of the male body, and of "man's" ebbing power to resist encroaching "*castratism*."

Returning to the story of Christina, here we may see, by comparison, that Nietzsche's lack of "control" over his own text does not—perhaps cannot—have the significance that Derrida wishes to attach to it. We would argue that such control is not necessary to constitute a "body" or a "style," anymore than a minute, conscious attention to the movements of the body can constitute proprioception. The Heideggerian hermeneut who is the ostensible object of Derrida's critique in *Spurs* (including that aspect of Nietzsche that seems to take hermeneutics at its word) may think that an "author" establishes and underwrites the unity and ultimate coherence of a text. Derrida writes as if to demonstrate that, if the "author" constructed by hermeneutics does not exist, and if as a consequence of that development the unity of the text is undermined, then, with it, the existence of a body of thought is undermined as well, rather than merely one particular account of that unity. Such a conception of the body, of the text, of a style, may even disclose an unacknowledged anti-perspectivist, metaphysical yearning, despite its professed aims. To stand metaphysics on its head is not necessarily to escape it. Such a reversal may merely reinscribe it instead.

Most of *Twilight* is a dialogue with the men whom Nietzsche either admires or deplores. We have in mind one of the latter in particular: Nietzsche's violent and, to use one his favorite terms, "mocking" denunciation of Carlyle. It is well known that many critics of both authors find notable similarities—in "style," if nothing else. So, given the concerns of our present discussion, Nietzsche's remarks are of special interest:

> I have been reading the life of *Thomas Carlyle*, this unconscious and involuntary farce, this heroic-moralistic interpretation of dyspeptic states. Carlyle: a man of strong words and attitudes, a rhetor from *need*, constantly lured by the craving for a strong faith and the feeling of his incapacity for it (in this respect, a typical romantic!). The craving for a strong faith is no proof of a strong faith, but quite the contrary. If one has such a faith, then one can afford the beautiful luxury of skepticism: one is sure enough, firm enough, has ties enough for that. Carlyle drugs something in himself with the fortissimo of his veneration of men of strong faith and with his rage against the less simple-minded: he *requires* noise. A constant passionate dishonesty against himself—that is his *proprium*; in this respect he is and remains interesting. (*TI* "SUM" 12)

This passage brings together many of the strands we have been following throughout this book, not the least in its intriguing conversion of the bodily theory of humors with the theory of rhetoric and romanticism. The intensity of Nietzsche's attack on Carlyle also deserves comment, especially since Carlyle's choleric/hyperbolic style has often been seen by critics as Nietzschean (and vice versa), and since Carlyle's stridency seems at least superficially like Nietzsche's own. Yet this is not atypical. Nietzsche's harshest attacks seem to be reserved for those in whom we might be tempted to see something of himself. In Carlyle's case in particular, Nietzsche may be trying to separate himself from some element of the parodic, or rather self-parodic. Indeed, Nietzsche's critique of Carlyle echoes many of the particulars of Derrida's remarks on the parodic in Nietzsche.

Nietzsche's remarks on Carlyle's romanticism are especially telling. Nietzsche insists upon the symptomatic nature of striving after belief. Carlyle insists on commitment and belief, castigating others for their diminished capacity for them, and yet all the while suspecting his own incapacity. Nietzsche's readers see the problem: by the internal logic of Nietzsche's own writings, this diatribe, "accurate" though it may be, also serves as a penetrating self-analysis and inadvertent self-criticism. For Nietzsche, recall, Western culture will not avoid the consequences of the decline of the Christian/ascetic order through the posturing of such misguided "believers" as Carlyle. Western culture could only avoid decline through a self-overcoming and transformation that none, not Nietzsche, not even Zarathustra—and surely not Carlyle—has achieved. In other words, Nietzsche, ambiguously the highest of "the higher men" and forerunner or prophet of the *Übermensch*, remains one of us. Put differently: if only the *Übermensch* can evade the painful self-division ascribed to romanticism, then he-she-it is uniquely post-Romantic, as Nietzsche appears not to be, according to his own self-description.

The awareness that separates Nietzsche from Carlyle, that stands between irony and (self) parody, and the faith in a future self-overcoming that makes his skepticism and his criticism possible might even be considered versions of Romanticism, perhaps a sort of postmodern romanticism (to coin an oxymoron). They are, taken together, traits of a "higher" Romantic type, we suggest. For the emphasis on faith in the quoted passage is central also to Nietzsche, who, it could be argued, adverts to and wants to claim for himself a kind of natural and preconscious faith, a "body confidence." The degree of Carlyle's choler, his rhetorical "noise," betray the lack of such a confidence, Nietzsche suggests, and his lack of self-awareness renders him "farcical"—a term which could just as easily have been "parodic" or even more cuttingly, "self-parodic," since Carlyle's loud assertions of faith become self parodies in light of the lack or need that drives them. Much is also made in the quoted passage of self-awareness, or of Carlyle's lack of it and Nietzsche's repeated claims to possess it. Carlyle is a Romantic unawares (despite his call to "put down your Byron") as Nietzsche is a self-aware, perhaps ambivalent Romantic—a Romantic under

protest, a postmodern romantic. But how much difference is there really between the choleric hyperbole of Carlyle and the mocking hyperbole of
Nietzsche? Between the exuberant body of *Ecce Homo* and the "clothes philosophy" of *Sartor Resartus*? Here, everything turns on the "ironic difference" of
awareness, or rather of whether irony makes a difference.

Whether we are discussing the choleric hyperbole of Carlyle or the gaiety,
the mocking hyperbole of Nietzsche, we seem to encounter the same range of
possibilities. Hyperbole rounds back on itself, as in irony, yielding a self-
awareness which, we are tempted to believe, sets us apart from the unaware.
Or hyperbole transgresses a boundary between awareness and unawareness,
yielding parody which, as Derrida points out "always presupposes a naïveté
withdrawing into an unconscious, a vertiginous non-mastery."[24] Or, beyond
even parody, one becomes—unaware—the butt of one's own joke, yielding
self-parody. But what if the ironist, who thinks that her refined awareness, her
self-consciousness, makes a difference is simply unaware that this distinction
finally does not make a difference? That her irony is also self-parody?[25] This
may well be what is at stake in Nietzsche's late works, especially *Ecce Homo*: the
value of this ironic consciousness that grows out of Romanticism's consciousness of its own failings, which we have come to call "modern" and with the
collapse of modernism, "postmodern."

Once the subject of Carlyle has been raised, Nietzsche's work beckons to and
calls up—from among all of his many, spirited writings—*Sartor Resartus*. Carlyle's most Nietzschean, most Zarathustran work, *Sartor Resartus* is, in fact, the
source from which we have taken the central metaphor of the present discussion: the body of thought. Carlyle's figure of "clothing" is, of course, famous.
Clothing is an emblem; but then, for him, "all visible things are emblems." Life
itself is characterized by clothing, for the spirit, "like a light-particle," descends
from above "to be clothed with a Body." Indeed, "the whole External Universe
and what it holds is both Clothing, and the essence of all Science lies in the
PHILOSOPHY OF CLOTHES." Insofar as this sounds Platonic, we might
understand Nietzsche's disdain; but it also sounds Emersonian, and, as we
read in the very next section of *Twilight*, Nietzsche admired Emerson. Just as
the body is clothing, for Carlyle, so is its means of expression. That is, clothing
expresses itself by other clothing: language as "cover" or clothing":

Language is called the Garment of Thought: however, it should rather be, 'Language is
the Flesh-Garment, the Body, of Thought'. I said that Imagination wove this Flesh-
Garment; and does not she? Metaphors are her stuff: examine Language; what, if you
except some few primitive elements (of natural sound), what is it all but Metaphors,
recognized as such, or no longer recognized; still fluid and florid, or now solid-grown
and colorless? If those same primitive elements are the osseous fixtures in the Flesh-
Garment, Language,—then are metaphors its muscles and tissues and living integu-
ments. An unmetaphorical style you shall in vain seek for: is not your very *Attention* a

Stretching-to? The difference lies here: some styles are lean, adust, wiry, the muscle itself seems osseous; some are even quite pallid, hunger-bitten and dead-looking; while others again glow in the flush of health and vigorous self-growth, sometimes (as in my own case) not without an apoplectic tendency. Moreover, there are sham Metaphors, which overhanging that same Thought's-Body (best naked), and deceptively bedizening, or bolstering it out, may be called its false stuffings, superfluous show-cloaks (*Putz-Mantel*), and tawdry woollen rags: whereof he that runs and reads may gather whole hampers,—and burn them.[26]

Carlyle begins with the familiar Christian metaphor of the body as clothing for the soul or "divine ME"—a metaphor which adverts to the ascetic tradition of denigrating body in favor of spirit. Similarly, language can be considered the garment of thought, which obliquely refers to an anti-rhetorical tradition of considering language, style, as something superficial, like clothing, to be put on and taken off. But Carlyle suggests that the relationship between language and thought is more fundamental. Language, he writes, is a "Flesh-Garment" or "Body of Thought." Now, if language is a body, does it not take on some of the characteristics of the body—solidity, for instance? In what looks like a very Nietzschean passage, Carlyle argues that metaphor, whether still striking and fluid or solidified by time and familiarity, is the raw material of language; indeed, it is claimed that all language is metaphor (and all thought too?). In the body of thought the primitive sounds out of which language is made are the bones, and metaphor is the flesh and muscle.

Moving from the language/thought relationship in general to specific instances of this relationship, or style, Carlyle maintains that different styles are like different bodies or physiognomies: lean/wan, healthy/vigorous, apoplectic (like Carlyle's own). In style, Carlyle seems to say, the inner person is inscribed on the body, the outward appearance. Yet clearly, Carlyle must regard his own "apoplectic" style as only a partial revelation of the reality truly attested to by the lean or healthy styles. Is this body a reliable or an at least partly deceptive indication of the inner thought? And what, after all, is the relationship of the metaphysical body to the physical body, so rapidly being lost to the mobility of metaphor? Does Carlyle share with the wracked Nietzsche a conviction that the linguistic body is a "truer" standard than the physical—at least in his own case? But, Carlyle continues, not all metaphors "embody" in this way. "Sham" metaphors are not part of the body of thought. They are, instead, at a farther remove: clothes on the body of thought and ridiculous or puffed-up clothes at that, costumery. But doesn't this distinction call all metaphor and language—and even the body itself—once more into question? At just this point, Carlyle's fictional editor interrupts: "Than which paragraph on Metaphors did the reader ever chance to see a more surprisingly metaphorical?" How is one to get hold of rhetoric, to gauge the relationship between metaphor and body when one is always already metaphorizing? What happens to the body when it is submitted to the seamless, boundless field of figuration? Perhaps Carlyle answers this question when (in the close of this passage), after having toyed with the body metaphor, he "puts on" the clothing metaphor as his own. In a universe of clothing, what else can he do? Life and words clothe the same "light."

Carlyle's larger purpose in *Sartor Resartus* is to reassure his contemporaries that their faith, and the assurance that flows from it, will survive the wearing out of the Christian suit of clothes. Beneath the inevitable changes in worn out metaphysical garments, the human form and its faith remains the same. This is change without self-overcoming, which is precisely what Nietzsche, who regards our language and ideology as body parts, argues against. For him, Carlyle's insistence merely cloaks his despair. Only self-overcoming is sufficient to describe the needed change. *For Nietzsche, nihilism is Romanticism without self-overcoming.*

In a sense, Carlyle's importance to us is that he brings out and underscores what is commonplace in Nietzsche. And this, in turn, enables us to isolate what stands out—Nietzsche's insistence on the fundamental difference of self-overcoming, which in "The Greatest Stress" takes the form of overcoming our ambivalence about life—an ambivalence everywhere apparent in this passage from Carlyle. In Carlyle, the body is *just* a garment; the body is the inscription of the soul, the only manifestation we have of the soul within. And Carlyle's deployment of the figure indirectly asserts the powerful point that the ideas of spirit/mind/imagination lead us to treat the body like clothing: as something at once essential (who goes naked willingly?) and disposable—perhaps like life itself. But insofar as humankind has an "essence," the body is disposable. Insofar as humankind is self-creating, then it must have the visible results of that creation in order to be itself.

In the end, "the body of thought" as a metaphor and as a distinct idea is consumed by the complexities of the lived body, as "style" is consumed (in Derrida) by the complexities of our relationship to texts. In metaphorizing the textual body, we imagine it *like* a body; and in metaphorizing the physical body, we imagine it *like* a textual body. Consequently, we do not so much *have* it as *use* it, as in asceticism, for some other purpose, especially for the purpose of creating meaning. In Nietzsche's view, in the tradition that culminates in Romanticism, the body is thoroughly dissolved in language—too much flesh has been traded for meaning to go back now. But it is also clear that, for Nietzsche, meaning flows from figuration, not the other way around, that meaning is engendered in a relationship of disparates.

In "Description of Ancient Rhetoric" (1872–73), Nietzsche remarks on the artificial distinction between rhetoric and conception, arguing that there is no state of language prior to figuration. Implicit in Nietzsche's description is an even more challenging assertion: the modern approach to rhetoric is given over to "dilettantism and crude empiricism"[27] not just because non-rhetoricians are insensitive to the rhetorical character of language per se, but because even our rhetoricians lack a sophisticated sense of how vital, fluid, and unmanageable "rhetoric" is. Indeed, even today rhetorically-oriented critics operate largely within the limits of classical rhetorical terminology.[28] A straightened taxonomy of figures is accepted as constituting "rhetoric" in much the same way that, for a certain kind of English teacher, aversion to split infinitives seems to be an expression of natural law.

Our description of key Nietzschean concepts—eternal recurrence, the *Übermensch*, will to power, perspectivism—as self-consuming (in chapter 1 and thereafter), though it may seem idiosyncratic to some, is entirely descriptive of the conceptualizations of rhetorical events which are the critic's stock-in-trade. Nietzsche's neologistic (or neotropic) hyperboles reopen rhetoric not only to new examples of existing tropes but to entirely new categories as well. Rhetoric is now open-ended—proximately as a consequence of the freedom Nietzsche claims for himself as a writer, ultimately as a consequence of the freedom he seems to envision for a future state of humanity. Nietzsche himself is not unambivalent about this open-endedness of rhetoric without the illusion of "truth." For a time, writing (his version of *Dichtung*) stands between Nietzsche and the threat of self-parody, even—some critics might argue—the threat of nihilism. This is especially true of *Thus Spoke Zarathustra,* in which he avails himself of so many forms of writing that the role of writer seems to take on a life all its own. But finally, this "difference" of the writer cannot be sustained, even by the most extreme means. After all, writing can be understood as that symptom identified in "The Greatest Stress": it is the model for the profound acceptance/affirmation of eternal recurrence; it is also the sign of its absence, of a profound desire to be elsewhere or otherwise.

Writing by means of "style"—in the way we have been talking about it—may try to restrain rhetoric. But, in the end, it is overtaken by hyperbole's remorseless demand for the unattainable: "more." Not just another trope, hyperbole violates or transcends the ordinary demands of "rhetoric." Thus, in the form of litotes, Socrates transgressed the limits of Sophism to found philosophy. One might even claim that the binary, hyperbole/litotes, marks the limits of perspectivism; indeed, it offers an insight into their apposite function; and, we think, that appositeness makes Nietzschean perspectivism possible, for within the broad limits of their twin functions operate Nietzschean irony, parody, and self-parody.

Parody is inherent in the persistent "pas au dela" or step beyond of hyperbole/litotes. Each of Nietzsche's major hyperboles, the stones he casts at the edifice of metaphysics, derives considerable impact as a deep parody of current attitudes, ways of comprehending and self-descriptions. Nietzsche's recurrent discourse of the body—his emphasis on the *différence* between intellectual and moral pretensions to "health" and the myriad disorders of the body in ascetic/metaphysical culture—goes beyond ironic difference into parody, as the example of Christina helps us to see. Her clumsy attempts to reconstruct proprioception guided only by sight result in a parody of "normality," parody of the typical integration of consciousness and body, which in turn helps us to see the limitations of philosophy (or any other discourse) in its attempts to create "health" on its own narrow foundation. This powerful example also betrays the link between parody which, as Derrida argues, implies a "vertiginous non-mastery," and self-parody, which is the result when this non-mastery is unconsciously turned back on the self in the movement of irony.

In chapter 4, we quoted Nehamas's observation that Nietzsche's written character "does not provide a model for imitation. . . . To imitate him directly would produce a caricature." (Yet self imitation is an inevitable consequence of trying to produce a body of work.) Nietzsche takes this hyperbolic step beyond: in *Ecce Homo*, he contrives to imitate himself and in doing so, to transcend by exploiting the caricature or self-parody that results. (Self) imitation is indeed the sincerest form of parody. So powerful is our ascetic/metaphysical culture (which is our very being, has become our bodies themselves) that the more "accurate" or "rigorous" the representation, including self-representation, the closer it gets to caricature. Or, to put it slightly differently, the closer such a project comes to realizing its own ideal, the more self-parodic it is.

In *Ecce Homo*, just as metaphorical language in the service of asceticism has dissolved the body into "likeness," so must even Nietzsche's own language result in the self-parodic "Nietzsche." Realizing that self-representation can only be self-parody, Nietzsche cleverly, hyperbolically attempts to exploit this fact to raise *Ecce Homo* to a "higher level," to transcend himself. Nevertheless, the vexing question remains, Does this awareness really make a difference? Does this difference really make a difference? If so, what difference does it make?

This way of framing the issue may still be received as "essentially" the Romantic question, on which criticism and philosophy often converge. For example, in his helpful book on Nietzsche and Romanticism, *Nietzsche Contra Nietzsche*,[29] Adrian del Caro argues that Nietzsche actually owes more to the earlier German Romanticism of Friedrich Schiller and the Jena School than than to the later, nationalistic, and contemporary Romanticism of Wagner. According to del Caro, where Nietzsche departs from and goes beyond the Romantics is on the question of art. The Romantics typically regarded art as the highest expression and ultimate form of the human project. And as we have seen, Nietzsche has few illusions about art and artists. Instead, Nietzsche seems to elevate the task of self-creation to the highest status. It may be the case that del Caro exaggerates the novelty of this innovation in relation to Romanticism, particularly English Romanticism. But at the same time, he seems to us to underestimate the significance of moving it so explicitly to the forefront of the agenda as Nietzsche does. For in Nietzsche's writing and thought the very self, not merely art, appears to be at stake. A new state of awareness and new forms of art will not meet Nietzsche's demand; unlike Coleridge, Wordsworth, Shelley—unlike even Wagner—although interested in artistic innovation, Nietzsche seems unwilling to concentrate upon it as his sole—or even his major—concern. For him, nothing short of self-overcoming will do. And yet, as we suggested in chapter 1, self-overcoming—in Nietzsche's sense of saying "yes" to eternal recurrence—is impossible.

As we observed in our discussion of *Toward the Genealogy of Morals*, Nietzsche redeems the negativity of his account of ascetic culture and of the symptomatology of nihilism by arguing that asceticism itself was initially a defense of life. But if this is the case—and is a result of Nietzsche's "departure" from Romanticism—then we must also wonder if the nihilism/self-overcoming contrast constitutes a distinction without a difference or, that is, whether self-overcoming is not just one more defense, perhaps even shakier than asceticism, erected against the despair of an animal, sick with despair. We have even suggested that this self-overcoming, which is a figure so self-consuming that neither its nature nor its goals can be foreseen, entails some version of progress, a version that nurtures, exploits, and finally consumes our salvific yearnings for secular redemption. The end of that "progress," which is endless and so, imaginatively, circular, remains yet "unimaginable."

Viewed from this perspective, Nietzsche's future-directed *Toward the Genealogy of Morals* can itself be read as a metaphoric excursion from the historical perspective (of genealogy) into an ahistorical "non-prospective of [a]morals": a daring prospect of a Dionysian alternative to nothingness. This is, of course, at once a radicalization of our inherited idea of progress (now bereft of its specifically Platonic-Christian motivation and sanction) as well as a powerful challenge to our secular idea of progress, for at best it allows an ultimate goal that must—given our human limitations—remain "unimaginable." And yet, as we have also suggested, the "unimaginable" exists, just as Hamlet and Lear and Zarathustra exist, only in a fictive sense. For only in the imagination does the "unimaginable" take shape. And from Plato on, neither philosophers nor literary critics have had the final say on—or should we say the "God's eye view of"—the "unimaginable."[1] By this we mean only to say that the "unimaginable" is one of many hyperbolic expressions indicating a human interest in ideas of the imagination.

Current critical discussion of Nietzsche in the English-speaking world has suffered—and our shared culture's imagination has, in consequence, been impoverished—not only as a result of the mutual shunning of "analytical" and "continental" approaches to Nietzsche's texts, to the body of his thought. There is another, deeper, older, even more pervasively institutionalized mutual shunning so ubiquitous that it hides in plain view: the separation of "literary" from "philosophical" discourse. That mutual shunning is as old, as unquestioned (and hence as "venerable") as Plato's decision to banish "poets" from the polis the "philosopher" is destined to rule. And it is only a slight exaggeration to say that this very shunning is the founding gesture of philosophy as it has been delivered over to us: "I, Plato, *am* the truth," Nietzsche reminds us helpfully in *Twilight of the Idols*. The impact on Nietzsche has been lamentable, however, for each—"poet" and "philosopher" (or writer and thinker, critic and philosopher)—continues to regard the other with suspicion. As a result of this hermeneutics of suspicion, philosophers—especially those inclined to what we called "the Official View" in chapter 1—typically regard "literary-critical" appropriations of Nietzsche as, at best, simple-minded misappropriations, or, at worst, practicing without a license. And for most "literary critics" the philosopher's carefully domesticated "Nietzsche" either looks hopelessly naive, uninteresting, or both; he looks hopelessly "thin"; he looks like someone to place in the wax museum of great dead (white male) "philosophers." The philosopher typically looks for coherent meaning in Nietzsche's texts, and, above all, for evidence of rigor; the critic looks for novel new ideas, new insights, for fractures, fissures, and ambiguities in Nietzsche's texts, for opportunities or connections missed. Thus, mutual shunning of our literary and philosophical cultures continues.

This book has marked our first attempt to contest this baleful shunning, or, to vary the figure, to suture the body of Nietzsche's institutionally dismembered literary/philosophical thought. To extend this figure, we have treated the body of Nietzsche's thought as thoroughly permeable and suturable, available to thoughtful intervention whether the means be marked "literary" or "philosophical." Indeed, one of our guiding aims has been to render ultimately uninteresting and inappropriate the question, "Is this philosophy or is it literature?" Only in this way, in our view, can there be a genuine recuperation, a convalescence, a restoration of the body of Nietzsche's (institutionally dismembered) literary/philosophical thought that is both robust and nuanced. We have, to put it simply, attempted in these pages a kind of suturing, even a kind of healing, but above all a kind of thinking that has a rigor of its own—a rigor which, one hopes, has left mortis behind.

Notes

Pre(post)face

1. We have substituted the gender neutral term "humankind" for "man" (Kaufmann's usage) primarily to keep faith with Nietzsche's equally gender neutral "*Mensch*" in the German text. For further discussion, see our footnote in chapter 1 which explains our retention of the German "*Übermensch*."

2. Two important institutional interventions have recently occurred to contest and reverse this state of affairs, to privilege collaborative research in the humanities: the founding of the University of California Humanities Research Institute (at UC Irvine), and the Center for Ideas and Society (at UC Riverside).

Chapter 1

1. See Arthur C. Danto, "Some Remarks on *The Genealogy of Morals*" in *Reading Nietzsche*, eds. Robert C. Solomon and Kathleen Higgins (New York: Oxford University Press, 1988); Alexander Nehamas, *Nietzsche: Life as Literature*, (Cambridge, Mass.: Harvard University Press, 1985); Jacques Derrida, *Spurs: Nietzsche's Style*, (Chicago: University of Chicago Press, 1979).

2. Danto, *Nietzsche as Philosopher* (New York: Macmillan, 1965) p. 13.

3. Eric Blondel, "Nietzsche: la vie et la metaphore," *Revue Philosophique*, 1971. (Translated as "Nietzsche: Life as [sic] Metaphor," in David Allison's *The New Nietzsche*, [New York: Dell Publishing Co., 1977] pp. 150 ff.).

4. Danto, *Nietzsche as Philosopher* p. 19.

5. It is only recently that the careful structuring of Nietzsche's individual works has begun to receive some attention. Indeed, until recently the word "aphorisms" was typically used to characterize the body of his work despite the fact that probably less than ten percent of his jottings conform to this genre. We still lack a single word in our language to characterize the sort of writing of which Nietzsche's works consist (and many of Wittgenstein's, for that matter).

6. For a discussion of this point see Magnus's "The Use and Abuse of *The Will to Power*" (in Solomon and Higgins's *Reading Nietzsche*, cited above) and the literature referred to there, especially the work of Mazzino Montinari.

7. Danto, *Nietzsche as Philosopher* pp. 13–14.

8. Alan White's recent *Within Nietzsche's Labyrinth* (New York: Routledge, 1990) comes close to sharing this concern, articulating such a problematic. However, as will be evident in

the pages that follow, White's approach to many of the texts and issues we discuss is markedly different, and at critical points incompatible with our approach.

9. For an interesting discussion of Nietzsche in France, see Alan D. Schrift's *Nietzsche and the Question of Interpretation* (New York: Routledge, 1990), especially chapters 3 and 4: "The French Scene," and "Derrida: Nietzsche Contra Heidegger" respectively.

10. This is, of course, a *leitmotif* with him, but see Ludwig Wittgenstein, *Philosophical Investigations*, trans. G.E.M. Anscombe (Oxford: Basil Blackwell, 1958), p. 8e.

11. We are aware of the fact that much of what we have now said appears to undermine itself, for to characterize Derrida's work as resisting characterization just *is* to characterize it; and to assert that his writing may be read as a generalization of this point—a challenge to the familiar procedure of paraphrasing and characterizing philosophical writers and their writings in general—simply deepens the appearance of oddity.

12. Jacques Derrida, *The Ear of the Other* (Lincoln: University of Nebraska Press, 1988), pp. 86–88.

13. Ibid., p. 120.

14. Ibid.

15. Most of Derrida's "deconstructions" can be read as instances of this same gesture enacted and reenacted in different settings. This example was selected simply because of a prescribed economy—it took only a paragraph or two to characterize. In a similar vein, Derrida's much-discussed reversal of the priority of writing over speech—his overcoming of Saussurean "phonocentrism"—can be read with profit as a strategic move, one in which it is pointed out that one would not be able to recognize sounds as meaningful phonemes unless "traces" of intelligibility had already been "inscribed" (i.e., "written") in the psyche—as in Plato's theory of recollection.

16. *Of Grammatology*, (Baltimore: The Johns Hopkins University Press, 1974) pp. 17–18.

17. Ibid.

18. KGW III 2, pp. 374–375: "On Truth and Lies in the Non-Moral Sense." This entire discussion, in Nietzsche's as well as in Derrida's case, prefigures Donald Davidson's work on the literal/metaphorical contrast. To think of literal speech as a platform built up out of dead metaphors, to think of it as one would a coral reef composed of dead organisms, chimes well with Nietzsche's and Derrida's suggestions. That also helps to explain why Rorty much prefers the contrast between the familiar and unfamiliar to the literal/metaphorical contrast. See, for example, Rorty's *Contingency, Irony, Solidarity*, chapter 1 (Cambridge: Cambridge University Press, 1989) and his "Deconstruction and Circumvention" in *Critical Inquiry*, 1987.

19. "Différance," in *Margins of Philosophy*, p. 27.

20. It makes no difference to the coherence of the argument whether "origins" is understood by Heidegger and his commentators chronologically, causally, ontologically or phenomenologically. "Origins" itself is the problem.

21. Alexander Nehamas, *Nietzsche: Life as Literature* (Cambridge, Mass.: Harvard University Press, 1985).

22. The first numbered section of *Ecce Homo* concludes, in italics: "*Hear me! For I am such and such a person. Above all, do not mistake me for someone else.*"

23. It would be interesting to pair this sentence, which concludes *Ecce Homo*, with the one which ends the first section, quoted in the previous footnote.

24. Alexander Nehamas's otherwise fine discussion of *Beyond Good and Evil*, in Solomon's and Higgins's *Reading Nietzsche* (cited above), which argues that Nietzsche's book itself constitutes the philosophy of the future rather than envisioning it seems highly implausible in the light of what we have just said, since the text's subtitle would simply have to be ignored or explained away to give Nehamas's argument force.

25. Z I "OYW." It is a continuing mystery why elementary principles and courtesies that apply to the interpretation of utterances in other writers's texts are routinely ignored in the Nietzsche case, as in the example just cited, which ignores the fact that this is a statement made by an old woman to Zarathustra within a particular dramatic setting and narrative structure. To take but a single contrasting example, as is well known, Plato has Glaucon argue in Book Two of *The Republic* that justice is not wanted for its own sake but is instead a compromise between two extremes. What everyone wants intrinsically, Glaucon argues, is the satisfaction with impunity of each and every desire, as if we had the powers of the gods, no matter what harms and injuries we inflict upon others. What is least desirable, in stark contrast, is to suffer harm without the power to retaliate. And when we have had a taste of each extreme, Glaucon goes on to argue, we settle for a compromise neither to inflict harm nor to suffer it; and we call this compact "justice." But—so the argument goes—justice is really never wanted for its own sake, despite our shared social hypocrisy.

Our point in assembling this familiar reminder from Plato's *The Republic* is straightforward. No commentator has ever suggested, to the best of our knowledge, that Glaucon's embryonic contract theory of justice ought to be attributed to Plato as his settled view on the question of justice, any more than the utterances of Thrasymachus are thought to play that role. And yet, when it comes to interpreting Nietzsche, especially his *Thus Spoke Zarathustra*, context, speaker, dramatic intent and narrative placement are simply ignored or set aside.

26. This is an aphorism in the proper sense of the term. It appears as aphorism #8 in the opening "chapter" of *Twilight of the Idols*, a chapter marked "Maxims and Arrows" (*Sprüche und Pfeile*). It reads: "*Out of life's school of war*: What does not destroy me, makes me stronger."

27. For example, some would be inclined to argue that certain commentators have put the argument of the first critique better than Kant had put it. A good illustration of this point is the critical reception of Henry Allison's discussion of the transcendental unity of apperception in his *Kant's Transcendental Idealism* (New Haven: Yale University Press, 1983).

28. Stanley E. Fish, *Self-Consuming Artifacts: The Experience of Seventeenth-Century Literature* (Berkeley: University of California Press, 1972).

29. "The word 'satisfies' is meant literally here; for it is characteristic of a rhetorical form to mirror and present for approval the opinions its readers already hold. It follows then that the experience of such a form will be flattering, for it tells the reader that what he has always thought about the world is true and that the ways of his thinking are sufficient . . . whatever one is told can be placed and contained within the categories and assumptions of received systems of knowledge" (ibid., p. 1).

30. "A dialectical presentation . . . is disturbing, for it requires of its readers a searching and rigorous scrutiny of everything they believe and live by . . . it does not preach the truth, but asks that its readers discover the truth for themselves . . . the experience of a dialectical form is humiliating" (ibid. pp. 1–2).

31. "Self-Consuming Artifact . . . is intended in two senses: the reader's self is consumed as he responds to the medicinal purging of the dialectician's art, and that art, like other medicines, is consumed in the workings of its own best effect . . . it disallows to its productions the claims usually made for verbal art—that they reflect, contain or express Truth—and transfers pressure and attention from the work to its effects, from what is happening on the page to what is happening in the reader. A self-consuming artifact signifies most successfully when it fails, when it points away from itself to something its forms cannot capture" (ibid. pp. 3–4).

32. We shall be saying *Übermensch* and *Übermenschlichkeit* instead of "overman" and "what it is like to be an overman." In what follows as in what precedes, we shall continue Magnus's habit of using the German instead of "overman" or "superman" because the word "superman" seems to us to have been preempted by Clark Kent in English. "Overman", on the other hand, merely adds the prefix "over" to the stem "man" and conveys few of the superlatives which are so super when we use the prefix "super," as in the following cases, for example: superhuman, supernatural, superlunary, superego, supernova, superpower, superstar. The term "overman" never found its way into common usage, as "superman" did, despite the fact that it is almost eighty years old, for Walter Kaufmann merely adopted Thomas Common's usage, from the earliest English translation of Nietzsche. It is an interesting irony that the index to the inadequate Oscar Levy edition of Nietzsche's collected works, in which Common's translation of *Also Sprach Zarathustra* appears, refers all entries for *Übermensch* in the index to "superman" not "overman." Finally, one important additional reason for using the German expression throughout and its surrogates is that *Übermensch* is not gender specific. It is gender neutral. The expression can apply with equal linguistic force to women and men alike, which the English translations have not managed to do to date.

33. Our use of the notion of a self-consuming concept bears only a family resemblance to Fish's sense and was arrived at independently of his work. In our usage, concepts are *themselves* self-consuming in Nietzsche's works, not merely the structure his texts display or presuppose.

34. This is a further point of contrast between our use and Hegel's use of the notion of negation. If one subtracts the elevating optimism from Hegel's *Aufhebungen* one is left with self-consuming concepts in our sense.

35. Perhaps the contrast between seeing something different and seeing the same thing differently is out of place here. As we shall see below, in our discussion of eternal recurrence, seeing the same thing differently can sometimes be indistinguishable from seeing something different, a classic instance of a distinction that makes no difference.

36. It is worthwhile to remember that this was the penultimate entry of the first published version of *The Gay Science*, followed by an entry which is—literally—incorporated into *Thus Spoke Zarathustra*, and with which the tragedy begins. *Incipit Tragödia!* Book Five of *The Gay Science* was added years later.

37. *EH* "WIWSGB."

38. *TI* "SUM" 51.

39. For different readings of the notion of eternal recurrence, ones which seem to us unsatisfactory in the final analysis but are nevertheless powerful, see Nehamas's text cited above and Maudemarie Clark's *Nietzsche on Truth and Philosophy* (Cambridge: Cambridge University Press, 1990), chapter 8.

40. For detailed discussion of the textual and conceptual issues in the doctrine of eternal recurrence, see Magnus's *Nietzsche's Existential Imperative* (Bloomington: Indiana University Press, 1978) or the texts of Nehamas or Clark.

41. For a fuller discussion of this point see Magnus's "Eternal Recurrence," *Nietzsche Studien* 8 (1979).

42. Nietzsche has Zarathustra summon his most abysmal thought throughout the text of *Thus Spoke Zarathustra* and try repeatedly to summon up the courage to confront its abysmality.

43. Clark, *Nietzsche on Truth and Philosophy*.

44. Ibid., p. 269

45. Ibid.

46. Ibid., pp. 269–270.

47. Nehamas, *Nietzsche: Life as Literature*, p. 7.
48. Ibid., p. 179
49. The most illuminating contemporary discussions of the issues involved in the "problem of free will" and moral responsibility are to be found in John Martin Fischer's (ed.) excellent *Moral Responsibility* (Ithaca: Cornell University Press, 1986). Fischer's introduction is especially helpful and incisive; but, of course, he is absolved of any responsibility for the use made here of his work.
50. Nehamas, *Nietzsche: Life as Literature*, p. 179
51. Nehamas's discussion of the connection between eternal recurrence and *Übermenschlichkeit* represents a considerable advance in the Nietzsche literature, as does Clark's, despite our criticism and disavowals. For earlier commentators could not resist assimilating Nietzsche to one or another version of virtue ethics. So, for example, Walter Kaufmann was able to characterize the *Übermensch* in the following words, in his influential *Nietzsche: Philosopher, Psychologist, Antichrist* (Princeton: Princeton University Press, 1974):

> The unphilosophic and inartistic mass remain animalic, while the man who overcomes himself, sublimating his impulses, consecrating his passions, and giving style to his character, becomes truly human or—as Zarathustra would say, enraptured by the word *über*—*super*human (p. 312) . . . The *Übermensch* . . . is the "Dionysian" man who is depicted under the name Goethe at the end of *Götzendämmerung* (IX, 49). He has overcome his animal nature, organized the chaos of his passions, sublimated his impulses, and given style to his character—or, as Nietzsche said of Goethe: "he disciplined himself to wholeness, he created himself" and became "the man of tolerance, not from weakness but from strength," "a spirit who has become free." (p. 316)

This construal of the *Übermensch* as creative self-perfection has also been endorsed by philosophers of markedly differing temperaments and orientations. Consider, for example, the following assessment from the pen of Arthur Danto, in his *Nietzsche as Philosopher* (New York: Macmillan, 1965):

> The *Übermensch*, accordingly, is not the blond giant dominating his lesser fellows. He is merely a joyous, guiltless, free human being, in possession of instinctual drives which do not overpower him. He is the master and not the slave of his drives, and so he is in a position to make something of himself rather than being the product of instinctual discharge and external obstacle. (pp. 199–200)

But precisely this reading of *Übermenschlichkeit* defeats Nietzsche's originality in its triumph. For what we are left with is a most unoriginal formula of sorts:

> A sultry heart plus a cool head, minus the human-all-too-human. But this, divorced from the extravagant language and the rushing cadences of Zarathustra's singing, turns out to be a bland and all-too-familiar recommendation, rather squarely in a moralistic tradition. It says only that we should seek to keep our passionate as well as our intellectual life in our command, not to deny one at the price of the other, and that we should not be petty and "merely" human. Here is an ancient, vaguely pagan ideal, the passions disciplined but not denied, in contrast with the life and attitude of guilty celibacy which has been an official moral recommendation until rather recent times. (p. 199)

Many philosophers find irresistible the temptation to assimilate Nietzsche and his *Übermensch* to something like the virtue ethics tradition. For Schacht, for example, the *Übermensch*

represents the greatest and richest enhancement of life Nietzsche considers possible. . . . Overflowing vitality and great health; powerful affects and the ability to
control and direct them; high spirituality and refinement of sensibility and manners; independence of mind and action; the capacity to befriend and to respect
and disdain and deal justly with others as they warrant; intellectual honesty and
astuteness; the strength to be undaunted by suffering and by disillusionment; persistence in self-overcoming; the resources to undertake and follow through on the
most demanding of tasks; and the ability to love and to esteem, and above all to
create. (*Nietzsche* [London: Routledge and Kegan Paul, 1983], p. 340)

While reading these characterizations of *Übermenschlichkeit* one could scarcely avoid
picturing Clark Kent on his way to a telephone booth. And yet even the least action-
guiding interpretations of Nietzsche's *Übermensch* can't seem to resist the temptation to
read tacit imperatives into his tropology.

The doctrine of eternal recurrence uses aesthetic criteria to evaluate the significance of an individual life. The events of one's life gain significance when one approaches them as artistic raw material, appropriated in aspiring toward some indi-
vidually determined vision of greatness. This vision is symbolized, in Zarathustra's
scheme, by the overman. . . . We can find our lives meaningful if we approach their
events as aesthetic material; and according to Zarathustra's tragic position we *ought*
to do this. [Kathleen Higgins. "Reading Zarathustra," in *Reading Nietzsche*, pp. 145–
146]

52. As this remark suggests, our study places us close to the spirit of Gary Shapiro as reflected in *Nietzschean Narratives* (Bloomington: Indiana University Press, 1989) and his
powerfully provocative *Alcyone: Nietzsche on Gifts, Noise, and Women* (Albany: State University of New York Press, 1991).

53. An earlier version of the remarks that follow appeared in Bernd Magnus's "The Use
and Abuse of *The Will to Power*," in *Reading Nietzsche*.

54. Richard Schacht, *Nietzsche* (London: Routledge and Kegan Paul, 1983), p. xii. These
observations are not meant as a direct criticism of Schacht's valuable book, to which all
Nietzsche scholars are indebted. Given his task, to write a book in "the arguments of the
philosophers" series—a Herculean task which took him the better part of a decade—it
is natural that he should be drawn to the "book" which we shall argue below consists of
those notes Nietzsche elected neither to publish *nor* to work up for publication. In further defense of Schacht and other "lumpers" who precede him, it is worth remembering that we did not have an adequate textual basis until 1979 on which to set *The Will to
Power* notes aside, when the Colli-Montinari edition was first completed. By that time
Schacht had been at work on his study for nearly six years. Hollingdale and Schlechta—
who had earlier pleaded that "Nietzsche" ought to mean the published corpus only—
were voices crying in the wilderness. They had no authoritative textual basis—as we
now do have—on which to base their urgings. Schlechta—for example and with more
than a touch of irony—published his selections from Nietzsche's *Nachlass* under the title
"notes of the eighties" (in his famous three volume Nietzsche edition) and his selections
derive *entirely* from *The Will to Power* notes, the very items Schlechta would have us
(rightly) discount!

55. Schacht, *Nietzsche*, p. xiv.

56. Martin Heidegger, *Nietzsche*, trans. David Krell (New York: Harper and Row, 1979), pp.
8–9 (our italics).

57. See note 1, above.

58. Harold Alderman's thought-provoking *Nietzsche's Gift* (Columbus: Ohio University

Press, 1977) comes closest to expressing this point of view in English-language commentaries, as do some of Magnus's own recent and past writings.

59. This is Walter Kaufmann's characterization of eternal recurrence, in the "Editor's Notes" to Z IV. It reads: "Nietzsche wants the eternity of *this* life with all its agonies—and seeing that it flees, its eternal recurrence. As it is expressed in sections 9, 10, and 11 [of part IV], the conception of the eternal recurrence is certainly meaningful; but its formulation as a doctrine depended on Nietzsche's mistaken belief that science compels us to accept the hypothesis of the eternal recurrence of the same events at gigantic intervals."

60. It is important to mention that the lumpers/splitters distinction does not cut with equal force for each theme in Nietzsche's writings. Put simply, without the *Nachlass* it is virtually impossible to read eternal recurrence and will to power as first-order descriptions of the way the world is in itself, as a description of the world's intelligible character. For eternal recurrence, for example, see Magnus, *Nietzsche's Existential Imperative*, Studies in Phenomenology and Existential Philosophy (Bloomington: Indiana University Press, 1978), chap. 3; and Alexander Nehamas's "The Eternal Recurrence," *The Philosophical Review*, 89.3 (July 1980). Perspectivism, in contrast, can perhaps be read as a "theory of knowledge" whether one relies on the published or unpublished remains. The concept of the *Übermensch* is the most difficult in many ways, including the philological dimension, precisely because—while it is central to the book Nietzsche regarded as his most important one, *Thus Spoke Zarathustra*—the notion virtually disappears in the published and unpublished manuscripts of 1886–89. In consequence, it is not the case that being a lumper is a necessary condition for reading the *Übermensch* as an ideal type, a realizable goal manifesting certain "virtues," or the result of passing a "life affirmation" test.

61. Harold Alderman's and Alexander Nehamas's books (cited above) address this issue in different ways. Magnus addresses this issue as well in "The Deification of the Commonplace: *Twilight of the Idols*," in *Reading Nietzsche*.

62. We refer to the *Werke: Kritischegesammtausgabe* and the *Studienausgabe*.

63. Kaufmann and Hollingdale translated these materials long after they had appeared in E. Förster-Nietzsche's biography of her brother (second edition versions) and after Kröner had incorporated them into the *GA*.

64. Many items are pertinent here, including *KGW* VIII 1, "Vorbemerkung der Herausgeber," all of KSA *Band* 14; but especially relevant is Mazzino Montinari's "Nietzsche's *Nachlass* von 1885 bis 1888 oder Textkritik und Wille zur Macht" in his *Nietzsche Lesen* (Berlin: de Gruyter, 1982), pp. 92–120 as well as his entry in KSA 14, pp. 383–400.

65. See, for example, *KSA* 14, pp. 29–35.

66. Montinari suggests this in his *Nietzsche Lesen*, and documents it very well.

67. *KGW* VIII 1 and the literature cited there tell that tale well.

68. The careful reader will have noticed a discrepancy between the 374 entries we refer to and the 372 entries we claim Nietzsche numbered. The discrepancy is Nietzsche's, not ours. He inadvertently repeated two numbers in selecting *374* entries for further polishing. Hence he thought he had selected *372* entries, while he had in fact selected 374.

69. *KSA* 13, *KGW* VIII 2 Fragment 12 [2].

70. R. J. Hollingdale makes this point in his excellent study *Nietzsche: The Man and his Philosophy* ([Baton Rouge: Louisiana State University Press, 1965], p. 298). He claims that Nietzsche had instructed his landlord to dispose of—as waste—manuscripts for which he had no further use as he left Sils in September 1888; that Durisch instead "brought out armfuls of this paper and invited them [i.e., interested visitors] to help themselves"; that this fact was reported in the 1893 (autumn) *Magazin für Literatur*; that Elisabeth put a stop to this at once after hearing the news; and that "when the *Will to Power* was prepared, it was among the 'manuscripts' from which selection was made."

Michael Platt and Bernd Magnus have tried to reconstruct this scenario, with mixed results. To begin with, the autumn 1893 *Magazin für Literatur* article does not say precisely what Hollingdale claims it does. Rather, it is Fritz Kögel's account of his accidental discovery of an (at that time) unpublished variant of the Preface to *Twilight of the Idols*, a page he discovered while perusing the *proofs* Nietzsche had left at Sils. Moreover, neither the name nor behavior of the landlord is described as Hollingdale alleges. As far as Platt and Magnus can determine, Hollingdale's source must be Carl Albrecht Bernoulli, who recounts a similar but by no means identical tale in his *Franz Overbeck und Friedrich Nietzsche: Eine Freundschaft* (Jena: Eugen Diederich Verlag, 1908). See especially pp. 301–302.

71. *The Will to Power*, 1067. *KGW* VII 3, pp. 338–339; *KSA* 11, pp. 610–611.

72. *KGW* VII 1, 2 [41] and 3 [1].

73. *KGW* VII 1, 12 [1] 114.

74. *KGW* VII 3, 31 [52].

75. *KGW* VII 3, 32 [9].

76. *Z* IV "AF" 1.

77. Adrian del Caro focuses on the tension between Nietzsche's early "romanticism" and his later anti-romanticism in his interesting study *Nietzsche Contra Nietzsche: Creativity and the Anti-Romantic* (Baton Rouge: Louisiana State University Press, 1989).

78. We do not wish to suggest that being a lumper is a necessary condition for treating the *Übermensch* as a human ideal, because some splitters are bewitched by the same idealization project. We do think it is a *sufficient* condition, however. That is, if one views the task of philosophers to be that of giving an account, among other things, of the generic features of experience, the origin, nature and limits of knowledge, and how we ought to live our lives—if, that is to say, one is in the grip of a picture of philosophy as the search for a permanent neutral matrix addressed to timeless questions, in Rorty's sense—one is inevitably destined to read the *Übermensch* as the goal of human striving or as a recipe for achieving greatness. It should also be stressed that whereas one cannot easily extract an ontology from Nietzsche without *The Will to Power*, one can certainly extract a normative view of the *Übermensch* without that non-book.

79. For some discussions of Nietzsche's relationship to postmodernism, see *Nietzsche As Postmodernist*, Clayton Koelb ed. (Albany: The State University of New York Press, 1990).

Chapter 2

1. For a contrasting approach to many of the issues discussed in this chapter and taken up in subsequent chapters, see Henry Staten's *Nietzsche's Voice* (Ithaca and London: Cornell University Press, 1990).

2. G. E. Moore, "Autobiography," in *The Philosophy of G. E. Moore*, ed. Paul Schilpp (La Salle, Ill.: Open Court, 1968), p. 14.

3. We are thinking here of Jeremiah, John the Baptist, Zarathustra, and the seer of *The Antichrist* (to mention only one such speaker).

4. For instance, Bacon, Milton's "Son of Joseph," Zarathustra, and the author in *Twilight of the Idols*.

5. We are thinking here of such figures as Jesus of the Gospels, Bacon's proto-type of the scientific "Governor" in *New Atlantis*, and, again, Zarathustra.

6. Lawrence's "man who had died," and, of course, Zarathustra.

7. Milton's Son in the "pathless Desert" would be a case in point.

8. Michael Lieb, *Poetics of the Holy: A Reading of "Paradise Lost"* (Chapel Hill: University of North Carolina Press, 1981), passim, but see esp. chap. 3.

9. Op. cit., p. 162.

10. For a contrasting discussion of *Thus Spoke Zarathustra*, here and throughout the remainder of this book—but especially in chapter 4—compare Laurence Lampert's *Nietzsche's Teaching: An Interpretation of "Thus Spoke Zarathustra"* (New Haven: Yale University Press, 1986).

11. Kathleen Marie Higgins, *Nietzsche's "Zarathustra"* (Philadelphia: Temple University Press, 1987), pasim, esp. pp. 166–74.

12. Gary Shapiro, "The Writing on the Wall: *The Antichrist* and the Semiotics of History," in *Reading Nietzsche*, ed. Robert C. Solomon and Kathleen M. Higgins (New York: Oxford University Press, 1988), pp. 192–217.

13. Ibid., p. 214.

14. Ibid., p. 213.

15. *A*, op. cit., p. 213.

16. Ibid., p. 196.

17. Shapiro, p. 195.

18. Shapiro, p. 210.

19. We are indebted to Paul J. Spaeth, Rare Books Librarian of Friedsam Memorial Library at St. Bonaventure University for permission to examine Manuscript No. 9, a Latin Bible (ca. 1200), and for his expert remarks on the manuscript, which was presented in 1945 by Very Rev. Matthias Faust O.F.M. in honor of the twenty-fifth Anniversary of Rev. Thomas Plassman O.F.M. as President of St. Bonaventure University.

20. For a more extensive discussion of this subject, see Stanley Stewart, *The Enclosed Garden: The Tradition and the Image in Seventeenth-Century Poetry* (Madison: University of Wisconsin Press, 1966), chapter 1, esp. pp. 16–18.

21. Edward Calamy, Preface to Thomas Wilson, *A Complete Christian Dictionary*, 8th ed. (London, [1678]), sig. A5; cf. John Cowell, *The Interpreter* (Cambridge, 1607), sig. 3.

22. Thomas Wilson, *A Christian Dictionary*, 2nd ed. (London, 1616), sig. 2.

23. John Milton, *A Treatise of Civil Power in Ecclesiastical Causes*, ed. Robert W. Ayers, in *Complete Prose of John Milton*, gen. ed., Don M. Wolfe, 7 vols. (New Haven: Yale University Press, 1953–80), 7:243.

24. Ibid., 7:243.

25. E. D. Hirsch, Jr., *Validity in Interpretation* (New Haven: Yale University Press, 1967), esp. chapter 1 and Appendix 1, "Objective Interpretation."

26. Milton, op. cit., 7:242.

27. John Hales, *Golden Remains*, 2nd ed. (London, 1673), p. 4.

28. Hales, op. cit., p. 3.

29. George Herbert, *The Works of George Herbert*, ed. F. E. Hutchinson (Oxford: Clarendon Press, 1953), p. 58.

30. Richard Popkin, *The History of Scepticism from Erasmus to Descartes*, rev. ed. (Assen: Van Gorcum & Co., 1964); the actual title of chapter 1 is "The Intellectual Crisis of the Reformation," but Popkin's thesis is that questions regarding "the criterion of knowledge, made paramount by the Reformation," renewed interest in the "theories of the Greek sceptics," and resulted in an epistemological crisis "extended from theology to philosophy" (p. 16).

31. For instance, George Herbert was an admirer of Francis Bacon, who in turn dedicated his verse translation of *Certain Psalms* to Herbert; and Bacon, a great favorite also of English Puritans, was numbered among Nietzsche's four great architects of philosophical methodology (the other three being Aristotle, Descartes, and Comte).

32. Francis Bacon, *The Works of Francis Bacon*, ed. James Spedding et al., 14 vols (London: Longman's, 1861–1901), 4:20; unless otherwise indicated, all citations from Bacon will be from this standard edition.

33. Ibid., 5:116.

34. Ibid., 5:117.
35. Francis Bacon, *New Atlantis: A Worke unfinished* (1626), bound with *Sylva Sylvarum* (London, 1626); all citations from *New Atlantis* in our text will be from this, the first, edition.
36. Elizabeth McCutcheon, "Bacon and the Cherubim: An Iconographical Reading of the *New Atlantis*," *English Literary Renaissance*, 2.3 (1972):334–55; our discussion owes much to this ground-breaking essay.
37. *New Atlantis*, sig. A1.
38. Ibid., sigs. A1-A1v.
39. Ibid., sig. A1v.
40. Ibid.
41. Ibid., sig. A2.
42. Ibid.
43. Ibid., sig. A1v.
44. Ibid., sig. A2.
45. Ibid., sig. A3.
46. J. Weinberger, "Science and Rule in Bacon's Utopia: An Introduction to the Reading of the *New Atlantis*," *American Political Science Review*, 70 (1976): 865–85.
47. *New Atlantis*, sig. a2v.
48. Ibid., sig. a2.
49. *Julius Caesar* (hereafter *JC*): 2.1.256; all citations from Shakespeare in our text will be from *The Riverside Shakespeare*, ed. G. Blakemore Evans et al. (Boston: Houghton Mifflin, 1974).
50. *JC*, 2.1.252–55.
51. *JC*, 2.1.10–34.
52. *Novum Organum, The Works of Francis Bacon*, 4:54.
53. Ibid.
54. Ibid., p. 60.
55. Ibid., pp. 60–61.
56. Ibid., p. 61.
57. Lisa Jardine, *Francis Bacon: Discovery and the Art of Discourse* (Cambridge: Cambridge University Press, 1974).
58. Bacon, *Works.*, 4:63.
59. Ibid., p. 64.
60. Ibid., p. 66.
61. Jardine, *Francis Bacon.*, p. 148.
62. Charles Whitney, *Francis Bacon and Modernity* (New Haven: Yale University Press, 1986), p. 43.
63. Ibid., p. 203.
64. Ibid., p. 157.
65. Ibid., p. 196.
66. Ibid., p. 197.
67. Ibid., p. 198.
68. But for a discussion of the role played by *New Atlantis* in defense of "natural religion" later in the seventeenth century, see Richard S. Westfall, *Science and Religion in Seventeenth-Century England* (New Haven: Yale University Press, 1958). chap. 5, esp. p. 116.
69. Whitney, *Francis Bacon*, p. 203.
70. See Stewart, *The Enclosed Garden*, chapter 3, esp. pp. 88–96 and figs. 29–33.
71. John Milton, *Paradise Regained* (hereafter *PR*), 1.18-19; unless otherwise indicated, all citations from Milton's poetry in our text will be from *John Milton: Complete Poems and Major Prose*, ed. Merritt Y. Hughes (New York: Odyssey Press, 1957).

72. Milton, *PR*, 1.23.
73. *PR*, 1.24–25.
74. *PR*, 1.30–31.
75. *PR*, 1.186–88.
76. Many distinguished critics have debated the issue here. All recent commentary owes much to Barbara Kiefer Lewalski's seminal study, *Milton's Brief Epic: The Genre, Meaning, and Art of "Paradise Regained"* (Providence: Brown University Press; London: Methuen, 1966); see esp. chapters 8–12. See also E. W. Tayler, *Milton's Poetry: Its Development in Time* (Pittsburgh: Duquesne University Press, 1979); chapter 6; Louis L. Martz, *Milton: Poet of Exile* (New Haven and London: Yale University Press, 1986), chapter 15; and Christopher Grose, *Milton and the Sense of Tradition* (New Haven: Yale University Press, 1988), chapters 7–8.
77. Milton, *PR*, 1.269.
78. *PR*, 1.187.
79. *PR*, 1.282–89.
80. *PR*.1.217.
81. *PR*, 1.217.
82. *PR*, 1.296.
83. *PR*, 1.290.
84. *PR*, 1.290–94.
85. John Milton, *Paradise Lost*, 9.710.
86. *PR*, 4.517–20.
87. *PR*, 4.540.
88. *PR*, 1.221–23
89. *PR*, 4.4.
90. *PR*, 4.161.
91. *PR*, 4.229–32.
92. *PR*, 4.240–41.
93. *PR*, 4.321–42.
94. *PR*, 4.348.
95. *PR*, 4.613.
96. *PR*, 4.635.
97. *PR*, 4.638–39.
98. Higgins, *Nietzsche's "Zarathustra,"* esp. chapter 6.
99. Tracy B. Strong, *Friedrich Nietzsche and the Politics of Transfiguration* (Berkeley: University of California Press, 1975).
100. Jacob Burckhardt, *The Civilization of the Renaissance In Italy*, intro. by Hajo Holborn (New York: Random House, 1954), p. 79.
101. Strong, *Nietzsche and the Politics of Transfiguration*, p. 167.
102. Strong, ibid., pp. 167–68.
103. We are thinking here of *Illuminations: Essays and Reflections*, ed. Hannah Arendt, trans. Harry Zohn (New York: Harcourt Brace Jovanovich, 1955); his influential statement on "The Work of Art in the Age of Mechanical Reproduction," from *Illuminations*, appears in *Marxism and Art: Writings in Aesthetics and Criticism*, ed. Berel Lang and Forrest Williams (New York: David McKay, 1972).
104. *Ben Jonson*, ed. Ian Donaldson, in *The Oxford Authors*, gen. ed., Frank Kermode (Oxford: Oxford University Press, 1985), p. 222.
105. Ludwig Wittgenstein, *Philosophical Investigations*, trans. G.E.M. Anscombe (Oxford: Basil Blackwell, 1958), p. 19e.
106. The *locus classicus* is, of course, Michel Foucault, *Language, Counter-Memory, Practice: Se-*

lected Essays and Interviews, ed. Donald F. Bouchard, trans. Donald F. Bouchard and Sherry Simon (Ithaca: Cornell University Press, 1977), p. 121.

107. Ibid., p. 120n.
108. Ibid., p. 123.
109. Ibid., p. 142.
110. Ibid., p. 146.
111. Ibid., p. 152.
112. John Milton, *Areopagitica*, in *Complete Poems and Major Prose.*, p. 720.
113. Ibid.
114. T. S. Eliot, *Essays Ancient and Modern* (London: Faber and Faber, 1936), p. 100.
115. Ibid., p. 108.
116. Milton, *Areopagitica*, p. 720.
117. Sir Thomas Browne, *Religio Medici*, in *The Works of Sir Thomas Browne*, 4 vols., ed. Geoffrey Keynes, 4 vols (London: Faber and Faber, 1963), 1:15.
118. Ludwig Wittgenstein, *The Blue and Brown Books* (Oxford: Basil Blackwell, 1958), p. 104.
119. For a fuller discussion of the confusion between "occurrence" and "recurrence," see Bernd Magnus, *Nietzsche's Existential Imperative* (Bloomington: Indiana University Press, 1978).
120. *GS*, p. 33n.

Chapter 3

1. Northrop Frye, *Anatomy of Criticism: Four Essays* (Princeton: Princeton University Press, 1957), p. 207.
2. Miguel de Unamuno, *Tragic Sense of Life*, trans. J. E. Crawford Flitch (New York: Dover, 1954), p. 328.
3. Frye, op. cit., p. 214.
4. Ibid., pp. 214–15.
5. Karl Jaspers, *Nietzsche: An Introduction to an Understanding of His Philosophical Activity*, trans. by Charles F. Walraff and Frederick J. Schmitz (Tuscon: University of Arisona Press, 1965), p. 434.
6. See "The Rhetoric of Crisis" in chapter 2, above.
7. John Milton, "Il Penseroso" (line 100), in *John Milton: Complete Poems and Major Prose*, ed. Merritt Y. Hughes (New York: Odyssey Press, 1957), p. 74.
8. Gilles Deleuze, *Nietzsche and Philosophy*, trans. Hugh Tomlinson (New York: Columbia University Press, 1983), pp. 30 and 202n.
9. In Book IV, the audience comes to him rather than the other way round, but the rhetorical apposition between the solitude of his cave and the world of others remains in play.
10. Rev. 3.13–16.
11. Here, the tablets as palimpsests come into play: written and broken, they prefigure the fate of Zarathustra's "gospel" as of all others.
12. Luke 13.19 ff..
13. Luke 13.31.
14. Luke 12.2–3.
15. Note that Nietzsche's highest hope, in *EH* is to be "a comedian of the [ascetic] ideal."
16. This episode invites comparison, too, with that other "teacher," that other founder of our shared tradition: Socrates, a figure in whom Nietzsche never lost interest.
17. See Alexander Nehamas's discussion of this aphorism in *Nietzsche: Life as Literature* (Cambridge: Harvard University Press, 1985), chap. 4, esp. pp. 114–15; see also Arthur

C. Danto, "Some Remarks on *The Genealogy of Morals*," in *Reading Nietzsche*, ed. Robert C. Solomon and Kathleen M. Higgins (New York: Oxford University Press, 1988), pp. 13–28, esp. 13–16.

18. Robert Burton , *The Anatomy of Melancholy*, 3 vols. intro. by Holbrook Jackson, (London: J. M. Dent, 1961), vol. 1, p. 19.

19. Martin Heidegger, *Nietzsche*, 4 vols., trans. David Farrell Krell (San Francisco: Harper & Row. 1984), vol. 2, p. 5.

20. Ibid., p. 6.

21. Ibid., p. 7.

22. See our discussion of the self-consuming character of this device in chapter 1.

23. Deleuze, *Nietzsche and Philosophy*, pp. 28–29. Many distinguished Nietzsche critics have commented on this passage; see, for instance, Shapiro, *Nietzschean Narratives*, chapter 3, esp. pp. 90–91; Maudemarie Clark, *Nietzsche on Truth and Philosophy* (Cambridge: Cambridge University Press, 1990), chapter 8; Bernd Magnus, *Nietzsche's Existential Imperative* (Bloomington: Indiana University Press, 1978), esp. pp. 111–54; and, of course, Heidegger, *Nietzsche*, vol. 1, esp. pp. 32–44.

24. George Wither, *A Collection of Emblemes, Ancient and Moderne* (London, 1635).

25. Ibid., p. 102.

26. Ibid., p. 157.

27. This line of thought would, of course, undercut recurrence, because it substantially confuses recurrence *of* a life with the *sense* of recurrence *within* a life.

28. And yet the *logic* of recurrence theories *requires* indifference as the only possible reaction (see chapter 1, above, and the literature cited there).

29. Shapiro, *Nietzschean Narratives*, pp. 83–85; Shapiro refers to Bernd Magnus's "useful phrase," "existential imperative," in elucidating the argument "that the thought of eternal recurrence does indeed violate the principle of identity" (p. 84); see Magnus, *Nietzsche's Existential Imperative*, pp. 98–110; and Magnus, "Nietzsche's Eternalistic Countermyth," *The Review of Metaphysics*, 26, no. 4 (June 1973), pp. 604–617.

30. See chapter 1, above.

31. Edmund Spenser, *The Faerie Queene*, 4.10.8–9; all citations from *The Works of Edmund Spenser: A Variorum Edition*, 8 vols., ed. Edwin Greenlaw et al. (Baltimore: The Johns Hopkins Press, 1932–57).

32. Ibid., 4.10.41.

33. Ibid., 3.6.30.

34. In his "Letter of the authors expounding," written to Sir Walter Ralegh, Spenser uses the figure of a "dark conceit" to suggest the many levels on which he expects his reader to understand his narrative figures.

35. Ibid., 3.6.31.

36. A. C. Hamilton, ed., assisted by R. J. Manning, *The Faerie Queene* (London and New York: Longman, 1980), p. 360n.

37. Spenser, *Works*, 3.6.8.

38. Ibid., 3.6.47.

39. Ibid., 3.6.33.

40. Ibid., 3.6.47.

41. D. H. Lawrence, *The Escaped Cock* (Paris: The Black Sun Press, 1929), p. 10; all citations from this work in our text will be from this, the first, edition; this short novel is more commonly published as *The Man Who Died*.

42. Ibid.

43. Ibid., p. 5.

44. Ibid., p. 4.

45. Ibid., p. 10.
46. Ibid., p. 5.
47. Ibid., p. 6.
48. Ibid.
49. Ibid., p. 7.
50. Ibid., p. 8.
51. Ibid.
52. Ibid., pp. 8–9.
53. Ibid., p. 10.
54. Ibid., p. 12.
55. Ibid., p. 28.
56. Ibid., p. 83.
57. Ibid., p. 29.
58. Ibid., p. 30.
59. Ibid., p. 32.
60. Ibid.
61. Ibid., p. 30.
62. John 20.17.
63. Lawrence, *The Escaped Cock*, p. 45.
64. Ibid., p. 54.
65. Ibid.
66. Ibid., p. 65.
67. Ibid.
68. Ibid., p. 66.
69. Ibid., p. 77.
70. Luke 7.37–8.
71. Lawrence, *The Escaped Cock*, p. 83.
72. Matt. 16.18.
73. Lawrence op. cit., pp. 87–88.
74. Op. cit., p. 93.
75. Op. cit., p. 94.
76. Op. cit., p. 96.
77. D. H. Lawrence, *The Complete Poems of D. H. Lawrence*, Collected and ed. by Vivian de Sola Pinto and Warren Roberts, 2 vols., (New York: Viking Press, 1964): 1:461.
78. Lawrence, *The Escaped Cock*, p. 96.
79. Eccles. 1.4.
80. Lawrence, *The Escaped Cock*, pp. 21, 34, and 71, respectively.
81. John 3.3.
82. Lawrence, *The Escaped Cock*, p. 96.
83. For an extensive and enlightening discussion of this motif, see Kathleen Marie Higgins, *Nietzsche's "Zarathustra"* (Philadelphia: Temple University Press, 1987), chapter 7.
84. Deut. 30.19.

Chapter 4

1. This thesis recurs in *The Anxiety of Influence* (Oxford: Oxford University Press, 1973), *A Map of Misreading* (Oxford: Oxford University Press, 1975), and *Deconstruction and Criticism* (New York: Seabury, 1979), where the Nietzschean origin may be easily inferred: " . . . there are *no* texts, but only interpretations" (p. 7).

2. Bloom, "The Internalization of Quest Romance," in *Romanticism and Consciousness*, ed. Harold Bloom (New York: Norton, 1970).

3. Daniel T. O'Hara, *The Romance of Interpretation* (New York: Columbia University Press, 1985).

4. For the view that the recent enterprise has been largely unsuccessful, see Steven Knapp and Walter Ben Michaels, "Against Theory II," *Critical Inquiry* 14 (Autumn, 1987): pp. 49–68; and for further discussion, see *Against Theory: Literary Studies and the new Pragmatism*, ed. W.J.T. Mitchell (Chicago and London: University of Chicago Press, 1985).

5. Paul de Man, *Allegories of Reading: Figural Language in Rousseau, Nietzsche, Rilke, and Proust* (New Haven: Yale University Press, 1979).

6. See Richard Rorty, *Contingency, Irony, Solidarity* (Cambridge: Cambridge University Press, 1989).

7. See Alexander Nehamas, *Nietzsche: Life as Literature* (Cambridge, Mass.: Harvard University Press, 1985), chapters 6–7, esp. pp. 194–99 and 226–34. Also see our discussion in chapter 1.

8. For a discussion of the view that the attribution to Nietzsche of an ontology of will to power depends almost entirely upon privileging texts and notes that he had discarded or set aside, see chapter 1, above.

9. Nehamas, *Life as Literature*, p. 3.

10. Ibid., p. 4.

11. Ibid., p. 8.

12. Ibid., pp. 20–21.

13. Ibid., p. 8.

14. Ibid., p. 5.

15. Ibid., p. 230.

16. Ibid., p. 232.

17. Ibid., p. 233.

18. The "mixed genre" has been a fixture in critical theory since the Renaissance, and, more recently, Clifford Geertz employs the figure of "blurred genres."

19. This text is set forward as an instance of what it recommends, a token of its type.

20. Just as we did in chapter 1, above.

21. Nehamas, *Life as Literature*, pp. 22–23.

22. Ibid., p. 26.

23. See chapter 1 for discussion of this point.

24. See Jean-Pierre Mileur, *The Critical Romance* (Madison: University of Wisconsin Press, 1991), and Harold Bloom, "The Internalization of Quest Romance."

25. Although these notions appear and reappear as themes in the writing of these critics, see, for instance, Paul de Man, *Blindness and Insight: Essays in the Rhetoric of Contemporary Criticism*, intro. by Wlad Godzich (Oxford: Oxford University Press, 1971); de Man *Allegories of Reading;* Michel Foucault, in many works, but see esp. "A Preface to Transgression," in *Language, Counter-Memory, Practice*; Jacques Derrida, *The Post Card: From Socrates to Freud and Beyond*, trans. Alan Bass (Chicago: University of Chicago Press, 1987); and Harold Bloom's texts, cited above.

26. See chapters 2 and 3, above.

27. For a more extensive discussion, see Mileur, *The Critical Romance*.

28. See chapters 1 and 3, above.

29. All citations from Browning in our text will be from Robert Browning, *Poems of Robert Browning*, ed. Donald Smalley (Boston: Houghton Mifflin, 1956).

30. Ibid.

31. Nehamas, *Life as Literature*, p. 188.

32. We examine this aspect of *Zarathustra* in chapters 2 and 3, above.

33. For a detailed discussion of this problem, see chapter 1.

34. His *Nachlass* notes suggest and trace this temptation—as well as its overcoming.

35. William Worsdworth, "Resolution and Independence," lines 22–25, in *William Words-worth*, ed. Stephen Gill (Oxford: Oxford University Press, 1984); all citations from Wordsworth in our text will be from this edition.

36. Henry David Thoreau, "Walking," *Great Short Works of Henry David Thoreau*, ed. Wendell Glick (New York: Harper & Row, 1982) p. 303.

37. Wordsworth, Ibid., lines 34–35.

38. Ibid., lines 43–49.

39. Ibid., lines 36–42.

40. Ibid., lines 113–26.

41. For a different but compatible reading of "On the Vision and the Riddle," see Magnus, *Nietzsche's Existential Imperative*.

42. Wordsworth, line 137.

43. Ibid., line 140.

44. To shift perspectives again, this same point is made about "Life"—when yoked to eternal recurrence—in chapter 1, in the notion of a self-consuming concept.

45. We should note that in a later chapter, "The Convalescent," Zarathustra remarks that *he* himself was the shepherd.

46. Wordsworth, lines 40–42.

47. Ibid., line 116.

48. William Blake, "The Marriage of Heaven and Hell," Plate 12, in *The Complete Poetry and Prose of William Blake*, ed. David V. Erdman (New York: Anchor Press, 1988); all citations from Blake in our text will be from this edition.

49. See our discussion of Milton and Nietzsche in chapter 3.

50. Blake, *Complete Poems*, Plate 13.

51. Kathleen Marie Higgins, *Nietzsche's "Zarathustra"* (Philadelphia: Temple University Press, 1987), p. 94.

52. Ibid.

53. Ibid., p. 96.

54. Ibid.

55. Ibid., p. 97.

56. Ibid., p. 98.

57. Harold Alderman, *Nietzsche's Gift* (Athens: Ohio University Press, 1977); see chapter 1, n. 59, above.

58. Edmund Spenser, *The Shepheardes Calender* (1579), in *The Works of Edmund Spenser: A Variorum Edition*, 11 vols., ed. Edwin Greenlaw et al. (Baltimore: The Johns Hopkins Press, 1932–57): 7, 5.

59. "To the most excellent and learned . . . Mayster Gabriell Harvey"; the identity of "E. K." is still the subject of spirited debate, with some critics holding that this earliest of Spenser critics was, at least in part, the author himself.

60. For further discussion of Spenser's self-presentation, see Stephen Greenblatt, *Renaissance Self-Fashioning From More to Shakespeare* (Chicago: University of Chicago Press, 1980) and Richard Helgerson, *Self Crowned Laureates: Spenser, Jonson, Milton, and the Literary System* (Berkeley: University of California Press, 1983).

61. Higgins, *Nietzsche's "Zarathustra,"* p. 208.

62. Ibid.

63. We adopted Kaufmann's (and Hollingdale's) "higher men" for the German *höhere Menschen* with some discomfort here and throughout our own text; for Nietzsche's expression is gender neutral. In German, it can apply with equal linguistic force to men

and women alike. Nevertheless, the English expression "higher men" has figured so prominently in discussions of Nietzsche's works that alternative expression seemed to us to invite further confusion—which was not the case in our translations of *Mensch* and *Übermensch*. If at all possible, therefore, we ask the reader to keep in mind that "higher men" need not refer to males in Nietzsche's text.

64. For a different perspective on this point, see Higgins, *Nietzsche's "Zarathustra,"* pp. 230–35.

65. The reader might compare this section with Nietzsche's discussion of ugliness in "The Problem of Socrates," *TI* 3.

66. Higgins, *Nietzsche's "Zarathustra,"* pp. 226–32.

67. Ibid., p. 234.

68. In a quite different genre, one is reminded of a remark attributed to John Lennon: "Life is what happens while you are making other plans."

69. Higgins, *Nietzsche's "Zarathustra,"* p. 234.

70. Ibid., p. 239.

71. See chapter 1, n. 23.

72. As spelled out in his popular book (admittedly designed for the general audience), *The Closing of the American Mind: How Higher Education Has Failed Democracy and Impoverished the Souls of Today's Students*, Foreword by Saul Bellow (New York: Simon and Schuster, 1987), part 2, esp. pp. 217–26.

73. Karsten Harries, "The Philosopher at Sea," in *Nietzsche's New Seas: Explorations in Philosophy, Aesthetics, and Politics*, ed. Michael Allen Gillespie and Tracy B. Strong (Chicago: University of Chicago Press, 1988), p. 40.

74. Harries, "The Philosopher at Sea," p. 40.

75. Ibid., p. 41.

76. Ibid., p. 41–42.

77. Ibid., p. 42.

78. Ibid.

79. Ibid.

80. Harold Bloom, *The Anxiety of Influence*, passim.

81. Harries, "The Philosopher at Sea," p. 43.

82. Ibid.

83. Alfred Lord Tennyson, "Ulysses," lines 31–32, *Tennyson's Poetry* (New York: Norton, 1971); all citations from Tennyson in our text will be from this edition.

84. Ibid., lines. 3–5.

85. Ibid., line 43.

86. Ibid., lines 36–38.

87. Ibid., lines 56–70.

Chapter 5

1. This is our conclusion in chapters 1–4, above.

2. For purposes of exposition and analysis, we are treating Zarathustra's *Werk* as Nietzsche's "work." The primary textual basis for conflating Nietzsche and Zarathustra here is that Nietzsche has Zarathustra say in "The Sign"—the closing "chapter" of *Thus Spoke Zarathustra*: "My suffering and my pity for suffering—what does it matter? Am I concerned with *happiness*? I am concerned with my *work* [*Werk*; in italics]." These words precede the book's inverse Epiphany: his animals draw near, his hour has come (he says), *his* morning, *his* day, is breaking: "rise now, rise, thou great noon!" (which, we could remember, is the moment of the briefest shadow, end of the longest error, as Nietzsche will later tell us in *Twilight of the Idols*).

What is remarkable in the conclusion of "The Sign" is Nietzsche's use of the German *Werk* for "work." Ordinarily, "my work" is *"meine Arbeit."* Work, in the more standard German usage, is *Arbeit*, not *Werk* (compare *Arbeit macht frei*, the horrific slogan that greeted all "newcomers" above the gate at the death camp Auschwitz)—although in some idiomatic contexts the noun *Werk* is appropriate. God's work alone is *Werk* that is not *Arbeit*; and, importantly for our purposes, Zarathustra's *Werk* may be regarded as his "work" in the sense of producing a literary corpus, the other standard sense of the word *Werk*. His (i.e., Zarathustra's) work is his literary production, or, alternatively, it is his creation of a new world. This shift from "readerly" to "writerly" perspectives is discussed by us in chapter 4, above.

3. Jean-Pierre Mileur, *Literary Revisionism and the Burden of Modernity* (Berkeley: University of California Press, 1985).

4. Ibid.

5. Tracy B. Strong, "Nietzsche's Political Aesthetics," in *Nietzsche's New Seas: Explorations in Philosophy, Aesthetics, and Politics*, ed. Michael Allen Gillespie and Tracy B. Strong (Chicago: University of Chicago Press, 1988), p. 167.

6. See previous chapter.

7. Cf. *BGE* 6.

8. Paul Bové, "Mendacious Innocents, or, The Modern Genealogist as Conscientious Intellectual: Nietzsche, Foucault, Said," in *Why Nietzsche Now?*, ed. Daniel T. O'Harra (Bloomington: Indiana University Press, 1985), pp. 371–72.

9. Wordsworth, "Lines Composed a Few Miles Above Tintern Abbey," lines 122–23; all citations from Wordsworth in our text will be from *William Wordsworth*, ed. Stephen Gill (Oxford: Oxford University Press, 1984).

10. See, Jacques Derrida, *The Ear of the Other* (Lincoln: University of Nebraska Press, 1988).

11. They touch on this matter in many places, but see, for instance, Foucault's "What is an Author," *Language, Counter-Memory, Practice: Selected Essays and Interviews*, ed. Donald F. Bouchard, trans. Donald F, Bouchard and Sherry Simon (Ithaca: Cornell University Press, 1977), pp. 115–38; and Jacques Derrida, "Otobiographies: The Teaching of Nietzsche and the Politics of the Proper Name," in *The Ear of the Other: Otobiography, Transference, Translation*, ed. Christie McDonald, trans. Peggy Kamuf (Lincoln: University of Nebraska Press, 1988), pp. 1–40, respectively.

12. Nietzsche addresses this point directly in "The Problem of Socrates" (*TI*): *"the value of life cannot be estimated.* Not by the living, for they are an interested party, even a bone of contention, and not judges; not by the dead, for a different reason."

13. Kathleen Marie Higgins, *Nietzsche's "Zarathustra"* (Philadelphia: Temple University Press, 1987), p. 241.

14. This discussion, in Nietzsche, prefigures later discussions in Heidegger and Sartre of "authenticity" (*Eigentlichkeit*).

15. For a discussion of Weir Mitchell, proprioception, and the connection of bodily identity with authorial and textual identity, see our chapter 6, above.

16. See her essay "Against Interpretation" in *Against Interpretation and Other Essays* (New York: Noonday Press, 1966).

17. Thomas Weiskel, *The Romantic Sublime* (Baltimore: The Johns Hopkins University Press, 1976).

18. For an acute "summary" of this view, see " 'Reason' in Philosophy" in *Twilight of the Idols*.

19. For a discussion, see our chapter 1, "A Fish Story: Self-Consuming Concepts."

20. Samuel Taylor Coleridge, *Biographia Literaria*, 2 vols., ed. John Showcross (Oxford: Oxford University Press, 1907), vol. 1, p. 202.

21. Of course, this forgetfulness is on the whole true primarily of "writers"—that is, of the writerly we are discussing here. Charles Manson, Jeffrey Dahmer, systemic child abuse,

not to mention the Holocaust, My Lai, Katyn Woods, and Vietnam, are eloquent testimony that "we moderns" have *not* forgotten how powerful a seduction to life inflicting pain can be. Indeed, some would argue, cruelty has *become* "our" narcotic!

22. We use scare-quotes to flag the peculiarity of Nietzsche's genealogical method, the assurance it claims for itself in the fame of Nietzsche's proclaimed perspectivism.

23. See Jacques Derrida, "Otobiographies," and *Spurs* (Chicago: University of Chicago Press, 1978).

24. See our more extended discussion of eternal recurrence in chapter 1.

25. From a literary point of view, the metaphor of the temple is itself crucial, since the inferiority of the second temple to the first was taken by Dryden and others as a sign of the inevitable running-down of the literary tradition, of the coming end of poetry.

26. "He which testifieth these things saith, Surely I come quickly. Amen. Even so, come, Lord Jesus" (Rev. 22.20).

27. See chapter 4.

28. Note our discussion of the subtitle of *Beyond Good and Evil: Prelude to a Philosophy of the Future* in chapter 1.

29. John Updike, *Hugging the Shore* (New York: Random House, 1984).

30. For different readings of these same passages see Alexander Nehamas, *Nietzsche: Life as Literature* (Cambridge, Mass.: Harvard University Press, 1985), and Arthur Danto, "Some Remarks on *The Genealogy of Morals*," in *Reading Nietzsche*, ed. Robert C. Solomon and Kathleen M. Higgins (New York: Oxford University Press, 1988).

31. We are aware that some commentators, e.g. Danto and Magnus, mark this distinction as relevant to the contrast between active and passive nihilism; but it is hard to see how that will help, hard to see how that is to be cashed out.

32. See chapters 1 and 4, above.

33. For further discussion see our chapter 6, below; and, perhaps Thomas Laqueur's *Making Sex: Body and Gender from the Greeks to Freud* (Cambridge: Harvard University Press, 1990) and the literature he cites, as well as Elaine Scarry's *The Body in Pain: The Making and Unmaking of the World* (Oxford: Oxford University Press, 1985).

34. Compare this discussion with the suggestion, in "What the Germans Lack" (*TI*), that all energy is finite, that whatever is spent in one direction will be unavailable for expenditure in another.

35. Harold Bloom, *The Anxiety of Influence: A Theory of Poetry* (New York: Oxford University Press, 1973), esp. chapters 2–4.

36. See, for example, Maudemarie Clark, *Nietzsche on Truth and Philosophy* (Cambridge: Cambridge University Press, 1990); Alexander Nehamas, *Life as Literature*; Bernd Magnus, *Nietzche's Existential Imperative* (Bloomington: Indiana University Press, 1978); Richard Schacht, *Nietzsche* (London: Routledge and Kegan Paul, 1983); and John Wilcox, *Truth and Value in Nietzsche* (Ann Arbor: University of Michigan Press, 1974).

37. See our chapters 1 and 4. For further discussion of this important matter, see authors cited in the previous footnote.

38. Compare, for example, Richard Rorty's suggestion—in his discussion of "Antipodeans" in his *Philosophy and the Mirror of Nature* (Princeton: Princeton Univerity Press, 1978)—that if the tactile sense had achieved the dominance in our tradition assumed by the visual the "problem" of mental representation might never have arisen; we might all "naturally" have been eliminative materialists in our philosophy instead, in this scenario.

39. We note, without further comment, that the history of recent philosophy is strewn with examples of instructive failures that attempt this "internal" perspective—from Bergson to Husserl to Heidegger.

40. For further discussion, see Bernd Magnus, "Jesus, Christianity, and Superhumanity," in

Studies in Nietzsche and the Judaeo-Christian Tradition, ed. J. C. O'Flaherty, T. F. Sellner, and Robert M. Helm (Chapel Hill: University of North Carolina Press, 1985), pp. 295–319.

41. Cf. "I fear we are not rid of God because we still have faith in grammar" (*TI*, " 'Reason' in Philosophy").

42. In addition, of course, attempting to "justify" truth presupposes it—like a snake attempting to devour itself.

43. Stanley Cavell, *Must We Mean What We Say: A Book of Essays* (New York: Charles Scribner's Sons, 1969), p 136.

44. John Milton, *Areopagitica*, in *Complete Poems and Major Prose*, ed. Merritt Y. Hughes (New York: Odyssey Press, 1957), p. 728.

45. Cf. "On Redemption" in *Thus Spoke Zarathustra*.

Chapter 6

1. Bernd Magnus, "The Deification of the Commonplace: *Twilight of the Idols*," in *Reading Nietzsche*, ed. Robert C. Solomon and Kathleen M. Higgins (New York: Oxford University Press, 1988), pp. 152–81, here, pp. 156–57.

2. Ibid., p. 156.

3. Ibid., p. 157.

4. Ibid., p. 155.

5. Ibid., p. 157.

6. Paul de Man, *Allegories of Reading: Figured Language in Rousseau, Nietzsche, Rilke, and Proust* (New Haven: Yale University Press, 1979).

7. For an extended discussion of this tradition, see chapter 4.

8. It is important to remember that Nietzsche's use of the term "realists" is meant in the vernacular sense, not in the philosophic sense of "realist."

9. Jacques Derrida, *Spurs: Nietzsche's Styles*, trans. Barbara Harlow (Chicago: University of Chicago Press, 1979).

10. Oliver Sacks, *The Man Who Mistook His Wife for a Hat* (New York: Harper & Row, 1987).

11. Ibid., p. 43.

12. Ibid., p. 43.

13. Ibid., p. 52.

14. Ibid., p. 49.

15. Ibid., pp. 45, 52, respectively.

16. Ibid.

17. Ibid., p. 48.

18. Ibid., p. 44.

19. Ibid. We are aware that in the passage cited, as often elsewhere, Wittgenstein is engaging a remark (here, one for which G. E. Moore was "famous"), as if with an interlocutor, rather than asserting it. His focus is on the anomalies which arise from multiple uses of such terms as "know" and "doubt." We need not pursue this matter in order to appreciate the value of Sacks's provocative line of thought here. What constitutes "feeling" one's "body"? How do we know that we are not "living" within the body of others? Can one have a toothache in someone else's body? And, of course, Wittgenstein, too, was interested in "shadow pains." Wittgenstein considers these questions in *The Blue and Brown Books* and in *Philosophical Investigations*. Even in *On Certainty*, we find a familiar focus on the way language "works": "The correct use of the expression 'I know.' Someone with bad sight asks me: 'do you believe that the thing we can see there is a tree?' I reply 'I *know* it is; I can see it clearly and am familiar with it' . . . 'Do you know or do you

only believe that your name is L. W.'" and so on. Ludwig Wittgenstein, *On Certainty*, ed. by G. E. M. Anscombe and G. H. von Wright, trans. Denis Paul and G. E. M. Anscombe (Oxford: Basil Blackwell, 1969), pp. 63, 64, respectively. We consider Sacks's remark, then, about the "haunting" quality of Wittgenstein's concern about the body as, at the very least, hyperbolic, perhaps even misleadingly so.

20. Derrida, *Spurs*, p. 139.
21. Ibid., p. 85.
22. Ibid., p. 87.
23. Ibid., p. 73.
24. Ibid., p. 101.
25. Richard Rorty provides an important (yet different) discussion of this problem, as well as a suggested direction for its resolution in chapter 4, "Private Irony and Liberal Hope," in his *Contingency, Irony, and Solidarity* (Cambridge: Cambridge University Press, 1989). He identifies his "ironist" as follows: "I shall define an 'ironist' as someone who fulfills three conditions: (1) She has radical and continuing doubts about the final vocabulary she currently uses, because she has been impressed by other vocabularies, vocabularies taken as final by people or books she has encountered; (2) she realizes that argument phrased in her present vocabulary can neither underwrite nor dissolve these doubts; (3) insofar as she philosophizes about her situation, she does not think that her vocabulary is closer to reality than others, that it is in touch with a power not herself. Ironists who are inclined to philosophize see the choice between vocabularies as made neither within a neutral and universal metavocabulary nor by an attempt to fight one's way past appearances to the real, but simply by playing the new off against the old" (p. 73).
26. Thomas Carlyle, *Sartor Resartus* (New York: Odyssey Press, 1937), pp. 73–74.
27. Fredrich Nietzsche, "Description of Ancient Rhetoric (1872–73)," in *Fredrich Nietzsche on Rhetoric and Language*, ed. and trans. Sander L. Gilman, Carole Blair, and David J. Parent (New York and Oxford: Oxford University Press, 1989), p. 3; here, the sections are too long to provide the Nietzsche's citation in the usual way.
28. We do not mean to imply that creation of a novel nomenclature would clarify anything. For suppose someone tells us that all the disciplines lack is a proper vocabulary. Insert this, and "the problem" of rhetoricians and non-rhetoricians alike will solve itself. And we respond by requesting a description of that vocabulary, in the preferred vocabulary, of course.
29. Adrian del Caro, *Nietzsche Contra Nietzsche* (Baton Rouge: Louisiana State University Press, 1989).

INDEX